JUNGIAN SYMBOLIC PSYCHOLOGY

The Voyage of Humanization of the Cosmos in Search of Enlightenment

CARLOS AMADEU BOTELHO BYINGTON

JUNGIAN SYMBOLIC PSYCHOLOGY

The Voyage of Humanization of the Cosmos
in Search of Enlightenment

———

Translation by Carlos Byington
Revision by Siobhan Drummond

Chiron Publications
Wilmette, Illinois
2012

Cover design by Vera Rosenthal
Book design: Ione Pereira
Printed in Brazil by JK Color Grafica e Editora

Byington, Carlos Amadeu Botelho.
Jungian Symbolic Psychology: the voyage of humanization of the cosmos in search of enlightenment. / Carlos Amadeu Botelho Byington. Translation by Carlos Byington. Revision by Siobhan Drummond. — São Paulo: JK Color Grafica e Editora, 2012.

385 p. il.

Originally published as Psicologia Simbólica Junguiana: A viagem de humanização do cosmos em busca da iluminação. © 2008 by Carlos Amadeu BotelhoByington. Published by Linear B Ed.

B997

Library of Congress Cataloging-in-Publication Data
ISBN - 978-1-888602-49-4 (pbk.)
1. Psychology. 2. Symbolic Psychology.
3. Consciousness. 4. Theory of Knowledge. 5. Jung,
Carl Gustav (1875 - 1961). 6. Freud, Sigmund. I. Title. II. Byington, Carlos,
Translation. III. Drummond, Siobhan, Revision.

Cataloging prepared by Wanda Lucia Schmidt - CRB-8-1922

Cover: "Cueva de las Manos" or Cave of the Hands, a cave situated in the valley of the Pinturas river, in the province of Santa Cruz in Patagonia, Argentina. It received its name and became famous for the paintings made by indian hands (probably the ancestors of the Tehuelche), 9000 years ago. Photo: Newton Guerra.

Carlos Amadeu Botelho Byington
c.byington@uol.com.br
www.carlosbyington.com.br

To my dear daughters
Elisa, Rita, Olívia, and Bianca
for who they are.

To the memory of Sigmund Freud,
I dedicate the concept of the normal and defensive structuring
functions.

To the memory of C. G. Jung,
I dedicate the concept of the archetype of alterity.

To the memory of Erich Neumann,
I dedicate the concept of the five archetypal positions of
consciousness.

To my dear wife
Maria Helena
with love and gratitude

To the Reader

This book is the result of daring. I dared to review the basic concepts of my masters. I dared to enter into the dimensions of other subjects.

This book is also the result of a life dedicated to the elaboration of symbols, which I encountered in my way. They called, guided, and authorized me.

To specialists, I ask for cooperation and benevolence to correct errors and fill gaps.

Carlos Byington

TABLE OF CONTENTS

Introduction

So God created him in His own image. (Gen. 1:27)

Kids were playing and accused him of eating earth.
He said it was a lie and asked his mother Yashoda to look in his mouth.
In doing it, she saw the universe and realized that the child was Krishna. (Jean Herbert, Yoga and Love)

Can a grain of sand understand the ocean or a neuron explain the functioning of the brain? Is a leaf able to describe the forest or an ant to imagine the animal kingdom? Is a raindrop capable of calculating the potential of the clouds or a ray of light of revealing the origin of the universe? Is it possible for a human being to inquire about the nature and the purpose of creation?

> According to the big bang theory, our universe was formed some 13.7 billion years ago, our sun five billion years ago, the earth 4.6 billion years ago, and life began around four billion years ago, when the ancestor of the DNA molecule was formed.
> For most of the four billion years since the origin of life, the dominant organisms were microscopic blue-green algae, which covered and filled the oceans. Sexuality began some two billion years ago . . . Then some 600 billion years ago, the monopolizing grip of the algae was broken and an enormous proliferation of new life forms emerged, an event called the Cambrian explosion. (Sagan 1980, p. 22)

Five hundred and forty million years ago, the Mollusca and the Arthropoda including the trilobites were formed; five hundred and five million years ago the first vertebrates and the fish appeared; four hundred and forty million years ago the Amphibia, the insects, and the tall plants appeared; three hundred and sixty million years ago the reptiles and the winged insects appeared; two hundred million years ago reptiles capable of regulating body temperature appeared; two hundred and forty-five million years ago the first mammals and the dinosaurs appeared; one hundred and forty-four million years ago, a meteor killed the dinosaurs and 75 percent of life on the planet. Plants and flowers spread; sixty-five million years ago came the whales and the first primates, which in time would include bats, lemurs, monkeys, apes, and finally humankind. The hominid family began with the genus Australopitecus and was followed by the genus Homo (Homo erectus and Homo habilis), and finally Homo sapiens neanderthalensis and Homo sapiens sapiens in the last one hundred thousand to two hundred thousand years (Tattersall 1995).

This process culminated in the creation of the human brain with one hundred billion neurons (10^{11}) able to form consciousness and undertake the search to know ourselves and the universe (Kandel 2000). The two mythological images that open this introduction encompass metaphorically the archetypal nature of consciousness and its instinctive journey in search of totality.

The creative archetypal power of our nervous system and of culture accumulated and transmitted through generations by collective consciousness has been capable of dominating the planet and of modifying its nature, fauna, and flora to a degree unthinkable for any other species. However, this extraordinary creativity and productivity can suffer fixations and form defenses and shadow with an immense capacity to express evil. This power is so great that it can destroy our existence. In the event that this happens, the universe will continue to experience creation without our participation. Natural events, such as a collision with a comet or meteor, earthquakes, hurricanes, tsunamis, or other catastrophes can dehumanize the cosmos, but human factors are equally threatening, with the difference that they depend on our behavior, for instance, fatally unbalancing the climate (Gore 2006). The great danger that darkens the horizon of modern times is our shadow which increasingly accumulates destructivity in spite of being foreseeable and rationally understood.

In this theory, evil is described within Jung's (1951) concept of the shadow, which is here modified to include symbols of both genders and to have its origin in the fixation of symbols, complexes, functions, and the formation of defenses discovered by Freud. From this perspective, evil originates from fixation during elaboration of normal individual and collective development of consciousness, which is understood as the path toward truth, self-fulfillment, and good. In this manner, we can accompany the ethical function in every symbolic elaboration and identify the formation of the shadow as evil starting from the distortion of development and never as an autonomous function. Good and evil are studied in the relation of consciousness and shadow within the concept of supraconsciousness. Searching to demonstrate that the conflict between them is present during symbolic elaboration in every step of our search for totality, I describe clearly the ethical function in psychology and in the general sciences as an archetypal function, rescuing it from its present ambiguity.

To be created in the image of God, as stated in Genesis, is the mythological, intuitive, and metaphorical way of expressing the notion that our consciousness is constituted by the same archetypal forces that make up the universe. The image of totality in the mouth of a child represents the same idea in Hinduism. The development of scientific knowledge enhances our perception of the grandiosity of totality. Physics teaches us that in our universe, over billions of years, billions of galaxies were formed, each one having billions of stars. The Milky Way, which is our galaxy, has 400 billion stars. One of them is our sun, a star of fifth magnitude, and Earth is its third planet. The fact that we know today that stars have been born and died for billions of years, that our sun has already lived one half of its life, and that Earth was born from it, is warmed by it, and will be absorbed into it when it dies unites us with the stars as companions of a cosmic voyage. Besides this, the discoveries that the stars generated the atoms that constitute our body makes our identity with the cosmos even more eloquent (Sagan 1980). It is this common voyage that allows us to acquire the knowledge of things together with the formation of consciousness and associates the neurosciences with creation myths, which from time immemorial describe symbolically and inseparably the formation of nature and of human beings. It is this knowledge too that allows us to associate life after death with the continuation of our atoms within the cosmos because from this symbolic perspective our atoms also express our mind and our body.

Over the course of more than four billion years, life on Earth developed and became increasingly more complex through mutations and survival of the fittest (Dobzhansky 1955). Our species appeared only about one hundred and fifty thousand years ago with a brain capable of perception, imagination, memory, communication, and creativity more developed than any other evolved species (Watson and Berry 2003). The theory of the transmission of acquired characteristics developed by Lamarck and often expressed in the writings of Jung and Freud was not confirmed by genetics. Even though one cuts off the tail of puppies for many generations, they are not born without it. In every human birth, we start again with approximately the same primordial brain of our species, and with this archetypal potential, we receive the culture accumulated by our ancestors, elaborate it archetypically, copy it or transform it, and pass it along to the next generation. Our brain does not inherit culture but can learn, modify, and store it in habits, folklore, myths, libraries, museums, and computers. Culture is the result of the interaction of our brain and the work of humanity and amplifies our creativity and our memory, cumulating it in an unlimited way (Watson and Berry 2003). Everything in our brain and in the work of humanity is symbolic. The symbol is the cell of the psyche. The concept of symbol is here enlarged to encompass all psychological entities. The word entity is derived from the Latin ens-entis, "a thing which has reality and distinctness of being either in fact or in thought" (*Webster's Dictionary*). In this sense, symbols include image, word, emotion, number, sound, nature, body, society, behavior, and silence. Symbols include also all representations of meaning, such as sign (restricted symbols), metaphor, figure, synonym, antonym, metonym, allegory, fable, illustration, simile, fiction, and so on.

The force of a symbol, that is, its dynamic action, is the function, which encompasses mental and physiological expressions. A dog attacks someone. The threatening dog is a symbol and fear is the function. The dog attacks and my heart pounds. The heart is a symbol and palpitation is a function.

Symbol and function are here considered the basic structural polarity of the psyche. They participate in the process of symbolic elaboration coordinated by archetypes to form consciousness, which makes them structuring symbols and functions. Together they form the cell of the psychic dimension.

A cluster of structuring symbols forms a complex. An inferiority complex, for instance, can be formed by bodily symbols of size, skin color, and aesthetics, of intelligence, of material possessions, of professional performance, and countless other symbols.

Polarity is an essential characteristic of psychic reality. All structuring symbols and functions are conscious and unconscious, subjective and objective, in varying degrees.

Genetics and culture, myth and materialistic science, elected to determine life, are unilateral approaches that simplify but deform knowledge. In spite of the unilateral development of consciousness, it seeks homeostasis, and, therefore, we have to be aware of the ego's tendency to attach to one pole of polarities. When exaggerated, this attachment can become fixated and generate defensive inflation or omnipotence, intolerance, and fanaticism, in which the ego loses access to the central path between polarities and tends to identify rigidly with one pole.

Symbols express polarities in all existential dimensions including science, art, religion, and psychology, the rational and the emotional, conscious and unconscious, in our search for self-fulfillment. When our consciousness operates unilaterally, it may radically separate energy from matter, mind from nature, conscious from unconscious, subjective from objective, and mind from body. In so doing, it functions more easily, but if this unilaterality becomes fixated, the price is alienation, which prevents the perception that our brain moves from unilaterality toward bipolar and multi-polar expression. In this way, it is important to avoid the unilateral formulation of certain concepts, such as id and archetype, which were reduced to "the unconscious," and to consider them always within the conscious-unconscious polarity.

The results of the interaction of the genetic or archetypal structure with acquired knowledge within existential experiences apprehend, transform, and transmit through symbols to the following generations the greatness and deformities of individual, family, and social development. When we can practice detachment and surpass unilateralities, we become aware that consciousness unites polarities through symbols expressed by archetypes, which include the relation of genetics and culture, mind and body, mind and nature, myth and science, energy and matter, reason and faith, and life and death.

Because of this, I shall not follow exclusively cognitive behavioral theory, which describes the unilateral conditioning of consciousness, nor those who see in "the unconscious" the truth of life. I shall follow the middle path, which describes the conscious and unconscious characteristics of symbols coordinated by archetypes conditioned through habit to form consciousness and shadow.

To avoid the great unilaterality of dynamic psychology, I amplified the concept of the archetype and of the id to include consciousness. This conceptual extension led me to relate ego and archetype permanently and inseparably. This was followed by the description of five ego-other archetypal positions in consciousness. Within them I differentiate in particular the insular matriarchal position, which expresses dominantly animism, pleasure, sensuality, participation mystique, magic, myth, and dream and which has been traditionally reduced to the unconscious dimension. I describe also the alterity archetype, which relates polarities dialectically and is one of the major contributions of Jungian symbolic psychology.

Normal structuring functions and systems elaborate structuring symbols and form consciousness and identity. When they are fixated, however, they become pathological and are expressed through defenses in the shadow.

If a car collides with a bus, both drivers, as well as the car and the bus, are structuring symbols and driving is a structuring function. Both drivers can have driven correctly or, on account of drinking, can have driven defensively, that is, acting out the shadow. These structuring symbols and function operate within the structuring system of traffic, which includes normal and defensive driving.

The process of symbolic elaboration, which forms consciousness through the interaction of structuring symbols, complexes, functions, and systems coordinated by archetypes, is here considered the center of all normal and pathological psychological activity. This led me to consider the structuring symbol and the structuring function the main psychological concepts to explain the process of individuation formulated by Jung in individual development, as well as the process of humanization described by Teilhard de Chardin (1947) in collective development.

Because of this, I named this theory symbolic psychology. I describe it as Jungian because the archetypal development of consciousness through structuring symbols, complexes, functions, and systems and the permanent confrontation with the shadow in search of the totality of our psychological capacity is the essence of that which Jung's genius transmitted in his concept of the individuation process, illustrated by his work, his dreams, and his life. Considering the concepts of the polarities of conscious-unconscious, eros-thanatos, puer-senex, and anima-animus too limited to describe the axis of the process of individuation, I conceived instead a regent archetypal quaternio formed by the matriarchal, the patriarchal, the alterity (anima-animus), and the totality archetypes coordinating all symbolic elaboration around the central archetype. In this respect, I reviewed the works of Neumann and Bachofen questioning the evolutionist connotation between the matriarchal and patriarchal archetypes and considering these two archetypes to be bi-gendered, that is, equally active in the personalities of men and of women. In this way, we can envisage all human experiences always related to subjective and objective, conscious and unconscious aspects and to psychic totality and create a new concept for dimensions of the Self other than the individual Self, such as the marriage Self, the family Self, the cultural Self, the therapeutic Self, the planetary Self, the cosmic Self, and so on. To avoid ambiguity, I have separated the concept of the Self, which encompasses all psychic entities including the ego, the other, all archetypes, and the shadow from that of the virtual central archetype which coordinates all symbolic elaboration.

The regent archetypal quaternio expresses the five ego-other archetypal positions of consciousness. Symbolic elaboration starts with the nondifferentiated or uroboric (Neumann) ego-other position, which corresponds to the central archetype. It is followed by the insular position of the matriarchal archetype, by the polarized position of the patriarchal archetype, the dialectical position of the alterity (anima and animus) archetype, and the contemplative position corresponding to the expression of the totality archetype.

The employment of the process of symbolic elaboration to form collective consciousness led me to conceive an archetypal theory of history with the same archetypes of individual development. This theory invalidates the traditional evolutionist connotation attributed to the matriarchal-patriarchal relationship in individual and collective development and conceives the psychological historical evolution of collective consciousness as the development toward the dominance of the dialectical position of the alterity archetype.

The description of the evolutionist connotation in the implantation of the dialectical position of the alterity archetype in collective consciousness, operating beyond the polarized position of the patriarchal archetype, allows us to relate this implantation to the myth of Buddha in the East and to the myth of Christ in the West. The implantation of the alterity archetype rooted in the Christian myth is prospectively related to the origins of the modern arts, sciences, love, social democracy, immunology, ecological balance, sustained economy, and dynamic psychotherapy.

Through the symbol-centered perspective, Jungian symbolic psychology studies the process of individuation and the process of humanization of the cosmos with their immense creativity and their shadow dysfunctions. This symbolic perspective allows us to include concepts from all psychological schools such as analytical psychology, psychoanalysis, individual psychology, psychodrama, Gestalt, transpersonal psychology, cognitive psychology, schools centered on body symbolism and phenomenology.

The extension of the concept of structuring symbol, complex, function, and system to include the subjective and the objective dimensions amplifies the concept of psyche to become a synonym of being as formulated in Heidegger's ontology (1927), and by the reunion of the objective concept of the universe with the subjective concept of god. From then on, we can conceive the polarities mind-body, mind-nature, energy-matter, and subjective-objective as structuring functions to form consciousness through symbolic elaboration within the dimension of being or of psyche.

In this theoretical perspective, illustrated in chapter 15 by the interpretation of the myth of Oedipus, the structuring of consciousness is conceived through a process of attachment-detachment in the formation of identity and of the ego-other polarity, which integrates progressively the archetypal potential of the central archetype, permanently confronting and trying to rescue the fixated symbols in the shadow. Its ultimate finality is to experience the grandiosity of creation and the humanization of the cosmos through the dialectical development of consciousness of infinity and eternity in enlightenment, including the experience of death and resurrection within wholeness.

Bon voyage!

Chapter 1

ADLER, JUNG, AND FREUD AND THE FRAGMENTATION OF DYNAMIC PSYCHOLOGY

"God is only one but through the ages, the sages have given Him many names." (Hindu saying)

The Theory of Knowledge in Psychology

A basic challenge to psychology is that it is the object and also the subject of study. Jungian symbolic psychology elaborates this methodological question by situating the ego facing the non-ego-the other-within consciousness and considering both an expression of the central archetype of the Self. This means that knowledge of all things and self-knowledge include the ego and the other within a permanent relation between themselves and the whole, always coordinated by archetypes.

Within this theory, the ego and the other are formed by the elaboration of symbols through structuring functions coordinated by the central archetype, by the archetypal quaternio comprised of the matriarchal, patriarchal, alterity (anima/animus), and totality archetypes, and by the remaining archetypes.

The ego is constituted by the representations of the subject. As it is structured, it differentiates itself from the non-ego, which expresses the representations of the other. In this manner, the ego and the other occupy the center of consciousness, are rooted in all symbols, and are the result of the fulfillment of the potential of the central archetype.

The methodical application of the theory of knowledge to psychology is difficult because, as the ego is formed and begins to operate, it cannot as yet consider its origin and take into account the other. In this initial stage, which includes elaboration through the matriarchal and patriarchal archetypes, the ego tends to consider itself the center of the psyche, what we call omnipotence in psychoanalysis and inflation in analytical psychology, and it can be normal or defensive. Reducing the psychic dimension considerably by so doing, the ego frequently considers itself the central archetype and relates to others as if they were autonomous entities.

Before the ego becomes aware of how it came to be and how it functions within the coordination of the alterity archetype, it is very difficult for it to be aware of its limitations and to operate without being inflated or omnipotent. To practice the "just measure" within the psychic dimension, the ego needs to learn to function in the dialectic position of the alterity archetype and in the contemplative position of the totality archetype. But the ego and the other begin every new transformation through the nondifferentiated position of the central archetype followed by the insular matriarchal and the polarized patriarchal positions, which are necessarily unilateral. Only after these three positions can the ego attain the dialectic and the contemplative positions, free itself from unilaterality, and relate on equal terms with the other.

The theory of polarities, valued from Heraclitus all the way to the alchemists and much emphasized by Hegel and Jung, also has central importance in Jungian symbolic psychology. It reminds the ego that it will never be alone because the other is its inseparable companion throughout life and indispensable to experiencing totality. This applies to every pole of all polarities.

The ego-other relationship is complemented by the other-other polarity in which the ego can be with either pole or with both, depending on circumstances. If I speak about the polarity of health and sickness, for instance, I relate myself with two others and at any moment I can be healthy or sick. The same occurs with all the polarities other-other, such as day and night, strong and weak, yesterday and tomorrow, right and wrong, life and death.

Knowledge is acquired through the relation of ego to other and of other to other within the dialectical position of alterity, and the contemplative position of totality guides the psyche to systemic symbolic knowledge, which is permanently open to relating creatively symbolic meanings with totality.

However, the acquisition of knowledge is frequently carried out within the insular matriarchal and polarized patriarchal positions which, as we shall see, are frequently unilateral, belong to natural development, and tend to be complemented during life. Think of the child's dependence on the parents which grows toward equilibrium and then inverts during life. The circumstantial unilaterality of opposites is quite normal and only becomes defensively inflated and omnipotent if, for one reason or other, it becomes fixated.

In such cases, ego-other or other-other dissociation occurs through fixations formed during symbolic elaboration which are the origin of defenses. They were discovered by Freud and I will here consider them always pathological, from the archetypal perspective of the shadow. After fixation, the ego-other or other-other polarities are subject to defensive behavior and become incapable of normal interaction. Let us imagine a case of claustrophobia in which the conscious ego is compelled by its fixed and defensive part in the shadow to climb up twelve flights of stairs for fear of the confines of the elevator. One part of the ego wants to go into the elevator while the other part, fixed and operating in the shadow through defensive fear, compels the ego to climb the stairs.

These initial considerations are important for understanding that the pioneers of dynamic psychology did not express many of their discoveries through a fully symbolic perspective, but rather within unilateral and reductive concepts, which must be reconsidered.

Some Reductive Formulations of the Pioneers

The discovery of the repressed unconscious which produces symptoms (Freud and Breuer 1893), considered by Freud to be the foundation of psychoanalysis, established the reductive approach that marked the psychodynamic concepts of the twentieth century (Freud 1914b). The consequences of this were that the unconscious, and especially the pathological unconscious, was deemed the most important part of the psyche to the detriment of consciousness and normality. Jung followed Freud in reducing the focus of psychoanalysis to the unconscious when he began his Terry Lectures with *The Autonomy of the Unconscious* (1940) and titled a central chapter of his memoir *The Confrontation with the Unconscious* (*Die Auseinandersetzung mit dem Unbewussten*), opening its prologue with: "My life is a story of the self-realization of the unconscious" (1961, p. 3). Nise da Silveira named her book on the paintings of psychotic patients *Images of the Unconscious* (1981). Frances Wickes, the pioneer of Jungian child psychotherapy, enhances the concept to the point of naming childhood *The Realm of the Unconscious* (1927). Ellenberger, who described the history of dynamic psychology, entitled his book *The Discovery of the Unconscious* (1970). Thus, the subjective dimension of symbolic psychology was reduced mostly to the unconscious pole by the pioneers of the field.

In this manner, twentieth-century psychology lost the symbolic bipolarity which includes the relation of unconscious and conscious psychic characteristics to form the identities of the ego and the other in consciousness and in the shadow.

This unilaterality greatly hindered the recognition of the importance of consciousness and its permanent dialectic relationship with unconscious characteristics in individuation and humanization, as well as in the understanding of psychological development side by side with psychopathological phenomenon. Obfuscated by the discovery of unconscious characteristics of the psyche, modern dynamic psychology did not fully realize that the great discovery of the nineteenth century, besides unconscious processes, was the rescue of the subjective dimension from subjective-objective dissociation and the dialectical functioning of the subjective side by side with the objective within the symbolic perspective of conscious and unconscious imagination. It is this unilaterality that Jungian symbolic psychology attempts to avoid through the formulation of the five ego-other archetypal positions in consciousness, which makes the ego-other relationship inseparable from archetypes.

Jung's concept of the collective unconscious rooted psychological reality in a transcendental dimension beyond the repressed unconscious of psychoanalysis. Jung's original vocation was archaeology, and the dream that gave him the idea of the collective unconscious in 1909 establishes the conscious-unconscious polarity through an archaeological metaphor. Here we see clearly the psychological stratification that reduced analytical psychology's concept of the archetype to the unilaterality of the unconscious.

> I was in a house I did not know, which had two stories. It was "my house." I found myself in the upper story, where there was a kind of salon furnished with fine old pieces in rococo style. On the walls hung a number of precious old paintings. I wondered that this should be my house, and thought, "Not bad." But then it occurred to me that I did not know what

the lower floor looked like. Descending the stairs, I reached the ground floor. There everything was much older, and I realized that this part of the house must date from about the fifteenth or sixteenth century. The furnishings were medieval; the floors were of red brick. Everywhere it was rather dark. I went from one room to another, thinking, "Now I really must explore the whole house." I came upon a heavy door, and opened it. Beyond it, I discovered a stone stairway that led down into the cellar. Descending again, I found myself in a beautifully vaulted room which looked exceedingly ancient. Examining the walls, I discovered layers of brick among the ordinary stone blocks, and chips of brick in the mortar. As soon as I saw this I knew that the walls dated from Roman times. My interest by now was intense. I looked more closely at the floor. It was of stone slabs, and in one of these I discovered a ring. When I pulled it, the stone slab lifted, and again I saw a stair-way of narrow stone steps leading down into the depths. These, too, I descended, and entered a low cave cut into the rock. Thick dust lay on the floor, and in the dust were scattered banes and broken pottery, like remains of a primitive culture. I discovered two human skulls, obviously very old and half disintegrated. Then I awoke. (Jung 1961, pp. 158-159)

In 1911 Freud and Adler separated, and in 1914 Jung renounced the presidency of the International Association of Psychoanalysis (Jones 1953). By this time, Freud had built up the pillars of his monumental work on the notion of the unconscious which would modify Western culture. He considered it to be the third limitation on humanity's self-esteem. The first was Copernicus's heliocentric system, through which we learned that the earth was not the center of the solar system, and that human beings had also lost this privileged position. The second was Darwin's discovery of evolution, by which we gave up our belief in our direct descent from God to become just one more species among all others. Freud considered the unconscious as important as these two earlier discoveries (Freud 1917).

However, if we include the polarity of the personal-collective unconscious in the symbolic dimension together with the conscious-unconscious and subjective-objective polarities, we can situate the importance of Freud's discovery within the symbolic dimension and avoid the damaging reduction of psychological reality to "the unconscious."

The Collective Unconscious and the Process of Individuation

In 1904-1905, Jung worked in the psychiatric department directed by Eugen Bleuler in the Burghölzli Hospital, Zurich, on experiments involving word association and other physiological measurements to uncover bodily manifestations of the repressed unconscious discovered by Breuer and developed by Freud. From these studies emerged the concept of the complex, which Freud (1909) used to describe the Oedipus complex. In 1916, Jung described the transcendent function which guides the imagination to go beyond the literal and operate in the symbolic dimension (1958). In 1919, Jung employed for the first time the term archetype. It comes from Plato's theory of forms, or theory of ideas (eidos), which represents categories of things. For the philosopher, these are the basic patterns of the mind. Passing from the complex to the archetype and from Freud to Plato, Jung revealed the direction in which his creativity would take him.

Through the concept of archetype, Jung formulated the theory of the collective unconscious and transcended pathology, which was initially predominant in the notion of the complex due to its origin in the dynamics of the repressed unconscious. He began to describe archetypal images in different cultures and in the dreams of patients. He discovered the images of totality in mandalas and conceived the central archetype, which he named the Self, and the archetype of the inner world of man, which he named anima, and of woman, animus. Discovering the meaningful association of archetypal images with psychological development in the second half of life, in 1928, Jung described the process of individuation (Jung 1928).

However, in conceiving of the archetype as exclusively unconscious, following Freud's concept of the id, Jung introduced unilaterality into analytical psychology, which was reinforced when he identified child development exclusively with the personal and nonarchetypal. The personal-archetypal polarity was described by Jung primarily to differentiate psychoanalysis from analytical psychology. This was a great error because it implied that personal symbols, such as mother, father, and child, were not archetypal and this proved not to be so when it was discovered in the 1950s that the ego is formed by archetypes.

As is well known, Freud and Jung parted after 1912, when Jung published *Symbols of Transformations* (1912), wherein he disagreed with Freud's reduction of libido to sexuality and instead equated it with psychic energy. This disagreement has been considered the explicit cause of their separation, but it does not express the many differences between their theories. It is incredible to think that these two great geniuses, with so many theoretical divergences to be creatively elaborated, never again spoke to one another. No doubt a huge pathological complex was constellated between them (Byington 2005a). Psychoanalysis went ahead without the creative structuring function of archetypes and individuation, and Jung developed his work unaware that the ego is formed by archetypes, that personal symbols such as father and mother are always also intensely archetypal, and that the fixation of symbols and the resulting defenses are the origins of evil and the shadow. Freud's separation from Adler (in 1914) reinforced the unilaterality and reduction of psychological development respectively to the drives of sexuality and power and prevented psychology from seeing them as archetypal structuring functions which normally operate side by side and, when fixated, form the shadow.

During the development of his work, Jung related the process of individuation to the symbols of individual development. It is important to note his discovery that the search for the philosophical stone in alchemy is a metaphorical process that expresses the search for totality in the individuation process and that he considered alchemy the forerunner of analytical psychology (Jung 1944).

The unilateral approach Jung took to alchemy is related to the reduction of the archetype to the subjective and to the unconscious, in keeping with the cultural subjective-objective dissociation, thus considering magical-mythical reality, dreams, and participation mystique as manifestations of the unconscious. In this manner, he could not identify that which I have named the insular matriarchal ego-other position as a position of consciousness. To analytical psychology, Freud's repressed unconscious and the collective unconscious could be differentiated through the personal-archetypal polarity.

The Experience of Analysis

During the first half of the twentieth century, psychoanalysis reduced itself to sexuality and aggression (incest and parricide), its discoveries centered mostly in childhood, with the parental complexes reduced to the Oedipus complex, describing the sexual development of the personality ending in puberty. Adler's individual psychology reduced itself to the power drive and social ascension, and analytical psychology centered itself on the individuation process in the second half of life.

The general connotations of the three main schools of dynamic psychology had their practical applications well laid out. In 1956, before graduating from medical school, I began analysis, psychoanalytically oriented, which lasted four years. During this process, I felt increasingly clear about my childhood and parental complexes but at the same time existentially limited by the method of regression and the reduction of my psychological life to childhood and parental complexes. My exuberant religiosity, creativity, and search for totality were insistently reduced to a childish longing for paradise and incest. Years later, I came to understand why Americans refer to analysis as head shrinking.

After four years of analysis, I participated for a few months in a group coordinated by Dr. Nise da Silveira to study Jung. As I read the initial chapters of *The Archetypes and the Collective Unconscious* (volume 9 of Jung's Collected Works), I felt a strong call and six months later arrived in Basel, coming from Paris by train. I had come to train at the C. G. Jung Institute in Zurich, Switzerland. Jungian psychology gave me back the symbolic meaning of life events in the search for totality. Recently, I understood that experience even better when I heard a Tibetan proverb in the film "Samsara" (2001): "The only way for a drop of water not to dry is to find the sea." However, this encounter with the archetypal dimension was only fully realized when I discovered that the archetype is also conscious and therefore can be not only consciously sought out but also taught. To capture the theory of this experience decades later, I wrote the book *Education from the Heart: A Jungian Symbolic Perspective* (2004).

Of course, my experiences were relative, comparing psychoanalysis in a Rio de Janeiro school and analytical psychology as practiced at that time in Zurich, but even so, for me this was very meaningful, mainly because during analysis I studied the authors of each school exhaustively. Through these studies, I was able to develop theoretical perspectives that integrated basic concepts of both schools: fixation, defense, and regression in psychoanalysis and symbolic life and the process of individuation coordinated by archetypes in analytical psychology. In this manner, I had the opportunity to experience the practical formation of analysts within the theoretical differences of these two schools. Freudian training analysis required four to five sessions a week and did not admit candidates over thirty years old, because it was based mostly on the method of regression. Jungian analysis required one to two sessions a week and the more mature the candidate the better, because it was based on the prospective meaning of symbols within the individuation process. At 28 years of age, I was in the acceptable limit of Jungian analysis. During my training, I was taught that children, adolescents, and young adults who came for therapy should be sent to a Freudian analysis "to finish up forming the ego" and only afterward undertake analysis based on the archetypes. At that time, the Jungian school in Zurich had not yet incorporated the studies of archetypal ego formation, which began in the 1950s, and on account of this it was still based unilaterally in the process of individuation in the second half of life as formulated by Jung (1943). The maternal and paternal complexes were treated as problems of adult life and not as primary archetypal factors in the structuring of the ego and the shadow (Byington 2008a).

I arrived in Zurich in April 1961. Jung died two months later. The Freudian, Jungian, and Adlerian fields were by now clearly delineated. The schism had been traumatic but was followed by relative peace, each school now flourishing and forming analysts according to the theoretical formulations of its founders and frequently surrounded by a wall of prejudice, sorrow, spite, reductions, and above all by ignorance of the other two. Worst of all was that each school equated its master's theories with truth and did not question the emotional reasons behind their separation, the theoretical meanings of their disagreement, or the possible gains of their reconciliation.

Europe had suffered two devastating wars in the first half of the century, and the field of dynamic psychology was intensely affected by World War II. In 1929, Freud wrote *Das Unbehagen in der Kultur (Civilization and Its Discontents)*, full of pessimism (Freud 1929). The Nazi party had 6 million votes that year in the national elections. In 1933, National Socialism came to power and installed a dictatorship that became increasingly fanatic, anti-Semitic, ruthless, warlike, genocidal, and suicidal (Byington 2003b). After much resistance, in June 4, 1938, Freud left Vienna with Ana, his youngest daughter, and went to Paris and then to London. England and France declared war on Germany in September 3, 1939, after the invasion of Poland, and

Freud died twenty days later. Four of his five sisters who remained in Vienna were killed in concentration camps (Gay 2006).

From the time he parted from psychoanalysis, the label of mysticism was applied to Jung's work, but after World War II, he was increasingly accused also of anti-Semitism and of having been a Nazi sympathizer. It was to no avail that he denied these accusations and was defended by many Jewish friends, some of whom had analyzed with him, such as the Kirsches from San Francisco. The greater his fame more was he attacked. I will not enter into details of this situation about which much has already been written, as can be seen in Deirdre Bair's *Jung: A Biography* (2003). I want only to emphasize the suffering inflicted by this rupture to all the three pioneers and their schools, which increased their emotional separation and prevented their creative association for the study of their differences. Although it may seem absurd to the scientific mind, it is frequently the case that specialists from one school of psychology are guided exclusively by its theoretical orientation and ignore all others.

The six years of creative relationship between Freud and Jung were characterized by close communion and intense fascination both felt for the unconscious dimension. Freud was admired as the founding genius and Jung as a brilliant psychiatrist who was consecrated and chosen by the master in his professional youth to be his main disciple and probable heir. In 1911, Jung was elected first president of the International Society of Psychoanalysis. The context was meaningful because Freud was a neurologist in Vienna and Jung was the chief psychiatrist under Professor Bleuler, director of the Burghölzli in Zurich, who had named schizophrenia (previously known as dementia praecox). At the time, Zurich was an important center of German psychiatry together with Munich, where Emil Kraepelin worked. Besides this, Freud was Jewish and Jung was Christian, which was a favorable aspect for the man intended to be the main proponent of psychoanalysis.

Much has been written about the Freud-Jung relationship for its historical importance in modern psychology (Moritz 2007). What I want to call attention to here is the immense emotional and professional expectation one had on the other and the frustration and grief which resulted from their nonelaborated rupture. It is notable that Jung did not associate his separation from Freud and his imminent withdrawal from the presidency of the International Society of Psychoanalysis with the murdering of Siegfried in a dream he had in December 18, 1913, which he interpreted as a collective problem of Germany:

I was with an unknown, brown-skinned man, a savage, in a lonely, rocky mountain landscape. It was before dawn; the eastern sky was already bright, and the stars fading. Then I heard Siegfried's horn sounding over the mountains and I knew that we had to kill him. We were armed with rifles and lay in wait for him on a narrow path over the rocks.

Then Siegfried appeared high up on the crest of the mountain, in the first ray of the rising sun. On a chariot made of the bones of the dead, he drove at furious speed down the precipitous slope. When he turned a corner, we shot at him, and he plunged down, struck dead.

Filled with disgust and remorse for having destroyed something so great and beautiful, I turned to flee, impelled by the fear that the murder might be discovered. But a tremendous downfall of rain began, and I knew that it would wipe out all traces of the dead. I had escaped the danger of discovery; life could go on, but an unbearable feeling of guilt remained.

When I awoke from the dream, I turned it over in my mind, but was unable to understand it. I tried therefore to fall asleep again, but a voice within me said, "You must understand the dream, and must do so at once!" The inner urgency mounted until the terrible moment came when the voice said, "If you do not understand the dream, you must shoot yourself!" In the drawer of my night table lay a loaded revolver, and I became frightened. Then I began pondering once again, and suddenly the meaning of the dream dawned on me. "Why, that is the problem that is being played out in the world." Siegfried, I thought, represents what the Germans want to achieve, heroically to impose their will, have their own way. "Where there is a will there is a way!" I had wanted to do the same. But now that was no longer possible. The dream showed that the attitude embodied by Siegfried, the hero, no longer suited me. Therefore it had to be killed. (Jung 1961, p.180)

We must consider also another amplification to further understand the dream. In Teutonic mythology, Siegfried was the son of Sigmund. This amplification strongly suggests the meaning of killing Siegfried as not only sacrificing and abdicating from the presidency of the International Society of Psychoanalysis, which soon followed, but also that Jung was giving up being the son of Sigmund Freud and the elected prince and heir of the psychoanalytic movement. Jung himself describes the nature of his emotional relationship with Freud: "But he still meant to me a superior personality, upon whom I projected the father" (ibid., p. 163).

Another amplification for the symbol of killing Siegfried, never mentioned by Jung, was to put a final end to the fantasy of Sabina Spielrein, who had moved to Vienna and belonged now to Freud's group. The fantasy was that Spielrein and Jung would become the central couple of psychoanalysis and have a son who would be called Siegfried (Carotenuto 1978). In a letter sent to Jung, together with her article on the death instinct (Spielrein, 1912), which Jung published side by side with the second part of his book, *Symbols of Transformation*, she expressed this clearly:

> Dear:
> Receive the product of our love, the paper (for you) is our little son Siegfried. It gave me a lot of work, but, for Siegfried, nothing would be too difficult (Carotenuto 1978, p. 115).

A key factor to understanding the dream, omitted repeatedly by Jung, and registered in one of Jung's black books, according to Sonu Shamdasani, was that the dream ended with Jung going up a mountain pulling Emma's hand. This and many other details of Jung's life in 1913 led Maria Helena Guerra to interpret this dream and Jung's *Red Book* as the expression of Jung's relationship with Toni Wolff, in her book *The Red Book - The Love Drama of C. G. Jung* (Guerra 2011).

To the suffering in the Freud-Jung separation we have to add that neither of them ever undertook analysis. This formed an ideal condition for the reciprocal unconscious projection of their defensive father complexes, which I think occupied an important role in their shadows (Byington 2005a). They did try to analyze each other, but that soon proved to be impossible, as we can well understand today, due to the concomitant personal involvement they were in.

> The trip to the United States which began in Bremen in 1909 lasted for seven weeks. We were together every day, and analyzed each other's dreams. At the time, I had a number of important ones, but Freud could make nothing of them. I did not regard that as any reflection upon him, for it sometimes happens to the best analyst that he is unable to unlock the riddle of a dream. It was a human failure, and I would never have wanted to discontinue our dream analyses on that account. On the contrary, they meant a great deal to me, and I found our relationship exceedingly valuable. I regarded Freud as an

older, more mature and experienced personality, and felt like a son in that respect. But then something happened which proved to be a severe blow to the whole relationship.

Freud had a dream-I would not think it right to air the problem it involved. I interpreted it as best I could, but added that a great deal more could be said about it if he would supply me with some additional details from his private life. Freud's response to these words was a curious look-a look of the utmost suspicion. Then he said, "But I cannot risk my authority!" At that moment he lost it altogether. That sentence burned itself into my memory; and in it the end of our relationship was already foreshadowed. Freud was placing personal authority above truth. (Jung 1961, p. 158)

What we know from their letters is that their separation occurred without any elaboration whatsoever of the mutual defensive projections of their father complexes (McGuire 1974). Consequently the great creative prospect of their joint work was frustrated and acted out defensively. Some of the gaps inherited by their followers have been since elaborated upon, mainly by Jungians. This is significant because the theory of archetypal ego formation, which had been left to psychoanalysis and to the "personal unconscious," applied to analytical psychology proved in time to be inevitable.

I consider myself a follower of these three pioneers to whose ideas I owe with immense admiration and gratitude my personal analysis and my theoretical training. In this book I want to examine the creativity that remained latent in their works and in the works of their followers, and which has not been clearly registered and developed. From the very beginning of my professional development, I have dedicated myself to this work. I have written and lectured about it for fifty years, primarily taking into account the archetypal foundations of psychoanalysis and even going so far as to invite Dr. Nise da Silveira to found a school of archetypal psychoanalysis. In the First Venezuelan Congress of Psychotherapy, I gave a lecture entitled "Freud and Jung: That Which Emotion Prevented from Uniting" in which I continued to study the complementary aspects of their theories that have always fascinated me (Byington 2005a).

During my analytical training, first in psychoanalysis (1956-1959) and then in analytical psychology (1961-1965), I lived deeply the two theories and their differences. As these were therapeutic but also training analyses, I experienced with intense suffering the degree to which the central themes of both theories were charged with the emotions of their authors and how their lack of analysis had limited deeper elaboration. In psychoanalytic parlance, we could say that the nonelaboration of these themes was due to fixations surrounded by defenses and much resistance. From the perspective of analytical psychology, it would seem that these difficulties constellated pathological complexes in their shadows. Whether the diagnosis is fixation or shadow formation, the important matter for this book was my perception of a great emotional resistance in dynamic psychology generally, in precisely that which I most needed and longed for-the integration of the different theories and practices to elaborate many important issues of my soul and many questions about the past and future of humankind.

To reiterate, during my training in Zurich the frame of reference characterizing the differences of analytical psychology and psychoanalysis, from the Jungian perspective, was the personal-archetypal polarity, with psychoanalysis reduced to the personal and analytical psychology to the archetypal dimension. The theoretical foundation of psychoanalysis was considered personal by Jung and analytical psychologists because it was centered on ego formation through primary relationships. Analysis in analytical psychology aimed to develop consciousness in the second half of life through the anima and animus archetypes as psychopomps of the individuation process, for which one had to detach from the ego and cultivate the Self, considered the main archetype (Jung 1943). On the other hand, hiding in my psychoanalytical luggage were the notions that Jung was labeled a mystic and that the concept of the archetype did not have anything to do with analysis, much less with psychoanalysis. There was even a great aversion to using the term analysis instead of therapy to refer to any therapeutic process based in Jungian psychology mainly because it did not work through defenses.

Experiencing and studying all three theories intensely, it became increasingly impossible to accept their differences as reciprocally exclusive. Although my mind was not clear on this question, I disagreed with the theoretical separation of the three schools and intuitively sensed a common denominator between the concepts of defense and repression in psychoanalysis, the process of individuation in analytical psychology, and the development of the personality through the power drive in individual psychology. The differences between Freud's and Adler's theories as explained by Jung through the extraversion-introversion polarity seemed to me insufficient because, although not mentioned, it was clear that Adler's power drive lay in the shadow of the Freud-Jung controversy. The possible bridges between the three schools were strengthened when I studied the works of Melanie Klein (1932), Erich Neumann (1955), and D. W. Winnicott (1964).

As the years passed, I formulated the concepts of structuring symbols, complexes, functions, and systems to express all phenomena in the psychological dimension, and this proved to be the common denominator I had searched for in dynamic psychology to articulate meaningfully the conscious-unconscious polarity. In this way, I also became aware that regression and prospection were a polarity inseparable from the structuring function of centroversion (Neumann 1949a). Regression occurs when the libido flows back to experiences of the past and centroversion occurs when the libido flows toward the central archetype. Of course, regression can occur together with centroversion and both functions can be normal or defensive, depending on how they become fixated and defensive, forming the shadow (Byington 2006a).

The Discovery of the Archetypal Formation of the Ego
The Archetypal Positions of Consciousness

In the second half of the 1950s an earthquake in analytical psychology shook the basis of Jungian theory and practice. These vibrations had a great influence on dynamic psychology and the consequences continue to produce waves of change even today. It all began with the studies of Jolande Jacobi (1965), Michael Fordham (1944), and Erich Neumann (1955) on the archetypal formation of the ego since life began. The differences between the personal and the archetypal dimensions crumbled and the theoretical separation between analytical psychology and psychoanalysis, which had permeated Jung's work for more than half a century as a barrier between his work and Freud's, disappeared. However, what I observed during the 1960s in Zurich was that the consequences of this discovery were not being absorbed, and the mere mention of the reintegration of these schools was felt by many as a lack of respect for the memory of Jung, recently deceased. I had no doubt then that the rupture between the three pioneers had constellated a collective defensive complex that was the great resistance, emotionally charged, which would need a long elaboration to be overcome.

However, this reunion seemed to me historically inevitable, and it has been undertaken by many authors, mainly Jungians in different ways. When I undertook it, I became aware that not only are the identities of the ego and the non-ego, that is, the other, formed through symbols, complexes, and functions coordinated by archetypes during the whole of life, but these archetypes express through symbolic elaboration five different positions of the ego-other polarity in consciousness. These positions participate actively in the process of symbolic elaboration and form the ego and the shadow (fixations and defenses) through the elaboration and fixation of symbols, complexes, functions, and systems, all of which express the central archetype of the Self.

The concept of the ego includes all representations of the subject and the concept of the non-ego, the other, all representations of objects. To understand this proposition, it is important to admit that the ego-other polarity occupies the center of consciousness, integrating and expressing the meanings virtually contained in the archetypes during the process of individuation. It is through symbolic elaboration that the identities of the ego and the other are formed and consciousness approaches totality, increasingly humanizing the genetic potential of the species. References to consciousness without an ego or the destruction of the ego, which we find mainly in Asian schools, correspond, as I shall describe later, to the passage of the ego from the polarized patriarchal position to the contemplative position, which does not mean disappearance or destruction of the ego but, on the contrary, to an extraordinary degree of ego development, abstraction, and detachment.

James Hillman (1975) created archetypal psychology, centered on countless amplifications and denying the utility of developmental psychology with ego and shadow formation, fixation and formation of defenses, and disregarding also the functioning of defensive transference. In this manner, it seems to me that archetypal psychology postulates a radically unilateral perspective reduced to the collective unconscious, which makes it very difficult to imagine it as a psychological reference to psychotherapy. Another methodological problem it poses is the preference given to polytheism, without relating it dialectically to monotheism and to the archetypal positions of consciousness. In spite of the brilliant and extensive symbolic elaboration of archetypal psychology, its reduction of symbols to archetypal images, without reference to ego formation and shadow formation through fixations and defenses, establishes enormous difficulties in understanding the individual and collective archetypal development dynamically, the formation of the shadow, the difference between the normal and defensive transference, and what archetypal psychotherapy is supposed to be.

It was the generalization of the symbolic perspective in the development of consciousness that led me to situate the process of symbolic elaboration, the conscious-unconscious polarity, and the difference of normal and defensive structuring functions including the transference in the center of Jungian symbolic psychology.

Jung and Polarities
The Reduction to the Unconscious

Although considering himself a thinking type (BBC interview with John Freeman, 1959), as far as I can see, Jung was an introverted intuitive thinking type with much mediumistic capacity. He had a special talent for understanding the symbolic meaning of things and their relation to psychological development, in spite of not having developed a systemic methodology, except for his theory of typology. He intuited that unilaterality unbalanced the experience of totality and was symbolically compensated within the Self, similar to Cannon's theory of homeostasis in physiology. Because of this, Jung gave great importance in his work to polarities and compensation. However, during the major part of his work (1902-1950), not knowing about the formation of the ego by archetypes and relegating the archetypes exclusively to the collective unconscious, he considered compensation reductively as the way the unconscious "corrected" the development of consciousness in the individuation process.

Jung formulated the theory that the psyche seeks the equilibrium of polarities in the search for wholeness through compensation carried out by the unconscious. However, when we acknowledge that consciousness is formed by symbolic elaboration coordinated by archetypal positions of the ego-other polarity, which participate significantly in any symbolic elaboration, we conclude that archetypes are both conscious and unconscious and, therefore, that compensation is not a function exclusively of the unconscious. Consequently, I conceive compensation as an archetypal structuring function, conscious and unconscious, coordinated by the central archetype during individual and collective development. In this manner, compensation is a prospective function inherent to symbolic elaboration. Jung's capacity to intuit the unilaterality of a symptom and to seek its corresponding polarity during therapy, for instance, illustrates the degree to which compensation can also be exercised consciously and should not be reduced exclusively to the unconscious. When we fully admit that archetypes and symbols are both conscious and unconscious, we understand that the same thing happens to compensation and imagination. The application of the concept of compensation consciously and unconsciously in the five archetypal ego-other positions of consciousness is the necessary condition for understanding the dialectic and systemic perspective of symbolic development.

The two reductions present in Jung's work are the concept of the archetype, of dreams, and of compensation limited to the collective unconscious and the concept of psyche dominantly encompassing subjective reality. As we shall see from the description of the five archetypal positions of the ego-other polarity, consciousness is formed by archetypes and functions through them. The ego is the fruit of the archetype. To conceive of the ego as a complex separated from archetypes is like wanting to have a fruit hanging in mid air. Therefore all archetypes here are conceived as being conscious and unconscious and operating through the ego in psychic reality, be it conscious, unconscious, personal or collective, subjective or objective.

In the practice of analytical psychology, many phenomena such as dreams were thus deformed because of their reduction to the unconscious. Side by side with the unconscious, the function of consciousness in dreams is also very important for it determines among other things whether they will be remembered or not. Why is it that many people do not remember their dreams? Sometimes this is due to a defense that blocks the perception of intimate reality. This hypothesis is reinforced when the person begins to become aware of his or her emotions and also his or her dreams during analysis.

I take great care when treating patients whose dreams remain totally unconscious and can never be remembered, because this can indicate a very serious dissociation. I can recall three patients who could never remember their dreams and each of whom had an intense repressive defense, which, when elaborated, precipitated a psychotic episode. This shows how much conscious and unconscious participation in dreams is normal and necessary.

There are cases of people who normally remember their dreams but who find they cannot remember them during certain periods, although we know they dream because they exhibit REM, that is, rapid eye movement, during sleep. The conscious-unconscious characteristics of dreams change with time. I have been in the habit of writing down my dreams since my first analysis, and I have observed that late in life I have begun increasingly to create while dreaming, mostly thinking about theoretical questions in my professional writing which develop during sleep as though I were awake, compensating unilateralities and deepening symbolic elaboration (dialectic position). This led me to think that dreams can also be expressed in any of the five archetypal positions of consciousness, and I stopped considering the unconscious a region of the mind and began to consider it a characteristic of psychic events side by side with conscious attributes in varying degrees in all symbols and archetypes, including dreams and symptoms.

The same can be said of the concepts, from psychoanalysis, of the repressed unconscious and the id, which together with the collective unconscious contributed to making the unconscious a place and to radically separating conscious from unconscious characteristics. It is important to acknowledge that Freud always treated defense mechanisms such as repression as universal phenomena which is the same as considering them to be archetypal. Defense mechanisms are considered by many to be exclusively unconscious, but I did not find this to be the case in clinical practice. A defense may be primarily unconscious, but when it is recognized and elaborated upon it can become conscious even as it continues to be active and to show resistance as a defense. A defense mechanism generally has taken many years to form and its conditioning has to be undone to revert it to a normal structuring function. Symbols, archetypes and normal and defensive structuring functions cannot be considered exclusively conscious or unconscious because their conscious and unconscious characteristics are always present and changing in varying degrees (Byington 2006a).

Cases of Defense Mechanisms

A twenty-six-year-old woman suffered depression related to her marriage relationship. When she had married one year earlier, she discovered that she was sexually frigid and that her sexuality was intensely repressed. She had learned from her mother that "sex was a dirty thing that only men enjoyed." She had never masturbated or had sexual fantasies and felt irritated whenever sexual matters were mentioned. She never had sexual dreams. She became depressed after realizing that she could not give herself up to her husband, whom she loved deeply. During therapy, I recommended her to read romantic books and to watch films with implicit and explicit sexuality. Her husband helped her with his understanding and companionship. She began masturbating during these readings and films and progressively rescued her repressed sexuality. Finally she began to have erotic dreams and overcame her frigidity.

Before she married, the repression of her sexuality had been almost totally unconscious; during therapy, the repressive defense became progressively conscious, but continued to be active due to the intense conditioning during her youth. To consider her repressive defense exclusively unconscious would have made her treatment more difficult and it would have prevented her treatment from being oriented by the conscious and unconscious characteristics of her repression. The mere fact that she felt irritated whenever sexuality was mentioned and was frustrated about not feeling sensual and orgasmic demonstrated that the repression was not completely unconscious, for if it had been, she would not have felt anything at all related to sexuality.

I have had patients in analysis whose defensive repression was almost totally unconscious and in each case it proved to be an extreme condition. These cases are rare, probably because they almost never seek therapy on their own initiative, and they are very difficult to treat when they do show up.

I remember the case of a fifty-year-old man who was sent to therapy by his sister "to develop spontaneity and joy of life and to relate better to his daughter." He was of Japanese descent, and like his father and his two brothers, he had been educated to work hard and that he did. His was the most intense case of workaholism I had ever seen. He suffered from a very intense repressive defense, which initially was almost totally unconscious and which, little by little during therapy, became more conscious, although always very resistant.

He had become a widow two years before. During the twenty years of his marriage, his wife, who he loved and respected, took care of their home and their daughter who was now seventeen. He worked as a manager and provided for the family. His sister sent him for therapy because she found to be true her niece's complaint that her father could not exchange more than two words with her at a time.

Even in this extreme case, however, I do not consider the defensive repression to be totally unconscious; when his sister mentioned the situation to him and recommended therapy, he recognized the logic of her argument and called me up. Although he felt unable to do it, he wanted very much to be able to talk intimately to his daughter, who he felt he loved very much. This led me to think that he was at least a little conscious of the repression of his emotions. Many of the cases of severe repression that we see are sent to therapy by doctors on account of physical symptoms and these are harder to treat.

The treatment of a repressive defense that is mostly unconscious demands much dedication and creativity of the therapist. As expected, this patient did not remember his dreams and the subject was so foreign to him that, reacting to my insistence, he asked me whether I had any patients who remembered dreams. Our dialogue was restricted to a few words describing daily events. After a detailed anamnesis, in which I searched but did not find the least manifestation of joy or spontaneity, I went again over his life history trying to discover the existence of any pleasurable event. After much effort he remembered an episode in his adolescence when he had learned how to play poker and had enjoyed it. From this session on, I began to play poker with him. (Cards and card playing is an expressive technique often used in child psychotherapy [Byington 2008a].) After a few sessions of intense resistance, we began to extract a few emotions. He taught the game to his sister and daughter, and they began to play poker and other card games with friends (Moccio 1980).

Through the structuring function of card playing, his repressive defense began to give way, and he began to recover a few sensations of joy and pleasure. During one game, I intentionally provoked him by cheating, and he expressed anger and indignation. To stress the importance of the loosening up of his repressive defense, I stood up and hugged him. Caught by surprise, he laughed heartily and then I hugged him again to congratulate him doubly for his spontaneous reaction, and we had a good laugh over it. In subsequent sessions,

I employed other expressive techniques to continue the elaboration of the repressive defense of his emotions. One technique that produced good results was a literary technique that consisted of writing letters to his relatives, including the deceased. He was especially moved by the letters he wrote to his wife, his daughter, and to the Japanese immigrants who came to live in Brazil. In the course of his therapy, during which the proportion of conscious and unconscious characteristics of his repressive defense varied intensely, it became clear to me how much this defense had limited the creativity of his imagination together with pleasure and spontaneity. As we overcame the defense through his intense conscious cooperation, he felt more and more the desire to participate affectionately in life, although he became aware that he did not know why. Gradually he realized that he needed to learn and train these new functions, and he dedicated himself to them with much enthusiasm. His creative capacity defensively imprisoned in workaholism was now engaged creatively to search for affection, pleasure, and happiness with very good results.

To elaborate any defense involves the conscious-unconscious polarity. The reduction of the concept of defense to unconsciousness limits the therapeutic alliance and hinders our ability to understand the psychodynamics of the Self and the working through of fixations, defenses, and shadow together with the prospective creativity of the personality.

The Illusion of Insight and the Defensive Omnipotence of Interpretation without Elaboration

The use of the unconscious pole as a separate location for the id, repression, and all the other defense mechanisms discovered by psychoanalysis, together with the reduction of the archetype to the unconscious by analytical psychology, has restricted our understanding of normal and pathological psychological development. This reduction has led to the illusion of insight, which is possibly the greatest disappointment and anticlimax of psychoanalysis.

Interpretation was treated as though it had the power of a magic wand. Apparently, it sufficed to make unconscious characteristics conscious for the symptom to disappear. This supposition arose with the disappearance of the phobia of water in the treatment of Anna O., the famous case by Breuer that inaugurated psychoanalysis. Through hypnosis and the talking cure, the cause of the symptom was discovered and it immediately disappeared (Freud and Breuer 1893).

This is where the usage of defensive interpretation began. Defensive interpretation is a defense of the analyst; it arises to cover up a feeling of powerlessness for not being able to change symptoms and defenses whose symbolic content have been made conscious. The analyst repeatedly floods the patient with interpretations. They may be correct, but they do not bring about any change of the symptoms. Although defenses have been made conscious, their conditioning has not been undone, and therefore they do not change. Defensive interpretation prevents analyst and patient from realizing that they are identifying symbols without really experiencing them emotionally.

The reduction of defenses to the unconscious prevented the understanding of the capacity of the conscious ego to elaborate pathology symbolically. This limitation favored the development of cognitive-behavioral psychology to modify symptoms without elaborating their unconscious aspects. In this manner, there emerged a new unilaterality, this time reduced by cognitive-behavioral psychology to the conscious pole, which also limits the symbolic elaboration of symptoms within the totality of the Self (Skinner 1953). When we elaborate symptoms symbolically related to the conscious-unconscious polarity, we can then systemically employ cognitive-behavioral psychology to undo the conditioning of defenses (symptoms) (Byington 1996).

Today, a growing number of analysts consider the unconscious dimension to be a characteristic of symbols together with the conscious dimension. In this manner, we can ascertain that what diminishes symptoms in most cases is not simply the conscious designation of their unconscious contents, but rather the emotional experience of their conscious and unconscious meanings, within the transference relationship, complemented by the ethical attitude and the conscious effort to undo the conditioning of defenses. I call this process the symbolic elaboration of symptoms. It is often put to use in the verbal working through of defenses in psychoanalysis, but it becomes incomparably more productive when undertaken with expressive techniques to activate the normal structuring functions that were distorted when they suffered fixation and turned defensive, that is, when they became symptoms. When an analyst believes that defenses are exclusively unconscious, it is only natural to restrict all technique to verbal interpretations to turn the unconscious into consciousness. It is also natural that if, after many such interpretations, defenses do not change, the analyst concludes that patients do not improve because they do not want to. Once we become aware that defenses made conscious still need to have their conditioning undone, we conclude that the exclusively verbal method of psychoanalysis is based on a conceptual error, that what happened in the case of Anna O., where it seemed that defenses once made conscious subside, was an extraordinary exception. If the analyst admits this limitation, he will try to amplify his therapeutic method with expressive techniques to elaborate and undo conditioned fixations (Sándor 1974).

One needs to join the causal "why" to the prospective "what for" to elaborate any symbol with its respective structuring function, normal or defensive, within the search for totality of the patient. In this manner, we can add to our methods expressive techniques, including cognitive-behavioral therapy and drug therapy, with the advantage of using them symbolically within the process of the individuation of the patient (Byington 2008a).

Case Example

A middle-aged woman, a psychologist, who was married and had two sons, had an episode of depression together with alcoholism. She was treated with an antidepressant and an anti-alcoholic drug, and her psychiatrist told her to be prepared to be treated for the rest of her life. After six months, she felt better, but she came for psychotherapy because she continued to feel lack of justification to live. Examining her symptoms psychodynamically, I intuited that her depression probably had an important normal component that expressed her guilt about drinking and about leading a life that fell far short of her potential. This was confirmed by fits of anger she experienced whenever frustrated, which showed great vitality. I further suspected that, being the younger daughter with a couple of brilliant older siblings, she defensively adopted the role of being fragile and incompetent, as Adler repeatedly pointed out, to avoid competition with her siblings and to be protected by them. This was confirmed by a compulsive tendency she had to go home and lie in bed "exhausted" after any successful performance, which thus "proved" her fragility. Her pathological depression was the consequence of not elaborating her normal depression for missing out on life and success. Only after the elaboration and the removal of the conditioning of this defensive fragility, which covered up her fear of competition, did her depression improve, and she could then abstain from compulsive drinking and cease taking medication.

Jung's Personalities

Jung, at the age of ten, carved a little manikin on the end of a ruler, one of his first expressions of his appreciation of polarities. He painted the little man and placed him inside a pencil box together with a blackish stone that belonged to him. The stone was painted in watercolor and divided into upper and lower halves. Jung hid them in the attic beneath the roof, and they were his great secret (Jung 1961).

Jung's relationship with polarities was taken up again with his no. one and no. two personalities during and after his adolescence. Personality no. one was his identity as a student and young adult with all the characteristic expressions and immediate necessities of these roles. Personality no. two was much larger and encompassing, more mature and even ancestral, interested in philosophy, nature, and the grandiose themes of life, including dreams and God. These two personalities express, in my view, a basic polarity of the ego. On one side, the ego focuses on the obvious necessities of daily life; on the other, emphasis is laid on important themes, generally considered erudite or spiritual. To identify personality no. one with the ego and personality no. two with the Self, as is frequently done, seems to me unilateral and reductive. It is perhaps more correct to see in them the ontic and ontological identities of the ego with both conscious and unconscious characteristics, as we find described in the existential school of psychology (May 1958). Ontic identity refers to current identity characteristics while ontological identity is rooted in the profound characteristics of the personality, but both belong to the ego and to the Self, and both are personal and archetypal.

Polarities and Science
Mind-Nature and Subjective-Objective within the Self

Possibly the main event inaugurating the modern science was the discovery of the heliocentric nature of our world by Copernicus (1473-1543) in the beginning of the sixteenth century. However, it was another century before the method characteristic of consciousness in exercising science was described by Descartes (1596-1650) in his *Discourse on Method* (published in 1637). Why? The first event is a great discovery. The second is much more abstract and encompasses the symbolic elaboration to discover its causes and consequences, including the formulation of the method that made it possible and which it inaugurates. Descartes continued the search of truth within the scientific method and arrived at the methodological separation of the subjective from the objective. Unfortunately, the understanding of this brilliant formulation has been impaired by the pejorative connotation Cartesianism has acquired, unjustly accused of proposing the dissociation of polarities, whereas it only proposed the necessity of differentiating them.

In this discrediting of Descartes, we see the importance of differentiating the normal from the defensive structuring function. The structuring function here refers to the differentiation of polarities. Descartes proposed the normal separation between mind and nature in order to reason correctly. Quite different is the fixation and dissociation of mind and nature that turns the normal structuring function of separation into dissociation, which is its defensive aspect. In fact, the subject-object dissociation was practiced extensively in the materialism of the nineteenth century, but Descartes did not have anything to do with it.

In the *Discourse*, Descartes establishes the necessity of separating thinking (*res cogitans*) from nature (*res extensa*) to differentiate scientific thinking from the magic-mythic mentality. Truly, the essential condition for elaborating anything away from the magic-mythic mentality is to separate it into polarities, primarily the ego-other or subjective-objective polarities, as a way to organize consciousness. If we confuse the objective nature of whatever it is we want to know with our own impressions, as we do in magic, our scientific observations will easily lead to confusion and error. How can the ego exercise its main function in scientific thinking if it does not completely differentiate itself from others, that is, the subjective from the objective? However, to separate the ego from the other is not an easy task; one needs to know the archetypal positions of the ego-other relationship in consciousness as described in chapter 4.

It is important to remember that the *Discourse on Method* was conceived in a historical period in which scientists were watched and persecuted by the Congregation for the Doctrine of Faith. Galileo (1564-1642) was humiliated and condemned for heresy in 1616 for having endorsed the heliocentric system and, in 1633, again judged and condemned for the rest of his life to house arrest on the same charge. Giordano Bruno (1548-1600) was condemned for heresy and burned in Rome in 1600 (Byington 1991a). Descartes himself feared persecution by the Inquisition, and in the last sixteen years of his life he fled to Norway and later to Sweden where he died. In this context we can understand the Discourse also symbolically; beyond its injunction to "think well" and separate the mind from nature, it is also a declaration of consideration for the other. At the same time he affirms the nature of the ego and separates the mind from nature, Descartes protects nature, that is, the other methodologically from the fanatical omnipotence of the Inquisition, which abused it by imposing the mythical perspective of the scriptures to violate objective reality. Descartes's "good thinking" is inseparable from the search for truth within freedom, which is the very oxygen of scientific mentality. As the Enlightenment expressed it so well afterward: "I disagree with everything you say, but I will defend with my life your right to say it."

The famous sentence of Descartes -"I think, therefore I am" - can be seen as the self-perception of the ego inseparable from the description of the scientific method. The more objectivity is identified in a scientific discovery, the more can one detect subjectivity, but both have to be well differentiated to practice the Cartesian method to "think well."

Freud pointed this out when he interpreted the resistance of collective consciousness to the discoveries of heliocentrism, evolution, and the unconscious dimension and pointed out the degree to which they affected the self-esteem and vanity of humanity. We can even say that the reaction of the Church to heliocentrism was based, among other things, on the threat that science would diminish its power over the knowledge of the universe. What the Church knew was based on the mythical revelation of the scriptures mixed with traditional knowledge, which it continued to repeat as though this were objective knowledge. The scientific method revealed through heliocentrism was new to the Church and rooted in the dialectical relation of truth and error exercised in the experimental method. This new method of reasoning threatened the power of the Church because it began to reveal the truth transcendent to conscious will and prevented its dogmatic manipulation for political convenience.

Psychology and Polarities

To function in polarities is a basic need of consciousness to differentiate and coordinate the representations of the subject (ego) and those of the dimensions of nature, body, society, and emotions, that is, of the object (the non-ego or other). The ego needs to separate from the other so that each can form its identity. Afterward, as taught by the great masters of Tao, Zen, and Nirvana, consciousness, including both the ego and the other, will have to detach and transcend all polarities to reunite again within totality.

The rise of sexual polarity in the evolution of life was an important phenomenon that increased considerably the diversity of species and the capacity for adaptation and survival. During the first two billion years of life on earth, the reproduction of living organisms occurred by parthenogenesis, that is, without sexual differentiation. Gender appeared in evolution two billion years ago and favored genetic diversity from one generation to another.

Many of the organs of the human body are anatomically bipolar, such as the cerebral hemispheres, arms, legs, lungs, the sense organs, kidneys, sexual glands, and so on. The coordination of these polarities and their harmonious operation is one of the main functions of the body.

It is because these polarities are necessary that their effective coordination is so important. Similarly, in the psychological dimension, without the coordination of the ego-other polarity, consciousness cannot function properly. One of the characteristics of psychotic delusion, for instance, is the confusion of the ego-other polarity. However, symbolic elaboration which forms the identity of the ego-other polarity is always initially unilateral, which makes the tendency for the equilibrium of polarities a permanent psychological characteristic. This does not prevent from living countless polarities unilaterally on a day-to-day basis, and this inclines us often to forget that both poles are necessary for totality.

To avoid the unilaterality of polarities in the formulations concerning being, Heidegger (1927) abolished them altogether. This was the way he chose in philosophy to keep the unity of being intact in the search for knowledge of the world and for self-knowledge. Heidegger even avoids mentioning the poles of polarities in the description of phenomena and refers only to their existential dimensions. Instead of formulating the polarity mind-nature, for instance, he refers to the human condition *(Dasein)* as being-in-the-world *(Dasein ist in-der-Welt sein)*. I shall never forget a panel discussion between Heidegger and the Swiss psychiatrists that I attended when I was training in Zurich. After much arguing, some of it surprisingly emotional, the disappointing conclusion that "no conclusion was possible" was accompanied by remarks colored by defensive arrogance on both sides, according to which philosophers ignore mental disease and psychiatrists are not capable of understanding philosophy.

I realize and admire Heidegger's genial capacity for abstraction and his theoretical effort to remain always within the integrity of being, without dividing it into polarities (Heidegger 1927). For philosophers it is possible to deal with metaphysics avoiding polarities because they do not have to deal methodologically with either the ego or shadow formation nor with consciousness-shadow interaction as something indispensable to treating people and differentiating good from evil and normality from pathology. However, in psychology and psychiatry, it is not possible to avoid polarities because, from beginning to end of the developmental process, we need to accompany the ego's differentiation from the non-ego. Psychology can only transcend polarities at the end of every symbolic elaboration, when consciousness operates in the contemplative position. In the proximity of physical death, this transcendence is not only fully possible but necessary, as we shall see in chapter 12.

Polarities and the Symbolic Dimension

Polarities frequently present a relation of opposition within their dimensions, which unfortunately led us to refer to them in common parlance as opposites: beauty and ugly in the aesthetic dimension; day and night in the cosmic dimension; love and hate in the emotional dimension; legality and crime in law; good and evil in the ethical dimension; health and disease in medicine, and so on. In this way, polarities coexist within unities, which is sometimes difficult to conceive. It is common, for instance, to see doctors treating symptoms objectively only with drugs without elaborating simultaneously their emotional subjective counterpart. Even when behavioral techniques are also applied, the subjective dimension is not fully considered because unconscious characteristics are left out. We also frequently see specialists in the natural sciences who study nature without relating their observations with their subjective aspects. Without a doubt, the forms of observation of only one pole separated from its counterpart tend to divide and alienate being.

Therefore, psychologists and psychiatrists who need polarities to describe the differentiation of the ego from the other must undertake a great methodological effort to avoid remaining on only one pole. When, however, we fall into dissociated unilaterality, we increase considerably the power of the ego through defensive omnipotence (inflation) but we also fall prey to alienation. In such cases, we lose the dialectic and systemic perspective and, consequently, the integrity of being. Health and disease, for instance, are polarities of being in the world, but when we deal exclusively with symptoms as something dissociated from health, we become alienated from the human reality of our patients, a fact unfortunately frequently found today in medical practice. Here the patient is equated with his or her symptom, becoming just one more case of depression, phobia, or schizophrenia. We stop seeing the patient in all his or her human complexity, and we miss the unique way in which every person suffers and reacts to disease and to medication. In cases of depression, for instance, this frequently occurs when the depression is treated pharmacologically or through cognitive therapy exclusively as a pathological symptom. The structuring function of depression is then reduced to a disease, which prevents the correlation of normal and defensive depression within the mood dimension of each specific personality (Byington 2007). Taking into account these considerations, it is easy to understand why Heidegger and the Swiss psychiatrists could not understand their differences in the approach to mental disease.

In this manner, as Descartes postulated, we need to separate the subjective from the objective. On considering the reality of polarities, Jung gave them a place of honor in his work. However, in considering the unconscious dimension completely separate from the conscious, the archetypal dimension excluding the personal dimension, and individuation exclusively in the second half of life, he fell into methodological unilaterality. As a result, Jung left to his followers the mission of redeeming analytical psychology from these unilateral positions and the task of situating them methodologically within the symbolic systemic and ontological dimension through the relationship of the polarity that has the ego-other as one pole and the central archetype as the other pole, that is, the symbolic axis. In this undertaking, the dialectic encounter of the works of pioneers in dynamic psychology must be addressed to reunite "that which emotion did not allow" (Byington 2005a).

Jungian Diplom Thesis

My diploma thesis at the Jung Institute in Zurich was *Genuineness as Duality in Unity* (Byington 1965), wherein I began to unite Heidegger and psychiatry through the dialectical interaction of polarities within several human dimensions, including the psychological and the philosophical. It was a search to find the ways polarities interact in such a way that being preserved genuineness (Heidegger 1927). This was the first formulation of my later conception of the archetype of alterity, which includes the anima and animus archetypes within the dialectical position of the ego-other relationship in consciousness.

In the chapter on psychology, I related the works of Freud and Jung as complementary. A few analysts in the institute reacted with such aversion that it almost prevented the presentation of my thesis. In the dissertation, I sketched the notion of the complementarities of analytical psychology and psychoanalysis as a vast theme whose study had to be undertaken. On one side, the meeting of the two bodies of work expressed the synthesis, mostly intuitive, of my professional and analytical experience. On the other, it pointed to the future direction of my creativity in search of a theoretical formulation, which included not only the work of the pioneers but also of their major followers, who I considered to be Melanie Klein and D. W. Winnicott in psychoanalysis and Erich Neumann in analytical psychology. This synthesis was later formulated through the extension of the concept of archetype, of symbol (structuring symbols), and of the archetypal nature of all psychological functions (structuring functions) which coordinate normal development, but which, when fixated, originate defenses (psychoanalysis) and the shadow (analytical psychology) (Byington 2006a).

The Jung Institute first assigned the examination of my dissertation to three colleagues, presided over by my own analyst, who did not accept at all the idea of the complementarity between psychoanalysis and analytical psychology. This led to the traumatic end of a profound analytical relationship, which by itself shows how the C. G. Jung Institute in Zurich at the time did not take into account the meaning of the defensive transference of analyst and of analysand in the analytical relationship (Byington 1985). New examiners were nominated and my thesis was approved, but the damage had been done, forming a defensive complex and a creative block which lasted ten years. I only became conscious of its intensity when, after having returned to Brazil, I was asked to write the foreword to the translation into Portuguese of Jung's *Memories, Dreams, Reflections*. I remained with the book for a whole year, at the end of which I returned it to the publisher without the foreword and with many apologies.

The rebirth of my creativity from this nigredo occurred with synchronicity when I was asked to give a lecture at the celebrations in Rio de Janeiro and São Paulo of the one hundredth anniversary of Jung's birth. When I started hesitantly to write, a theme occurred to me immediately and my writing became fluent again; the title was "Freud and Jung: Two Opposites Which Make a Whole" (Byington 1975). After this lecture, I was invited to coordinate the study of Jung and Neumann by a group of psychologists and psychiatrists in São Paulo. From this group was born the Brazilian Society for Analytical Psychology, which has trained more than one hundred analysts and contributed to the formation of Jungian analysts, study groups, and societies in Uruguay, Venezuela, Argentina, Chile, and Ecuador.

However, my reencounter with analytical psychology needed further elaboration of the defensive complex formed in the aftermath of my analysis in Zurich. Paradoxically, destiny determined that this elaboration should occur during my third analysis, this time with a Kleinian analyst. I felt the necessity to continue my analysis and, due to the ambivalence toward my preceding

Jungian analysis, I looked for a Kleinian practitioner, with whom I elaborated my needs at that time and also the interruption of my Jungian analysis. The analyst and her husband had belonged to the original Freudian group in Germany. They came to Brazil to found the Brazilian Society of Psychoanalysis in Rio de Janeiro. During this analysis, I experienced the method of regression in the Kleinian School, which Neumann (1955) described as the disturbance of the archetype of the great mother in early childhood. Surprisingly, my analyst told me that she admired Jung very much, and, perhaps as an exception due to my particular process, she told me a dream: she was in a sailing boat on the high seas; the captain was an old man with a white beard-the captain was Jung.

During these four years of analytical didactic and therapeutic holding, I had a very important dream: I was within the womb of my analyst. The walls were rosy and the atmosphere twilight, as in Bergman's film Cries and Whispers. I was fascinated by the works of Jung and Freud side by side on a bookshelf.

I immediately associated the film, in which a woman dies, asphyxiated by asthma, and returns to life, with my Zurich crisis and the "resurrection" of my creativity through the transference in my Kleinian analysis (Byington 1996). A mythological amplification of this transference wound, which also came to mind, was the wound of Telefo which could only be cured by the lance of Achilles that had inflicted it.

The reunion of Freud's and Jung's works within the transference womb were quite clear as part of my creative project, but why it should occur within a Kleinian womb was not clear to me at the time. Afterward I understood this symbol better by studying the emphasis Melanie Klein laid on child imagination and her formulation of the schizo-paranoid and depressive positions of the ego. They became the basis of my concept of the five archetypal ego-other positions in consciousness, undoubtedly an encounter of analytical psychology and psychoanalysis within the symbolic axis. These positions join dynamically the ego and consciousness with archetypes, which thus become conscious and unconscious, forming a central tenet of Jungian symbolic psychology. From this perspective, we realize clearly that the central archetype is virtual, the ego of consciousness is its normal creation, and the ego of the shadow is its deformed expression due to fixation and defense formation.

In chapter 4, the detailed study of the five archetypal positions and the four regent archetypes of symbolic elaboration will lead us to a systemic understanding of normal and defensive structuring functions, of normal and of pathological unilaterality, fixated and expressed through defenses in the shadow.

Chapter 2

THE SELF AND
THE CENTRAL ARCHETYPE
THE TRANSINDIVIDUAL DIMENSIONS
OF THE SELF

Jung named the totality of the personality - which includes consciousness, ego, persona, shadow, and the archetypes - Self. However, he also frequently used the concept of the Self as the main archetype. Because he focused on the developmental process in the second half of life, this ambiguity had fewer consequences in his work than in the work of Fordham (1944), Neumann (1955), and Edinger (1972), who studied the archetypal formation of the ego and decided to maintain it. Fordham, for instance, writes:

> In the present book, I shall demonstrate, I hope conclusively, that individuation processes are active in infancy and childhood and that they are an essential feature of maturation.
>
> In setting out to show this, I shall make use of a concept of the Self somewhat at variance with Jung's, though his formulations are not consistent . . . . On the one hand he defined the Self as the totality of the psyche, comprising the ego and the archetypes, a conception which means that these structures are parts of the whole. On the other hand, he thought of the Self as an entity which organizes all parts and is super ordinate or transcendent to them-a separate entity. The two conceptions cannot be easily reconciled . . . It was in the later growth of his ideas that Jung developed a different idea: the

Self was an organizer, the central archetype. (Fordham 1944,
pp. 27-28)

In spite of this, Fordham continued to use the word Self for both
functions. This ambiguity added confusion to Neuman's work and those, like
Edinger, who adopted his concept of the ego-Self axis. If the ego is part of the
Self, how can we have an ego-Self axis? Because of this, I use the term Self
exclusively for the total psyche and denominate the main archetype, the central
archetype, as did Jung (1912), Fordham (1944), and, more consistently, Perry
(1974). To correct Neumann's ambiguity, I refer to the expression ego-Self
axis as the ego-central archetype axis or simply the symbolic axis.

This semantic imprecision which superimposes the Self and the central
archetype is specially confusing when applied to ego development because
frequently, although unwillingly, it gives the idea that the ego lies outside of
the Self and so induces the crucial error of denying the archetypal root of the
ego. Fordham started this when he described ego formation through
deintegration of the Self. Neumann continued it by formulating the ego-Self
axis. I suppose that what Jung wanted to express with the concept of the Self
was all the parts of the psyche within a unity. When we name the whole Self
and describe the ego deintegrating from it or having an axis on which to relate
with it, we are situating the ego in and out of the Self at the same time. This
creates countless opportunities to express confusing situations while describing
ego development within the Self. Edinger also sees this ambiguity and
maintains it, trying uselessly to justify himself, when he writes:

These diagrams represent progressive stages of ego-
Self separation appearing in the course of psychological
development.

Ego-Self Axis

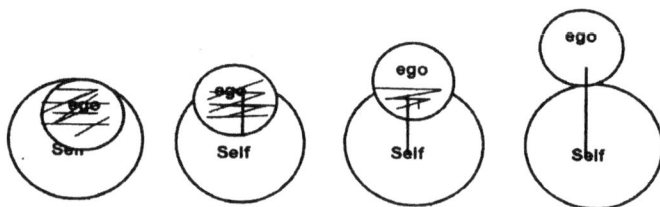

Diagram 1

The shaded areas designate the residual ego-Self identity. The line connecting ego-center with Self-center represents the ego-Self axis-the vital connecting link between ego and Self that ensures the integrity of the ego. It should be understood that these diagrams were designed to illustrate a particular point and are thus inaccurate in other aspects. For example, we generally define the Self as the totality of the psyche which would necessarily include the ego. According to these diagrams, and to the method of this presentation, it would seem as though ego and Self become two separate entities, the ego being the smaller lump and the Self the larger lump of totality. This difficulty is inherent in the subject matter. If we speak rationally, we must inevitably make a distinction between ego and Self which contradicts our definition of Self. The fact is, the conception of the Self is a paradox. It is simultaneously the center and the circumference of the circle of totality. Considering ego and Self as two separate entities is a necessary rational device for discussing these things. (Edinger 1972, pp. 5-6)

The use of the term Self for the main archetype and also for the whole personality did not generate much ambiguity until the 1950s, because it was not yet known that the ego was formed by archetypes. At present, however, it is a great source of conceptual confusion, and correcting this situation is of the utmost importance for analytical psychology.

This semantic indiscrimination exacted a high price, for example, in Edinger's oversimplification, highly confused and contradictory, when he writes:

It is generally accepted among analytical psychologists that the task of the first half of life involves ego development with progressive separation between ego and Self; whereas the second half of life requires a surrender or at least a revitalization of the ego as it experiences and relates to the Self. The current working formula therefore is, first half of life: ego-Self separation; second half of life: ego-Self reunion. (Ibid., p. 5)

The whole matter can be corrected if we designate Self the factual totality of the psyche and central archetype, the virtual coordinating center of the developmental process.

As we shall see in chapter 4, the relation of the ego with the central archetype and with the four regent archetypes characterizes five archetypal positions in consciousness, which vary in every life situation and in the developmental life stages of symbolic elaboration in the individual and in the cultural Self. This conception becomes very distorted when we separate the ego from the Self, and worse, when we reduce their relationship to a typical pattern in the first or second half of life.

From Archetypal Image to Structuring Symbol

Considering the archetype a virtual pattern, Jung conceived its expression through archetypal images. Consequently, the image was reductively elected as the only symbolic expression of archetypes to the detriment of all other possible means. This reduction of archetypal expression to images created imaginal psychology and limited significantly the perception of the countless meanings of symbolic archetypal expression.

Jung developed the method of amplification in which the archetypal image to be interpreted appears in different cultural contexts to reveal different meanings. For this reason, Jung's works are full of cultural parallels to serve this purpose. I acknowledge the value of amplification, but I believe it can be applied to any psychological representation and not only to images.

After the discovery of archetypal ego formation, the polarity personal-archetypal became senseless. From then on, it became clear that individual and collective consciousness are coordinated by archetypes and, therefore, that everything in the psyche is archetypal. Is there, for instance, anything more personal and, at the same time, having the greatest archetypal capacity to form our ego than our parents? One poet almost four hundred years ago realized that small events may have great capacity to influence our lives when he gave Hamlet the line: "There is a special providence in the fall of a sparrow" (*Hamlet*, act 5, scene 2). Part of the resistance toward realizing the senselessness of the personal-archetypal polarity may be that, if one does so, the main barrier that Jungians used for decades to keep analytical psychology in nobler territory than psychoanalysis disappears. However, although psychoanalysts may never admit it, aren't all defense mechanisms used to form what was once called the personal unconscious also archetypal? Is there any human being in any culture immune to repression, idealization, displacement, reactive formation, defensive projection, defensive introjection, or defensive transference?

Considering that the ego and consciousness are formed by the central archetype, as the coordinator of psychological representations present in all life experiences, it follows that archetypes are always present and can be expressed not only by images but also by representations in all the other senses of society, nature, body, words, ideas, emotions, numbers, behavior, and even by silence. In other words, archetypes express themselves through anything that has meaning in the psychological dimension. Because of this, I chose the traditional concept of symbol to express archetypes and extended it to encompass all polarities, such as subjective-objective, conscious-unconscious, literal-transcendent, personal-collective, concrete-abstract, life-death, mind-body, mind-nature, and energy-matter.

Symbol, from the Greek *syn* "with" and *ballein* "to throw," meaning "to throw with," is the ideal concept to express the union of each and every psychic polarity. Considering all psychological representations to be archetypal, this obviously includes all symbols. There are symbols that are only imaginary, for example, the dragon; there are those that can be concrete, for example, the rhinoceros, but also imaginary, like the rhinoceros totems of certain African tribes. In this context, complexes are defined as a cluster of symbols.

In this extended form, symbols also include concepts that involve meaning, such as metaphors, signs, allegories, emblems, parables, illustrations, and so on. Signs are limited symbols. The traffic light, for instance, generally only considered as a sign is also a symbol which can be codified as a sign or not. Although the meaning of its red, yellow, and green lights is set and internationally codified, they can also be used as figures of speech. "Watch out, for if you repeat the insult, you may turn on a red light in our relationship," says the enraged friend. "I have called him up and given him the green light to start the project," remarked the company CEO. The main extension of the concept of symbol that I propose is the inclusion of objective representations together with the subjective representations that are typical of the traditional concept. In this way, oxygen and blood are just as symbolic as an emotion or an experience and medicine is as symbolic as art. One can say, for instance, "I never had enough oxygen in my family." Or "soccer is in the blood of the Brazilian people." My medical colleagues, mainly orthopedists and neurologists, generally find their hair standing on end when they hear me say this. Their strong reaction seems to me to be part of the subjective-objective dissociation which medicine inherited from materialism, and which does not admit body symbolism in any way whatsoever. And yet how can we conceive psycho-somatic medicine without body symbolism?

This extension of the traditional notion of symbol led me to formulate the concept of the structuring symbol which expresses archetypes to form consciousness. When symbols suffer a fixation and are acted out through defensive functions, they become pathological structuring symbols in the shadow.

I have called the transformation of symbols forming the identity of the ego and the other in consciousness the process of symbolic elaboration, and I consider it to be the central operation of the psyche. At the same time I have named all subjective and objective functions structuring functions because they work on the structuring symbols to extract meanings that structure consciousness. Someone gets in his car and turns on the motor; the car is a structuring symbol and driving is a structuring function. The heart beats sixty times per minute and pumps blood into the arteries; the heart is a structuring symbol and circulation is a structuring function. I hear a song I love; the song is a structuring symbol and the love of music is a structuring function. I take a sun bath; the sun is a structuring symbol and heat is a structuring function. I hate someone; this person is a structuring symbol and hate is a structuring function. I admire a politician; this public figure is a structuring symbol and admiration is a structuring function. Newton discovered gravity; Newton is a structuring symbol and gravity is a structuring function. Symbols and structuring functions form complexes and have countless meanings; when seen working systemically, they reunite duality or multiplicity in unity. To consider life experiences as structuring symbols and functions leads us to see the interaction of all things systemically within the Self forming individual and collective consciousness in the individuation and humanization processes. A cardiologist must elaborate the symbol of the heart during every consultation to distinguish the objective from the subjective heart. If he cannot see the heart symbolically and only sees it objectively he will be a very limited professional.

Categories of symbols and structuring functions form structuring systems of consciousness. A citizen commits a crime, stands trial, and is convicted; his crime is a symbol, the trial is a structuring function, and the law is a structuring system. A youngster breaks a leg and needs surgery; the fracture is a structuring symbol, surgery is a structuring function, and medicine is a structuring system to organize consciousness.

When Jung rescued the concept of libido from its reduction to sexuality and redefined it as psychic energy, he freed the psyche to be studied and understood in its creative grandiosity. However, the concepts of archetype, complex, archetypal image, psychic energy, individual Self, and individuation are insufficient to express the psychic interaction of all parts. The concepts of energy (including mental and physical energy), archetype (including the subjective and objective consciousness and unconsciousness) structuring symbol, function, and system, individuation process (individual Self), humanization process (cultural Self), fixation, defenses, and shadow, encompassing all experiences of being-in-the-world allow us to build a theoretical dialectical and systemic framework to study and understand psychic vitality and its limitations when it suffers fixations. At the same time, they show that fixed unilaterality and reduction are the black holes and cancer of knowledge. A doctor incapable of conceiving the symbolic body will never be able to treat his patients as human beings.

The Ego-Other Polarity

The reduction of the concept of archetype to the collective unconscious reduced consciousness to an epiphenomenon of secondary creative importance.

When we examine the concept of consciousness within dynamic psychology, we see that it was conceived and employed structurally and functionally in a unilateral way. Freud (1914a) described ego formation from the beginning of life through narcissism. Jung saw the importance of consciousness when he remarked: "Man's capacity for consciousness alone makes him man" (Jung 1954a, par. 412) and "the attainment of consciousness was the most precious form of true knowledge, the magical weapon which gave man victory over the earth, and which will give him a still greater victory over himself" (Jung 1934a, par. 289). Jung also tried to reunite psyche and matter in his work through the concepts of unus mundus, the psychoid, and synchronicity. However, the fact that he followed Freud in conceiving the ego as the center of consciousness (Jung 1923) prevented him from apprehending the representations of the subjective-objective interaction, that is, the relation of the interior and exterior world as a characteristic of the structure of consciousness necessary to form the identity of the ego and of the non-ego, that is, the other.

When we consider that the ego and individual and collective consciousness are formed by the elaboration of structuring symbols, complexes, functions, and systems coordinated by archetypes through polarities, including the subjective-objective polarity, we conclude that what occupies the center of consciousness is not only the ego complex but the ego-other polarity. In this polarity, the ego expresses the representations of the subject and the other, of the object, and through the formation of their identities consciousness incarnates the central archetype.

Jung was completely aware of the formation of the object together with the subject in consciousness:

> If one reflects upon what consciousness is, one is deeply impressed by the extremely wonderful fact that an event which occurs outside in the cosmos produces simultaneously an inner image. Thus it also occurs within, in other words, it becomes conscious. (Jung 1934b)

However, the difficulty of seeing the representation of objects as the non-ego in permanent interaction with ego formation in the center of consciousness prevented Jung from perceiving the ego-other and inner-outer polarities as representations of all psychological events within consciousness.

The existence of the ego-other polarity in consciousness was not seen before, possibly due to the subject-object dissociation that traditionally kept nature, body, people, and the other in general out of the psyche. Psychoanalysis treats this other as introjected objects in the ego and therefore continues to ignore the reality of the ego-other polarity in consciousness. However, even ignored as an an-sich reality, the other is always there, not inside the ego, but side by side with it in consciousness. Let us examine briefly, as an illustration, the polarity man-woman in the consciousness of a man. His masculine identity was formed during his lifetime. In the same way, the identity of his non-ego, of woman, was formed through his many life experiences with women beginning with his mother. We can say the same about the symbol of man as other in the ego-other polarity of a woman's consciousness.

In this perspective, that which distinguishes consciousness from the shadow is not the nature of structuring symbols, complexes, functions, and systems but what happens with them during the process of symbolic elaboration, that is, whether they become fixated and defensive or not. The determining factor is therefore dynamic and not structural, that is, it is acquired and not inborn. The fixation that originates the shadow also involves the ego-other polarity. In this way, we see that the shadow also has an ego as subject always associated with an object, the other.

We analysts generally talk to our patients about their shadows, and we seldom give voice to the ego and the other in the shadow. It is a very important initiation for an analyst to animate the patient's shadow or his own in active imagination and let it give full voice to its identity. In that moment, the analyst will be convinced through his own experience that the shadow really has an ego-other polarity in the service of evil, which when seen in mythological Christianity is the devil. Of course, such practice of active imagination must be carried out only with patients who do not have anything more serious than a neurotic psychopathology and who have undergone enough analysis and shown that their conscious ego-other polarity has the strength to undergo such an "animated" encounter with their shadow. It is of paramount importance that the analyst has gone through this initiation himself before proposing it to his patients (film *The Exorcist*, 1973, which represents the devil as the psychotic shadow).

The Extension of the Concept of the Individual Self

Having situated the theory of archetypes in the collective unconscious, Jung went on to describe his theory of individuation in the individual Self. Jung's concept of the process of individuation enriched the psychoanalytic id with the possibility of an exuberant instinctive spirituality and creativity, which had not been imagined within the psychoanalytic theory of drives.

As far as I know, Erich Neumann (1949a) was the first who referred to the group Self. Although Jung reduced the comprehension of many cultural processes exclusively to projections of the individual Self to explain cultural factors, as in his introduction to alchemy (Jung 1944) without mentioning a transindividual Self, he also refers many times to a collective dynamic without reducing it to individual dynamics. In his interpretation of Nazism, in *Wotan* (1936), and of Christianity, in *Aion* (1951), he also recognizes and describes primary collective characteristics in social phenomena. However, perhaps because he was personally affected by National Socialism and communism which devastated Europe in the first half of the twentieth century, he shows at times an almost phobic aversion to the collective dimension. This reaction prevented him from studying the archetypal roots of social movements in the humanization process and how these roots could form collective consciousness and shadow above and beyond the individual Self. Jung's devaluation of social movements, labeling them "isms," expressed, in my view, a defensive prejudice to the collective dimension which he equated with the masses.

> If the subjective consciousness proffers the ideas and opinions of collective consciousness and identifies with them, then the contents of the collective unconscious are repressed . . . And the more highly charged the collective consciousness, the more the ego forfeits its practical importance. It is, as it were, absorbed by the opinions and tendencies of collective consciousness, and the result of that is the mass man, the ever-ready victim of some wretched "ism." (Jung 1954b, par. 425)

> I have been blamed in many quarters for allowing myself to speak of German "psychopathy." I am-and always was-of the opinion that the political mass movements of our time are psychic epidemics, in others words, mass psychosis. (Ibid., par. 465)

The theory of individuation and the differentiation of the individual from the collective dimension proposed by Jung can be complemented by the concept of transindividual dimensions of the Self, irreducible to the individual Self, of which there are many, for instance, atom, cell, family, society, culture, planet, and cosmos among others. When such reduction is attempted, collective symbols become centered on the individual. To avoid this reduction, a theory within Jungian symbolic psychology that describes the process of humanization of the cosmos, based on the work of Teilhard de Chardin (1947), complements Jung's theory of the individuation process together with the development of the cultural Self based on the same archetypes. This theory is centered on the symbol and prevents reducing conscious development to the individual dimension. In all the other dimensions of the Self, the elaboration of structuring symbolic functions and systems is coordinated by the same central archetype.

When symbolic elaboration expresses the individual Self, it furthers the development of individual consciousness primarily and collective consciousness only secondarily. However, when symbolic elaboration occurs within the cultural Self, it propitiates the direct development of collective consciousness. Let us imagine, for instance, the elaboration of the symbol of water. Each of us has many associations with water as a result of the individuation process, which for Westerners may include taking pleasure in bathing and saving water for the benefit of all. However, from the perspective of the cultural Selves of India and China, which depend on irrigation to cultivate rice to feed more than two billion people, the symbolic meanings of water can be seen in a quite different perspective. When the water symbol is studied on the level of the planetary Self, the symbolic meaning of water may be even more complex, because we must then relate the aquifers of the planet with climate changes, underground pollution of rivers, water springs, and general climate changes, as when governments and world councils meet to deal with the water symbol. In such cases, the needs of the individual Self come second after considerations that primarily concern the cultural Selves, the continental Self, and, in ultimate analysis, the planetary Self and the cosmic Self. In this manner, we clearly see that the elaboration of all the dimensions of the Self is centered on structuring symbols, complexes, functions, and systems coordinated by the central archetype. These symbols include the differentiation of the individual Self but transcend it by far to include all other dimensions of the Self.

In the extension of the concept of the Self to encompass the totality of all existential dimensions it is of fundamental importance to include the individual-planet and individual-cosmos polarities with all their meanings in the formation of consciousness. Only in this way can we avoid the unilaterality of cultivating the individual pole to the detriment of the collective dimension, which unduly separates psychology from sociology, politics, law, economics, astronomy, chemistry, and physics.

The scope of transindividual consciousness can only be correctly formulated with the representation of the world around the individual. The central archetype is situated in the nervous system of every person. Due to its totalizing capacity, it can group representations of phenomena from all existential dimensions that have a meaningful relationship (diagram 1). In this sense, the cosmic Self is the subjective and objective representation of the universe in consciousness. The subjective-objective dissociation in Western culture led us into the materialism of science and to the separation of science from religion. This is, however, a pathological defensive split, because the subjective representation of totality projected onto a divine figure cultivated emotionally through faith is symbolically inseparable from the objective characteristics of the universe studied through scientific truth within the cosmic Self.

The Process of Individuation and of Humanization

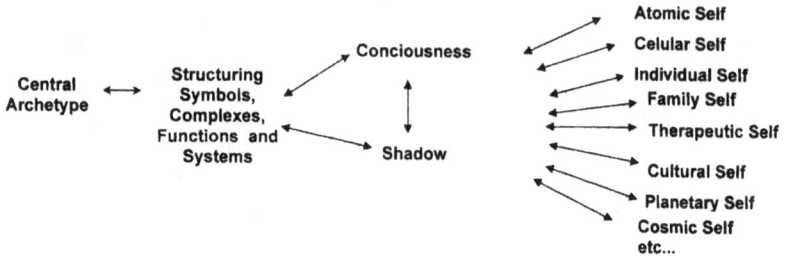

```
                                                              Atomic Self
                                       Conciousness           Celular Self
  Central        Structuring                                  Individual Self
  Archetype  ←→  Symbols,                                     Family Self
                 Complexes,                                    Therapeutic Self
                 Functions and                                
                 Systems          →    Shadow                 Cultural Self
                                                              Planetary Self
                                                              Cosmic Self
                                                              etc...
```

Diagram 2

The concept of the cosmic Self allows consciousness to think of the universal being as proposed by Heidegger, Einstein, Teilhard de Chardin, and many other important thinkers. We can do this only because we have within our nervous system a central archetype that forms our consciousness with representations acquired through the elaboration of subjective and objective, individual and transindividual symbols. As any psychiatric or neurological examination shows, time and space are the most important structuring functions for expressing either mental health or mental dysfunction in the adult personality. Within the cosmic Self, time and space can express eternity and infinity, which relate our consciousness to the symbol of the universe in physics, to the concept of being in psychology, and to the concept of God in religion. The larger dimensions encompass the smaller ones but each one must prevail in the existential dimension that is elaborating the symbol in question.

Including the subjective and the objective dimensions in the symbolic paradigm, Jungian symbolic psychology formulates the epistemological opening to encompass polarities but at the same time to maintain them related within the integrity of the Self. This perspective keeps the ego-other polarity permanently within consciousness and shadow in all dimensions, which allows psychology to understand transcendence of death and the experience of totality (see chapter 12). In this way, we can understand through reason and emotion the search for enlightenment within the humanization experience of the cosmos.

Chapter 3

ARCHETYPAL DEFENSE MECHANISMS NORMAL AND DEFENSIVE STRUCTURING SYMBOLS, COMPLEXES, FUNCTIONS, AND SYSTEMS

One of the big differences between analytical psychology and psychoanalysis can be expressed as a polarity that has at one pole image and at the other pole function, represented by the concept of archetypal image in analytical psychology and by the concept of ego defense mechanism centered on repression in psychoanalysis. Archetypal images give central importance to the archetype, while defense mechanisms give central importance to the ego; in both theories, however, the root of archetypal images and defense mechanisms were reduced to the unconscious pole of the psychic dimension. In chapter 2, we explored how the image is but one manifestation of the structuring symbol and is conscious and unconscious in varying degrees. Here we will do the same for defense mechanisms.

The image-function polarity is very important in the scientific theory of knowledge; it received central attention in the work *Process and Reality* by the English philosopher of science Alfred North Whitehead (1929). We know today that the dominant brain hemisphere, which contains the center of speech and is generally the left hemisphere, is relatively more verbal, rational, abstract, and logical, while the nondominant hemisphere, generally the right one, is more imaginal, intuitive, emotional, and musical. It has been observed that many personality types are dominantly imaginal and others dominantly verbal.

Jung displayed both types in his personality but the imaginal was very strong and possibly dominant. His choice of the image to express archetypes, his dedication to painting, sculpture, alchemy, active imagination, and the imaginal nature of his most important concepts, such as persona, shadow, anima, and animus, illustrate the imaginal type. On the other hand, Freud's preference for concepts is characteristic of the verbal type. Applying the theory of polarities, as Jung did in typology, the dominance of the imaginal type does not exclude the expression of the verbal side of the personality, as Jung's extensive verbal capacity demonstrates. The corollary is also true. The imaginal type in Jung and the verbal type in Freud show up in the interpretation of dreams: while Jung took dream imagery at face value, Freud gave it a secondary role (manifest meaning) and chose instead as more important the rational process underlying dreams (latent meaning).

Jung's preference for image led him to praise the poetic abundance of mythology while Freud's choice of process can be seen in his theory of the defensive neuropsychosis rooted in the pillars of the hysteria-obsessive neurosis polarity.

In this manner we see a relation of polarities in which we observe a complementary relation between the right and left hemispheres of the brain and, in the same way, between entity and process, that is, between image and function. This complementarity is the pillar of symbolic elaboration involving the interaction of structuring symbols, complexes, and functions, forming psychological structuring systems.

Jung's typological preference for images had been expressed since his childhood in the exuberant and detailed nature of his dreams, fantasies and artistic talent for painting, sculpture, and architecture, this last laboriously carried out in the work of building the Bollingen Tower. His talent for painting was expressed with great diligence in the composition of the *Red Book*, which contains images from his dreams and visions, painstakingly decorated with golden words written in old German. His typology appears also in the poetic choice of the terms shadow, persona, anima, animus, and child archetype.

> I had in those days a yellow, varnished pencil case of the kind commonly used by primary-school pupils, with a little lock and the customary ruler. At the end of this ruler I now carved a little manikin, about two inches long, with frock coat, top hat, and shiny black boots. I colored him black with ink, sawed him

off the ruler, and put him in the pencil case, where I made him a little bed. I even made a coat for him out of a bit of wool. In the case I also placed a smooth, oblong blackish stone from the Rhine, which I had painted with water colors to look as though it were divided into an upper and lower half, and had long carried around in my trouser pocket. This was his stone." (Jung 1961, pp. 20-21)

Freud, instead of image, emphasized the value of functions and concepts to express the nature of the psyche. At the very beginning of his work in 1892, he and Breuer attributed great importance to the function of repression in the discovery of unconscious processes, followed by projection and sublimation. He made the story of Oedipus central to his work, but he extracted from it mainly the functions of aggression (parricide) and sexuality (incest), with which he constructed his theory. The imaginal use Freud made of the figure of Oedipus was so limited that he did not amplify its meaning even with Laius's and Iocaste's filicidal attempt. Nor did he make use of the meaning of Oedipus's life as expressed in the plays *Oedipus the King*, Antigona, and *Oedipus at Colonus* by Sophocles, wherein the Oedipus complex is significantly amplified (see chapter 15).

Jung became conscious of Freud's unilaterality but, in my view, he went astray when he relegated psychoanalysis to the personal dimension and attributed analytical psychology to the archetypal dimension. His own typological unilaterality, present in the reduction of archetypal expression to images, prevented him from recognizing that the functions Freud preferred - repression, projection, sublimation, dislocation, condensation, and repetition compulsion-are also archetypal. No psychoanalyst would consider ego defense mechanisms absent in any culture past or present, which is sufficient to admit their archetypal nature.

Admitting that it makes no sense to differentiate psychoanalysis and analytical psychology along the personal-archetypal polarity, we see that the image-process polarity is important for separating these theoretical approaches. Another important point in the comprehension of both theories was Jung's lack of admission that defense mechanisms were archetypal. However, we must recognize that this lack of admission was greatly influenced by many significant reductions present in the psychoanalytical theory.

The first reduction is the well-known emphasis on sexuality, which is equivalent to Alfred Adler's reduction of libido to the power drive. This reduction was brilliantly identified by Jung and corrected by conceiving libido as psychic energy. However, besides the reduction of libido to sexuality, there are two other very important ones: the reduction of the id to literalization, and pathologization, which led to the fixed unilateral usage of structuring symbols, complexes, functions, and systems.

In describing the castration complex very close to literal castration, Freud reduced the threat of injury to the developmental process of being so well described by phenomenology in the existential school of psychology (May 1958). This reduction was so literal that Freud based feminine identity on penis envy and a castration complex as a result of being born without a penis (Freud 1905). Lacan's concept of the phallus corrected this distortion, for women can also have a phallus, meaning power. However, Lacan's many contributions to psychoanalysis, although much more symbolic, that is, metaphoric, continued the reduction to unconscious processes and to sexuality.

Another reductive literalization was Freud's interpretation of the primal scene as the actual or imagined sight of parental coitus by the child. The primal scene as structuring symbol and function of the parental couple, when seen in its full symbolic dimension is not exclusively sexual but an existential model of interaction within the mother-father bond and consequently of all polarities. It is so far-reaching because the parental bond is one of the main structuring symbols of ego formation as part of the primary quaternio, which includes the maternal and paternal figures, their relationship, and the reactions of the child in ego formation (see chapter 5). Therefore, to interpret the primal scene as the discovery of parental coitus is an emblematic example of symbolic reduction to literality. This is not to say, however, that structuring symbols, complexes, functions, and systems do not include literal, concrete, and reified meanings. In fact, from this perspective, the symbolic dimension includes a spectrum that extends from the very literal to the quite abstract and metaphoric. What I am criticizing is the reduction of symbols by defensive literality and not symbolic literality itself.

To these reductions of symbolism to sexuality, and literality, a third reduction can be found in the theory and practice of psychoanalysis, and it too greatly deformed psychic reality. It is the phenomenon of pathologization, that is, erroneously considering certain normal structuring symbols, complexes, functions, and systems to be pathological.

Within the subjective-objective dissociation of scientific materialism, the effort in psychology to rescue subjectivity when psychology became an academic field was met with great resistance. Academic objective science had difficulty recognizing the extraordinary richness and vitality of psychological creativity, emotion, and intuition expressed in the structuring transcendent function of the imagination. Within an atmosphere of prejudice and ideological control of knowledge, it was natural to invalidate the subjective dimension, and to consider it a source of insecurity and error. Even though admitted into the university to be studied scientifically, subjectivity and intuition were treated then and today as a scapegoat onto which many dysfunctions of scientific error are projected. These cultural conditions favored the reduction of the subjective to pathology. It is important to become aware that this disqualifying projection of scientific knowledge onto the subjective dimension was an extension of another projection which during the millennia of patriarchal domination was defensively projected onto sensuality and onto women as the depository of the emotional dimension. This defensive projection reminds us of the adage that to identify any social problem one should first look for a woman (*cherchez la femme*).

The beginning of acceptance of subjectivity in the academy occurred with madness. Phillipe Pinel (1745-1826), in France, and Anton Mesmer (1734-1815), from Vienna, entered Paris synchronistically in the 1778 (Zilboorg and Henry 1941). Mesmer practiced the treatment of mental disease using a method of suggestion, later called hypnosis, which he named animal magnetism, and Pinel began treating madness by separating patients from criminals. Although hypnosis, first named by James Brady in 1843, was established as a method of psychotherapy in the nineteenth century, Pinel is now considered the patron of psychiatry while Mesmer is mostly remembered as a charlatan. This illustrates the prejudice against hypnosis as a result of its dynamic penetration into the subjective realm where the conscious and unconscious function of imagination is found. Nonetheless, the treatment of the insane as patients was undoubtedly a gigantic step into the study of subjectivity.

During the nineteenth century, the subjective dimension emerged from the dungeons of Europe and was treated partly through hypnotism. Practiced in more than ten thousand cases by members of the Nancy School, initially Liébeault (1823-1904) and later Bernheim (1837-1919) and their assistants, the study of hypnotism convinced them that normal people can also be hypnotized. It seemed that the moment had arrived for the study of the subjective dimension to be received by the Paris Academy of Sciences. However, the prejudice against subjectivity prevailed, and this did not happen. The famous neurologist Charcot (1825-1893), heir of Pinel at the Bicêtre and Salpêtrière hospitals in Paris, prevented it. He presented a paper on hypnotism which was accepted by the Academy on the basis of his reputation. Unfortunately, his paper had a gross error: it asserted that only hysterical patients could be hypnotized. At the same time, Bernheim's paper, which affirmed that everyone can be hypnotized, was rejected (Zilboorg and Henry 1941). Was this the fault of the Academy? Hardly so. The misguided pathologization of the subjective was the real villain. Hypnosis, which entered into conscious and unconscious subjectivity, was accepted by the Academy, but only because it came with the label of pathology.

For a whole century it had been demonstrated that normal people could be hypnotized but at the point where it might have been recognized as capable of showing the richness and the creativity of conscious and unconscious imagination, it was pathologized. The fact that it subjectively expressed emotion, imagination, and conscious and unconscious suggestion was enough to consider it pathological.

Freud (1856-1939) was a student of Charcot. He was in Paris in 1885 and 1886, translating his teacher's books into German and learning to practice hypnosis. Returning to Vienna, he worked with his colleague and family friend Joseph Breuer, who also practiced hypnosis. In 1892, Breuer told him about the successful treatment of Anna O.'s phobia ten years earlier. As we know, this case was published by Freud and Breuer in a book on hysteria, and psychoanalysis was inaugurated.

Psychoanalysis and the discovery of repressed unconscious contents came to light from studying mostly cases of hysteria in women. Freud was a scientist educated in Helmholz's materialist positivism, by which irrational emotions were considered a disease and treated but not cultivated within the normal transcendent creativity of myth, poetry, love, and intuition. According to Jung, Freud once remarked,

> "My dear Jung, promise never to abandon the sexual theory. That is the most essential thing of all. You see, we must

make a dogma of it, an unshakable bulwark." . . . In some astonishment I asked him, "A bulwark-against what?" To which he replied, "Against the black tide of mud"-and here he hesitated for a moment, then added-"of occultism." (Jung 1961, p. 150)

The id could not contain the wonders of imagination and whenever it tried, it was stigmatized as occultist. From this perspective, it was inevitable that the concept of the archetype would also be considered esoteric.

It must be born in mind that Freud received from Breuer and Anna O. the discovery of the repressed unconscious which produces symptoms. At the time, general attitude within the scientific mentality about subjectivity and the creative imagination included an intense prejudice. It was perhaps within this prejudice that Freud conceived but did not duly praise that which I consider one of his major discoveries, that is, the formation of ego identity and consciousness from the beginning of life through primary relationships. More than infantile sexuality and the repressed unconscious, this concept inaugurated modern psychology and introduced into science the formation and development of the most extraordinary phenomenon of our species: consciousness!

As described in the preceding chapter, individual and collective consciousnesses are the final products resulting from the interaction of the vital prospective force of the central archetype and the symbolic work of past generations. By discovering its origin and formation in the beginning of life, Freud showed us the starting point of the great voyage of the humanization process in search of enlightenment. Although denied in many schools of psychology and ignored in philosophical treatises, without ego identity formation, psychological differentiation is impossible. However, as frequently happens, such an extraordinary discovery proved to be too much for one person to apprehend with all its simplicity and grandiosity, even one as capable as Freud. When we cannot bear the impact of a structuring symbol or function, whether because of pain and suffering or because of its greatness, there follow fixations, defenses, and shadow formation during its elaboration. When this happens, part of the Self is imprisoned in fixation and prevented from advancing freely in the way of knowledge and growth of consciousness. How could Freud value the greatness of the discovery of the development of consciousness when he himself and the philosophy of the scientific worldview within which he worked had not the slightest idea that our species is archetypally endowed to develop consciousness, to study and contemplate through reason and emotion the miracle of the creation of life and of the universe? In reality, Freud in his genius discovered the sunrise of a glorious day whose zenith and sunset he did not have the personal and cultural openness of mind and heart to contemplate. The sunrise was reduced to a perverse polymorph through the pathology of incest and parricide.

Defending himself from the impact of his spectacular discovery, Freud's work became so limited that his theory of ego formation ended in puberty, limited by the reduction to sexuality, to literality, and to pathologization through the Oedipus complex. Defensive pathologization reduces structuring symbols, complexes, functions, and systems to their pathological aspects by fixating their symbolic elaboration and restricting their total meaning.

Freud's scientific formation, guided by the principle of rational causality, led him to recognize the importance of Breuer's discovery of the repressed unconscious. This great discovery became the heart of his creative work, and when he plunged into himself to develop it further, he discovered the Oedipus complex. This discovery was an astounding feat of auto analysis. Incapable of once more bearing the burden of this discovery due to extraordinary moral suffering, Freud followed Oedipus, symbolically blinded himself through fixation and fell victim to the pathologizing defense. "I have the Oedipus complex," he could have said, "but all children are born with it, are perverse polymorphs and need repression and sublimation to form the superego and become normal."

Was not the human being considered criminal and expelled from paradise in Genesis, the myth of patriarchal dominance, for having eaten of the tree of knowledge of good and evil which had been placed there by the Creator? Did not Christianity, theologically deformed by the puritan defense that rendered it patriarchal, transform Adam and Eve's transgression into original sin from which children can be liberated only through baptism? And now Freud, an heir of the Enlightenment, an atheist who considered religion an obsessive-neurotic infantile regression, came to declare human beings evil and to recommend they be educated through repression and sublimation in order to mature and become civilized!

Due to the idea that the Oedipus complex should be repressed during childhood, psychoanalysis went on to conceive the ego defense mechanism of repression as something not only normal but necessary. Unfortunately this application of defenses to normal development contaminated most theories of psychodynamic personality formation.

The first pathologizing of normal development by psychoanalysis was the reduction of primary relationships to the Oedipus complex. The second was the application of defenses to normal development. The third instance of pathologizing normal development in psychoanalysis occurred with the theory of primary narcissism (Freud 1914a). We know today through much research that child development occurs through symbiotic relations (Mahler, Pine, and Bergman 1975, pp. 13-14). Based on these observations we can say that narcissism is a structuring function that reinforces ego development operating side by side with ecoism, which reinforces identity of the other during symbolic elaboration (Montellano 1996). On account of this, primary narcissism, which considered the ego independent of the other in the beginning of ego formation, is the projection of defensive narcissism on child development, which corresponds also to a defensive pathologization.

The fourth defensive pathologization of psychoanalytic theory occurred with another of its great discoveries, that of imagination. It was as though the grandiosity of the psychic dimension could not be acknowledged and had to be limited by defensive pathologization.

> When this etiology (of seduction) crumbled down by the weight of its own improbability and contradiction, in clearly verifiable circumstances, we became initially disoriented. Analysis had taken us to these infantile sexual traumas through the current way, and, however, they were not true. We stopped standing on firm ground. At that time (see letter to Fliess in 9/21/1897) I almost decided to give up my work. If hysterical patients refer their symptoms to traumas which are inventions, then the new fact which emerges is that they create such scenes in their fantasy and this psychological reality. This reflection was soon followed by the discovery that these fantasies were intended to cover-up auto-erotic practices of early childhood, to embellish and situate them on a higher plane. (Freud 1914b, pp. 27-28)

This episode illustrates how Freud discovered the conscious and unconscious structuring function of the imagination in psychic reality, but unfortunately reduced it to a defensive mechanism. Considering the Oedipus complex to be normal was a disaster because it pathologized and crippled the discovery of normal ego formation through primary relationships. If Freud had recognized in himself and in psychological development that the Oedipus complex is a defensive, that is, pathological, variation of the normal structuring function of the primary quaternio, the story of psychoanalysis and the whole field of dynamic psychology would have been much more creative. The structuring functions of aggression and affection occur frequently in symbolic elaboration of the maternal and parental complexes in the primary quaternio and also in the whole of life. Aggression and affection only become pathological, for instance, as in the Oedipus complex, when they become fixated and defensive.

Pathologizing the structuring quaternio through the Oedipus complex became a defensive model that greatly deformed the whole theory of psychological development. Its worse consequence was that children were deemed structurally sick and evil and needed repression and sublimation to behave normally and to mature in a healthy fashion. No doubt, this justified the repressive patriarchal tradition that permeated education and social systems since the beginning of the Christian era. As I shall describe ahead, symbolic elaboration coordinated by the alterity archetype instead of the patriarchal archetype does not describe any structuring symbol or function as innately pathological, as Freud did with the child-parent relationship. Coordination by the alterity archetype first examines symbolic elaboration carefully. If it is fixated and defensive, it is considered pathological (shadow); but if it operates freely (no matter what its content is), it is taken as normal.

The cultural tendency to pathologize the subjective, which underlined Charcot's erroneous interpretation of hypnosis and Freud's tendency to pathologize psychological development, also affected Alfred Adler's individual psychology. As is well known, he constructed his theory of psychological development based on a goal of compensating for overpowering feelings of inferiority, which explains feelings of ambition and all neurotic symptoms. For Adler, we can say, that the original sin is the inferiority complex present in all children.

The structuring function of power is one of the most important for psychological development. It is the drive that stimulates us to search for things we need and to build our normal sense of self-esteem and dignity. As with all structuring functions, the will-to-power is coordinated by the regent archetypes and finally by the central archetype to fulfill the urge toward self-realization in individuation (individual Self) and humanization (cultural Self). When Adler describes it mostly as the lifeline with the final purpose of fighting feelings of inferiority with the goal of superiority, he does not focus on the power drive as a structuring function for self-realization, but rather situates it as a defensive reactive formation. He followed this tendency in his explanation of all neurotic symptoms as reactive formations of the will-to-power to "arrange" the compensation for feelings of inferiority.

It is as though Adler did not recognize a genuine creative function for the power drive and had to reduce it to a defensive reactive formation. This attitude pathologizes it. In the following passage he clearly expresses this reduction:

> Thus the child arrives at the positing of a goal, an imagined goal of superiority, whereby his poverty is transformed into wealth, his subordination into domination... . In our present civilization both the girl and youth will feel themselves forced to extraordinary exertions and maneuvers. A large number of these are admittedly of a distinctively progressive nature. To preserve this progressive nature but, to ferret those by-paths that lead us astray and cause illness, to make these harmless that is our object and one that takes us far beyond the limits of medical art. It is to this aspect of our subject that society, child education and folk education may look for germs of a far-reaching kind. For the aim of this point of view is to gain a reinforced sense of reality, the development of a feeling of responsibility and substitution for latent hatred of a feeling of mutual good will, all of which can be gained only by the conscious evolution of a feeling for the common weal and the conscious destruction of the will-to-power. (Adler 1914, pp. 14-15)

Another epistemological distortion of psychoanalysis was the defensive unilateralization of the parent-children relationship in the way the Oedipus complex was taken to form identity. The Oedipus complex relates the prophecy of parricide by the Delphic oracle and of the attempted filicide of Oedipus by Laius and Iocasta. The myth relates that his feet were swollen (misshapen) because they had been pierced with a golden pin when, as a baby, he was given to a servant to be killed.

Therefore, long before Oedipus acted out parricide and incest, the inspiration for Freud's term Oedipus complex, his parents acted out a psychopathic filicide defense against him. In this manner, placing the Oedipus complex at the center of the formation of child identity independent of parental reactions introduced an accentuated defensive unilaterality in the theory of psychological development (Masson 1984).

Ego Defense Mechanisms and the Structuring Functions

During World War II (1939-1945) London was severely bombed by Germany. It became commonplace for people on hearing sirens to interrupt their work and rush to air-raid shelters. When this happened, analysts and patients of all types would abruptly terminate their sessions and, helmet in hand, run together for shelter. The hatred for a common enemy diminished the rivalry between schools of psychotherapy and built bridges for some common work.

Michael Fordham, one of the founders of the British Society for Analytical Psychology, very much influenced by the Kleinian school of psychoanalysis, was the first Jungian to analyze children based on the concept of ego formation by the Self (deintegration). He adapted many concepts such as the Oedipus complex, castration complex, primary anxieties, and defenses in the same reductive way as had Freud and Melanie Klein. Fordham realized that ego defense mechanisms described by psychoanalysis are not only of the ego but are also archetypal and, therefore, are defenses of the Self. However, considering that defenses are part of normal development, he repeated the pathologizing reduction of psychoanalysis and wasted a great opportunity to rescue ego archetypal development from pathological reduction (Fordham 1995).

The tendency to pathologize subjectivity defensively is very strong and became deeply rooted in materialistic science. In order to bypass this reduction, Jungian symbolic psychology emphasizes the importance of considering the concept of the structuring function to be archetypal, thus avoiding its undue pathologization by postulating that all structuring functions are normal; only when fixated during symbolic elaboration do they become defensive and pathological and form the shadow (Byington 2006a).

Defensive Structuring Functions Result from the Fixation of Normal Structuring Functions

The concept of structuring function describes normal formation of ego and consciousness by the primary quaternio without considering necessary repression or any other defense. Primary relationships form ego and other identity through the normal structuring functions of identification, imitation, projection, introjection, and so on, which, when fixated, become defensive and form shadow, as for instance in the case of Oedipal defenses.

The prejudice against subjectivity expressed in psychoanalysis is analogous to the Puritan concept of humans being born evil. It seems to me that Freud was so obsessed with defending himself from incestuous and parricidal fantasies that he not only projected them defensively on every child but constructed a defensive genetic theory to include the guilt of parricide for the killing of the ancestral father (Freud 1913). The coincidence of this work with the separation from Adler and Jung strongly suggests that they were also targets of the defensive parricide projection. The extraordinary fact in this work is that this defensive fantasy was included within a scientific theory to explain exogamy and totemism (ibid.).

Analysts today, who have learned through daily dedication and suffering what it is to elaborate the shadow and defenses within ourselves and in our patients, can well imagine that the pioneers, who did not have any analytical sessions, would be liable to project their defenses and their shadows through their theories.

In this sense, we can rightly suppose that Freud discovered the Oedipus complex in his shadow but did not elaborate it in any analytical session. We see from his letters to Fliess how psychological themes were rationally approached with very little personal insight. Freud's defensive projection of his unelaborated Oedipus complex was so vast that it encompassed many areas of the psyche, such as the religious dimension. Due to this defensive approach, he projected defensively his Oedipus complex on the Father God image and concluded that religion was not genuine but defensive because it covered up parricidal tendencies with the love of God (Freud 1913, 1939).

The Oedipus complex is a brilliant discovery that explains many disturbances of primary relationships through the fixation of structuring functions and shadow formation within the primary quaternio (Byington 2008b).

The concept of structuring function expresses, then, the normal development of the personality, and its pathological variable is the defense mechanism, here conceived as a defensive structuring function. It is archetypal and it is a conscious and unconscious defense of the Self and not exclusively of the ego as postulated by Freud (A. Freud 1927).

Structuring functions may have normal or defensive expression depending on how they function in the symbolic axis. When they operate normally, they extract meanings from structuring symbols to form ego-other identity in individual and collective consciousness. When they are fixated, they become defensive and express structuring symbols forming the identity of ego-other in the shadow. It is obvious that all fixated symbols in the shadow are necessary for normal development, but, in order to do so, they must be first elaborated and rescued from fixation and defenses which imprison and deform them in the shadow. These defenses always include resistance and compulsive repetition, two other remarkable discoveries by Freud.

My observation that the defenses are always pathological has received much opposition. This resistance seems to me to be rooted in Freud's traditional formulation that defenses help out the ego and that, therefore, they are normal and beneficial, and only in extreme cases do they become pathological. I agree that defenses contribute toward mitigating the ego's anxieties and sufferings, and because of this they were called ego defense mechanisms by Freud. However, they help the ego by diminishing the productivity of the Self and sooner or later this will fall back on the ego. Painful walking can be alleviated by limping, but this will in time have dire consequences for the body, and in no way can limping be considered a normal way of walking.

We cannot go on employing the same concept for both normality and pathology because of the danger of confusing health and disease as well as consciousness and shadow and good and evil (Byington 1997).

Aggression, jealousy, envy, sexuality, projection, breathing, digestion, vision, mysticism, repetition, rejection, and resistance are among the countless structuring functions that can operate normally or defensively (Byington 2006 c). When they operate freely and form consciousness with the meanings they contain even though amidst suffering, I consider them normal. However, when they are fixated and become defensive, even when they diminish suffering, they form the shadow and operate in an inadequate and deformed way. This is frequently destructive, even though the diminished anxiety and suffering is well received by the ego and by the social group.

To illustrate: take a very loving mother who suffered to see her newborn baby cry. She imagined that it cried because she did not have enough milk and she began to feel depressed. She ignored the pediatrician's recommendation and started to breast-feed the baby whenever it cried, complementing the feeding with a bottle. The crying diminished and she felt better, but the next time she consulted her pediatrician, the baby was far overweight. No doubt the defensive feeding of the baby diminished her suffering for a while, but the end result was negative.

The inadequate action of structuring functions operating defensively will fall back on the ego. Defenses are a bank check given to destiny which will one day be charged to the account. In fairy tales this theme is represented by cases in which the devil helps someone out of a difficult situation. The problem is solved and the person is relieved. Time passes by, and one day the devil appears and presents his bill, which is never cheap. Symbolically seen, this means that defenses, even when expressing help, fall prey to the shadow and block the individuation process.

When fixation and defenses are reactions to a difficulty which is resolved in time and when the defenses can be elaborated and done with, we have the circumstantial shadow. But when fixations and defenses become entrenched, are expressed by repetition compulsion, strongly resist elaboration, and require therapy, we have the chronic shadow. However, no matter to what degree the shadow, whether circumstantial or chronic, is acted out by defensive projection and introjection and alleviates inner tension, it will always divide the Self and will always be abnormal and pathological. It does not matter if the symbols fixated in the shadow have small or great value, are negative or positive; if they are fixated and cannot be adequately elaborated and expressed in life, they will be lived in a deformed way. We can even say that the more valuable the symbols fixated, the more pathological is the shadow and the more suffering and existential dysfunction it will bring.

Another example: a forty-year-old man had been married for twelve years. The couple had two children, and he began to feel he did not love his wife anymore, that he was still young and needed to have more loving experiences. He began to have affairs to come home late, and in so doing he felt greatly satisfied. One night he arrived home to find his wife desperate and in tears. She told him that she knew of his love affairs, had tolerated them because she loved him, but now she could not stand it any longer and wanted a divorce. He went to sleep very happy, feeling that now he could have all the women he wanted. During the night, he dreamed of the death of a twelve-year-old girl who was very sweet. He began to cry with such intensity that it woke up both him and his wife. He continued crying, compulsively imagining the girl being buried. He had loved his wife very much, but had not cultivated their love, which is how he came to feel that their love had died. His love for her had become fixated and defensively repressed, and it took form in his shadow. Could there be anything more valuable than his shadow? Yet he could not live this love as before, because it lay in the darkness, deformed and forgotten. In its place came a feeling of existential suffocation from dragging a corpse, which could only be alleviated by defensive acting out of many love affairs. Each affair looked wonderful before going to bed, but afterward vanished like a soap bubble accompanied by frustration, disgust, guilt, and malaise. He compulsively had to find a new one, and that he did, with no avail. The girl in the dream was his dying love for his wife, which now, compensating for his insane acting out, came to show him, in the desperate imminence of its burial, how much it was still alive. The saying goes that the way to hell is paved with good intentions. Unconscious of his real love, he was certain that his love affairs were the way to heaven.

In this manner, I have conceived the shadow as a disturbance due to fixations of individual and collective psychological development, inseparably linked to the fixated structuring function of ethics. In this sense, the shadow is always pathological, and it is the representation of evil in the psyche. Within this framework, we can understand why the fixation of any structuring function will also affect the structuring function of ethics. This theoretical approach permits the distinction within the psychological dimension of health and disease, as well as good and evil in science and in humanism (Byington 1997).

Chapter 4

THE REGENT ARCHETYPAL QUATERNIO
THE FIVE ARCHETYPAL POSITIONS OF
THE EGO-OTHER POLARITY

The five archetypal ego-other positions are inseparable from the central archetype on the symbolic axis (Neumann's ego-Self axis). They relate individual and collective consciousness permanently with the central archetype, and so they demonstrate that everything which is personal and collective in the psyche is also archetypal.

The five archetypal positions of individual and collective consciousness are the five ways human consciousness deals with life. To know and understand the way they function enables the psychologist to understand the normal and pathological ways of being in the world. If archetypes in general are human types of behavior, the five archetypal ego-other positions are the five types of behavior, of intelligence, of consciousness, and of fixations in the shadow.

Like archetypes, the ego-other positions in consciousness are virtual and cannot be defined clearly and logically. Therefore, the method for describing them will be circumambulation, the "walking around" recommended by Jung to describe archetypes.

Through the five archetypal positions of consciousness, the process of symbolic elaboration follows the saying of the famous alchemist Maria Prophetissa (well known for the bain-marie): the one (the nondifferentiated position) transforms into two (the insular position), the two into three (the polarized position), the three into four (the dialectic position), which is again the one (the contemplative position).

Due to its archetypal quaternary nature, this axiom represents, through the relationship of detachment and attachment of the ego-other polarity, the five phases of every symbolic elaboration common to individual and collective consciousness. The same axiom expresses the five stages of the humanization process. These five ego-other positions are the expression of the five main archetypes. They are said to be regent archetypes because they participate in every symbolic elaboration. One of them can be dominant either because of the stage of life or because of particular circumstances.

The first ego-other position is called nondifferentiated or uroboric, following Neumann (1949a), and expresses the constellation of a symbol by the central archetype. The Ouroboros is a mythological figure, appearing also in alchemy, of a dragon biting its own tail, showing symbolically the nearness of beginning and end. In this position, the meanings or representations that will form and become incorporated into the identities of the ego and the other are still fused. The second position, the insular position, expresses the sensuality of the matriarchal archetype. In this position, consciousness takes the form of islands, in alchemy it is the scintillae, which are intuitively related by unconscious characteristics that correspond to the metaphor of the sea. The third position, the polarized position, expresses the organizing capacity of the patriarchal archetype. Its polar opposites are situated hierarchically with a rational logic that forms systems. In these two positions-the insular and the polarized-the ego considers itself to be the center of consciousness and the other to be an outsider, forming a narcissistic theoretical frame which is frequently subject to inflation (analytical psychology) or omnipotence (psychoanalysis).

The fourth position, the dialectic position, expresses the capacity of the alterity archetype to relate all the poles found in polarities with equal right to express their nature, including the matriarchal-patriarchal polarity. In this manner, the dialectic position includes the anima and animus archetypes and a spectrum of polarities varying all the way from opposition to equality. In this position, the ego begins to consider the other as the non-ego and also as its inseparable partner in the center of consciousness. Finally, the fifth position, the contemplative position, expresses the ego and the other reunited in a single relationship, but one very different from the original, nondifferentiated position; on the contrary, here ego and other are highly differentiated but so abstract that they lose their boundaries and become incorporated in totality. This position marks the end of the process of every symbolic elaboration and the end of physical life.

The Process of Symbolic Elaboration of the Self

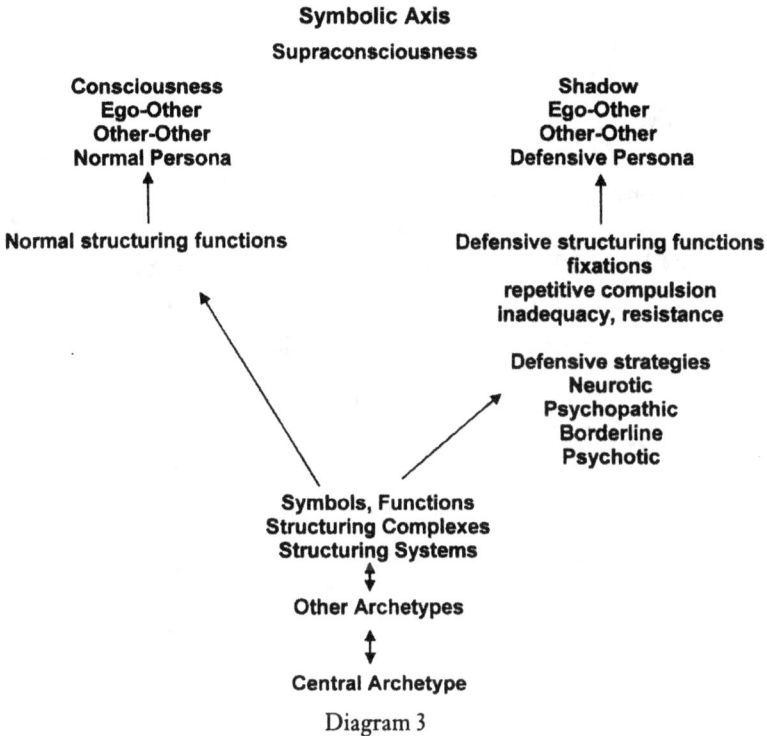

Symbolic Axis

Supraconsciousness

Consciousness	**Shadow**
Ego-Other	**Ego-Other**
Other-Other	**Other-Other**
Normal Persona	**Defensive Persona**

Normal structuring functions

Defensive structuring functions
fixations
repetitive compulsion
inadequacy, resistance

Defensive strategies
Neurotic
Psychopathic
Borderline
Psychotic

Symbols, Functions
Structuring Complexes
Structuring Systems

Other Archetypes

Central Archetype

Diagram 3

The representations of symbolic elaboration through structuring symbols, complexes, functions, and systems reveal two great polarities, shown in the vertical symbolic axis in diagram 3. Below we have the central archetype representing all archetypal potential, and above we have supraconsciousness, with consciousness and shadow as polar opposites. On the horizontal axis we find the normal structuring functions on the side of consciousness and the normal persona, and on the side of the shadow, with its ego-other polarity, we find the defensive persona and the defensive structuring functions with fixation and compulsive repetition.

As we can observe, what determines whether symbols will form consciousness or shadow is not their nature but how they function. If the elaboration is normal, which does not exclude suffering and conflict, the libido (psychic energy) flows freely in the service of developing consciousness and the Self. If fixated and turned defensive, the libido expresses the shadow. In both cases the ego-other polarity is present.

Diagram 4 presents a synthesis of the concepts of persona, shadow, archetype, and Self from analytical psychology with those of fixation, defense, and repetitive compulsion from psychoanalysis, dynamically related through the concepts of structuring symbols, complexes, functions, systems, and supraconsciousness from Jungian symbolic psychology.

The Archetypal Positions of Consciousness
The Regent Archetypal Quaternio
Process of Symbolic Elaboration

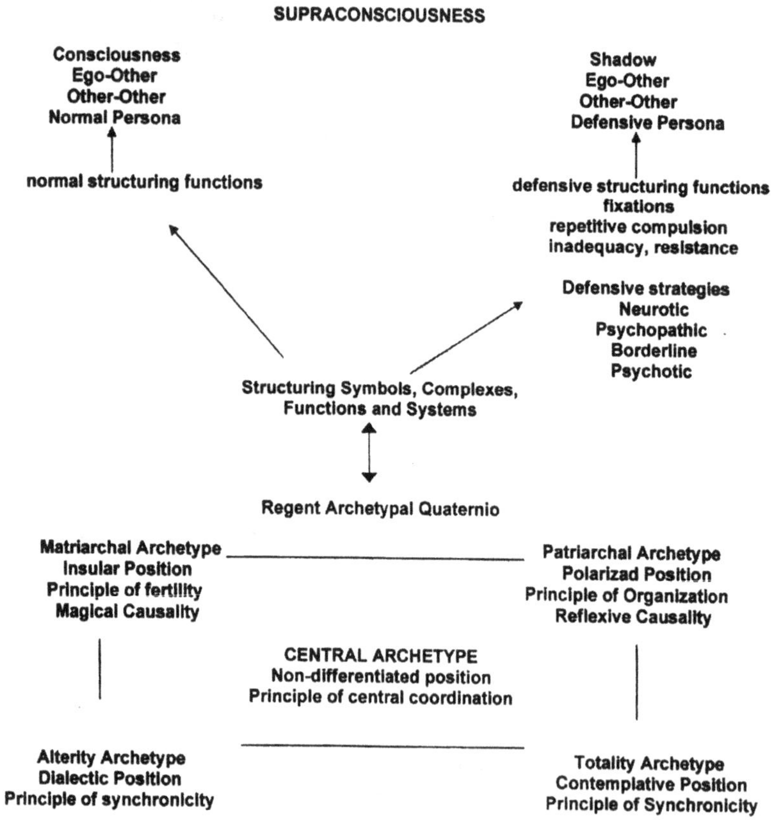

SUPRACONSCIOUSNESS

Consciousness
Ego-Other
Other-Other
Normal Persona

Shadow
Ego-Other
Other-Other
Defensive Persona

normal structuring functions

defensive structuring functions
fixations
repetitive compulsion
inadequacy, resistance

Defensive strategies
Neurotic
Psychopathic
Borderline
Psychotic

Structuring Symbols, Complexes,
Functions and Systems

Regent Archetypal Quaternio

Matriarchal Archetype
Insular Position
Principle of fertility
Magical Causality

Patriarchal Archetype
Polarizad Position
Principle of Organization
Reflexive Causality

CENTRAL ARCHETYPE
Non-differentiated position
Principle of central coordination

Alterity Archetype
Dialectic Position
Principle of synchronicity

Totality Archetype
Contemplative Position
Principle of Synchronicity

Diagram 4

Deepening the study of the symbolic elaboration process, I shall now describe two very important structures represented in diagram 4. The first is formed by the subdivision of the central archetype into four archetypes subordinated to it and which also take part in every symbolic elaboration. This means that there cannot be any content of consciousness or attitude of the ego that is not related to archetypes. Because of this, they are called the regent archetypes and form the regent archetypal quaternio. They are the matriarchal archetype, the patriarchal archetype, the alterity archetype (which encompasses the anima and the animus archetypes), and the totality archetype. This quaternio coordinates the symbolic orchestra with all other archetypes to create the symphony of symbolic elaboration under the conductor-the central archetype.

The second structure represented in diagram 4 is formed by the five archetypal positions which express all possible ego-other relationships in consciousness and in the shadow.

Diagram 4, then, represents the articulation of the process of symbolic elaboration of the Self with the functioning of consciousness, persona, and shadow related to the central archetype and the four regent archetypes in all dimensions of the Self. The supraconsciousness is a special concept intended to emphasize the capacity of consciousness to accompany the confrontation of consciousness and shadow.

We shall continue our circumambulation of symbolic elaboration by amplifying each of the five ego-other positions of consciousness.

The Nondifferentiated Position and the Central Archetype

And the earth was without form, and void; and darkness was upon the face of the deep. And the Spirit of God moved upon the face of the waters. (Gen. 1:2)

The central hypothesis of Jungian symbolic psychology is that the psyche is a human energetic field permeated by symbolic meanings in elaboration. According to this formulation, the main psychological force is the drive coordinated by the central archetype to develop consciousness toward the realization of the full potential of the Self through the elaboration of symbols, complexes, functions, systems, and their polarities.

When an event occurs, be it within or outside the personality, and is referred to the ego or the other (the non-ego), it suffers the influence of the energetic field and becomes a structuring symbol or complex subject to the action of structuring functions or systems coordinated by archetypes, and ultimately by the central archetype.

At the beginning of every symbolic elaboration, consciousness is not differentiated because the potential meanings of the ego and the other are not yet actualized; this characterizes this condition of consciousness as unitary. An unknown song on the radio next door, a shadow on the porch, an explosion in the neighborhood, arrival at an unknown place, a sharp abdominal pain, the imminent announcement of important news are all examples of circumstances that get our attention and signal the start of symbolic elaboration. Why symbolic? Because one thing is certain: whatever it may be, it will have many meanings which will amplify the connection of the ego to the existential process, of the part to the whole, and which will enhance the actualization of the archetypal potential of the psyche.

The beginning of elaboration may occur with symbols coming from outside the person that simply occur along the way. Or the symbols may spring from an inner necessity that creates a sense of emptiness or longing. Adolescence begins, a boy and a girl cross paths, and out of the blue an affectionate relationship is sparked.

In the nondifferentiated position, the ego and the other are still fused within the new symbol and their future meanings are rooted in the archetypal infinite. In any of the examples listed above, the event cannot yet be known or explained. In the affectionate relationship just begun, the boy and the girl form a unit. The one cannot clearly identify feelings separated from the other. They know they are together, but as to whether they will love each other, get married, and have children or forget each other the next day and never meet again, they do not have the slightest idea.

The fixations that occur in this position are very difficult to elaborate exactly because consciousness in a nondifferentiated position cannot confront the shadow. Elaboration here generally depends on some special expressive technique, such as hypnosis or an altered state of consciousness, to activate the imagination and enter into the insular position. It occurs frequently in traumatic neurosis in which the fixated symbol has just begun to be elaborated (Byington 1993a, 2008a).

A case example: a teenager couple had just begun their love affair. They went out for a car ride and got involved in a violent accident. The girl died and the young man arrived at the hospital in a state of emotional shock. He was released and days later began to have nightmares, fainting episodes, and panic attacks characteristic of traumatic neurosis. It took him years for this elaboration to pass from the nondifferentiated position to the positions that follow.

One fixation in the nonelaborated position of the planetary Self involves the symbol of survival of our species. In spite of the repeated warnings by specialists, humanity is fixed in an infantile, dependent, irresponsible, and predatory attitude toward nature and presents great resistance toward elaborating this fixation. However, the existential pressure on the consciousness of the planetary Self is increasing, and every day it claims more need for this elaboration.

The Insular Position and Matriarchal Consciousness

Each shining leaf, all the beaches, every veil of fog in the dark forests, each clearing in the woods and all buzzing of insects are sacred in the traditions and in the conscience of my people. - Chief Seatl, Duwamish Tribe, 1855

The adjective insular refers to "island" (*insula*, in Latin) and to a pattern of the functioning of consciousness that corresponds to the matriarchal archetype, in which polar opposites are not necessarily associated and, therefore, the ego may relate to each pole separately. Without any split such as we find in fixations, the insular position is binary or dyadic, because in it the ego relates to the other as one pole of a polarity, independent of its polar counterpart.

Case Example

A woman traveled to a foreign country. She was twenty-five years old and had just graduated in psychology. She had worked hard to help her family, taking care of her dying mother, but she had received a scholarship and now she was in Zurich. She had entered the central station to take a train to the outskirts where she lived when suddenly she felt an intense desire for freedom, which made her shiver. Adventure, knowledge, experience! She went to the ticket window and saw that the next train for Paris would leave in half an hour. She bought a ticket. As she walked along the platform, slowly noticing everything and everyone around her, she felt like the character in Caetano Veloso's song, *Joy, Joy*:

> Walking against the wind
> Without either handkerchief or papers
> In a sunny summer day
> I go
> ...
> Without handkerchief or papers
> Without anything in my pocket or in my hands
> I want to go on living, love
> I go
> Why not, why not?

Another example: a man, when asked if he liked his neighbors, said he loved them. When asked again after a noisy party that ended at daybreak and to which he had not been invited, he said he hated them. Admiration and aversion, although they form a polarity, live on different islands, which are visited by the mood of the day.

The insular position is comparable to Melanie Klein's schizoparanoid position from object relations theory, in the British school of psychoanalysis. She denominated it so, perhaps due to the division of polarities.

The matriarchal archetype is the archetype of sensuality, of desire, and of the survival instinct, equally present in the personalities of men and women and in culture, and its expression in consciousness occurs through the ego-other insular position. The motivations of the ego are emotional, kaleidoscopic aspects of the imagination, rooted in magical wishful thinking and devoid of objective impartiality. To try to understand the matriarchal dimension through logical reasoning is a fruitless undertaking. In order to understand it, one has to employ empathy, emotion, intuition, and feeling in lived experiences. Because poles of polarities are not articulated between them, creativity and spontaneity are its essence, as we can observe in the play of children. Things are not done out of duty or as a task to accomplish something, but simply to be lived with its sensuous experience, the way we eat, dance, and make love. The proximity of the ego with the other sometimes mixes and confuses them, making it difficult to understand how adult people and civilized societies can think in this position of consciousness. Perhaps because of this, Jung followed Levy-Brühl (1922, 1938) and called this way of mental functioning participation mystique or unconscious identity, because it leads the personality to function within magic causality. However, only when we do not recognize the insular matriarchal position in consciousness as the most basic and important pattern of consciousness for the intimate relationship between ego and other can we consider it to be unconscious identity (Jung), primary process and infantile (Freud), or sensory-motor intelligence (Piaget).

Due to the frequent expression of sensuality, desire, and aggression in the insular position, independent of coherence with the world around it, it propitiates a high degree of spontaneity, pleasure, lightness, faith, and high spirits, as was so well expressed in the film *Zorba the Greek*, with Anthony Quinn. Activities like eating, sleeping, intimate conversation, domestic occupations, living in nature and with animals, and physical action may bring satisfaction and pleasure due to the sensuality of the insular position.

The absence of a conjugated opposition between poles (the polarized patriarchal position) allows them to be experienced separately, forming binary relationships with the ego. Because things, which include body and nature, are not experienced in a permanent polarized position with the mind, emotions can easily mix with them. This fact propitiates magical causality, in which emotions "animate" things that can then act upon imagination and desire. Because it is not systematically separated from the non-ego, the ego desires something and is sure that the non-ego will correspond to this desire. Magical thinking functions with the logic of "I want it (power) or I wish it (eros), and things will behave accordingly." It expresses magical causality as a principle to deal with all that is non-ego, be it nature, people, body, or emotions. It expresses the imagination subjectively and can be used in any life situation. It is completely different from objective causality (the polarized patriarchal position), which is based on the permanent association of the poles, maintained in straight separation and permanent rational opposition. This is why James Frazer (1890), studying magic, concluded that it is a bastard science and that cultures who practice it (he called them savages and primitives) cannot think correctly. Within magical causality, the imagination is dominated by subjectivity and associates the islands of matriarchal consciousness through will and desire to determine behavior.

   Malinowski (1979) studied the natives of the Trobriand Islands in New Guinea and gives an interesting example of magical causality in the functioning of this society.

> There is one aspect which is very important for the social life of the Trobriands. It occupies a separate position as something peculiar and specific. The natives distinguish a certain category of facts and a type of human behavior and use to designate it the megwa which can be adequately translated as magic. It is intimately associated with economic life, and truly, with all interests of daily life: it is also an instrument of power and a sign of importance for someone who practices it. The position which women occupy in magic must be examined with special consideration.
>   Magic is a certain aspect of psychological reality. It is considered indispensable in all activities and important enterprises whose results are not completely under human control. Therefore, one can resort to magic in agriculture and fishing expeditions, in the construction of a big canoe or when one dives to search for precious shells; it is also for magic that one asks to appease the winds and improve the climate; its assistance is invoked in times of war, in questions of love and personal attraction, to have safety at sea, to guarantee success in any enterprise of great importance and finally-which does not mean that its utility is less important-to preserve or recover health and also to make enemies get sick. Success and security in all these occasions depend in great part-sometimes completely-upon magic to control these adequately. There is the conviction that a successful or unsuccessful ending, abundance or need, health or disease depends mainly on the magical procedures applied correctly in the right moment. (p. 69)

   Although magic functions well within the domain of wishful thinking and cannot be understood within the Cartesian abstract objective logic, it can be individually and socially very useful whenever applied to emotions. Although much less efficient than reflective causality when dealing objectively with reality, it is much more efficient when dealing with subjective reality. Due to the fact that any undertaking depends frequently on subjective characteristics such as self-esteem, will power, self-assurance, dedication, faith, and hope, the emotional reassurance produced by magic can influence and significantly affect the end result of any human enterprise.

Therefore, action based on the insular matriarchal position, although mostly the result of desire and not logically and directly articulated with the poles of polarities, can be very satisfactory from the standpoint of joy and pleasure and also of successful results when the situation depends heavily on the subjective dimension.

This is not to endorse the principle of magical causality in all issues, for when it becomes dominant in individual and collective behavior regarding the objective dimension, it may limit the concomitant use of objective causality and condemn culture and the individuation process to stagnation in superstition, ignorance, and underdevelopment.

The Insular Matriarchal Position and the Central Archetype

Although expressing islands of consciousness, which isolate the ego and the other in a binary symbiosis exclusively with one pole of polarities, this does not mean that the parts in the insular matriarchal position remain restricted and isolated within the whole. The liberation of intuition within spontaneity gives the insular position great power over the conscious and unconscious imagination, and this endows it with an extraordinary capacity to contact the central archetype and the whole Self. Just as islands connect with each other through the sea, so the parts operating in the insular position are interrelated through unconscious intuition and imagination among themselves and with wholeness.

The development of unconscious intuition and its connection with the whole Self and the central archetype in the insular matriarchal position activates the mediumistic structuring function, which can become very prominent. The lack of objective Cartesian logical reasoning, which frequently functions as a straitjacketed rationalism to the mind, liberates our thoughts from rationally preformed modes of thinking and can fly within totality through harmony with life, leading us to the structuring function of divination. This explains why certain tribal societies, which are deeply invested in the insular matriarchal position, have oracular systems operated by soothsayers. The Afro-Brazilian Yoruba, for example, have an Orixá (god) called Orunmilá as patron of the oracle of Ifá. Through the game of cowrie shells (buzios) and other methods, the priests (babalawos) inspire themselves in the mystical tradition and produce odus, oracular revelations that guide the lives of the believers. Let us also remember the Delphic oracle, which first pertained to the dragoness Delphine, then to Dionysus, and finally to Apollo and which for centuries guided many crucial events in ancient Greek society, based on the state of mental possession inherent to the divinatory ritual of the Pythia (priestesses).

The Insular Matriarchal Ego-Other Position and Dreams

The insular matriarchal position expresses myths and dreams and great part of the formation of psychopathological symptoms. Unfortunately, it has been confused with the unconscious, and this has largely prevented its study and usage in teaching as an active ego-other position in the participation of consciousness.

To consider the dream as "the royal road" to the unconscious and to not study simultaneously its conscious characteristics is a reduction that greatly deforms the understanding of its nature.

We identify the participation of the ego in dreams which indicates the presence of consciousness. We know, too, that without consciously remembering dreams, we cannot elaborate their symbols. The concept of the structuring symbol, which includes all psychological entities as conscious and unconscious, personal or collective but always archetypal, allows us to study dreams also in this perspective.

Some years ago, I formed a group to study the dimension of dreams through their sensuous experience (Byington 1991b). We soon realized that the natural tendency of the group, whose members were all teachers undertaking analysis, was to emphasize the fantastic nature of dreams and to begin their interpretation at the level of rational, logical thinking. It did not take us long to realize that in so doing we lost many of their characteristics, which include the representation of dreams through the imaginal, emotional, and sensorial dimensions. We decided to avoid interpretation, trying as much as possible to emphasize the meaning of dreams through our senses, intuition, and fantasy. This experience was most enriching and opened for us a new dimension we had until then completely ignored. This dimension was discovered as we experienced the dreams in the insular matriarchal position of consciousness. Had we continued our conventional rational dream interpretation, considering the essence of dream to be unconscious, we would have never had this sensual experience. As a result of this research and following Jung's example, I ask my patients to paint important dreams and to hang them up where they can look at them every morning (see also Marion Galbach, *Learning with Dreams* (2003), which addresses this issue).

When I conceived the insular matriarchal position, I became aware that this state of consciousness speaks the language of dreams (Freud's manifest meaning) and that our mental work to express dreams in logical discourse transposes them to the polarized patriarchal position (Freud's latent expression). It is very important that both positions of consciousness are used to elaborate dreams symbolically. In his *Interpretation of Dreams* (1900), Freud practiced the transposition with a detective-like strategy he considered necessary to decipher the work of a censor who camouflages the latent meaning to protect the sleep of the dreamer. From the symbolic perspective, this is one more reduction of psychoanalysis.

Jungian symbolic psychology considers dreaming to be a structuring function of consciousness and its language to be mostly a symbolic expression of the insular position of consciousness, which like any other symbolic expression can be normal or defensive. Therefore, in order to interpret a dream, it is very productive to experience first its sensorial aspects through expressive techniques and only then to elaborate it in the polarized patriarchal position through free association and amplification. This method favors constructing the interpretation from within the symbol and not from outside it in the mind of the analyst or the analysand. During this elaboration, dream structuring symbols, functions, and systems become contextualized in the individuation and in the humanization processes, and only then will it be revealed whether they are normally functioning in consciousness or fixated and operating defensively though repetitive compulsion in the shadow.

Based on this essential metaphoric and matriarchal characteristic, dreams can also be expressed dominantly in the polarized patriarchal, in the dialectics of alterity and in the contemplative totality positions. Jung's extraordinary dreaming capacity, for instance, includes countless passages expressed in the dialectical position of the alterity archetype.

Regarding dreams and the primary process of the id in a general manner, Freud had a tendency to see them defensively, and Jung saw this quite clearly:

> I was never able to agree with Freud that the dream is a "façade" behind which its meaning lies hidden-a meaning already known but maliciously, so to speak, withheld from consciousness. To me dreams are a part of nature, which harbors no intention to deceive, but expresses something as best it can, just as a plant grows or an animal seeks its food as best it can. (Jung 1961, pp. 161-162)

Jung as we know had a vivid experience with dreams and elaborated their symbols with the help of the insular matriarchal position of consciousness by expressing them through painting and sculpture. However, as with all symbols, Jung also interpreted dream symbols by using the patriarchal polarized position, the dialectical position of the alterity archetype mainly through the method of active imagination, and also in the contemplative position.

Many of the symbols from my dreams in analysis in Zurich were significantly elaborated through painting, and this elaboration therefore began in the insular matriarchal position. Undoubtedly, however, one of the most profound or perhaps the most profound dream revealed its meaning to me through the dialectical position of alterity in active imagination. I dreamed I was with Jesus, undertaking a journey across a very high mountain accompanied by a gorilla, a wolf, and a deer. After painting and doing free association and amplification, my analyst suggested that I practice active imagination with the dream. I had begun practicing this method of symbolic elaboration a few months before and was most impressed by the dramatic way in which the figures became animated and responded to the ego. Today I realize that this animation is an archetypal structuring function that is present in all forms of animism and expresses intensely the insular matriarchal pattern in consciousness and is not simply a manifestation of the unconscious.

During the exercise, I invoked Christ and asked him about the reason for his presence in the dream and the meaning of his journey over the mountains. The animation of his figure and his sayings during our dialectical interaction affected my whole life. I had had a formal Catholic education in my youth, and although very much impressed by the figure of Jesus, I had never had anything like a religious experience. The elaboration of the dream in active imagination activated the structuring function of religiosity in my Self with intensity. Since then, I have always been in contact with the mythological figure of Jesus during important moments of symbolic elaboration. This experience inspired and guided the interpretation of Christianity in my archetypal theory of history, summarized in chapter 13, and its patriarchal fixation and defensive deformation during institutionalization.

Unfortunately, Jung followed Freud and reduced many important issues such as dreams, archetypes, compensation, participation mystique, and many important psychological manifestations to the unconscious and did not situate these structuring functions in the archetypal positions of consciousness, especially in the insular matriarchal position, which he tended to consider as a synonym for the unconscious.

The insular matriarchal position expresses mythic reality, the poetic and fantastic dimension of being magically in the world. For many years, on Christmas eve, I dressed as Santa Claus to bring gifts to my grandchildren. Annually I accompanied their magical experience of the dear old man who arrived in a farm wagon (we usually spent Christmas on a farm) to excite their imaginations and pleasure. My arrival was always merry. I saluted them by name and asked about their studies as I distributed the gifts. Then I said farewell as they accompanied me to the porch, promising that I would return in the following year. I observed that when they were about six or seven years old they began to form a polarity which represented me and Santa Claus. Through the polarized patriarchal position and reflexive causality, they then came to the conclusion that these two poles were related because I dressed as Santa Claus. This was accompanied by disillusionment, sadness, and sometimes even anger, which inclined me to associate it with Melanie Klein's depressive position. To compensate for this frustration I secretly promoted them to be my "assistants" to help me dress up and distribute the gifts to the younger children.

During my adolescence, I began to play soccer, and I became fascinated with my favorite players, who could perform miracles and with whom I identified. Together with a dear cousin, I accompanied my team, Flamengo in Rio de Janeiro, to every game in the nearby towns. We resorted to little magic tricks like sleeping with our team uniform and putting pictures of the players in our schoolbooks for luck. We cherished victory and suffered with defeat, crying in the stadium until closing time. It was a significant phase of symbiotic identification with our heroes. Observing how important cheering was for the performance of the players, I later came to the conclusion that magic can produce significant results in human enterprises through emotional mobilization. Because science, psychology, and medicine did not initially recognize this important subjective factor in the placebo effect of drugs, and in the therapeutic relationship, a gap developed in cultural knowledge which became a gold mine for the development of propaganda and marketing and the million-dollar business of self-help literature. All these activities are centered on the structuring function of magic and the functioning of the insular matriarchal position in consciousness.

The insular matriarchal position depends on desire, sensuality, and imagination to maintain a binary intimacy in the ego-other relationship. The structuring function of ritual involves practice with the imagination and enhances and maintains this magic intimacy. Among the Afro-Brazilian Yoruba, before spiritually receiving his Orixá (god), the believer must present a sacrificial offering with ritually prepared food and must be dressed with characteristically colored clothes and adornments. The ritual continues with specific dancing and singing accompanied by sacred drums, all of which pertains traditionally to the believer's Orixá. Only then will the ritual of normal possession occur through which the adept receives the Orixá (Verger 1981). This ritual can only be understood and practiced by one who believes in the magic dimension of the insular matriarchal consciousness; in the polarized patriarchal position, the ritual does not make any sense because the association of specific food, dressing, singing, and dancing cannot rationally cause emotions, much less possession.

The Insular Matriarchal Ego-Other Position and Psychopathology

The binary attachment inherent in the insular matriarchal position favors intense symbiotic relationships in which the non-ego represents only one pole of such polarities as, for instance, love-hate. At one moment you can hate someone intensively and an hour later love that person heartily. Explanations? No explanations required because these are "matters of the heart." This aspect makes this position very possessive, jealous, and characteristic of intimate relationships. It can become fixated with defensive reactions expressing the shadow, including defensive affectionate possession, pathological envy and jealousy, defensive gossip, and slander, which can reach the point of phobic intolerance and pathological hate (Byington 2002a).

The main disturbances that result from the fixation of the insular matriarchal position are dissociated clinical conditions, traditionally considered hysterical. The metaphor adopted by Hippocrates, wherein he imagined the frenzied womb (hystera) floating around the body to explain the great variety of hysterical symptoms, can be explained by fixations and splits of the matriarchal islands affecting defensively body parts and emotions and resulting in specific modes of defensive behavior such as compulsive seduction, frigidity, histrionic personality disorder, manipulation, and lying, which become part of the shadow and are frequently expressed by defensive projections. Sleepwalking is an illustrative hysterical symptom of the defensive insular position: a part of the mind, although unconscious, awakens and coordinates walking while other parts are asleep. Hysterical cases of multiple personalities behave autonomously, living the shadow mostly unconscious (some illustrations of this can be seen in the films *Zelig* by Woody Allen and *Vertigo* and *Psycho* by Alfred Hitchcock).

The case of Anna O. inaugurated psychoanalysis and became very well known. Bertha Pappenheim (her real name) was a young patient who suffered very much as a result of her father's terminal illness; she fell ill with a hysterical psychosis which included a phobic reaction to drink water and many other symptoms. Joseph Breuer, a friend of the Freud family, was her doctor and relieved her of many of her symptoms through hypnosis. Bertha referred to this technique as "chimney sweeping" and the "talking cure."

One of the symptoms that appeared one day was a phobia of drinking water, as a result of which she drank only fruit juice. The phobic symbol (water) was plainly conscious but the motivation for it was completely unconscious. Hypnosis revealed the unconscious motivation. Bertha had seen her governess's little dog, which she disliked, jump on a chair and drink from a glass of water on the table. On awakening from the hypnotic state, the phobia of water had disappeared (Freud and Breuer 1893).

This symptom is famous because it was the first one to be cured psychodynamically. Breuer treated Bertha in 1882 and told Freud about it ten years later. Freud considered this discovery so important that for many years he considered Breuer the founder of psychoanalysis (Freud 1914b).

A case example: a fifty-year-old lawyer came to analysis because of morbid obesity, anxiety crises with intense sweating, and very low self-esteem. After being in therapy a few weeks, he dreamed of a tiger which persecuted him. We associated it with his voracity and obesity. We then elaborated the symbol in active imagination, and the tiger turned into a vigorous prosecutor who insulted the patient with pejorative and humiliating language. We concluded that his repressed aggression was turning against himself as a function of his obesity and low self-esteem. Elaborating the symbol more deeply, the tiger was revealed to be both the ego and the other, fixated and fused. The aggression was against others who rejected him and against himself who ate too much and could not take care of himself. Such fixations of structuring symbols and functions in the insular matriarchal position generally present this fusion of ego and other which has to be elaborated correctly in order to separate them. Being a lawyer, the use of active imagination together with dramatic techniques, sand play, and marionettes of the Self were very productive in his therapy (Byington 1992a).

Knowing the archetypal positions of consciousness, we become aware that symptoms are frequently formed through the defensive imagination, chiefly unconsciously. To be worked through, their meaning has to be understood correctly for the adequate expressive techniques to be applied productively.

The Polarized Ego-Other Position and the Patriarchal Archetype

Called to untie the Gordian knot, which until then no one had succeeded in doing, according to legend, Alexander raised his sword and with one stroke cut it in half. (Bulfinch's Mythology)

The patriarchal archetype is here conceived, in the personality of man, of woman, and of the ternary coordination of the ego-other and other-other in consciousness. As we saw, in the matriarchal position the ego mixes relatively with the other. The polarized patriarchal position, on the contrary, always expresses itself through both poles of any given polarity, very clearly separated, in opposition and hierarchically positioned. This polarization enables consciousness to perform within the principle of reflexive causality. Descartes'

Discourse on Method recommends the strict separation of thinking (subjective) and the objective (nature) to practice the scientific method. Beautiful is always employed having ugly in mind, night is always referred to day, victory to defeat, good to bad, gratitude to ingratitude, loyalty to treason, construction to destruction, strong to weak, tall to short, health to disease, and so on. The polarized position can be compared to Melanie Klein's depressive position. It is ternary because the opposites are always related within the same symbol, and thus the ego relates to one pole inseparably from the other. While in the insular position the ego relates to mother and father in different islands of sensuality, in the polarized position the ego relates to mother inseparably from father. I do not refer to this position as necessarily oedipal, because this would reductively predetermine the relation of the ego with parents, that is, as attraction for the opposite sex and antagonism of the same sex. All arrangements in the triad are possible, including one which may form the Oedipus complex, in which case the triadic relationship becomes fixated, that is, defensive and pathologic.

The polarities always in hierarchical opposition enable patriarchal consciousness to organize symbolic elaboration through reflective causality and form logical systems based on polarities. This logical capacity, which is rational and systemic, endows personal and collective consciousness with an extraordinary efficiency in the formation of knowledge and in the execution of tasks that call for abstraction. In this manner, this position establishes great control over the body, emotions, ideas, people, and nature. All binary computer systems, for instance, function in the triadic polarized position. The banking system, hospitals, airports, traffic, communications, television, and computers could not do without it. The systems are objectively binary but psychologically ternary, because it is the ego that operates them. If polarities did not have a strictly binary meaning, the whole computation system would be impossible. When we review our bank statements, we want to see our credit and debit accounts always in clear and strict opposition and without the least confusion between them. When we board an airplane, we trust that the flight controllers will articulate takeoffs and landings with precise exactitude. When we undergo surgery, we trust that all surgical instruments will be completely sterilized, and so on.

The polarized patriarchal position can function only through a great abstraction of the ego-other polarity from the insular matriarchal position.

This abstraction is articulated through the transcendent function of the imagination, through the sacrificial function (Viveiros de Sá 2000), and through the structuring function of power. In this sense, rigid (or Spartan) methods of education are employed to tame emotions and drives, to control desire (the insular matriarchal position), and to strengthen willpower. While cleaning a child's wound with an antiseptic that causes pain, the motto "that which hurts, cures" may be repeated several times like a mantra, and if a boy cries, he is accused of being a freak, a sissy, or gay.

In this manner, the result of exercising the polarized patriarchal position in life is the formation of systems in which polarities are hierarchically organized under the structuring functions of power, planning, and execution. Therefore, the persona or the superego, here defined as collective morality, guides the personality and collective consciousness to do that which is politically correct. In this manner, the polarized position coordinated by the patriarchal archetype establishes traditional morality by being critical, puritan, always judgmental and full of prejudice in such a way that the inferior poles are always socially disapproved to some degree, which frequently leads to defensive unilaterality, repression, and shadow formation.

It so happens that when the matriarchal-patriarchal polarity undergoes patriarchal dominance in culture or in the individual, the insular matriarchal position tends to be discriminated and stigmatized in the child, in culture, and in the humanities, including the field of psychology. The result is that the polarized patriarchal position tends to be considered an expression of the ideal of truth, maturity, perfection, honesty, reason, erudition, progress, and dignity, and that which is related to the insular matriarchal position tends to be disqualified as infantile, immature, irrational, lazy, irresponsible, ignorant, superstitions, wrong, savage, primitive, and promiscuous.

Abstraction and hierarchical relation of polarities, memorization of results of the work of others through written records, cults of traditions, prevision, planning of tasks, responsibility, the search for perfection, being overly demanding, aversion to error, workaholism, ambition, competition, pride for work accomplished, guilt, and fear of failure are natural sequences of the patriarchal polarized position.

Because of all this, we can say that symbolic elaboration coordinated by the patriarchal archetype endows consciousness and the Self with extraordinary powers of organization within the processes of individuation and humanization, but also hinders significantly the full creativity and spontaneity of the Self and becomes a most powerful source of shadow formation.

Why is it that most people do not play at work? Because responsibility and demand permeate tasks in such a way that frequently joy and play are considered to be irresponsible and to lack seriousness. This is cruelly illustrated by Jean de La Fontaine's fable in which the workaholic ant condemns the singing locust to death by freezing. This logic is born within a system that articulates will ("where there is a will, there is a way"), dedication, planning, responsibility, programmed time, success, persistency, and determination. The polarized position is in permanent and austere opposition to sensual pleasure, which favors doing spontaneously what one enjoys, respecting one's own rhythm in the search of well-being and satisfaction-characteristics of the insular matriarchal position.

The polarized patriarchal position can be compared to abstract intelligence (Piaget 1954) that transcends sensory-motor intelligence, which we can associate somewhat with the insular matriarchal position. This evolutionary perspective present in the polarity between sensory-motor and abstract intelligence and the matriarchal-patriarchal relationship stigmatizes the insular matriarchal position and sensory-motor intelligence as primary, inferior, and merely a stage to be transcended. We cannot deny that the sensory-motor intelligence and the insular matriarchal position are dominant in early childhood and, depending on the culture, tend to be more or less transcended by abstract intelligence and the polarized patriarchal ego-other position. However, sensory-motor intelligence and the insular position are rooted in the matriarchal archetype and continue to participate in symbolic elaboration as emotional intelligence throughout life. The disregard for the insular matriarchal position and sensory-motor or emotional intelligence in adult life is a great limitation (Goleman 1995). Regarding the capacity to plan and organize life, control emotions, and explain the world objectively and rationally, the polarized position is far more efficient, but when we consider the art of living with spontaneity, intuition, empathy for the feelings of others, bodily sensations, ecological consideration, humor, joy, pleasure, and community participation, the insular matriarchal position is by far more efficient.

The polarized patriarchal position very efficiently produces quantity in symbolic elaboration. This capacity coordinated line production and industrial development. However, the power drive behind ambition and perfectionism frequently becomes defensive when it favors repression of important existential dimensions that frustrate its goals. We find this repeatedly in unrestricted capitalism, in autocratic government, in war, in the devastation and pollution of nature, and in the disregard for social welfare, emotions, health, and well-being.

The Dialectical Ego-Other Position and the Archetype of Alterity

And the scribes and Pharisees brought unto him a woman taken in adultery; and when they had set her in the midst, they said unto him, Master, this woman was taken in adultery, in the very act.
Now Moses in the law commanded us, that such should be stoned: but what sayest thou? This they said, tempting him, so that they could accuse him. But Jesus stooped down, and with his finger wrote on the ground, as though he heard them not.
So when they continued asking him, he lifted up himself, and said unto them, He that is without sin among you, let him first cast a stone at her. (John 8:3-7)

The tension existing in the psyche between sensuality and the satisfaction of desire inherent in the insular matriarchal position and the austere power of organization inherent in the polarized patriarchal position of consciousness propitiates the activation of a third way for the brain and the psyche to elaborate life and coordinate the ego-other and other-other polarities. This is the dialectical position of the archetype of alterity, which includes the anima and animus archetypes described by Jung and can coordinate the relationship of polarities in all their ways of relating. This pattern of relationship forms a spectrum that varies from opposition to equality. In this manner, symbolic elaboration coordinated by the archetype of alterity can attain the maximum of productivity in the creativity of the psyche.

Both the insular matriarchal and the polarized patriarchal positions treat the poles of polarities unequally. They are dominantly narcissistic when they privilege the ego and dominantly echoistic when they give preference to the other during elaboration. The narcissist-echoistic polarity is inspired by the myth of Narcissus and Echo, in which Narcissus is centered on the subject and Echo on the object. The unilaterality of the narcissistic-echoistic polarity occurs, in this case, in two different ways. In the insular matriarchal position it is due to the sensual preference of one pole over the other inherent in desire. In the polarized patriarchal position, due to the power hierarchy between the poles, one pole is considered inferior and the other superior, one ordering and the other obeying, and this leads to a unilaterality of the narcissism-echoism polarity subordinated to the power drive. It is only in the dialectic position of the alterity archetype that the unilaterality within the narcissism-echoism polarity is transcended and the polarities ego-other and other-other relate in the middle path with equal rights for each pole to express itself. It is here that Echo and Narcissus finally encounter one another.

In the dialectical position of the alterity archetype, the process of symbolic elaboration can reach the climax of its productivity because the polarities can be situated in a spectrum of meaning all the way from opposition to equality, giving their poles equal rights to express their differences, and therefore enabling the expression of all characteristics conceivable by the imagination. This position is quaternary because the ego and the other admit that both can be right or wrong. Each one accepts the other to point out his or her shadow and they dedicate themselves to elaborating it. This permits consciousness to work both in magical causality and in reflexive causality and to open itself to the principle of synchronicity. In this manner, the production of meanings by symbolic elaboration is unlimited because in synchronicity meanings are as numerous as reality. Its world vision occurs in the dimension of mystery that reveals totality through reality.

The polarized patriarchal position can be systemic but it will be so hierarchically and unilaterally, whereas the dialectical position of alterity is systemic, holistic, and dialectical, which permits it to be democratic within wholeness.

The dialectical position of alterity of the ego-other polarity occurs, for example, within biofeedback systems, identified by von Bertalanffy (1969) in biological systems and applied to the theory of communication as a foundation of systemic theory (Watzlavick, Bavelas, and Jackson 1967). The multiple biofeedback system, applied within the symbolic dimension, permits us to see, through the dialectical position of alterity, that structuring symbols, functions, complexes, and systems are part of the essence of the nervous system and of mind-body, mind-nature, mind-emotion, and energy-matter polarities (Bateson 1972).

Within the dialectical position of alterity, opposites and paradoxes can frequently be found to be true. Creationism and Darwin's theory of evolution, for instance, which have been two poles of a ferocious battle since the nineteenth century, can be understood through the polarity of the religious magic-mythic perspective (insular matriarchal position) and the scientific, logical, objective perspective (polarized patriarchal position).

The dialectical position of alterity encompasses the confrontation of myth and science, parallel to the matriarchal-patriarchal relationship. In La Fontaine's fable only the dialectical position of alterity could have reached a consensus between the locust and the ant before the ant condemned the locust to freeze to death. Consensus between reason and emotion is also the backbone of my book *Education from the Heart: A Jungian Symbolic Perspective* (2004), where I describe how the dialectical transference relationship between teachers and students unites reason and emotion and therefore has a most important effect on the learning process. The essence of the book is to show that reason and emotion, science and magic, rational knowledge and myth, are polar opposites that can operate in complementary ways through the dialectical position of alterity with a significant increase in the efficiency of symbolic elaboration. Therefore, instead of exclusively polarizing, proponents of creationism and the theory of evolution have to admit the importance of both in knowledge.

Propitiating such expansion of consciousness, the dialectical position of alterity coordinates within symbolic humanism some of the most important issues in modern society regarding civil rights, social democracy, sustainable economy, regulation of the financial market, and the world fight against the collective planetary shadow expressed in poverty, political oppression, aggression against all forms of life, exhaustion of planetary reserves, accumulation of waste, and obsessive consumerism (Brown 2000).

The fixation and defensive expression of the dialectical position of the alterity archetype forms a shadow expressed in demagogy and in the manipulation of communication systems to distort information, expressed as treason, lying, and in all forms of defensively disregarding the other in the name of love and civil rights.

The Contemplative Ego-Other Position and the Archetype of Totality

Those who know, do not speak anymore. (Chinese saying)

The contemplative position and the archetype of totality are the end of elaboration of all symbols including the end of the physical life process. When meanings of structuring symbols, complexes, functions, and systems have been sufficiently worked through and integrated by the Self, whether in circumstantial events or at the end of physical life, the ego and the other undergo extreme detachment, lose their boundaries, become one again, and reunite with totality through contemplation, as the tai-chi symbol, a mandala, so well illustrates.

It is important to differentiate the contemplative position of the totality archetype from the nondifferentiated position of the central archetypal that coordinates all elaboration. The central archetype encompasses all symbolic elaboration coordinating the four regent archetypes which vary from primary nondifferentiation to completeness. The totality archetype coordinates only one part of the central archetype, which refers to the end of symbolic elaboration including the end of physical life in the conscious-unconscious reunion of the individual with the cosmos. The reunion of consciousness with the totality of the Self, in this case, is part of the movement of centroversion which integrates the result of psychological production and propitiates the continuation of the process.

Fixations in this position form defenses in which people cannot adequately put an end to what they do and so become dependent and linked in defensive symbiosis to unresolved situations. This is the case, for instance, of compulsive collectors. I remember a very intelligent middle-age woman who became compulsively incapable of detachment from personal objects. Eventually the compulsion came to include newspapers, and a few months later she had to sleep in her living room because her bedroom had been filled up.

At the end of life, fixations of the contemplative position and of the archetype of totality prevent the detachment needed to activate the sacrificial structuring function and prepare to die (Viveiros de Sá 2000). Fixations of the contemplative position, detachment, and the sacrificial function in old age can transform this stage of life into compulsive and desperate attachment, permeated by anxiety and depressive nihilism. In creatively detaching from everyone and everything at the end of life, the ego and the other mix together. In this way they prepare for the proximity of death, which transcends the circumstantial limits and opens the soul for the experience of eternity and infinity.

Meditation is the main structuring function that exercises consciousness in detachment and in contemplation. Oriental humanism, in which meditation is practiced and detailed observations are made of all sensations, sometimes postulates that in the contemplative position the ego is destroyed. In my view this is an error because the ego is archetypal and, therefore, cannot be destroyed. I consider that the attitude of consciousness that is meditation does not destroy the ego-other polarity. Rather, the contemplative position transcends the other four positions of consciousness and represents the fifth intelligence of being in which the ego attains a highly developed way of functioning through detachment.

Meditation: Part 1

Any meditation, with or without mantras, serves to detach one from things and activities and to open consciousness for the experience of transcendence and totality. Some meditations are focused on determined images and experiences, but they also can practice the experience of detachment and transcendence. The structuring function of meditation is the central spiritual practice of the great religions and traditional philosophies of India, China, Japan, and Tibet.

As an expressive technique to elaborate fixations, meditation can be used for many clinical situations in psychotherapy, for instance, in cases of anxiety and stress. Anxiety is a structuring function that accompanies fear. The word phobia comes from god Phobos, which in Greek mythology is the god of fear. Disturbances of anxiety are very frequent in modern life due to intense competition and countless activities we carry out every day in increasingly shorter periods of time. This tension generates chronic states of overwork and fear of failure. The person who suffers from stress due to workaholism or guilt feelings for not being able to cope with life's tasks is an exhausted traveler threatened with conscious or unconscious fear of failure.

The stress syndrome reaches its extreme in the panic syndrome which may include terror of dying.

In the first part of the meditation that follows, one practices detachment from doing followed by contemplation of breathing and circulation. This part is very useful for fighting stress and can be practiced during a short time (10 minutes) before sleep. It reproduces, while awake, the psychological and neurological state of sleep. It can also be practiced at any time during the day in periods of 10 to 30 minutes or more. In this manner, it is capable of diminishing feelings of being overly in demand and bringing about a mental and physical state of intense relaxation. In this theory the psyche includes the mental-physical polarity.

Contemplation of the Miracle of Life

And the Lord God formed man of the dust of the ground, and breathed into his nostrils the breath of life; and man became a living soul. (Gen. 2:7)

Place yourself in your preferred position for meditation. It can be in the lotus position or in any other. This meditation includes active imagination (Hannah 1981).

Imagine a sunny day with a beautiful blue sky. You are taking a walk in an enchanted forest. The trees are tall and the paths among them are very well kept. A gnome comes to meet you. He calls you by your name because he has been taking care of your life tree since you were born. He asks you to follow him, walks along the forest, and takes you to your tree. You accommodate yourself under the tree, and he goes away, wishing you a good meditation.

Your tree is enormous and its first branch is about ten feet over your head. The crown is large and among the leaves you can see countless little apples which stand for all your activities. Jumping around them is a little monkey representing your ego. He carries a little flannel cloth with which he rubs the little apple that corresponds to your activity at that moment. You get up in the morning, he polishes that little apple. You brush your teeth, another apple is polished. You eat your breakfast, a third one, and so on all day long.

But now it is time for detachment. You ask the little monkey to interrupt his activities and come and lie down on the first branch above your head, right beside his cousin, a sloth which started climbing the tree when you were born.

The monkey comes down to the branch, closes one eye, and leaves the other one open to accompany your meditation.

The little monkey is lying down. This means that your ego has ceased all executive functions that are active attitudes. From now on, your ego will function only in the passive attitude. Focus your attention on your breathing rhythm (*pranayama* means "the control of breathing"). Your mind ceases all executive activity of the cerebral-spinal nervous system and opens to contemplation exclusively using the vegetative nervous system through breathing and circulation. Inhale. Exhale. Relax. Focus on your breathing movements. If you feel like it, you can put one or both hands over your stomach to accompany your breathing.

Pay attention to air containing oxygen entering your nose and going to your lungs. Imagine oxygen crossing the alveoli and entering the capillaries. The hemoglobin from your red cells unites with oxygen and the blood becomes red. Through circulation, oxygen is taken to all your tissues and body cells. Inhale. Exhale. Carefully accompany the oxygen arriving at every part of your body. This is the life energy. Rejoice with it and relax. If any other thought enters your mind, do not fight it, but don't pay attention to it and it will go away. Your mind becomes increasingly empty. Concentrate on your breathing rhythm and relax.

Oxygen is being used in the tissues and becomes carbon dioxide. It joins the red cells, which turn blue, and returns to the heart and then the lungs through your veins. The carbon dioxide passes through the capillaries, enters the alveoli, and is exhaled into the atmosphere. Inhale. Exhale.

This is the cycle of life within the body. Now comes the cycle outside. Continue contemplating the marvelous reality of being alive through the breathing rhythm. The carbon dioxide you exhale is absorbed by plants which use it along with sunlight in photosynthesis to produce food and oxygen, which is returned to the atmosphere for you to inhale again. This is the cycle of life outside of your body, establishing the symbiotic relationship of your body and the rest of nature. It expresses the humanization of the cosmos, which has lasted four billion years. Be aware of this miracle and rejoice!

The physical life cycle begins in conception and ends in physical death. But the spirit, the mind, the emotions, and the soul want more. They know that the body will disintegrate with physical death and that its matter will remain in the universe. To continue this journey, practice the second part of this meditation, described in chapter 12, (page 269).

Chapter 5

THE CONIUNCTIO ARCHETYPE AND THE THREE STRUCTURING QUATERNIOS DURING THE INDIVIDUATION PROCESS

The Primary Quaternio

In his last great work, *Mysterium Coniunctionis* (1955-56), Jung defined the archetype of the coniunctio as the archetype of the reunion and separation of opposites. In this chapter, I will describe the structuring function of this archetype through the three quaternios that succeed one another during the process of individuation and the seven archetypal phases of life described in chapter 14.

Of all the structuring systems that propitiate symbolic elaboration in order to form the identity of the ego-other polarity within the Self in the individual and at the collective level, the family Self is one of the most powerful. The structuring function of the primary quaternio prepares the individual Self to assimilate the family Self so that the individual will become able one day to reproduce it in the adult quaternio, starting with the love affairs of adolescence.

The identification of structuring functions in the formation of the ego is very difficult because we are trying to describe verbally a process that occurs together with nonverbal neurophysiological development. It is an effort to describe through the polarized patriarchal position and the dialectical alterity position that which happens within the intimacy of the insular matriarchal position including its preverbal state. As Mahler, Pine, and Bergman (1975) point out:

The question of the kind of inferences that can be drawn from direct observation of the preverbal period is a most controversial one. The problem is complicated by the fact that not only is the infant preverbal, but that the verbal means of the observer lends itself only very little to the translation of such material. (p. 13)

The Primary Quaternio:
Imitation, Projective and Introjective Identification
The Identity Formation of the Ego and of the Other

When we admit that the ego is not the center of consciousness because it shares this position with the other, we are prepared to realize that the identity of the other is also formed through primary relationships. This fact is important to show that just as the ego is formed through the symbolic representations of the subject, so the other or non-ego is formed through the symbolic representations of "objects." In this manner, we conclude that the other is just as symbolic as the ego. The food we like to eat, people we like or dislike, subjects that attract our interest and may one day become our profession are all examples of symbolically meaningful "objects" whose identity began to take form in our early life in the same way as our ego.

It is true that when we want to know something, we search for its objectivity; this does not mean that we want to know the object by itself but rather that we want to know the object with all its meaning. In the same way, when we search for inner truth we want to know the profound and countless meanings of our subjectivity.

Due to the fact that the ego and the other spring from symbols in which they initially have an undifferentiated relationship, throughout life they will continue to differentiate one from the other. Therefore, we must be careful when using the concept of projection not to think that the other is already separated from the ego which projects parts of itself. When we elaborate parts of the symbol projected onto the other, we, at the same time, elaborate parts of the symbol introjected in the ego. The structuring functions of projection and introjection are inseparable and form the identities of the ego and of the other. They follow primary identification through imitation which is the basic function of identity formation.

These two different perspectives of projection and introjection in the ego-other relationship must take into account that, on one side, the ego sees the other as completely different from itself, but on the other side, when the ego learns about their common origin within the Self, it also will see the other as its twin, permanently coordinated by the potential of the central archetype.

The fact that the ego and the other emerge from symbols through the coordination of the central archetype is their common secret, which will be revealed to them during the life process. They are the expression of the cosmic creative principle that guides the psyche to reveal and to know itself through the formation of ego and the other. Their differentiation coordinated by the central archetype forms consciousness of the person and of the world in the individuation process. In the end, ego and other detach progressively from this identity and lay bare the cosmic creative principle.

Primary Quaternio
The Family Self and the
Emergence of the Individual Self

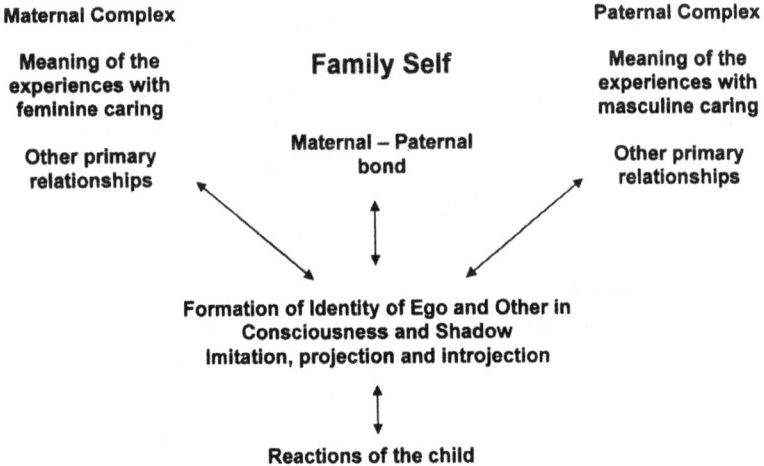

Maternal Complex

Meaning of the experiences with feminine caring

Other primary relationships

Family Self

Maternal – Paternal bond

Paternal Complex

Meaning of the experiences with masculine caring

Other primary relationships

Formation of Identity of Ego and Other in Consciousness and Shadow Imitation, projection and introjection

Reactions of the child

Diagram 5

Many authors, most of them influenced by psychoanalysis, have described the primary relationships of the first year of life. Melanie Klein, for instance, postulates the functioning of the ego in the first year of life, first in the paranoid-schizoid position (dyadic) followed by the depressive position (triadic). In her theory, the main mechanism of ego formation would be projective identification (Klein 1932). In this respect we can complement projective identification with introjective identification to avoid unilaterality in the parent-child relationship. While children project and identify, they also introject and identify, following the first structuring function, which is imitation.

The parental complexes are very much influenced by countless symbols rooted in the archetype of the child, which we all have and which is extraordinarily activated in the selves of the parents, of the family, and of society. This theoretical concept does not determine how identity is formed, but rather formulates parameters through which it is formed. The complexity of these variables is so great that we must view identity formation in each case through synchronicity rather than trying to set rules through causality. One approach is to suppose that certain structuring functions affect child identity. Another, quite different, approach is to attribute our fantasies to a child in its nonverbal stage and affirm the motivations of its behavior, like psychoanalysis did with the Oedipus complex.

Jungian symbolic psychology proposes the development of identity through the symbols, functions, complexes, and systems coordinated by the primary quaternio and formed mainly by the maternal complex, the paternal complex, the bond between them, and the reactions of the child.

Jung (1948b) emphasized that the symbol of the quaternio frequently expresses the central archetype which he called Self. We have the four cardinal points, the four seasons, the four functions of consciousness, the regent archetypal quaternio, and many others. We also use the geometry of the quaternio in many other objects of our daily lives such as books, documents, chairs, tables, doors, windows, beds, and countless others. It is meaningful that rooms of all kinds, including those in houses and offices, tend to have a quaternary form. It is as if the central archetype needs a quaternary structuring function to express its totalizing developmental function.

Therefore, I conceive the primary quaternio formed by the maternal and paternal complexes, the bond between them, and the reactions of the child as a structuring system encompassing the primary relationships of the child to coordinate the formation of the identity of the ego and the other in consciousness and in the shadow in the beginning of life.

The maternal and paternal complexes are here conceived as the meanings of feminine and masculine caring parental figures, which can include siblings, grandparents, and other primary relationships, including animals. Complexes are clusters of symbols that include the objective figure of parents and the subjective meanings experienced by the child. The parental complexes do not exclude the shadows of the parental figures because they are formed by their entire individuation process, including the frustration of that which they dreamed but did not realize.

Another important aspect of the archetypal quaternio is that the reactions of the child can also contribute to form his or her identity together with the characteristics of the parental complexes and the bond between them. One very difficult patient I had who suffered from obesity and a defensive identification with evil was a woman who at the age of two had felt much joy when her younger sister died. The reactions of children with frustrations of various kinds, anger, jealousy, envy, and feelings of inferiority and competition can mark their identity significantly (Byington 2006c).

It is important for the gender of the parental figures to be only relatively considered in identity formation because, contrary to what we might imagine, many characteristics of the parents are incorporated by the ego independent of gender, perhaps because they occur before the child has structured its sexual identity. A boy can perfectly identify with important characteristics of his mother without affecting his masculinity, and likewise a girl with characteristics of her father. There are identifications however with characteristics of the parent of the other sex that do affect sexual identity significantly.

The main difference between the concept of the primary quaternio here described and most other theories of child development is the inclusion of the representation of the father figure together with the mother and the bond between them from the very beginning of the primary relationships. Traditionally the primary relationship has been reduced to the child-mother dyad with the father entering later to form the oedipal triad.

Freud included both the father and mother figures in the Oedipus complex from the very beginning of life, but later studies by Melanie Klein

(1932) anticipated the primary relationship to an exclusive relation with the breast. Other theorists posited the primary dyad with the mother, considering it preoedipal. The absence of the father figure from the primary relationship was maintained in almost all approaches, such as those of Anna Freud (1927); Fairbairn (1952); Fordham (1944); Neumann (1955); Jacobson (1964); Bowlby (1969, 1973, 1980); Mahler, Pine, and Bergman (1975); Stern (1985); and Jacoby (1999). The only exception I know of is Dorothy Dinnerstein (1945).

I believe that centering the primary dyad on the mother-child relationship is not structural and is due to historical circumstances that are today undergoing a great change. During the millennia of patriarchal dominance, the identities of man and woman were reduced to their family and social roles. Due mainly to pregnancy and breast-feeding, women's activities were restricted to the home while men assumed public roles. Based on this traditional bias, developmental psychology frequently described the mother-child dyad as a structural characteristic of the primary relationship. It seems to me that this perspective, which ratified the role of the distant father and of the exclusively domestic mother, was responsible for the systematic deformation of the father and mother identities and of their complexes in the formation of the identity of the child.

In the lives of modern young couples, in which women are likely to have professional educations and work outside the home, the traditional family roles of man and woman are changing radically because both tend to support the family financially and to divide child and home care between them (Byington 1986). From the beginning of pregnancy, the companionship of man and woman is present in visits to the gynecologist to verify the embryo's growth, in listening to medical advice and in preparing the baby's room. There are fathers who caress their wife's belly, attend to her complaints, talk to the baby in the womb, and even describe themselves as "pregnant." A friend of mine talked to his baby boy and tickled his feet and one day declared that the boy was left-handed. To everybody's surprise, the diagnosis was confirmed after birth.

There is no doubt that this new man-woman relationship comes from the progressive social implantation of the dialectic position of the alterity archetype in civil rights and overall collective consciousness, diminishing the dominance of the traditional patriarchal polarized position (which is described in greater detail in the archetypal theory of history in chapter 13). No doubt

Jung contributed significantly to this modern social transformation when he conceived the anima and animus archetypes at the center of the individuation process. Jung's contribution was amplified when post-Jungian authors began to describe symbols of both genders present in the archetypes of the anima and animus. This amplification happened either by describing the anima and animus archetypes present in the personalities of men and women (Hillman 1966, Whitmont 1969) or seeing these archetypes as bi-gendered (Byington 1986).

Within this new father role, the importance of the obstetrician was partly reduced. Instead of the doctor handing the newborn baby to the mother and then going outside the delivery room to announce the birth to the father and the rest of family, today it is often the father who receives the newborn and takes it to its mother, participating in their happiness. From there on, waking up at night to change diapers, preparing the baby for breast-feeding or warming a bottle, and bathing the baby are activities that can become part of the new father function. As can be easily understood through the concept of the archetypal quaternio, the child's identity will be greatly affected by the figure of the intimate father to the point of sometimes beginning to talk with the word daddy, to the family's surprise. This new parental role in child care during primary relationships confirmed a very interesting fact that Jungian symbolic psychology had already described. When both parents take care of the baby, it is not unusual for the father to be more skilful and to have more pleasure than the mother in doing so. Generally this occurs in situations where the mother is professionally more successful and earns more money than the father. I have associated this with the matriarchal-patriarchal archetypal typology, where the father can be a matriarchal dominant type and the mother a patriarchal dominant type (Byington 2008).

The traditional social roles of man and of woman aside, another difficulty of admitting the father into the intimacy of the primary relationship was that researchers realized that the infant is capable only of a dyadic or binary relationship; it can relate only to one part (one person) at a time (pars pro toto). However, with the archetypal concept of the insular matriarchal position and the inclusion of the matriarchal archetype in the personalities of man and of woman, we now can conceive the dyadic (binary) relationship of the baby with the mother in one island and with the father in another island. This explains why sometimes the primordial human image appears as a hermaphrodite in children's dreams and drawings. This can happen when father and mother and gender islands become (con)fused.

With the concept of the archetypal quaternio we avoid a great bias in the theory of archetypal development which has traditionally ratified the patriarchal deformation of the distant father in the formation of identity. A case that illustrates this situation was that of a middle-aged married man who had the perverse compulsion to kiss men sensually in public. He came from a very traditional European family and was educated at a great distance from his father. One day, at the age of seven, he was told to dress up and come solemnly kiss his father's hand. It was their first real meeting.

One of the consequences of this deformation of the father complex in primary relationships was that the identities of both boys and girls were distorted by the distant father figure and by the exaggerated predominance of the mother figure ambiguously condemned to domestic activities and crowned the queen of the home. This ambiguity came with corollary stigmatizations, which included defensive projection of professional incapacity and limitation of women in intellectual, political, social, and religious participation crowned by the prohibition to study, because "a girl who studies would have difficulties in getting married." Of course, this social position of women has changed considerably in the last two centuries in many countries, but it continues relatively unchanged in others, and its archetypal development has not been duly absorbed by psychological theory. Let me only emphasize that the deformation of the distant father complex and the omnipresent but inferior mother complex induces a defensive polarized relationship between men and women that greatly affects married life as well as the parental complexes in the primary structuring quaternio and in the identity formation of the child.

We know that the dynamics of boys and girls are very different during the developmental process because boys have to separate from their mothers to differentiate their masculine traits while girls do not. This explains in part the aggressiveness of boys, which later develops into cruel initiation rites in so many cultures, while girls typically remain near their mothers and imitate them from early childhood with the maternal caring of dolls. In this context, we can see that the figure of the distant father distorts the identity of children in two ways: first, it lengthens the period of mother-child dependence; second, it limits the differentiation of boys from their mothers and exaggerates girls' identification with them.

Of course, these observations do not cover all variations of the primary quaternio; these are countless if we take into consideration modern changes in the family, with women often working outside of the home in most Western societies and with so many blended families as a result of divorce and subsequent remarriages. But they serve to help us avoid the traditional reductions and to establish a structuring primary archetypal quaternio which, because of its quaternary all-encompassing nature, provides a basic reference to elaborate all symbolic forms of primary identity.

Dorothy Dinnerstein (1945) was an American Kleinian analyst who recognized the deformation of the primary relationship and its disturbing effect on the man-woman relationship in adult life. She described this limitation in her book *The Mermaid and the Minotaur*, the title of which is an inspired metaphor describing this limitation.

If a man must differentiate from the original symbiosis with his mother to form his identity and does not do it adequately for the lack of reinforcement from his distant father figure, he probably will not have sufficient maturity to relate to a woman on equal terms, and he will either remain obediently dependent on her as a mother figure or defensively antagonize her in different ways of misogyny, including exaggerated control, repression, prepotency, affectionate rejection, indifference, defensive autism, pathological jealousy, abandonment, humiliation, betrayal, sadism, and overt aggression. With a distant father and an overprotective mother, a woman may tend to be submissive to men and to consider men the repository of all social, political, religious, artistic, or scientific creativity. Being little differentiated from her mother and defensively symbiotic to her children, she may present great difficulty in developing professionally and fail to acquire the capacity for self-support.

Beyond the reactions of the child and of the parental complexes, the concept of the primary quaternio gives great importance to the bond between the mother and father complexes. This bond expresses a model for the ego-other relationship and for all other polarities. It will significantly influence the child's capacity to develop the dialectical position of the archetype of alterity and thus to deal democratically with polarities in general and with the man-woman polarity in particular.

Applying the concept of the primary quaternio to the structuring of the child's Self also contributes to evaluating the interactions of the child and its parents. The interpretation of the Oedipus complex by Freud led him to concentrate on the reactions of children and to disregard or even cover up the behavior of parents. In this respect, it is important to register Masson's (1984) emphatic criticism of the attitude of psychoanalysis and the seduction theory, which according to him has contributed to covering up cases of child sexual abuse by parents. We must add that the reduction of child development to the Oedipus complex has also contributed to covering up the extraordinary frequency of parental aggression (Parish 1996). Based on American statistics, Teixeira (2008) estimated an annual 400,000 cases of battered child syndrome in Brazil, 40,000 with severe injuries and 4,000 resulting in death.

One more contribution of the concept of the primary quaternio is the application of the dialectical position of the alterity archetype and of the principle of synchronicity to the study of symbolic elaboration in child development. When we apply these two concepts, we see that the insular matriarchal position is dominant in the initial structuring of the child's Self, but this is not to say that it does so alone.

The patriarchal position also influences the primary quaternio from its very beginning. The importance of hygiene and the appropriate use of all objects in regard to child care are generally coordinated in the polarized patriarchal position. But this can also take a defensive stance. For example, one patient related this traditional complaint: she was upset to the point of tears listening to her son yell in hunger while milk dripped from her breasts, waiting sometimes more than an hour to adhere to the scheduled four hours between feedings recommended by her pediatrician and strictly imposed by her husband. It is still very common today to instruct parents not to hold babies who cry at night because this is thought to pamper them; rather one is instructed to let the baby cry until exhaustion so that it will learn to control its frustrations. Of course, such rigid measures vary from pediatrician to pediatrician, from family to family, from culture to culture, and from generation to generation. But it is obvious that these injunctions and others that will certainly follow them-based on the polarized patriarchal position imposed on the baby, who is totally open and subject to any influence because it relates within the insular matriarchal position-will have a significant influence on the formation of identity. The dialectic position is also an important part of the primary relationship, and it increases every day when parents are conscious of the feedback pattern when relating to the child. In this position, parents and pediatricians cannot treat a child as a being separated from the parents (polarized patriarchal position) but as part and parcel of the primary quaternio which responds to the structuring functions contained therein (the dialectic position of the alterity archetype).

Finally, the primary relationship also includes the contemplative position, which expresses the overall purpose of life for the parents and their experiences with the life processes of their families and cultures. These experiences will be projected consciously and unconsciously by the parents onto the child.

It is very important to take into account that the primary quaternio includes the shadows of the father and mother figures, which can become part of the ego-other polarity of the child. Jung's preface in Frances Wickes's book *The Inner World of Childhood* (1927) called attention to the projection of the parents' shadows on their children together with other archetypal contents. However, Jung and Wickes did not consider these contents as structuring symbols of ego formation and treated them as pre-egoic. The influence of the parent's shadow on the formation of the child's shadow makes it very difficult for the child later on to confront and elaborate its shadow, because the child considers it to be very much a genuine part of its identity. To confront such fixations and defenses, great therapeutic effort using expressive techniques is necessary to elaborate them. In this manner, the patient may come to realize that these defenses express a shadow that came from his or her parents and from the bond between them quite unconsciously. These complexes are also very difficult to elaborate because they are not necessarily the expression of something the parents actually did with the child, but rather something they lived, consciously or unconsciously, and with which they contaminated the child through the symbiotic intimacy of the imitative structuring function within the insular matriarchal position with the child's ego in the passive attitude.

Case Example

A forty-five-year-old married woman is an artist has three children. She herself was the oldest of five children in her family. When she came to me, she had already undergone analysis with other therapists of different orientations over the course of many years. She said she knew all about her childhood, her parents, and herself and now wanted something different. She suffered from anxiety episodes that bordered on panic attacks. During these crises she repeatedly felt that she was no one. She had taken various antidepressants but did not want them anymore because she felt that they affected her sense of identity and disturbed her creativity. I persuaded her to take five drops of clonazepam only when she felt that an anxiety episode was coming on. During these crises she felt a great fear that her children might die, and she recalled the deaths of her parents, repeating the suffering she went through at the time. She also suffered insomnia, compulsive nail-biting, smoking, and aggressive fits during these anxiety crises.

Her life story was that of an upper-middle-class family with a good standard of living, well adapted and without any extraordinary events except for the death of her parents from cancer in old age. Her dreams were very rich but did not offer any clues to her suffering. What most impressed me in her life story was the intensity of her symbiosis with her mother with whom she quarreled daily but whom she loved very much. As the eldest daughter, she had been an only child until the age of three. To her dismay, I told her that we had to elaborate more profoundly the mother-daughter relationship. The mother came from a very poor family and had suffered great need, even hunger, in childhood. Everything changed when she married, but she remembered those terrible days and told her daughter about them many times. It seemed that the mother never got over that suffering, and during her married life as a rich woman in high society, not for a day did she forget her past, and she passed this suffering to her daughter very precociously.

It soon became quite clear to me that the patient was fixated on a symbiosis with her mother and that in spite of or precisely because of all the quarreling during their lives, this fixation continued. Therefore, treatment had to explore this fixation, consciously and unconsciously, to see two points. The first was the unconscious nucleus of her anxiety syndrome. The second was the relationship, if any, of this nucleus to the symbiotic defensive mother complex. My intuition was that they were one and same complex, but only the experience of them during regression could clarify this central issue.

Normally, I work in the Jungian face-to-face setting but the next chapter of the treatment was to convince the patient that her treatment would require expressive techniques, the couch, regression, and hypnosis among others. At first she was very resistant and reluctant to do this, saying that she had already "analyzed" this aspect of her personality a thousand times, but she finally agreed when I explained to her that it was one thing to talk about symbiosis and quite another to elaborate it through regression using expressive techniques. We increased therapy to two sessions a week.

The regression on the couch with exploratory hypnosis soon showed the degree to which the symbiosis was fixated on a complex with many symbols of poverty, suffering, and empathic compassion for her mother's childhood, stained with guilt for feeling happy not to have had such a childhood. In one session, I employed the technique of using marionettes of the Self (Byington 1992a). This technique is different from sand play because the puppets represent the ego and stand near to the symbols related to them. Next, I employed active imagination with her mother. "Yes, I love you very much, but I abhor your suffering and your past, and every day of my life I thank God that I never went through that, for which I feel very guilty and cannot excuse myself" was what she finally told her mother.

Once the fixated symbiosis was partly elaborated, we began working on the nucleus of the anxiety syndrome to discover what it was she really feared unconsciously. The techniques employed to start with were the couch, hypnosis, centroversion, and regression. It soon became clear why she felt, during her crises, that she was no one. Through hypnosis we entered the anxiety state bordering panic attack and, through much suffering, the regression revealed that her fear was linked to the discovery of the horror and disgust she had always felt for her mother's childhood and suffering. She also felt that such an emotion was accompanied by immense guilt and the terrible judgment that someone who felt this way about one's own mother should not exist. This explained her effort not to exist which was at the center of her anxiety crises.

After articulating the elaboration of the mother-daughter fixation and the anxiety syndrome, we began to work to undo their conditioning within a cognitive behavioral perspective. After one year of therapy, the patient began to handle her anxiety successfully, felt very much reassured, did not feel anymore that she had to be no one, and could do without medication.

The Identity of the Ego and of the Other:
The Precocious Manifestations of Anima and Animus

If we admit that the identity of the non-ego, that is, the other, is part of consciousness together with the ego, it is reasonable to suppose that the identity of the other begins also to be formed through the structuring functions of the primary quaternio. This hypothesis is corroborated when we compare the relationships we have in adult life with the ones we had in our earliest years.

Jungian analysts see countless cases in which the anima is projected by a man onto a woman who resembles his mother, or the animus is projected by a woman onto a man with characteristics of her father. In psychoanalysis this could be interpreted as an incestuous tendency. Frequently, the opposite occurs, and one marries exactly the opposite type of one's mother or father, but this can also be seen as an aversive reaction to one's mother or father complex formed during the structuring function of the primary quaternio. In psychoanalysis, this could be diagnosed as a reactive formation to an oedipal fixation.

We know that the anima and animus archetypes, mainly when conceived as bi-gendered, are normally influenced by the parental complexes, and this can be seen as a quite normal occurrence. The difference between a normal and a defensive anima or animus projection can be seen in the harmonious or conflicting nature of the relationship. Already in early infancy children may show typical expressions of the anima and animus archetypes. Teachers of kindergarten are frequently amazed by the poetic tenderness of the expressions of love among small children.

Identity, Imitation, and Imprinting

The structuring function of imitation is very important for the formation of the ego-other polarity in consciousness and in the shadow. Imitation is similar to imprinting in animals. The insular matriarchal position approximates the ego and the other and frequently superposes them, (con)fusing their identities. Within this intimacy, empathy can be very intense and favors imitation.

The structuring function of imitation operates throughout the life span. It can hide individual identity, mainly ontological identity, and because it avoids the more profound elaboration and differentiation of identity, which frequently brings great effort and suffering, it is very attractive and tempting. People who imitate their friends and remain nondifferentiated personalities, sometimes called "wishy-washy," are much more numerous than we normally imagine. Would it be an exaggeration to consider that among ten people, nine remain subject to imitation and only one develops creative differentiation? The frequency of the habit of imitation illustrates the power of this structuring function and the degree to which it is activated by the central archetype. Children are prone to imitation because they have not yet learned the more sophisticated functions of analysis and criticism and are less able to judge another's behavior before imitating it. It is very important that parents and educators understand the power of the structuring function of imitation in the formation of identity. This understanding stimulates them to propitiate intelligent and cultural experiences and surroundings for their children and avoid negative, sick, and mediocre people and situations. I have seen children acquire phobic symptoms hours after seeing a phobic reaction from a parent.

Case Example

I once treated a thirty-year-old, good looking, male patient who was a brilliant university professor. He came for therapy because he did not understand why girls quickly rejected him. During a detailed anamnesis of his affectionate relationships, I registered an extraordinary comment made by one of the girls -"Your problem is your underwear," she remarked. Examining symbolically such odd statement, I asked him to give me exact details of his underwear. He told me that they were quite normal except that he very seldom changed them, because "I rarely wash myself up."

Continuing the elaboration, he added that since early childhood he had not liked washing up below the waist. When asked why, after a pause, he remarked that this was perhaps due to the fact that he had always slept in the same room with his older brother, who was paraplegic and had great difficulty washing himself below the waist. We were then able to identify his unconscious imitation of his brother, treating the lower part of his body as if it were also paralyzed and did not need or deserve much attention and care.

Another hypothesis as to what might have reinforced this defensive avoidance of washing up could be his aversion to his brother's paraplegia, leading him to ignore the lower part of his own body. With this elaboration of the symptom and some cognitive-behavioral orientation to undo the conditioning of the defense, he began to wash himself below the waist with ritual daily exercises, taking great care and noting precisely how his muscles functioned normally, a clear demonstration that he was not paraplegic. After this elaboration of the symptom and daily ritual washing of his underwear and of himself, he began dating again with very high spirits, and very soon became engaged.

Creative Family Tree

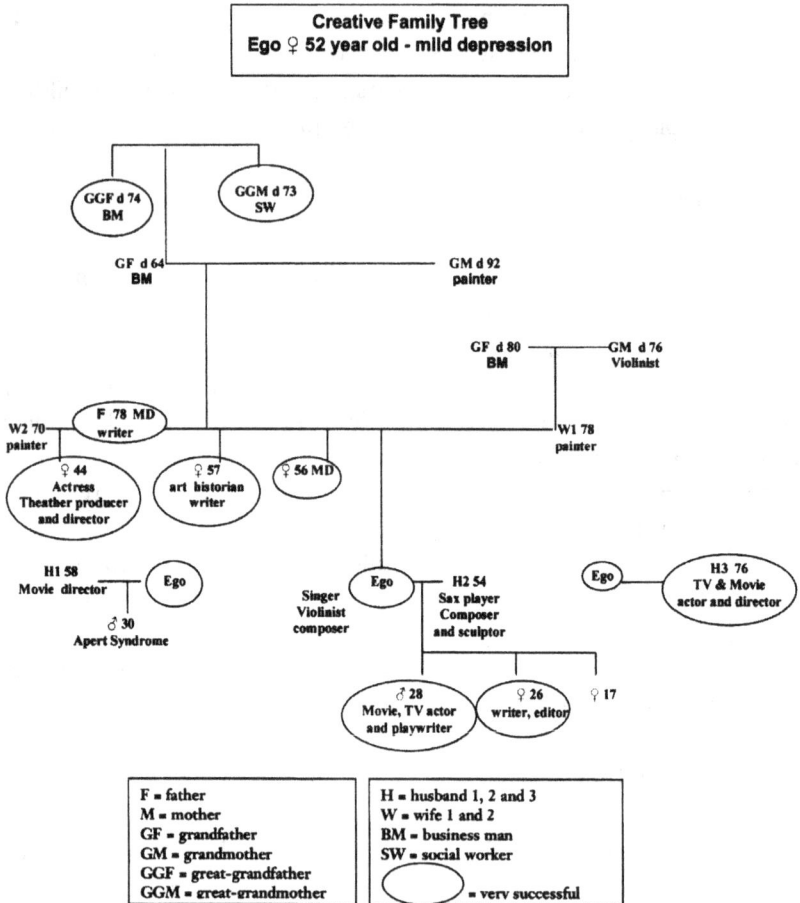

<table>
<tr><td colspan="2">Creative Family Tree
Ego ♀ 52 year old - mild depression</td></tr>
</table>

GGF d 74
BM

GGM d 73
SW

GF d 64
BM

GM d 92
painter

GF d 80
BM

GM d 76
Violinist

W2 70
painter

F 78 MD
writer

W1 78
painter

♀ 44
Actress
Theather producer
and director

♀ 57
art historian
writer

♀ 56 MD

H1 58
Movie director

Ego

Ego

H2 54
Sax player
Composer
and sculptor

Ego

H3 76
TV & Movie
actor and director

♂ 30
Apert Syndrome

Singer
Violinist
composer

♂ 28
Movie, TV actor
and playwriter

♀ 26
writer, editor

♀ 17

F = father M = mother GF = grandfather GM = grandmother GGF = great-grandfather GGM = great-grandmother	H = husband 1, 2 and 3 W = wife 1 and 2 BM = business man SW = social worker ⬭ = very successful

Diagram 6

Pathologic Family Tree

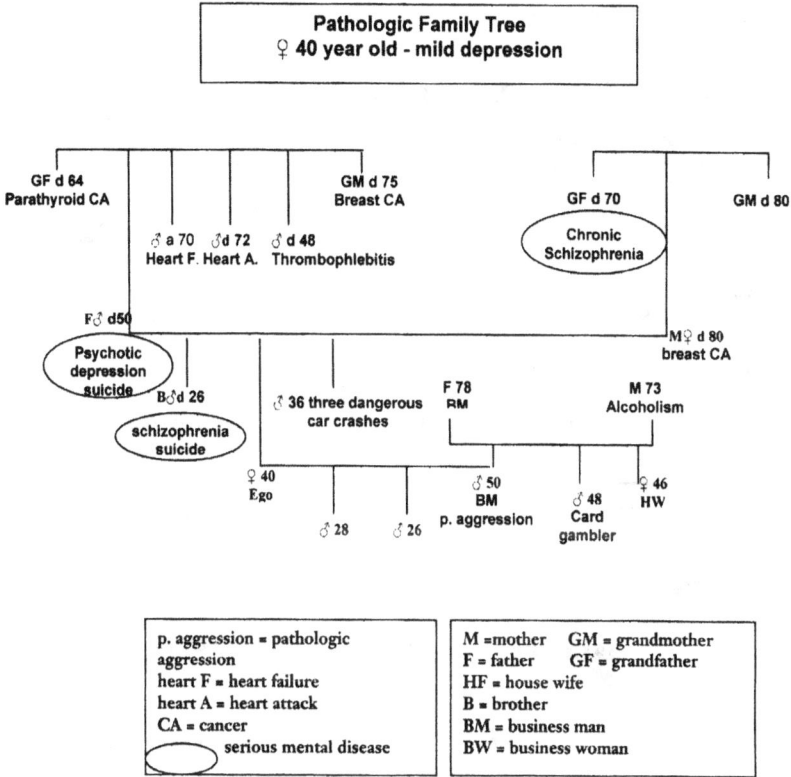

```
┌─────────────────────────────────────────┐
│         Pathologic Family Tree           │
│      ♀ 40 year old - mild depression     │
└─────────────────────────────────────────┘
```

GF d 64
Parathyroid CA

♂ a 70 ♂ d 72 ♂ d 48
Heart F. Heart A. Thrombophlebitis

GM d 75
Breast CA

GF d 70

Chronic
Schizophrenia

GM d 80

F♂ d50

Psychotic
depression
suicide

B♂ d 26

schizophrenia
suicide

♂ 36 three dangerous
car crashes

M♀ d 80
breast CA

F 78
RM

M 73
Alcoholism

♀ 40
Ego

♂ 28   ♂ 26

♂ 50
BM
p. aggression

♂ 48
Card
gambler

♀ 46
HW

p. aggression = pathologic aggression	M =mother GM = grandmother
heart F = heart failure	F = father GF = grandfather
heart A = heart attack	HF = house wife
CA = cancer	B = brother
⬭ serious mental disease	BM = business man
	BW = business woman

Diagram 7

Identity Inventory of the Primary Quaternio

In the beginning of analysis, I ask every patient to sketch a family tree signaling the creative members of the family (diagram 6) and another signaling the pathological cases in the family (diagram 7). After a few sessions, I ask the patient to list positive and negative characteristics of both parents and of the parents' relationship (diagram 8). Next, this list is complemented by negative and positive characteristics of the parents and their relationship that appear inthe personality of the patient (diagram 9). This inventory is very useful for revealing a great deal about the patient's creativity and pathology and his or her parental complexes in order to work through normal complexes and the shadow.

Parental Complexes Described by the Pacient

Mother Complex Mother and/or mother figures		Father Complex Father and/or father figures	
Positive Characteristics	Negative Characteristics	Positive Characteristics	Negative Characteristics
_____ ( )	_____ ( )	_____ ( )	_____ ( )
_____ ( )	_____ ( )	_____ ( )	_____ ( )
_____ ( )	_____ ( )	_____ ( )	_____ ( )

Relationship Between them

Positive Characteristics	Negative Characteristics
_____ ( )	_____ ( )
_____ ( )	_____ ( )
_____ ( )	_____ ( )

Diagram 8

List of Characteristics of the Patient's Personality

From Mother and/or mother figures		From Father and/or father figures	
Positive Characteristics	Negative Characteristics	Positive Characteristics	Negative Characteristics
_____ ( )	_____ ( )	_____ ( )	_____ ( )
_____ ( )	_____ ( )	_____ ( )	_____ ( )
_____ ( )	_____ ( )	_____ ( )	_____ ( )

From the Relationship Between them

Positive Characteristics	Negative Characteristics
_____ ( )	_____ ( )
_____ ( )	_____ ( )
_____ ( )	_____ ( )

Diagram 9

The Adult Quaternio

The primary quaternio is the main structuring function of the coniunctio archetype in the first three phases of life, that is, in the intrauterine phase and in the second (up to 2 years old) and third (from 2 to 12 years old) phases of childhood. The symbolic elaboration of the first two phases is coordinated primarily by the matriarchal insular position, while the third phase is coordinated mainly by the patriarchal polarized position. From puberty onward, beginning in the fourth (from 12 to 20 years old), continuing in the fifth (from 20 to 40 years old), and ending in the sixth archetypal phase of development, the archetype of conjunction (coniunctio) suffers a great change with the activation of the sexual glands and the intense existential drive toward a partner and the world, which is characterized by eroticism, affection, curiosity, and later by the raising of a new family. This phase of the archetype of conjunction corresponds to the matriarchal and patriarchal archetypes in the active position and to the anima-animus and alterity archetypes in the passive position that make up the conjugal or adult quaternio.

The Second Quaternio. Adult Quaternio. Marriage Self

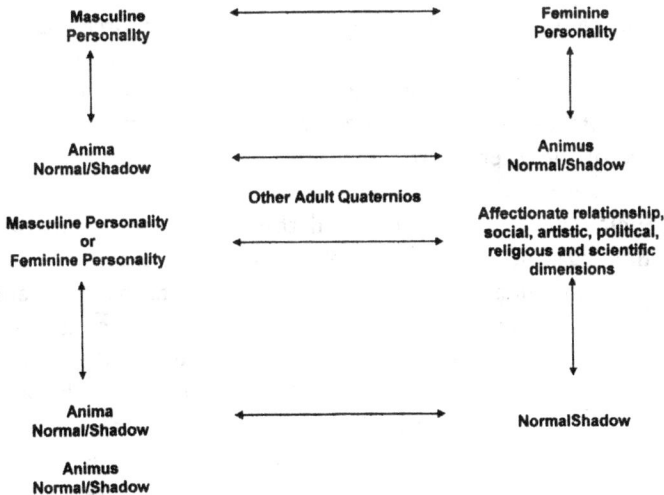

Diagram 10

This is truly an existential revolution with a change in the archetypal paradigm. While in the primary quaternio the two great others that confront the child are the parental complexes and their relationships, in the adult quaternio the main others are of the same age or stage and the cultural Self which lays beyond the family Self. Instead of being coordinated almost exclusively by the parental archetypes in the passive position, from now on, the ego will increasingly operate the matriarchal and patriarchal archetype in the active position. In the passive position, the child's ego is mostly passive and the parent's ego is mostly active. This change will be accompanied by a great activation of the anima, animus, and hero archetypes within the dialectical position of the alterity archetype, mostly in the passive position which will continue developing after adolescence in adult and mature life.

The structuring capacity of the adult quaternio will differentiate identity through detachment from the original family, but it will reinforce, now in the active position. many of the characteristics acquired through the primary quaternio. From adolescence onward, we will encounter a dispute within the regent archetypal quaternio, which will be essential during the whole process of individuation. The development of the matriarchal and patriarchal archetypes in the adolescent and adult personalities in the active position will be highly influenced by a competition between the matriarchal and patriarchal archetypes to be or not to be subordinated to the dialectical position of the alterity archetype. If the matriarchal and patriarchal archetypes strongly resist the influence of the alterity archetype, they can reinforce characteristics acquired through the primary quaternio, and, in this situation, the process of individuation can remain limited to traditional collective mentality. On the other hand, if the parental archetypes are open in adult life to the coordinating influence of the alterity archetype, the individuation process will flow creatively to great differentiation. Unfortunately this second possibility is still much rarer than the first and this diminishes significantly the differentiating structuring capacity of the adult quaternio.

The adult quaternio propitiates the confrontation of the anima and animus archetypes and of the shadow in the man-woman relationship. This pattern of relationship is very productive to the extent that it occurs in a quaternary manner within the dialectical pattern of alterity. The progression or stagnation of a love relationship frequently depends on its quaternary functioning. It is quaternary because the ego of one can relate and question the ego and shadow of the partner, and at the same time be open to relate and be questioned in the same way in return. In addition to heterosexual or homosexual relationships, the adult quaternio can also coordinate the dialectical relationships of creative professional life and any other relationship, including the body and nature. This can be better understood when we admit that the anima and animus archetypes are bi-gendered.

In the sixth phase of life, (from approximately 40 to 60 years old), we have a secondary adolescence in which the anima, animus, alterity, and hero archetypes, now in the active position, polarize again with the matriarchal and patriarchal archetypes, and the individual has the opportunity to attain full individuality and ontological identity. Here we begin the important transition from the dominance of anima, animus, alterity, and hero archetypes to the third and last quaternio.

The Third Quaternio: The Cosmic Quaternio and Death

In the final life quaternio, which encompasses the seventh and last archetypal phase of life, the central archetype activates once more the coniunctio archetype. This is the third and last quaternio in the individuation process. It is the cosmic quaternio that relates the personal body and the cosmic body in the interaction of life and death.

The decline of sexual and existential vitality diminishes the structuring capacity of the adult quaternio and transforms the relationship of man with woman and with all living things into a relationship of companionship. During this phase the subordination of the individuation process to the humanization process is fully revealed.

In this quaternio, the conjunction archetype propitiates detachment from the total incarnation that occurred during the second quaternio and elaborates the end of physical life.

As physical death draws near and we become increasingly detached from this incarnation, the coniunctio archetype constellates the relationship of the extinguishing body to the universal body and the finitude of incarnation to the eternity of being .

The Third Quaternio

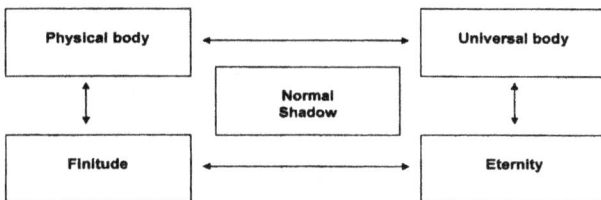

Diagram 11

During the structuring function of the third quaternio, the ego-other polarity detaches from this incarnation coordinated by the contemplative position of the totality archetype and the central archetype fuses again with totality, propitiating the ecstatic consciousness of creation which is the finality of the individuation and the humanization processes. This state of consciousness can be conditioned through various types of meditation, which encourage complete detachment. The relationship of the aging personal body with the permanence of the cosmos coordinates the interaction of finitude and eternity in the last conjunction (I have elaborated this quaternary relationship in the meditation described in chapters 4, 12, and 14).

The elaboration of this quaternio is generally handled through myths and religions in most cultures. Psychologically it calls forth the development of consciousness of our relationship with the universe with all its infinite and eternal symbolic meanings. Up to this point, we may have understood duality to be an illusion; this is intellectually correct but existentially unavoidable as a transitory state of consciousness. From now on the urge for nirvana and enlightenment is an existential necessity that can be obtained. Our increasing scientific knowledge of matter, space, time, energy, electromagnetism, gravity, and the extent and nature of the cosmos together with all the revelations of the mystics about the endless nature of the world spirit are very valuable to this transformation.

During my long dedication to developing my creativity and confronting my shadow, there were many episodes of great effort and suffering. A recent episode while writing these lines illustrates the nature of this process. My shadow, like that of most people, manifests itself under many forms. During years of elaboration, I came to illustrate the relationship of light and shadow in fantasy with two mythic beings-one of extraordinary creativity, the other with an equivalent destructivity. In this latest encounter, I used active imagination to enter into their origin. It was a long voyage which culminated when I arrived at their nest and they were revealed as twins within my Self and the cosmic Self. An encounter and a union occurred within the body of a great bird, which took flight and entered the flux of primordial energy beyond space and time. The experience brought peace and meaning.

Chapter 6

THE PROCESS OF SYMBOLIC ELABORATION

This above all: to thine own self be true, and it must follow, as the night the day, thou canst not then be false to any man. (Polonius's advice to his son Laertes in Hamlet, act 1, scene 3)

Jungian symbolic psychology unites and extends the concepts of archetype and archetypal image from analytical psychology and of fixation, defense mechanisms, compulsive repetition, resistance, and working through from psychoanalysis. This brings forth the concepts of structuring symbols and complexes, structuring functions and systems to form the process of symbolic elaboration coordinated by the central archetype in order to form consciousness and shadow in the symbolic axis of the Self. This process produces the countless meanings, which form the identities of the ego and the other in consciousness and in the shadow. This makes Jungian symbolic psychology symbol-centered rather than ego-centered or archetype-centered. Structuring symbols, complexes, functions, systems, and archetypes are formed by polarities that separate and reunite around the polarities of ego-other or other-other. Symbolic elaboration is an existential system of relationship. The fixation of polarities to one of its poles breaks up the system, transforming it into a disarticulated whole and forming the shadow. In such a case, one may construct a logical model through rationalization, but it will lack existential integrity. Furthermore, any life experience becomes a structuring symbol, complex, function, and system when elaborated.

Case Example

Walking along a street near his home, a man in his forties was attacked by a Rottweiler dog. He was terrified, but the owner of the dog held it tightly by the collar. The dog is a symbol, and the symbols closely related to it form a complex; fear is the structuring function, and the protective measures of the dog's owner form a structuring system. The elaboration of this experience continued. In time, the man became opposed to breeding these dogs. He heard that one attacked a child, hurting it badly. He happily followed the discussion of the law forbidding such dogs to go out in the street without a muzzle.

Through the structuring function of fear, he was elaborating the structuring symbol of the frightening dog and forming the identity of the scared ego and the Rottweiler dog (the other) in his consciousness. This began to take part in his thoughts, emotions, and attitudes in his daily life (the process of symbolic elaboration). These various experiences with the Rottweiler dog formed a complex that was initially normal but which, in time, due to the tension and difficulty in its elaboration, became fixated and defensive, that is, pathological.

Three months later, he was walking home and came across another Rottweiler dog. It was aggressive but had a muzzle on. The man became very pale, his heart throbbed, and he almost fainted. The elaboration of the symbol and of the complex of the Rottweiler dog now presented anxiety reactions beyond the control of the conscious ego, which showed that a fixation had taken place and that the ego-other polarity had begun to express itself through defensive anxiety in the shadow; in this case, a severe phobic defense bordering on panic.

We examined the story of fear in his life but there were no important memories, except for a film with a threatening shark he had seen a few years before and three nightmares of threatening biting animals in the month that followed.

Under my symbolic and cognitive behavior guidance to undo the conditioned anxiety defense, he phoned a Rottweiler dog breeder and began to visit and play with puppies twice a week for two months. Soon he felt that his anxiety reaction was under control.

Situated in varying degrees of elaboration along the symbolic axis, structuring symbols, complexes, functions, and systems relate consciousness, shadow, and the ego-other polarity with the central archetype. When something comes into the psychological field of the Self and becomes a structuring symbol, the first function activated is the transcendent structuring function of the imagination, which positions the symbol within the symbolic axis. During elaboration, symbols produce meanings (Fordham's deintegration) that, through imitation, introjection, and projection, form and transform the identity of the ego and the other. When this operation is inadequate, and the ego introjects what should be projected to form the other or vice versa, it is repeated and improved through the evaluation function. In this manner, consciousness accumulates countless representations in the individual, family, cultural, planetary, and cosmic dimensions, permanently growing and transforming under the coordination of the central archetype. As life goes on, self-consciousness and knowledge of the world walk hand in hand with the expanding identity of the ego and the other. Fixations of symbols and shadow formation impoverish, jeopardize, diminish productivity, and threaten the developmental process.

Union and separation, attachment and detachment are polarities of basic functions that elaborate symbols and form consciousness. In the beginning of the process, this occurs in symbolic relationships, where parts separate and become differentiated within the whole, metaphorically called Uroboros (the serpent biting its tale) by Neumann, and suffer the action of the sacrificial structuring function. This sacrificial separation from the old, which is gone, is just as important as incorporating the new. Union and separation coordinated by the conjunction archetype express the central archetype (Jung 1955-1956).

Exaggerated attachment to what we already are and resistance to detaching from the old and receiving the new are important causes and consequences of the formation of fixations, defenses, and the shadow and of the stagnation of symbolic elaboration. This is why most methods of psychological or spiritual development, explicitly pedagogical or not, are in one way or another based on the detachment structuring function, subordinated to the sacrificial function. Christianity, Buddhism, Judaism, and Islamism, for instance, have detachment as one of their central functions. Fixation of the normal sacrificial function prevents normal exchange of the old and the new and simply eliminates the old, giving rise to mutilation, which expresses deformed and insufficiently elaborated symbols through the shadow, preventing their normal transformation.

The Time of Symbolic Elaboration

The elaboration time of structuring symbols and complexes varies considerably and may last from moments to a lifetime or more. The sound of dripping water can sometimes be very irritating. You close your eyes to sleep, but the dripping in the bathroom sink reminds you that there is one more thing to be done while still awake. The drop is the symbol, dripping is the function, and plumbing is the structuring system. The elaboration is rapid, and the conclusion is immediate. You get up, go to the bathroom, and tighten the faucet. The complete elaboration and the resulting action takes may be forty seconds. In the case of the parental complexes, elaboration occurs during the whole life and continues even after the parents have passed away. This difference in duration explains why the symbolic axis presents countless structuring symbols in differing degrees of elaboration. There are structuring symbols in the cultural dimension, such as the relationship of man and woman, or in the planetary Self, such as our relationship with nature, which have been elaborated since the birth of consciousness in humankind and will be elaborated for as long as humankind exists, not to mention our relationship of the cosmic Self with the stars and the universe. These rich and unlimited symbols have infinite potential meanings. They are themes studied by science and expressed in works of art, social constructs, and religions, and they are the subject of permanent cultural elaboration.

The Unilateral Development of Consciousness
The Active-Passive Attitude in Symbolic Elaboration

Within the phenomenon of bipolarity expressed in the ego-other differentiation from the cosmos, the development of consciousness occurs unilaterally. During the process, however, in both the short run and the long run, it tends toward the equilibrium of the poles. This fact reminds us of

Cannon's principle of homeostasis, present in all living matter. The ingestion of food, for instance, causes an increase in gastric acid. After digestion, the production of acid returns to normal. Enthusiasm or an emotional experience can increase the blood level of adrenalin and the heart rate, but when it passes away, adrenalin blood level and heart rate return to normal.

The four functions and the two attitudes of consciousness described by Jung (1923), that is, thinking, intuition, sensation, feeling, introversion, and extraversion, are systemically organized to operate unilaterally as structuring functions in symbolic elaboration, forming the psychological types. This unilaterality tends to diminish during life. The natural attraction for the opposite sex in adult love relationships, subordinated to the anima and animus archetypes, for instance, almost always constellates around someone of the opposite type and diminishes typological unilaterality. This also happens in friendships between adults of the same sex, as in the classic companionship of Don Quijote and Sancho Panza.

The tendency to search for the equilibrium of typological unilaterality continues until the end of life. Classic examples might be the introvert thinking grandfather, an electrical engineer who, after seventy, takes great pleasure in leaving behind computers to take his grandchildren to the zoo. Another example is the extrovert feeling type who one day decides to take a course in philosophy. There is the introvert intuitive who, late in life, becomes fascinated with activities involving extrovert sensation, such as repairing clocks and watches, or the introvert sensation types who, in old age, are very much attracted by occultism. These occupations are ways through which the central archetype compensates typological unilaterality to favor psychological integration of duality in unity (Byington 1965).

Most emotional relationships between human beings present significant unilaterality. The adult-child relationship is a good example. In pregnancy and early childhood, the unilaterality and asymmetry of power between children and adults is significant (Byington 2006b), but during growth, this asymmetry diminishes and develops toward inversion which will arrive at equality and then become once more asymmetrical. All teaching relationships also follow this pattern as students learn, graduate, and one day become specialists who will likely know more than their teachers.

The Active-Passive Attitude of the Ego-Other Polarity

As expected, one-sidedness in the development of consciousness affects the ego-other polarity and propitiates the appearance of passive and active attitudes.

During development, children are significantly passive and adults-the other-are proportionately active. A major part of the science and art of being a father or mother consists of being aware and caring for the passive attitude of children and of reassuring their daily transformation toward becoming increasingly more active. The same happens in education.

Practically speaking, the development of all structuring functions in childhood, and also in later life, stimulates the ego to operate increasingly in the active position. This requires that parents and teachers recognize and reassure children or students by being more passive as the children or students become more active (Byington 2006b). Of course, this is not a rigid recommendation, because during every new acquisition, the ego regresses and progresses. This prevents us from adopting a fixed automatic position in education and in life.

The advantage of having a more complex brain than that of other animals is that our neurological circuits are endowed with greater ability to produce meanings, change behavior, and adapt to new situations. The disadvantage comes in that the instinctual fixed behavior of animals is frequently more appropriate in many life situations in which humans can adopt mental options that are artificial and existentially inadequate. In this respect, one of the most frequent unilateral behaviors observed in the mother-child relationship, for instance, is overprotection due to anxiety. Compare this human inadequacy with the same relationship in dogs, in which the bitch is much healthier because it can avoid overprotection by rejecting and even biting puppies when they grow too big for nursing.

The Self, the Ego-Other Polarity, and the Beginning of Symbol Formation

Traditional psychology is in many aspects ego-centered as when, for instance, it considers that the process of symbol formation in the Self only begins when the ego is capable of exercising it in the active position. This reduction of symbol formation to a stage of ego development is very different from how I conceive the nature of symbols and their structuring capacity. When we practice a symbol-centered psychology and consider that symbolic elaboration forms the identity of the ego and the other, together with beginning of consciousness, we become aware that symbols start forming the ego of the child in the passive position long before the child is conceived. Many future characteristics of the child's ego are projections of the characteristics of its culture and family. These meanings have been conditioned over many generations and receive the mother's pregnancy with the future child with great projective expectation. Genetics is but one of these historical symbols.

I have mentioned that maternal and paternal complexes contain symbols that continue to be elaborated long after the parents pass away. Symbolic defensive reduction tends to make us see our parents exclusively through what they did to us during our lives. However, when we regard them as structuring symbols with their archetypal and cultural, personal and collective, conscious and unconscious meanings, we realize that they are much more significant to the formation of our identity than we could ever imagine. Their genetic qualities are in our bodies and the positive and negative identifications with them and, through them, with our ancestors and their history and cultures, will be part of many of our thoughts and emotions. Sometimes, the fact that we are more like our mother's or father's family will be of central importance to our identity. The fact that we may not inherit their intelligence, stature, skin color, or beauty is sometimes more significant than those features we do inherit. The most significant inferiority complex I've encountered belonged to a patient who was his mother's height, one foot shorter than his father. The ethnic groups to whom parents belong have enormous influence on the future ego's identity, especially if the parents belong to different ethnic groups. As Brazil is a country with perhaps the greatest miscegenation between the four races, the interethnic symbols in ego identity formation is of incredible variety and must always be carefully considered. Add to these characteristics the social class, education, socioeconomic status, and many other aspects and we have an idea of the countless meanings that will be projected onto the child, before and after it is born.

All these meanings reunite in the parents' relationship and in their imagination during pregnancy what they expect their child will be like. Sometimes, long before they meet, they have already had fantasies about how their children would or should be. After conception, during the sometimes exhausting nine months of pregnancy, they live and fantasize with their baby, helped by the varied opinions of their families, finally arriving at a name that will accompany the child from birth to death. All these characteristics are symbolic and very meaningful and will become part of the child's primary relationship.

This immense quantity of symbols will contribute to form the child's ego in the passive position. They will not be completely elaborated but will remain within the child's and the parent's Selves, as well as in the family and cultural Selves. When the development of the child's ego reaches the point where it acquires the capacity to react symbolically in the active position, around five years of age, it already has this immense array of meanings, which have formed the ego, mostly unconsciously in the passive position, as the capacity to act in the active position increases. Therefore, to restrict ego symbolic capacity to the active position is an extreme reduction.

The parents, who have such an important role in the primary structuring quaternio, are not limited to them but will form a bridge that will connect the child's ego with a permanent flow of symbolic meanings from the family, cultural, planetary, and cosmic Selves. From late childhood and especially in adolescence, the ego will acquire increasingly greater capacity to operate in the active position and participate extensively in the individuation process, but ego and other identities have and will greatly continue to be formed in the passive position.

The Structuring Transcendent Function of the Imagination

Melanie Klein formulated questionable and fantastic ideas describing the mental functioning in early childhood, but three of her ideas seem to me very creative. The first describes the paranoid-schizoid and depressive phases of ego formation in the child's first year, which she later changed to two ego positions during the whole of life. Influenced by this idea, I formulated the five ego-other archetypal positions of consciousness.

The second idea was that the child begins very early to fantasize about its experiences and the nature of the world. Although Melanie Klein describes these fantasies very reductively within the relationship of the child to the breast, which I find very difficult to accept, she can be credited with calling attention to this early capacity in children, which strongly suggests that the imagination is an archetypal conscious and unconscious structuring function. Melanie Klein's third great contribution, as I see it, was the development of play therapy that is, observing the child at play in the treatment of problems in childhood. This expressive technique led Winnicott to recognize the importance of play, seeing it as an archetypal structuring function of consciousness of central importance in child development (Winnicott 1971).

In the theory of Jungian symbolic psychology, everything in psychic life is symbolic. Our nervous system and our consciousness can function in a more literal or more metaphoric way, but our thoughts and the language we speak are always symbolic and never only objective. In fact, our nervous system can only operate symbolically. The less emotional and symbolic the elaboration of a symbol, the less our nervous system retains it in memory as though it reasoned that if it does not have emotion, the symbol in question is not important.

The ego can operate symbols in the active attitude, as for example when we use metaphors to better express ourselves, but even when our ego is in the passive, literal, or concrete dimension, psychological expression also is always symbolic. Because of this, Ernst Cassirer suggested that man should be defined as an animal symbolicum. As a representation of reality, spoken words and thoughts are always structuring symbols. In this sense, the development of language accompanies the development of consciousness. To borrow from Heidegger, if the expression of being is "being here" (*Dasein*), and if being is always in the world (*Sein ist in der Welt*), we then can also say that being is symbolically in the world (*Dasein ist sinnbildlich in der Welt*).

Symbols breathe within the function of imagination, which is the essence of creativity and the very nature of conscious and unconscious psychic life. As I have emphasized, the function of imagination and fantasy transcend image and encompass any form of psychological expression.

When we accept that the structuring symbol includes the subjective and the objective, because both are psychological representations of human reality, we see that the structuring symbol cannot live without the imagination; neither can the imagination express itself without the structuring symbol. We frequently refer to the expression "psychic reality" to emphasize a unique dimension. From this perspective, we can consider the polarity subjective-objective within the structuring symbol as the essence of reality and the functional unity of the imagination of being. It is within the imagination that we become fully aware of ego and other identity formation through symbolic elaboration and the Cartesian necessity to separate them during this process. Imagination and creativity are, therefore, inherent to symbolic elaboration. Imagination does not exclude realization, for they are complementary and inseparable in psychic life.

The notion of imagination always joined with thinking meets with great resistance due to the subject-object cultural dissociation within materialist science. This dysfunction is so intense that something imagined is, for many people, equivalent to its not existing. Frequently, we find in arguments between two people one saying to the other: "Stop exaggerating! You are out of reality. You are imagining things!"

This prejudice has prevented the recognition of subjectivity in many human contexts, including the creativity of scientific discourse. It has also led to the ideological control that causes many scientists to hide their fantasies and dreams during their creative process and to present their final objective conclusions as though they came directly from logical rational objective deduction. In this way, we ignore the importance of the imagination and intuition in the creative process and in life. However, it is worthwhile to try to evaluate the importance of conscious and unconscious imagination and to understand their creative expression in the symbolic dimension of the psyche.

The discovery of the imagination in science accompanied the scientific rescue of the subjective dimension, a process begun by Pinel and Mesmer at the end of the eighteenth century. As mentioned earlier (see chapter 3), Anton Mesmer arrived in Paris in 1778, in the same year as Pinel. Pinel came from the interior of France; Mesmer came from Vienna, fleeing accusations of quackery. Mesmer realized eventual cures by suggestion, which he attributed to a questionable theory of animal magnetism. Many of his clients experienced possession, and the phenomenon soon became very popular. There is no doubt that Mesmer was the precursor of hypnotism, which dominated British and French psychology during the nineteenth century. During his "sessions," between the eventual cure of symptoms and pure exhibitionism, lay the power of the structuring function of imagination (Zilboorg and Henry 1941).

The imagination was recognized and included in the form of suggestion in the practice of hypnotism, which followed Mesmer's animal magnetism in the nineteenth century. In the twentieth century, the imagination became an important issue in dynamic psychology. Parallel to Melanie Klein's description of it in fantasy in early infancy, Jung considered fantasy the main function of the symbolic dimension (Jung 1923, par. 78). Considering that the transcendent function described by Jung is the function that expresses symbolic reality, we can conclude that it is part of the function of imagination and call it the structuring transcendent function of the imagination. When elaborating the interpersonal relationship, imagination is frequently associated with the functions of suggestion, empathy, and feeling, which operate together in any method of teaching or treatment and in marketing.

Due to the subject-object dissociation of materialist science, medicine has great difficulty in recognizing the power of the imagination even in its role in placebos, in which the effect of a drug occurs through the imagination without objective foundation. Medical education in most Western countries generally does not teach that a placebo can be a powerful force acting together with objective medication, nor that it can be an expression of the creative transference in the medical therapeutic relationship.

Although little recognized and rarely taught in medicine, positive transference has great therapeutic influence and is always present in any human relationship (Jung 1946). When not recognized and not used consciously, the imagination can have very negative consequences which are likely to show up through the shadow. Medical transference includes suggestion, empathy, and feeling within the imagination of the symbolic representations of patient and doctor in each other's Self. If suggestion and empathy, which includes intuition and feeling, are not assumed and creatively used by doctors, an empty space is left which can be easily occupied by the shadow of the therapeutic imagination, suggesting the gravity of the disease and a poor prognosis, which can influence negatively the course of treatment.

When medical doctors are unaware of the functions of the imagination, they may communicate to patients their diagnostic fantasies, quite unconscious of the harm they may cause. The diagnosis aside, the imagined possibilities are many, some very simple, others very serious. When a final diagnosis is made and the result is normal or trivial, the patient and the family are relieved. However, if one of the diagnostic fantasies communicated was of a serious disease, the patient and the family, although relieved, will have carried it for days as a possibility and perhaps a fatal outcome, which may become a serious hypochondriac symptom afterward.

Iatros in Greek means "doctor," and iatrogenic disease is a disease caused by doctors. In this case, the disease is caused by the careless communication of the imagination of doctors to the imagination of the patient. This situation, which is not at all rare, teaches us that doctors must keep to themselves the various diagnoses they imagine and only tell their patients when they are quite certain of them. However, many doctors cannot hold back their imagination for many different reasons, some of which are very defensive. Some doctors are concentrated exclusively on objective medicine and do not give much importance to what their patients and their families feel, much less to what they imagine. Others exhibit themselves narcissistically and give patients many possible diagnoses to show how much they know. Others still- and these, although doctors, are very disturbed persons-use very serious diagnostic possibilities to terrify patients and their families, either to increase their value to the patient until the diagnosis is made or to charge excessively for having discovered the diagnosis of "such a difficult case." All these medical problems arise due to the fact that the transcendent function of the imagination is ignored and not sufficiently valued together with the objective dimension during medical training.

Case Example

From countless cases I have accompanied of inadequate attention to the imagination in medical practice, I offer the following for the sake of illustration.

A forty-year-old mother saw that her sixteen-year-old daughter was pale and took the girl to their gynecologist. The doctor asked for a blood test, which confirmed the diagnosis of anemia. The problem arose regarding the cause of the anemia. The doctor said that she was not certain of the cause and sent the girl to a blood specialist. When asked by the mother if the case was serious, she replied that it could be very simple, caused by, for instance, heavy menstruation, or very serious. The anxious mother then asked, "But very serious such as what?" Here the doctor could not control either her diagnostic imagination or the anxious imagination of the mother and answered, "It could be an aplastic anemia, but of course it is not," and sent the girl to a blood specialist. The mother and daughter went home. They phoned the blood specialist who, unfortunately, was attending a medical conference and could not see the girl for another week. Meanwhile, the mother and daughter could not control their anxiety and started to elaborate it, calling up friends and relatives to discuss it, and they discovered two families who had lost children to aplastic anemia. The father was summoned back from an important business trip. The grandmother reacted with a hypertension crisis and had to go to a hospital. The mother and daughter could not sleep and had to consult a psychiatrist, who medicated them with sedatives, and so on and on. The following week, the blood specialist asked for more blood tests and concluded that the anemia was caused by heavy menstruation; he prescribed iron sulfate and congratulated the girl, her sister, the mother, the father, and two grandparents who had all come to the consultation for having such a lovely daughter, sister, and granddaughter in such good health. The family cried, hugged each other as Latin people do in stressing situations, and went home to celebrate. Two months afterward the mother and daughter changed their gynecologist. The girl has had an anxiety attack before every monthly period and has to take sedatives. The situation aggravated the mother's chronic insomnia, and she now uses stronger medication. The symptoms of the mother and the daughter can be diagnosed as iatrogenic hypochondria. Such cases are so frequent that we cannot consider them either rare or extraordinary. They are due to the ignorance and lack of education of medical practitioners on the subjective dimension and the relation of the transcendent structuring function of the imagination with health, disease, and the transference in the doctor-patient relationship.

This medical case illustrates that the effect of doctors, and of all public figures, on the imagination of people must be symbolically elaborated to assess whether they are being productive or destructive. Professional figures must assume that their discourse, although apparently objective and emotionless, is always symbolic and will affect the imagination of the listener for better or for worse. In this respect, it is not absurd to associate the extraordinary growth of the means of communication with the present hysterical reactions in the money market to any economic crisis worldwide and with the epidemics of stress and depression, together with the irresponsible consideration of the symbolic power of the imagination.

The concept of the imagination as a structuring function greatly increases in importance because it unites the subjective and the objective within the symbolic dimension. In this manner, instead of conceiving the imagination as nothing but a subjective function, it is perceived as being both subjective and objective. The power the symptom of anemia had to activate so strongly the function of imagination in the girl's family in the case above was due to the conflation of an objective blood test showing anemia and the subjective possibility of aplastic anemia imagined by the gynecologist.

Experienced as both subjective and objective, the imagination can be very productively associated with the functions of empathy, suggestion, and feeling. To imagine and suggest an objective diagnosis to someone, we must use empathy and feeling. Empathy (*Einfühlen* in German, which means "to feel inside someone or something") has the capacity of experiencing the other objectively as well as subjectively. In order to do this successfully, the ego must employ the feeling function to realize how this objective other feels and suffers. The problem raised by many doctors who have difficulty empathizing with their patients' reactions is related to their predominantly objective training, separated from their feeling function. Without feeling, it is very difficult to empathize with the emotional suffering of the other and relate it to our ego to imagine what is occurring in the other person's Self.

The Unconscious Power of the Imagination

As with all structuring functions, Jung's concept of the transcendent function here included in the imagination, as the main starting function of the process of elaboration, can be seen subjective and objective, conscious and unconscious.

The structuring power of the imagination is extraordinary in childhood and also throughout the life of the individual and in culture. However, beyond its traditional usage as a conscious activity, we have to recognize its unconscious characteristics. They are as important, extensive, and intensive as the conscious ones. When we see in the consulting room patients complaining of parents, sometimes very objectively, we know that in time they will recognize this criticism as part of their maternal and paternal complexes, followed by their insight into the presence of those complexes in their shadow.

When we recognize the conscious and unconscious power of the transcendent structuring function of the imagination, we realize that not only is Jung's concept of the transcendental function part of it but also his theory of compensation. I have already called attention to the compensation function as a structuring function of the central archetype which activates prospectively structuring symbols to correct unilateral individual and collective development.

The wings of the psyche, which allow it to transcend the literality of the here-and-now through meaning, are the structuring symbols, complexes, functions, and systems, and their flight is guided by the transcendent function of the imagination. In the same manner, the compensation of psychological unilaterality of any symbol in fantasies, in dreams, or in attitudes is done through the coordination of the central archetype through the imagination. When we deny the power of the imagination, we become exposed to both its good and evil effects. For example, in the materialism of consumerism, the compulsive urge for profit can cause disregard for people's welfare and imbue them, through marketing, consciously and unconsciously, with the wish to consume.

When we become conscious of the immense extension of the imagination, we see that it explains the fabulous richness of the thinking process, of fantasy, dreams, and even the variety of psychological symptoms.

The Ego Capacity of Imagination

The ego's capacity for symbolization is firmly established at five years of age. As we have seen, this is valid for the active position of the ego but not for the passive position, which begins in the womb, when the ego receives many genetic inputs and countless projections of meanings from the ancestral universe that will contribute to the formation of its identity after birth.

The important fact to learn for the process of symbolic elaboration is that the identities of the ego and the other are formed and transformed by the impact of the meaning of symbols coordinated by archetypes, which express the main operation of the central archetype.

Winnicott (1964) distinguished the breast from the transitional object-the first object to which the child becomes attached, hugs, and sucks-and concluded that it inaugurates symbolization. I have amplified the concept of the transitional object as the first expression of the archetypal structuring function of detachment (from the breast) and attachment (to the transitional object), a process that will operate with countless symbols from the beginning to the end of life, coordinated by the transcendent function of the imagination. All things and persons, including the most intimate - the breast, the mother, the father, siblings - are archetypal structuring symbols that will be elaborated by the structuring functions of transition through the attachment-detachment and union-separation polarities, expressing the actualization of the virtual potential of being.

With the increasing capacity for symbolization and the formation of the ego-other polarity, consciousness and shadow acquire more and more power within the Self, which gives rise to normal or defensive inflation (analytic psychology) or omnipotence (psychoanalysis) of the ego-other polarity in every new symbolic elaboration. This experience of attachment and fusion of the ego with the other, which generates various degrees of omnipotence or inflation, leads to unilaterality in development and may become fixed, forming defensive inflation or defensive omnipotence through defenses and shadow. The Greeks called this defensive omnipotence hubris (Greek, *hybris*), which in mythology was punished in countless ways by the gods. The explanation for hubris is that the fixation of symbolic elaboration prevents the continuation of separation and union (detachment and attachment) and the dysfunctions that are formed are projected as divine punishment by the gods.

As the ego develops, it increases its capacity to symbolize and to express the imagination in the active position. However, this occurs only up to a certain point. We can easily observe that children experience the imagination very intensely, far more so than adults. They are so much more creative that playing with them for a whole morning can exhaust an adult, while children can still be motivated to play the whole afternoon and into the night, resisting going to bed and begging to play just a little more until they literally fall asleep. Accompanying the vitality of the growing body, children's openness to the new and their capacity to learn are much greater than adults, as we can see when they learn a new language.

This enormous superiority of the child is greatly denied by adults; because adults are socially so much more powerful and have the last say, it is difficult for them to admit such inferiority. Evidence is found when we see adults sitting for hours watching television, incapable of creative work, eating and drinking, to stuff with sameness the empty time created by leisure (de Masi 2000).

An explanation for the diminishing imagination in adult life is not easy to find. In the search for it, the first thing to overcome is the resistance to seeing how few continue to have the creative urge in adult life and how uncreative most people are, proudly hiding their mediocrity and chronic sameness under the label of maturity. Very creative adults frequently cannot find a persona to express them and end up expressing themselves through a bizarre or destructive shadow. Examples of this fact are countless and remind us of Nietzsche, who so praised the creative individual that he raised him to the ideal of the superman, while at the same time being himself incapable of finding peace and satisfaction in daily life (Nietzsche 1872).

The symbolic creativity of the imagination starts to diminish in children when they begin to adapt to social conventions in late childhood, from 2 to 12 years of age. It is not only schoolwork, which they must do to obtain good marks, that diminishes creativity, but also the social contexts, at home and outside, in which they must build a politically correct persona to be approved and admired. The building of the persona described in analytical psychology is equivalent to the formation of the superego described in psychoanalysis, a process which subordinates ego performance to moral social cannons and traditions. From an archetypal perspective, we would describe this crucial problem of maturation as being brought about by the encounter of the infant personality chiefly coordinated by the insular matriarchal pattern of sensuality, spontaneity, and pleasure with the polarized patriarchal personality of organization, responsibility, and duty. It seems clear to me that this process of social adaptation is the main cause of the diminution of children's imaginations and has many variants which depend on the child, the family, and culture. These variants can be better understood using detailed descriptions of the archetypal positions of consciousness.

The end result of socialization, education, and submission to collective rules, although variable as we shall see, significantly diminishes spontaneity, which is indispensable for the expression of the imagination and play. Repetitive work certainly diminishes this even more. The greater the extent to which patriarchal organization rules the individual and society, the more the matriarchal archetype is limited, diminishing the power of symbolization. In such cases, education may function as domestication and the senex paralyzes the puer, a situation Hillman (1966) has addressed extensively in his work.

Another great cause of diminished creativity during personality development is the structuring function of automatism through which learning is conditioned and transformed in behavior without spontaneity and reflection.

Symbolization, Creativity, and Centroversion

Creativity continues into the fourth, fifth, and sixth archetypal phases of life (chapter 14), through the anima and animus archetypes. The dialectic position of the alterity archetype summons the matriarchal insular position of sensuality to relate dialectically to the polarized patriarchal position and regain spontaneity, creativity, and the capacity for play. This is illustrated by the mid-life crisis Jung went through after he separated from Freud and renounced the presidency of the International Psychoanalytical Association in 1915.

> After the parting of the ways with Freud, a period of inner uncertainty began for me. It would be no exaggeration to call it a state of disorientation.
>
> . . . .
>
> Thereupon I said to myself, "Since I know nothing at all, I shall simply do whatever occurs to me." Thus I consciously submitted myself to the impulses of the unconscious.
>
> The first thing that came to the surface was a childhood memory from perhaps my tenth or eleventh year. At that time I had had a spell of playing passionately with building blocks. I distinctly recalled how I had built little houses and castles, using bottles to form the sides of gates and vaults. . . . To my astonishment, this memory was accompanied by a good deal of emotion. "Aha," I said to myself, "there is still life in these things. The small boy is still around, and possesses a creative life which I lack. But how can I make my way to it?" For a grown man it seemed impossible to me that I should be able to bridge the distance from the present back to my eleventh year. Yet if I wanted to re-establish contact with that period, I had no choice but to return to it and take up once more that child's life with his childish games. This moment was a turning point in my fate, but I gave in only after endless resistances and with a sense of resignation. For it was a painfully humiliating experience to realize that there was nothing to be done except play childish games. (Jung 1961, pp. 170, 173-174)

The detachment and sacrifice of the persona and from the professional status Jung had acquired in the psychiatric world as president of the International Psychoanalytic Association as well as the emotional separation from Freud as an important father figure disoriented Jung's personality and favored a regression and centroversion which would prove to be very creative. In 1913 Jung was 38 years old, and therefore we may suppose that the separation from Freud was an event synchronistic to his midlife crisis, which, as he himself described, activates many unconscious contents during the individuation process. In that year Jung began to live the experiences that, two years later, originated the *Red Book*.

During this regressive experience to his 10 and 11 years, Jung experienced his childhood "spell of playing passionately with building blocks." If we link his experience with the imagery in the *Red Book*, we realize that he not only was "submitting himself to the impulses of the unconscious" but was rescuing in his personality the exuberance of the insular matriarchal position which had been left behind during his academic education and his relationship with Freud. Unfortunately for analytical psychology and its theory of the individuation process, Jung did not recognize this imagery as pertaining to a conscious expression of the insular matriarchal archetype and reduced it merely to "the unconscious." This prevented him from becoming aware of the enantiodromic archetypal transformation going on in his personality and how the discovery of the patterns of consciousness so richly portrayed in myths, dreams, tribal cultures (participation mystique), and in himself expressed the matriarchal archetype and were in contrast to the patriarchal dominance in Freud's work and personality and his own education and university career.

The Ontic and the Ontological Identity

Based on Heidegger (1927), we can elaborate an important difference between ontic and ontological identity that contributes to our efforts in stressing the essence of symbolic elaboration, which is the conflict between genuineness of being and alienation during ego and consciousness development (May 1958).

I must excuse myself with Heidegger and Husserl for using *Sein* and *Seiendes*, being and entity, as a polarity. Everything they search for in their ontology is conceived so as to avoid polarities, which divide being and produce alienation. However, I promise them that the use of this polarity will be circumstantial and that at the end of the study, I will not leave reality divided in a dualistic perspective and shall reunite it again to preserve the integrity of being.

The development of the child's ego strengthens and differentiates the personality. Descartes' famous saying, "I think, therefore I am," is an assertion of consciousness that it exercises mental life because it coordinates representations of things. In the personality of the child, this motto is "I play, therefore I am." The growth of the child's ego occurs together with the development of the body with its psychological functions, which will become over time the symbolic body of the imagination. The acquisition of every detail of physical development forms symbols with meanings which are structuring symbols, complexes, functions, and systems and are the representations of the subject we call "ego" and of the objective non-ego we call "other" (Byington 1965).

The infant communicates first through sounds that are the beginning of language and asks for holding and caring and may express frustration and aggression. Through the movements of its fingers it develops the notion of its mental activity; it explores with curiosity the identity of objects with its mouth, the same mouth that receives milk and relieves hunger and experiences frustration, suffering, pleasure, and satisfaction. It opens its eyes to know people and the world, and day and night, which begin to link cosmic time with feeding time. It urinates and experiences relief and satisfaction. With the sensation of liquid and warmth and together with evacuation it realizes that it can produce things. Mental acquisitions represented by bodily functions continue to form identity and, at the same time, consciousness of the vitality of being through desire, action, receiving, and giving and eventually through selection and the capacity to say yes and no (Spitz and Codliner 1966).

The fantastic acquisitions of walking, sphincter control, sexual identity, speech, and self-feeding and the exercise of the imagination in play, in the control of rage and affection, and in seduction ratify the ego's growth and the construction of the motto "I exist because I think, that is, because I can operate the representations of the inner and outer world in my mind."

It is not my intention here to describe child personality development (see chapter 14) but only to call attention to a few important instances that contribute to form ego-other identity through physical experiences within the primary quaternio as described in the preceding chapter. It is remarkable that these physical experiences form the mind through representations in a symbolic field that roots the ego-other identity in the individual, family, cultural, planetary, and cosmic Selves coordinated by the function of the imagination. Initially passive and then active through all physical activities reunited in playing, imagination illustrates the vitality of the central archetype to form knowledge of the Self, which includes the world. It is through these countless meanings that the identity of the ego and the other are formed.

The representations of the other accompany the formation of the representations of the subject. During life, the ego and the other will receive many designations and titles, including an identity card, passport, and many other characteristics. They come from the family name, physical traits, religion, profession, nationality, home address, present job, positive and negative records, all of which form the ego's and other's ontic identity.

Within Heidegger's existential philosophy, things (*Seiende*) are the expression of being (*Sein*). In this manner, ontic identity expresses all characteristics of the physical, social, and mental dimensions that form our personality and appear in our persona, our social face. It expresses the way we adapt to society, to the superego, and to collective values. It is the identity of the social status, for which so many live and die-the car, the bank account, the way one dresses and poses.

"The habit does not make the monk" is the saying, but it is "in the habit that most people believe", the cynic might add. For most people, it is not enough to be; rather it is the appearance that is more important. In Rome, it was said that it was not enough for Caesar's wife to be honest. She also had to look honest.

The ontic identity, like the defensive persona, can become fixed and defensively form the shadow. In this case it is used to hide or represent false and deformed characteristics particularly intended to delude people.

However, the ontic identity is not enough to describe being. There is another characteristic of identity-the ontological identity-which is much harder to define or to describe. Whereas ontic identity is built through quite obvious characteristics of entities, the ontological identity is the identity of a hidden and virtual process. Ontic identity is mutable and circumstantial-it is constructed and destroyed day by day; ontological identity is unique and permanent because it is the identity of being inherent to the central archetype.

It is the profound identity of being, which can be conscious, but is also in great part unconscious; it is very difficult to perceive, and it is revealed during the individuation process. Frequently, people who know us intimately recognize our ontological identity better than we do ourselves. For instance, one may be on the verge of assuming an important attitude in a crucial life situation only to have an intimate friend remark, "You are wasting your time-this attitude is not you."

We could compare these two identities somewhat relatively with what Jung called his number one and number two personalities. He associated personality number one with the general occupations and interests of his life as a student and personality number two with philosophical and profound spiritual themes. Many Jungian analysts have associated number one with the ego and number two with the Self. However, taking into account that the ego is permanently expressing the central archetype, I consider it more appropriate to describe them as two different identities of the ego and to try to understand their differences as such. Number one is our ontic identity and number two is our ontological identity.

Ramana Maharshi, a very holy man in India, has written a small book with the title *Who Am I?* (2008). In this book he describes the method of the inquirer to search for "the happiness which is one's Self," which seems to me to refer to the ontological identity. He begins the method of inquiring who am I? by mentioning the gross body and the seven humors (*dhatus*) and saying that he is not them. Next, he mentions the five sense organs and all they can do, and he repeats that he is not them. He goes on listing all physiological and mental functions, and again says that he is not them. He ends by saying that after negating all the above-mentioned qualities, the awareness which alone remains is that I am.

It seems to me that the guru mentions as "not I" all that is circumstantial and ephemeral and can be regarded as samsara: thoughts and physical and mental sensations, and exactly because they are circumstantial, I define them as an expression of the ontic identity. On the other hand, once the inquiry *Who am I?* has discarded all these ontic characteristics of identity, what is left is pure awareness, which I find to be pure being, ontological identity related to the central archetype, to the Self and to *atman*. In order to experience such awareness as the essential identity of being, I ask the reader to close the eyes for a moment and meditate, asking you the question: *Who am I?* As literal characteristics come up, you should answer "Not this, not that," until finally there are no further answers to the question and a great void comes to mind. At that moment, you must concentrate fully to receive the pure awareness: "I am." This is the ontological identity of being!

If I consider the ontological identity as the identity of being (*Sein*) and if being encompasses all things, it follows that I cannot equate it with any entity, that is, with any part (*Seiende*), because a part cannot be equated with the whole. Heidegger tells us of genuineness (*Eigenartigkeit*) as the truth of being that is always the same. Ontological identity, then, is the genuineness, the immutable truth of being, the *atman*, because it expresses the relationship of the ego to the central archetype and is unique in every personality and culture. It is the singularity that guides the individuation process and the humanization process.

Many authors have described in literature the relation of the characters they create with ontological identity, such as for instance Camus, Graham Greene, Sartre, Dostoyevsky, Shakespeare, Cervantes, Tolstoy, and many others, including the Gospel. We can even say that in each case the plot and the many aspects of the characters they describe form a tortuous path of ontic identities, a true labyrinth which circumambulates and reveals during the course of the work the ontological identity of the characters, which lies hidden in the center like a pearl in an oyster. These great literary characters are covered up by a mysterious veil, which is drawn aside during the novel, in the same way that Ramana Maharshi considered and discarded many characteristics of being finally to answer the question, *Who am I?* through total awareness. Ontological identity cannot be defined through entities, and the art of existentially revealing it allows the reader to become aware of it through the depth of his or her own being. An example of this may be found by examining the romantic ridicule of Don Quijote's doings with his character and his adventures until we become exhausted and give up trying to pin down who that philosophical buffoon really is. Only then, perhaps, can we become aware of the essence of the character Cervantes wants to reveal to us. After dedicating much imagination and detachment to those fantastic adventures, I arrived at the archetype of hope as the ontological identity of Don Quijote (Byington 2003a).

Ever since he appeared to me in a dream a long time ago, I have often meditated upon Jesus and asked myself about his truth, and his ontological identity. One of the testimonies about him, which impressed me very much, was given by a minister who had lost his faith in one of Bergman's films, *Winter Light* (1963). Looking at a crucifix, he suddenly had an intense insight and exclaimed to himself, "How he must have suffered!"

It is obvious that the ontological identity, like all other structuring functions, also has an unconscious archetypal root, but it would be a mistake to reduce it unilaterally to unconscious identity or identity of the central archetype; if we do so, we lose its progressive revelation in consciousness during life as the identity of the process of incarnation of the central archetype.

Ontic identity and ontological identity cannot be equated with the ego and the central archetype respectively. They are rather two types of identity of the ego within the Self in the symbolic axis (ego-central archetype axis). Ontic identity centers on ego and its attachment to circumstantial acquisitions and doings, whereas ontological identity emanates from its root in the central archetype.

However, we must not dwell on the polar opposition of ontic and ontological identities, because that would be reducing symbolic elaboration and the self to the divisive polarized patriarchal position. If we do so, we lose the all-encompassing nature of being-in-the-world, which can only be experienced in the symbolic elaboration coordinated by the dialectic position of the alterity archetype. This position, as we can see, produces all the meanings contained in symbols, because it includes polarities with the poles in opposition but also in equality.

We have examined the ontic and ontological mostly in opposition, but now we must do it also in equality. To do this, we must abstract from what they have in opposition and relate them dialectically to discover what they have in common.

What they have in opposition, as I have pointed out, is that the ontic is dominantly that which the ego has acquired and done in life while the ontological is dominantly the process of relationship of the ego to the central archetype. What they have in common is that both express being in the symbolic axis of the Self through the main psychological activity of symbolic elaboration. In this sense, ontic identity is the expression of ontological identity and, in turn, affects it. Happy is the person who has traveled the great life journey without divorcing from his or her soul!

The great virtue of being is genuineness (Byington 1965), which can be jeopardized by dysfunctions such as fixation and shadow formation that bring hubris. Obviously, in such cases, ontic and ontological identities become dissociated and being is threatened by alienation, Sartre's *le néant* (nothingness) (1943).

This circumambulation in our symbolic elaboration of identity through the ontic-ontological polarity becomes clearer when we consider that great philosophers in all times have created systems of wisdom to avoid alienation between the poles of the ontic-ontological polarity.

The archer bends his bow, closes his eyes, and shoots an arrow at the center of the target (Herrigel 1948). This practice is an exercise of Taoism. Tao is being. Tao is the way of ontological identity. Archery, like any other human practice, is the exercise of ontic identity. How can one search for ontological identity through ontic identity without denying it thoroughly, as did Ramana Maharshi? Aim at the center, close your eyes, and shoot your arrow recommends the master of Taoism. If we understand that the concept of *wu wei* in Taoism is doing without doing, we see that when you aim at the center and close your eyes, through *wu wei*, you are undoing your controlling mind, characteristic of ontic identity, and propitiating ontological identity, characteristic of the center. In this manner, we are recognizing the opposition between the two identities and, at the same time, associating them in equality when the arrow hits the center through *wu wei*.

Let us now accompany a guru who had gone in pilgrimage to Benares and was returning to his little village in southern India. His favorite disciple had stayed home, practicing *yoga* exercises and meditating many hours a day to live up to his master's journey. When the master returned, the disciple eagerly went to him and asked, "After your pilgrimage what stage of consciousness have you reached on your search for Nirvana?" The master answered: "I continue to cut the wood to prepare my tea." The disciple was very disappointed. When the master turned around to cook his tea, in order to test his degree of awareness, the disciple took up a piece of wood and tried to hit the master on the head. The master turned around swiftly and grabbed the disciple's hand in mid air. Through Nirvana, he had acquired the vision of the opposites, the front and the back.

In a Zen monastery, every new disciple who entered the temple had to create a *koan*: A very bright young man began training. He woke up early every morning and exactly by sunrise sat in meditation in front of the master's door. The master went by him without saying a word. The disciple did this every day for many years searching for Zen, the master continued to walk past him without saying a word, but the disciple did not understand. One day, the master died of old age. The next morning, during meditation, the door did not open, and the disciple finally understood Zen and became a master himself. The speechless master had been his *koan*.

Centroversion and Regression

One of the many contributions of Erich Neumann (1949a) to analytical psychology was the concept of centroversion, which I believe to be the concept most necessary to approaching ontological identity. Centroversion is dominantly unconscious until the adult stage of life. It is the main structuring function of the Delphic "know thy Self" (*gnôthi s'autón*) which decorated the entrance of Apollo's shrine in Delphos. It is revealed during the process of individuation as ontological identity.

Centroversion is a structuring function that allows the ego to experience the direction and sense of the archetypal development of consciousness, and so is the compass of genuineness during the existential development of the truth of being.

Centroversion favors experiences of totality, which orient us to live our unique identity during our journey. These experiences are of great importance during our existential crises when we feel that we have lost our way.

Ontological identity can be revealed in genuineness through ontic identity (Byington 1965). Happy are those who have the privilege of this affinity. But the two identities can also enter into conflict. The meaningful events expressing ontological identity can be very smooth, chronic, and abrupt or intense, acute, and terrible. They are the profound manifestations of being described by Rudolf Otto (1917) within the experiences of the tremendum and the fascinosum which are characteristic of the dimension of the holy.

We can have experiences of the central archetype, that is, of the ontological identity, either through the ego or through the other as symbols of totality. During my training in Zurich, I became friends with a Jesuit doctor in theology with whom I had much affinity. One day, he asked to talk to me privately. I became worried because I sensed that he was very tense. I imagined that he had lost someone very dear to him or something of the sort. We searched for a free room in the institute, where we attended patients. When we sat down, he looked me straight in my eyes and began to cry with much intensity and suffering. He could hardly speak. After some time, he regained his self-control and said he wanted to share with me the most profound experience of his life. He had chosen the religious life following a strong vocation more than thirty years before. His faith was intense and permanent. He was doing analysis as part of his training to become an analyst and added that he began to have very intense emotions when he analyzed his judging reactions to many of our colleagues during training. His emotions were more intense when they were aggressive, and they were building up, to the point where he was becoming worried about their consequences.

On this morning he had gone to buy shoestrings. Back at home, he never bought anything, for all his needs were taken care of by the religious community in which he lived. But this morning, he had bought shoestrings and returned to his room. He knelt down to change the old shoestrings for the new, and then it happened. Like a bolt of lightning, he experienced his entire life of renouncing his will to attend the needs of others. Buying and changing his shoestrings, he realized he could also kneel before God and do things for himself. At that moment he became conscious that he could also live by doing, the opposite of *wu wei*. Then and there, Tao, his ontological identity, was paradoxically revealed to him.

Being, Shadow, and Supraconscience

In the perspective of Jungian symbolic psychology, fixation and defensive expression of ontic identity forms shadow. Now we may ask: How does shadow formation affect ontological identity?

I have conceived supraconscience as the structuring function of the Self that can become aware of the relationship of that part of being which operates freely in conscience and that part which is imprisoned in the shadow condemned to repetition compulsion.

Through the function of supraconscience then, we can become aware in time that the fixation of ontic identity affects ontological identity, bringing alienation to the Self.

Generally, in the fifth archetypal phase of life (20 to 40y years) we suffer fixations and struggle with the shadow in various dimensions of our ontic activities. It is not easy to see the extent to which these victories and defeats can affect our ontological identity with alienation.

In the sixth archetypal phase of life (40 to 60 years), however, with the increasing integration of the differentiation potential of the anima and animus archetypes within the process of individuation, we become more and more aware, through the structuring function of supraconscience, of the degree of alienation that deformed our ontological identity.

Shadow formation of ontic identity brings suffering because these symbols, which operate in the shadow, distort our adaptation to life, causing unhappiness and symptoms which frequently torture our everyday lives with mental disturbances, mythologically expressed in Christianity as the torments of the soul in Hell.

Shadow formation of the ontological identity, however, brings alienation of the life process and a different suffering to the Self. Its perception through supraconscience makes us aware of how much we have deviated from our capacity for realization of the potential of our being. From a mythological perspective, this is the perception of the greatest sin through which our soul has been estranged from God and become enslaved by the devil. Within a psychological and ontological perspective, this is the recognition of how much our being has suffered alienation and forfeited its creative urge for self-realization.

In this manner, I have fulfilled my promise to Husserl and to Heidegger that the subdivision of being in the ontic and ontological identities would not be definitive and bring alienation. Through the alterity archetype, we have seen that ontic and ontological identities, the part (*Dasein*) and the whole (*Sein*) are two ways of being that permanently interact and belong to wholeness during the developmental process.

Chapter 7

THE STRUCTURING FUNCTIONS OF DEFENSE MECHANISMS AND SHADOW FORMATION THE NEUROTIC DEFENSE AND THE PSYCHOPATHIC DEFENSE

Science sans conscience n'est que ruine de l'âme. (Rabelais 1483-1553).

It is perhaps in the description of the structuring function of ethics and in the formation of the shadow through fixation and defense mechanisms that we shall most creatively profit from the bringing together of analytical psychology and psychoanalysis proposed by Jungian symbolic psychology.

In banishing subjectivity from the search for knowledge and identifying it with superstition and error, science systematically excluded it from the scientific method and, in so doing, established a most serious fixation and dissociation of the subjective-objective polarity. This dissociation left a dark stain on the development of the Enlightenment, and it has haunted the Western cultural Self with materialism and reductionism since the end of the eighteenth century.

As a result of this dissociation, when science retook the study of subjectivity during the nineteenth century and created modern psychology, many prejudices were acted out defensively. The main one was the pathologization of the subjective dimension, which confused and deformed the study of ethics and psychopathology.

Jung began his experiments in the Burghölzli in Zurich to demonstrate the existence of the repressed unconscious and created the theory of complexes, which were initially defensive, that is, pathological. Progressively, however, he began to include normal phenomena in his experiments, which led him to describe the normal ego complex. Next, he conceived his theory of psychological types and archetypes, finally centering his work on the individuation process and subordinating pathology to it. This was a huge enantiodromic reaction to the pathologizing reduction begun by psychology in the eighteenth century.

Neuroscience in the second half of the twentieth century increasingly found drugs to be more efficient at diminishing symptoms of psychological suffering such as anxiety and depression, but the practitioners of neuroscience could not transcend the subject-object dissociation. Drug therapy, like any other structuring function, can be normal or defensive; it becomes a defensive therapy when we medicate symptoms without first elaborating their symbolic function within the Self. In such a case, a basic rule in medicine is violated: never treat symptoms autonomously, because this may cover up and reinforce pathology. Cognitive behavioral therapy (CBT), frequently used today as an accessory to drug therapy, can also reinforce pathology if symbolic elaboration of defenses with their unconscious components is not undertaken.

Jung's formulations of the ethical function and the shadow concept are perhaps the most confused and ambiguous portions of his work. He defines the shadow as the archetype that expresses psychological contents not accepted by consciousness or by the persona (Jung 1923). Unfortunately, he included in the shadow only aspects pertaining to the same gender as the ego. Contra sexual aspects of men not accepted by the persona were attributed to the anima archetype and of women to the animus archetype (Jung 1951). This generated confusion about the main characteristic of symbols expressed in the shadow-their lack of acceptance by the persona. What did this have to do with gender? If lack of acceptance is the main criterion, why exclude contra sexual symbols from the shadow? And why attribute the unaccepted characteristics of the opposite gender to the anima and animus archetypes?

A second ambiguity in the concept of the shadow occurred when other unconscious aspects were included in addition to those that were unacceptable or morally undesirable. This amplified the concept of the shadow to the extent of making it at times practically a synonym for unconscious processes (von Franz 1957). In this manner, the enantiodromic movement against defensive pathologizing went too far and disfigured the defensive (that is, pathological) nature of the shadow. This was unfortunate because it blurred the concept of the shadow in its capacity to differentiate clearly normal and pathological phenomena, which is essential for psychopathological theory and psychotherapy. In this manner it seems to me that analytical psychology wasted the precious concept of shadow as the depository of defensive ethics, pathology, and evil.

A third source of ambiguity came from Jung and the many Jungian analysts who found the presence of positive symbols in the shadow to be something extraordinary, to the point of conceiving a "golden shadow." However, recognizing that the shadow includes unaccepted symbols, there is no reason to differentiate the symbols themselves as being positive or negative, good or bad. If unaccepted symbols are taken up by symbolic elaboration and their meanings are integrated into consciousness, regardless of whether they are approved or disapproved, liked or disliked, they will become a creative part of the individuation process. The identification of good symbols in the shadow does not justify the concept of a golden shadow, all the more so because all symbols in the shadow, whether good or bad, need to be rescued and elaborated, their contents integrated to form the identity of the ego-other polarity in consciousness.

For example, an aggressive and destructive tendency in the shadow, if well elaborated, can become a positive quality of courage and determination in the personality, just as a depressive symptom, when elaborated and integrated, can become an affectionate function of self-esteem. A theological parallel would be a category of "good sins" equivalent to the golden shadow. However, neither makes sense because the positive characteristic of the shadow is implicit when we elaborate its symbols and integrate them in the individuation process, in the same way that the repenting of sins is part of the road to salvation.

The fourth reason for misunderstanding the concept of the shadow in analytical psychology occurred with Jung's "theological crusade" to contradict the Thomist concept of summum bonum and privatio boni, according to which God would be perfect and all imperfection, sin, or evil could be attributed to his absence. According to Jung, this would be equivalent to the absence of evil in the godhead. I shall take up this question in chapter 11 when we examine the theme of the paradox of the central archetype.

Finally, the fifth factor that confused the concepts of ethics and shadow in analytical psychology was Jung's reference to absolute evil in *Aion* (1951); he never explained what he really meant by this.

Erich Neumann, in his book *Depth Psychology and a New Ethic* (1949b), contributed greatly to clarifying the meaning of ethics in analytical psychology. He formulated a new ethic inherent to the moral values of the individuation process in contradistinction to ethics established by traditional collective values, somewhat analogous to the concept of the superego in psychoanalysis.

Unfortunately, Neumann did not address the concept of the shadow from the perspective of the five points listed above, nor did he refer to its formation within the Self as a result of ego fixation. It seems to me that with both new and traditional ethics in hand, we need to formulate a new psychodynamic concept of the shadow to match them.

Freud discovered the phenomenon of fixation and described it as a disturbance of psychological development that fixates the libido. He named regression the process of the ego returning to a fixation during life.

Jungian symbolic psychology conceives shadow formation as a result of fixation of structuring symbols, complexes, and functions. Fixations turn structuring functions defensive which form and express the shadow during the process of symbolic elaboration. This occurs mainly in childhood, but may happen in any stage of life. Through this, we may equate the shadow with the repressed unconscious and conceive its contents as structuring symbols and functions (complexes) of both genders, fixated and expressed by defenses within the pathological process of repetition compulsion as symptoms, sin, crime, error, and evil.

It is important to stress the distinction made here between normal and defensive structuring functions in order to preserve the theory of polarities. In this manner, for the normal structuring function of projection, we have the defensive structuring function of projection; for the normal structuring function of resistance, we have the defensive structuring function of resistance; and likewise for the normal structuring functions of aggression, envy, jealousy, treason, love, power, obedience, rebellion, and so on. If we have a function that already appears defensive-for instance, repression-we seek a denomination for its normal functioning, such as delimitation, contention, or restraint.

Once we have conceived a normal structuring function corresponding to each defensive structuring function, the next step to avoiding indiscriminate pathologizing in psychology is to sort out methodologically and accurately every normal structuring function in the formation and expression of consciousness and describe the formation and expression of a corresponding defensive structuring function in the shadow. In so doing, we apply the concept of fixation, defense, and pathology exclusively to the shadow, considering it therefore relatively equivalent to the repressed unconscious. I say "relatively" because this does not make the shadow an equivalent of the personal unconscious because in this perspective, all symbols are always personal and archetypal, and consequently the same occurs with any symbol fixated in the shadow and with any defense that expresses it.

Shadow Formation in Childhood

Children's normal transgression, frustration, anxiety, and depression express the pangs of growth. Those who question this proposition argue that children's anxiety reactions are so frequent and intense that they need defenses for normal development. I would counter this with the idea that the fact that defensive behavior is frequent during the developmental process of children does not make it normal.

My basic premise is that children's ego identity is formed by the primary quaternio coordinated by the central archetype. In this sense, the greatest conscious and unconscious desire of children is to grow up, that is, to develop their capacity to become adults. When they misbehave, most of the time they know they are transgressing, but they do not know how to adequately express what they want. Normal development includes transgression, and frequently children do not have the persona to transgress adequately. Indeed, the child should not always obey and submit, for normal ego development includes from its very beginning both yes and no (Spitz 1957). Therefore, instead of relying exclusively on sermons and punitive measures coordinated by the patriarchal archetype to correct dysfunctions of behavior, it is much more productive to try to elaborate the misbehavior of children through the dialectical position of the alterity archetype, trying to identify the reasons, difficulties, and purposes inherent in misbehavior and help the child in his or her elaboration and adequate expression. One great error in education is to think that when children misbehave, they know the meaning of what they are doing and must be repressed. Most of the time, children transgress, protest, and misbehave without knowing the meaning of what they are doing. In such cases, their reaction is a clumsy way to say that they disagree or want to do something else but do not know how to express themselves. This clumsy reaction should be seen as distorted and defensive behavior. If it is simply repressed or punished, children become guilty and confused and are not helped to learn how to elaborate difficult and unknown situations that involve suffering and frustration.

Children grow up withstanding the tension of desire and social organization coordinated by the matriarchal and patriarchal archetypes and, above them, by the central archetype. Most of time, they know very well what is morally expected of them according to traditional ethics. When they transgress this moral code, very frequently, they know that they are doing it, because it is a norm that every child easily learns. The structuring function of transgression is inherent to the creative and healthy growth process, and so the problem is not to avoid transgression, but to exercise it creatively, with a proper persona, and this is exactly what the child does not yet know, has to learn, and can be taught. This is one of the primary aspects of education and of building the persona.

Transgression expresses creative emotions in discovering the new, the power of self-assertion, and a taste of free will for breaking up dependence, acquiring the capacity of increased individuality, and pride for partaking of "the fruit of the tree of knowledge." In this respect, normal transgression is a very creative structuring function that is inherent to healthy vitality and propitiates necessary detachment from primary dependence.

Psychoanalysis follows the *Old Testament* and identifies transgression with sin expressed by oedipal parricidal and incestuous tendencies that generate anxiety and feelings of guilt through the castration complex. This leads to repressive education, to the sublimation of matriarchal desire, reduced to incest, and patriarchal disobedience, reduced to parricide, to form the superego and obey the traditional moral code.

The punishment of transgression by reinforcing the patriarchal code in traditional ethics educates through repression and does not teach the child to deal creatively with transgression. This pattern in education favors fixation, defense, and shadow formation. In this situation, what the child needs is not more limits and repression but help through symbolic elaboration in learning to express transgression creatively. For this to happen, adults, especially teachers, must have the experience of transgression and its difficulties, to have lived it symbolically in order to be able to express it as a normal aspect of creative life.

Normal transgression differentiates the child and propitiates detachment from dependence from the parents. This brings solitude, which-when not understood and affectionately reassured but instead censured and punished-turns into defensive rejection, abandonment, fixation, and shadow formation.

When we see an anxious child misbehaving, amidst rebellion and suffering, the approach indicated is not primarily sermon and punishment. A more efficient approach consists in confronting the child, questioning its insubordination with respect and firmness (the Hegelian logic of thesis and antithesis), and trying dialectically to extract the meanings of the transgression and channel anxiety to express it creatively so as to avoid fixation, defense, and shadow formation.

This does not mean that I do not recognize defense and shadow formation as a frequent occurrence; their formation, mostly as the circumstantial shadow, is a very frequent occurrence in childhood and also in adult life. The challenge is to recognize anxious normal behavior and help the child elaborate it, for when misbehavior becomes fixed, forming defense and shadow, it is always pathological. Instead of repression, what the child most needs is respectful confrontation and creative reinforcement in the task of elaborating the circumstantial shadow and preventing the formation of the chronic shadow, which is the basis of neurosis.

In his famous romance *Les Misérables*, Victor Hugo relates the story of Jean Valjean, who was condemned to nineteen years in prison for having stolen a loaf of bread. Living with criminals and treated as one, Jean introjected, fixated, and identified transgression with crime. This fixation led to compulsive repetition and a shadow with defensive criminal behavior.

Wandering through a small town in his way to Paris after leaving jail, Jean was hungry and homeless. He asked for shelter in a nearby church, and the bishop told a servant to feed him and give him a room for the night. In this room, there were two silver candlesticks. Waking up at dawn, Jean did not hesitate to steal the candlesticks. Discovered by two police officers during a routine inspection, Jean lied, saying that they were a gift from the bishop. He was taken back to the church where, to their surprise, the bishop told the police officers that Jean had told the truth, and he was freed.

Jean Valjean worked hard for many years and became a rich merchant. Although he found himself many times in great need, he never sold the candlesticks; they became a talisman. Whenever he had difficult moments, he held them tightly and remembered the bishop's lesson. Had Jean been punished and again imprisoned, he probably would never have been able to elaborate his criminal shadow and would have continued his ethical fixation in repetition compulsion.

Those who question this proposition argue that children's anxiety reactions are so frequent and their egos still so fragile that need defenses. However, just because they are frequent does not necessarily make them normal. Defenses are not normal because they include fixation and prevent full symbolic elaboration. When Jung refers to *réculer four mieux sauter* ("retreat to go forward") as a creative procedure, we have to understand it as a willful drawing back to go further and not as an autonomous and unconscious retreat, which is clearly defensive because it is accompanied by fixation and repetition compulsive and is therefore incompatible with a conscious intention to retreat in order to go forward.

Instead of seeing defensive behavior in children, labeling it normal, and then simply scolding and punishing them, it is much more intelligent and productive to empathize the child's difficulties and try to help the child's ego to elaborate them. One of the most precious things for children to learn is how to elaborate creatively anxious and depressive reactions in order to avoid defensive behavior that leads to shadow formation. Another issue no less precious is to teach children to deal with the circumstantial shadow in order to rescue symbolic elaboration from fixation and reintegrate it into normal development.

The Circumstantial Shadow and the Chronic Shadow

The concept of the circumstantial shadow is of great utility in recognizing circumstantial dynamics in the fixation and formation of defenses, which can be undone and reverted to normal structuring functions by affectionate understanding and ego reinforcement without specialized psychotherapy.

It is also important to recognize when defenses consolidate to form the chronic shadow; this calls for specialized therapeutic intervention such as dynamic psychotherapy. Although the circumstantial shadow is less serious than the chronic shadow, its identification is individually and collectively much more important, because this is the shadow that parents, family members, educators, and colleagues can detect during formation. To identify the circumstantial shadow and revert elaboration to normal is an invaluable way for parents and teachers to contribute to the prophylaxis of mental pathology. By recognizing the presence of a defensive structuring function, we can intervene to prevent it from becoming chronic, which is always much more serious, as we can observe daily in patients, relatives, and public figures. This is one more reason for us not to consider defenses normal; when we do so we leave children and society without psychological protection and orientation and prone to defenses becoming chronic, which is much harder to treat.

When we diminish a symptom but don't elaborate the fixation that underlines it, we run the risk of merely changing its expression or leaving the personality unable to exercise that function or to exercise it in a deformed way. Therefore, whenever I medicate a patient, I always elaborate the fixation of the defensive structuring function that expresses the symptom with the patient before, during, and after medication. The fact that clinical psychiatry considers generally many depressive and anxious reactions pathological and medicates them without elaboration frequently limits psychological development. However, in order to be able to identify a defense and separate it from its normal counterpart, the therapist needs to learn about the defenses in his or her own personality in analysis and apply the resulting knowledge in the transference relationship with his or her patients.

Depression and Anxiety

I shall now present a short description of the normal structuring functions of depression and anxiety so that we may have an idea of the difference from their corresponding defensive function. The pathologization of these two functions has been so intense in medical literature that even the idea of designating normal depression and normal anxious states seems strange to many people, including doctors and psychiatrists. In order to understand depression and anxiety as normal structuring functions, we have to know how they function psychodynamically. Their pathology is their distortion, and therefore their treatment must begin and end with understanding and expressing creatively the meaning of the symbols that they are having difficulty elaborating.

The Normal Structuring Function of Depression

Normal depression is the structuring function of sadness, guilt, suffering, and loss, and as such it is a most important function in the development of individual and collective consciousness. Through sadness and guilt, depression propitiates the elaboration of losses, errors, frustrations, and all dysfunctions of symbolic elaboration, including the most precious ethically-the symbols fixated in the shadow.

In all such cases, depression is a sign of mental health, mainly of ethical health and of psychological vitality. Its elaboration is so spiritually and ethically valuable because it goes hand in hand with the structuring function of ethics.

Normal depression begins as detachment from daily routine, irritation, bad humor, and lack of interest. The structuring functions of optimism, construction, enthusiasm, and pleasure recede and are replaced by emphasis on the bad, the ugly, sickness, pessimism, pain, suffering, destruction, evil, and death. It is a call to psychological initiation, to plunge into, know, and elaborate the dark side of the soul.

All symbols of eminent fixation or fixation in the shadow can only be elaborated by normal depression. Without depression it is practically impossible to become conscious of the evil we practice against others and against ourselves and to review and repair it. When a doctor systematically prevents a patient from suffering depression and thus from elaborating his or her shadow, he limits the ethical elaboration of evil and the growth of consciousness and, with the best intentions, he practices defensive omnipotence and acts iatrogenically at the service of the shadow and of evil. Doctors cannot restrict themselves to understanding the suffering of the body and ignore the meaning of the suffering of the soul without falling victim to the shadow.

To diminish the pain of physical suffering, medicine, to its great merit, discovered analgesics. Even lay people know, however, that the immediate relief of pain, before we discover its origin, can cover up serious disease and incur in malpractice. How many cases of cancer, cardiovascular disease, meningitis, appendicitis, and many other ills have had their diagnosis delayed, sometimes fatally, through the automatic prescription of medication against pain? The same happens with the suffering of depression when the doctor automatically diminishes the importance of the symptom and paralyzes the structuring function of ethics. Even cases of pathological depression should not be medicated without understanding of the normal depression that practically always accompanies them. People normally tend to resist depression and to see it as something bad or wrong that should be eliminated, the faster the better. The doctor naturally wants to avoid suffering, but he must not do it at the price of alienation. His duty, whenever he alleviates pain through medication, is to lead the patient medically and spiritually to examine his or her life led by the suffering of depression (Byington 2007).

The doctor, however, is not the only one contributing to human alienation by evading depression and suffering. The very paradigm of the affluent society of consumerism which has dominated the planet through globalization is also a very important factor. This paradigm of consumerism continues an age of materialism and of subject-object dissociation begun at the end of the eighteenth century. This dissociation has been greatly influenced by the suffering of two world wars and numerous other conflicts in the twentieth century and by the crumbling of the socialist democratic ideology rendered patriarchal in ruthless dictatorships under communism.

No doubt the consumerism in affluent societies, which now includes India and China, has become increasingly more defensive and manic, covering up the structuring function of normal depression and camouflaging the threatening warnings of risk to our very survival. The defensive denial of the necessity of living out normal depression is responsible for expressing it in the shadow through the worldwide epidemic pathological depression that is now underway and growing at an alarming rate.

The Normal Structuring Function of Anxiety

Anxiety is a function constellated to elaborate situations of fear. Phobic reactions are one of the most common defensive forms of anxiety. The word phobic comes from the Greek *phobos*, the name of the god of fear. All anxious situations normally include emotions that worry us and whose nature we fear one way or another.

Anxiety and depression complement each other and help us to understand them. They can be found together in cases of anxious depression. Generally, these two functions are directed in different or even opposite ways. Depression is directed through detachment from normal affectionate and pleasurable bonds toward inward themes of suffering, failure, disaster, disease, and death. Anxiety is directed to avoid any emotions that endanger our feelings of security and welfare. Being requires these two functions to protect itself and at the same time to elaborate difficult situations and grow. Apparently opposites, depression and anxiety can function hand in hand. Depression must dive to encounter and deal with evil, in the depth of being. Anxiety must keep ever alert in watchtowers to detect facts and emotions that menace being and learn to deal with them. This explains cases of anxious depression in which we have a tension between events that need elaboration through sadness and simultaneously through fear. These are cases in which the ethical elaboration is very threatening for fear of unbalancing psychological stability, one more reason why these functions have to be understood and exercised before or during medication. Therefore we must medicate anxiety and depression to diminish suffering while simultaneously elaborating their meaning and purpose.

The most difficult thing to learn in the psychopathology of structuring functions is that when they turn pathological they are painful but they do not have to be eliminated; rather they have to be lived, elaborated, and liberated from fixation and defense in order to be experienced productively. For those who are possessed by hedonism and the pleasure principle within our consumerist society, this may sound like masochism, but this is not the case at all for those who cultivate integrity, truth, and self-fulfillment of being.

The commonest cause of anxiety in modern times in my experience is the stress resulting from workaholism, perfectionism, fear of failure, and unemployment within a workplace atmosphere of extreme patriarchal competition. Defensive medication without elaboration prevents such cases from dealing with these difficulties intelligently. When people recognize that anxiety is a normal function, they can adopt a healthier way of life, including work, eating habits, exercise, sleep, meditation, and confrontation of defenses in general. Developed over millennia and practiced by the wise persons of ancient cultures in the East, meditation is one of the best expressive techniques for practicing detachment and relaxation within totality, which helps avoid stress and control anxiety.

There are two great difficulties in dealing with depression and anxiety in modern society. They are interdependent. The first is to recognize them as structuring functions that can be normal or pathological. The second is the role of fixations that are unconscious and unknown. This second can only be worked out by the correct exercise of the first, for we can only know the real content of depressive and anxious states by exercising their functions adequately and arriving at the meanings of the constellated symbols. Theoretical rational interpretations that do not penetrate in the emotional core of these symbols are useless most of the time. Expressive techniques, as usual, are priceless for deepening elaboration. In many cases, chronic anxious and depressive defenses can become quite conscious but do not give way because years of conditioning have ossified them and the hard work of symbolic cognitive behavior is necessary to undo this conditioning.

The Structuring Functions of Depression and Anxiety in the Cultural Self and in the Planetary Self

In contemporary times, the normal structuring functions of depression and anxiety are critical for the elaboration of many symbols in the dimensions of individual, cultural, and planetary Selves. World health organizations have lately referred to an epidemic of depression due to the global increase of pathological depression. However, if we also take into consideration normal depression, the significant rise in the statistics of depression strongly point out the need for normal depression in order to elaborate our worldwide problems (*Worldwatch Institute* 2010).

As noted above, normal anxiety and depression activate structuring functions of evaluation and of ethics which stimulate us to review our conduct and elaborate our shadow and lead us to become aware of what evil we and others are doing in the path of individuation and of humanization. At the cultural level, this permits us to empathize with the human suffering we see and feel in the great network of world communication - the worldwide misery and threats to humanity in planetary life.

The globalization process includes the generalization of information, which is quickly accumulating world data that allow us to evaluate the present and estimate the future. Nongovernmental organizations (NGOs), such as the *Worldwatch Institute* (www.worldwatch.com) which gathers together specialists to study national and international characteristics of food, health, security, irrigation, transportation, climate, housing, education, reproduction, longevity, material reserves, pollution, crime, and armament, have registered planetary dysfunctions rising in extraordinary numbers. Based on these studies-which continuously become more extensive, accurate, and serious and which show us to be increasingly liable-we realize that the richer countries consume approximately five times more in goods and energy than poorer ones like India and China, whose populations are much bigger. As these nations adopt the first-world models of consumerism and free market economy, we would need two or more planets like the Earth to supply them. These data point to the impossibility of civilization continuing this patriarchal capitalist orientation and to the recommendation that we urgently adopt a sustainability paradigm coordinated by the alterity archetype before it is too late. Blindness here is the major great risk. The problem is not only to dive deep enough into anxiety and depression to confront the shadow of patriarchally dominant civilization. The question is also whether we shall have time to confront this shadow, work it through, and reintegrate its contents productively through a massive elaboration of the archetype of alterity.

We are heading toward a catastrophe suicidal and genocidal in nature. Among other fixations, it presents a defensive involvement of the ethical function that has prevented the perception of the prodigious growth of the patriarchal shadow within the planetary Self, which until recently identified production with welfare. With the accumulation of data this gigantic shadow is being made conscious, and this coincides with the epidemics of depression and anxiety worldwide. The main consequence of this fixation of the ethical function is the incapacity to see that our immense creativity has turned defensive, fixated on the ambitions of production and consumerism. The massive investment of planetary creativity in social welfare, in the spiritual value of compassion for the millions who live in hunger and misery, in sustainable society, in consciousness of luxury and waste, and in ecological preservation are measures whose implantations are obvious when we elaborate planetary survival coordinated by the alterity archetype. To carry on this enterprise, the normal structuring functions of depression and anxiety are indispensable.

The Concept of the Unified Shadow and the Evil

One of the major consequences of fixations in the individual and collective dimension is the divided Self, which suffers with chronic frustration, guilt, and destructive behavior due to the repetition compulsion of defenses.

Perceiving these fixations of structuring symbols, complexes, functions, and systems in the individual and collective dimensions and their expression through defenses allows us to associate the shadow in the individual, cultural, planetary, and cosmic dimensions of the Self. I have named the reunion of these various manifestations the unified shadow, which expresses the shadow of being and allows us to become fully conscious of the systemic expression of evil in all dimensions of civilization.

The subjective-objective dissociation repeats its defensive model in all dimensions and forms a very much divided expression of the shadow in theory and practice. One of its consequences is a defensive formation of shadow patchwork which reminds us of a tower of Babel of the concepts and manifestations of evil. This dissociation prevents the acquisition of a common vocabulary for identifying the fruits of development and the shadow it produces.

Among the serious problems brought about by defensive compartmentalization is the difficulty of associating the shadows of different institutions and seeing their systemic aspects. This limits the perception of evil by systemic imagination and prevents the elaboration of the ethical function in each institution. The great antidote to this defensive compartmentalization of creativity and shadow has been the development of worldwide communication, which has laid bare this tower of Babel ethics.

To avoid the defensive compartmentalization, which hides evil by disguised diversification, I formulated the concept of the unified shadow, which includes sickness in health, criminality in law, misery and exploration in economy, evil in philosophy, sin in religion, error in science, and aggression toward nature in ecology, fixation and defenses in psychopathology of the self, and so on in all existential dimensions.

In this manner, the concept of the unified shadow becomes the archetypal ethical parameter of symbolic humanism which allows us to identify, study, and elaborate the shadow as evil during the process of individuation and humanization. In this perspective the capacity of the ego to experience anxiety and depression to elaborate suffering is a courageous and extraordinary acquisition in the art of living. These are extremely productive functions for experiencing the shadow in all human dimensions and dealing with it as an archetype that expresses itself in countless ways due to fixation and alienation in psychological development through the pathology of compulsive repetition.

When I conceived the unified shadow, Jung's intuitive mention of absolute evil in *Aion* (1951), which he left unexplained, came to mind. If we admit that the shadow is the representation of fixations and defensive formation in the personality and in culture, it follows that it is the best psychological representation of evil in humanism. In such a case, the common archetypal expression of evil in all dimensions of the personality and of culture within the unified shadow well expresses the concept of absolute evil.

Jungian symbolic psychology situates the structuring function of ethics in every symbolic elaboration and therefore inseparably from the process of individual and collective development of consciousness and of shadow formation. In this manner, the concept of the unified shadow situates evil and its elaboration as part of being in the psychological dimension of all individuals and of all cultures. The confrontation of shadow is then inherent to the search for full revelation of ontological identity together with the effort to avoid alienation in the self-realization of being.

The Structuring Function of Frustration and of Aggression

Frustration is the structuring function activated when the existential performance does not satisfy the existential necessity. When this happens, we normally repeat the behavior until our goal is reached. This is part of the function of normal repetition, which occurs frequently in normal elaboration and which, when turned defensive, becomes repetition compulsion.

Frequently, however we are not immediately successful with this effort and must withstand frustration until we can achieve the necessary performance. In this respect the function of patience is very useful for containing aggression, which is one of the daughters of frustration.

How many times does the baby learning to walk falls only to start again and again until finally it can walk and run? Frustration will be experienced countless times amid pain, suffering, and aggression. During this apprenticeship, the child may fixate many defenses, including learning to walk with deficient posture. This occurs so frequently that if we are not alert, we do not notice and neglect to educate the child correctly. Only later in life, when suffering from back pain and seeking orthopedic help, will we identify and try to correct lifelong posture deficiencies. Mental functions work in the same way, which is a strong argument against considering defenses normal in childhood.

Frustration is a function inherent to life and learning in such a way that when it is properly handled it becomes one of the most important functions to favor normal development and avoid shadow formation.

Normal transgression and aggression occur frequently and are necessary in human behavior, and they can be confused with defensive acting out. This happens frequently with children because they do not have the necessary culture and life experience to place transgression and aggression within a socially understood and acceptable creative persona.

The first thing to do to with the child's frustration, transgression, and aggression is to be emotionally open to understanding symbolically the meaning and the intention of its expression.

The main thing to understand in educating the child to express frustration and aggression normally is that, together with transgression, they are normal and necessary functions and adults have a much greater capacity for understanding their meaning. This, of course, is the opposite of repressing and sublimating them.

If frustration, transgression, and aggression are normal structuring functions, the adult's openness toward understanding them and helping the child to build a persona to express them normally can be most productive in their elaboration. If they are primarily seen as defensive, however, the lack of any sort of intellectual or emotional interchange will tend to dissociate the relationship. Even when outright defensive, however, the recognition that they are structuring functions and can be normal and productive will help elaborate them as defenses and find out what their normal meanings are. Of course, this second instance is much more difficult for parents to handle, but if they can do it, it will be very productive.

When we recognize the shadow in the defensive behavior of children with symptoms of social dysfunction prone to compulsive inadequacy, it is high time to help their symbolic elaboration. However, if the educator-parent, or teacher-considers defenses to be normal and not compulsive or pathological and frustration, transgression, and aggression to be wrong, he or she is liable to resort to scolding and punishment and in this manner propitiate fixation and chronic shadow formation.

This does not mean to say that we should go around interpreting children's inadequate behavior and transforming family life into group therapy. This would be absurd. Although Melanie Klein and Michael Fordham were in favor of infant analysis to elaborate the shadow confronting fixations and defenses, I agree with Anna Freud who was not in favor of child analysis, because the child's ego is not yet strong enough to confront the shadow. In this sense, Jung gives great importance to treating the family shadow in cases of child neurosis. His ideas on this were well expressed in the preface he wrote for *The Inner World of Childhood* (1927) by Frances Wickes, the first Jungian analyst of children. What parents, relatives, and therapists can do when defensive behavior appears in the psychological development of children is to try to understand what is going on in the family Self and give the child's ego support to elaborate its difficulties. Of course in such cases family counseling and even family therapy may also be necessary.

In giving this support, the main purpose is to teach the child to build its persona to express frustration, transgression, and aggression adequately instead of simply confronting the child's inadequate behavior with repressive traditional ethics or with analytical elaboration. Instead of saying, "don't do this" or "don't do that," try to empathize with what is frustrating the child and suggest, "why don't you express your wish or your anger in this or that way."

When we adopt the concept of the shadow as defensive behavior, we greatly increase a theoretical interchange between analytical psychology, psychoanalysis, individual psychology, and behavioral psychology, and also clinical psychiatry and the neural sciences. This is so because in such cases, if we establish clearly the concepts of normality and of pathology (fixation, defense, and shadow formation) within the symbolic perspective, we avoid confusing normality with pathology. In so doing, we emphatically endorse symbolic elaboration of defenses in the psychotherapy of adults with the help of expressive techniques, including cognitive behavioral therapy and medication.

The reformulations of the concepts of fixation, defense, and shadow as the expression of pathology are very much reinforced by the recognition of ethics as a structuring function whose fixation is always part of the shadow, a condition which allows us to equate the shadow with evil. These concepts have aroused strong resistance not only from psychoanalysis, which conceived the death instinct, incest, and parricide as inborn tendencies toward the expression of evil, but also from traditional ethics, which considers the human being born evil.

To conceive the shadow as the psychological representation of evil is of fundamental importance if we are to rescue evil from being reduced to something autonomous (to an *entia per se*) and if we are to consider Neumann's new ethics as a structuring function in the psychological development of the Self and in day-to-day symbolic elaboration. This is equivalent to situating the shadow and evil as a deformation of the normal search for truth within the scientific method and also as a function of the nervous system (Byington 2003c).

It is important to remember that the conception of defense mechanisms as pathological, mainly repression, within the nervous system is one of the main ideas of Freud's *Project* (1895), sketched and abandoned for lack of sufficient development of the neurosciences at that time.

Considering repression as a defensive deformation of normal development collides with the Western cultural prejudice according to which humankind is born evil and can learn proper behavior only through repressive education. This conceptual collision-which is religious, sociocultural, "scientific," and psychological-needs first to be fully recognized and repudiated in order to be reformulated.

In my perspective human beings are not in themselves either good or bad, but individual and collective development can be normal or pathological depending on the process of elaborating suffering to avoid fixation. Almost four hundred years ago, Shakespeare said: "Nothing is either good or bad, but thinking makes it so" (*Hamlet*, act II, scene 7).

It is important for us to consider the amount of evil perpetrated by human beings throughout history, and which continues to be perpetrated incessantly (Lorenz 1963). At the beginning of this book, I stressed the extraordinary capacity of our species to do evil as none other. In the practice of evil, we are an aberration in evolution for no other species has ever declared war against itself to the point of carrying out genocide. At the same time, I noted that our brain, which has evolved the greatest capacity for symbolization, has come to dominate many natural forces and most plant and animal life except for many microorganisms.

In this manner, we cannot make a genetic determination that we are good or bad because until today, with the same genome, we have been able to do and discover marvelous things for the welfare of humanity and, at the same time, practice incalculable cruelty and destruction against others and ourselves. Let us take up a hypothesis that requires great conceptual opening and absence of intellectual prejudice. Is it not incredible that we are equally inclined to good and evil? Is it possible that this equal inclination occurs by chance or because good and evil are interdependent? If this interdependence exists, what is the way that good relates to evil, and in ultimate analysis, how can one become the other? Is it not obvious that the explanation is the fixation of normal structuring functions which transform good into evil?

Ethics, Shadow, and Psychopathy

Our capacity to do evil intentionally is recognized in our penal codes and considered an aggravating factor when punishing criminals. In order to better understand the association of crime and intention, we must study the relationship of evil to fixation, defense, and shadow. This can be done by considering the functions of intention, feeling, motivation, and justification during symbolic elaboration involving the structuring function of ethics.

Forensic psychiatry was initially very much influenced by physical appearance, for example, in the work of Cesare Lombroso (1835-1909). In time, criminal motivation and action came to be considered within all other psychiatric disturbances. The consequence of these studies was that character and social dysfunction were separated from the categories of psychosis and psychoneurosis under the heading of psychopathic disturbances. I shall not discuss here the varieties of manifestations of psychopathy. The reader can find this in classical psychiatric texts. I recommend specially Silvano Arieti's *American Handbook of Psychiatry* (1959).

The important item I want to call attention to is that while psychopathy was classified in a group essentially different from psychosis and psychoneurosis, sexual perversions were included within psychopathy. Freud (1905) describes sexual perversions as the inverse of neurosis, because sexuality is overtly practiced in them while in neurosis it is repressed. Unfortunately, he thoroughly confused normality and pathology when he went on to consider every child to be normally a perverse polymorph before undergoing repression and sublimation of the Oedipus complex to form the superego and acquire morality at five years of age (Freud 1905).

Freud's pathologization of normality with the Oedipus complex confused the psychodynamics of psychopathy, of perversion, and of normal development. It is very important to realize that all this reductive pathologizing of normal development by psychoanalysis came after Freud's discovery of the Oedipus complex in himself followed by his defensive projection of it onto normal children, as if he thought: "I have it, but my Oedipus complex is not so serious because all children are also born with it."

The thesis I developed in chapter 5, which is fundamentally meant to separate normality from pathology in psychological development, is that the primary quaternio is formed by the maternal and paternal complexes, and their relationship is added to the reactions of the child to form primary identity without necessary repression, sublimation, or any other defense. In this perspective, the Oedipus complex is but one illustration of fixations and defenses in shadow formation within the primary quaternio and is therefore pathological.

Adolf Guggenbühl-Craig and James Hillman see psychopathy as a mental condition which they describe as emptiness of the soul (Guggenbühl 1980, Guggenbühl and Hillman 1995). In my view, on the contrary, psychopathy is a mental disturbance very puzzling to explain psychodynamically basically due to the disturbance of morality and of the feeling function in social relationship. Many authors in clinical psychiatry have faced this difficulty by considering it an organic inborn condition (Schneider 1950).

I consider functional psychopathy to be a defense based on fixation and dysfunction of normal structuring functions and separate it from the category of neurosis, not because of sexuality but because its fixation involves the volitive function (the will) together with the ethical function, the feeling function, and other functions depending on each case. In this manner, I have described the concept of functional psychopathic defense, which includes sexual perversions, character and social dysfunctions, and also many forms of sadomasochism, mostly centered on the sexual impulse or on the power drive. When it involves the major part of the personality, instead of psychopathic defense I use the concept of psychopathic personality.

Considering defenses and the shadow conscious and unconscious helps us in the formulation of these concepts because the great challenge of studying the psychodynamics of psychopathy is that it involves character and the volitive function and therefore is also partly conscious and voluntary. This voluntary practice of the defense is an important factor that has prevented psychopathic behavior from being considered a defense because neurotic defenses, even when partly conscious, are never voluntary.

Once we have decided to consider psychopathic behavior an acquired defensive mental disturbance due to fixation, we can see that its central characteristic is to have the volitive function fixated together with the feeling and ethical functions and other structuring functions, whatever the case may be. In this manner, the will becomes fixated and subject to repetition compulsion, without necessarily being completely conscious even when it is dominantly voluntary.

The fact that psychopathic behavior was not considered a defense in clinical psychiatry prevented it from being seen as a defensive pathological variation of normal behavior varying from mild (adolescents lying) to very serious conditions (criminal perversions).

Psychopathy and Neurosis
Matriarchal and Patriarchal Dominance
in Psychopathology

Although Jungian symbolic psychology is open to any psychological theory or occurrence based on the concept of structuring symbol, complex, function, system, and archetype, there is one aspect in particular that establishes many differences with other schools of psychology and also of humanism. This is the recognition of the matriarchal archetype as being bi-gendered and of its coordination of symbolic elaboration on equal terms with the patriarchal archetype; as discussed in chapter 8, I have named the conscious matriarchal pattern as the insular matriarchal ego-other position in consciousness.

In order to attain this basic symmetry between the matriarchal and patriarchal archetypes, Jungian symbolic psychology has described the alterity archetype and its dialectical position in consciousness which is perhaps its main contribution to psychology. The alterity archetype is the archetype of the syzygy, described by Jung in *Aion* (1951), which includes the anima and animus archetypes and is responsible for the dialectical relationship of polarities (see chapters 8 and 11).

The dialectic pattern of consciousness is the most developed method of symbolic elaboration and is the most productive form of intelligence of the Self. Its incarnation in individual and collective consciousness is a fundamental part of the great historical search for individual and collective development. As will be seen in chapters 8 and 11, the development of the intelligence of alterity differs strongly from the asymmetrical implantation of the matriarchal and patriarchal archetypes during individual and collective development.

The catastrophic error in the study of human evolution was that the patriarchal archetype was equated with the ideal aim of civilization. The lack of knowledge of the alterity archetype and its search as the final goal of progress and of civilization did not allow us to see patriarchal dominance as a circumstantial stage on the way to alterity. Therefore, patriarchal dominance and matriarchal submission were frequently seen as psychological structural realities. This gross error of the science of history brought about a great distortion in the comprehension of many dimensions of the cultural Self and of humanism.

Such a gigantic distortion in scientific perspective was primarily a result of the tremendous impact of Darwin's theory of evolution on knowledge, which was applied to the individual and collective transformation of conscience in the nineteenth century.

Freud's greatest discovery was perhaps the development of the psyche starting with the formation of the ego in primary relationships. Jung's greatest discovery was perhaps the discovery of the continuation of psychological development until the end of life based on the individuation process coordinated by archetypes. The limitation of both of these theories was the lack of recognition of the importance and permanence of the matriarchal archetype throughout life, its brutal collision with the patriarchal archetype during individual and collective history, and the knowledge of the alterity archetype for understanding archetypally the goal of human development. In the next chapter, we will look at the relation and collision of these two great archetypes in a general way. For now, we will look at them in ethics, in psychopathology, and in the shadow as we have conceived it so far.

The notion that "savages," from the beginnings of human settlement, have been progressively civilized through increasing patriarchal and technological development has been massively believed and has been defensively projected onto the process of development by all dimensions of culture throughout time. Therefore, it was no surprise that this cultural perspective was radically transposed to psychology and to the study of child development. Children received the same treatment as "primitives." Patriarchally oriented adults were considered mature and civilized. Modern anthropology since Franz Boas has been rescuing the matriarchal qualities of hunting-gathering groups and tribal cultures from the pejorative labels of savagery and primitivism. Child psychology and psychopathology followed the same way. Common to this modern tendency is the recognition of the importance of the function of the matriarchal archetype in individual and collective consciousness before, during, and after patriarchal dominance.

Freud's projection of the Oedipus complex on normal children was a massive defensive projection of the normal and pathological organizing polarized patriarchal position onto the primary relationship. Mother and father were strictly identified as polar opposites, each one illustrating the roles men and women had exercised during the millennia of patriarchal dominance. A pattern of incestuous and parricidal tendencies within the Oedipus complex was erroneously considered a normal inborn occurrence and not a defensive and deformed reaction to patriarchal repression.

The sensuality of the matriarchal archetype present in the psyches of men and women-included in the instinctive nature of the id and in sexuality, aggression, and desire-was treated as an unbridled animal that had to be framed by the organized law of patriarchal restraint. This coercion was not to be carried out lightly but, on the contrary, with the physical metaphoric model of repression and sublimation.

Although describing the matriarchal world in the dimensions of myth and of psychological development, Neumann (1949a, 1955) reduced it to the feminine, to the great mother archetype (1950, 1952a, 1952b), and subordinated it to the solar masculine father archetype during individual and collective development.

In this manner, the insular position of the matriarchal archetype as the expression of bi-gendered sensuality throughout the whole of life was not adequately related on equal terms to the polarized position of the patriarchal archetype as the expression of the bi-gendered pattern of organization.

As far as the archetypal application of the concept of evolution to the humanities is concerned, the great difficulty is that there exists a clear dominance of the sensuality pattern of the matriarchal archetype in the beginning of symbolic elaboration in individual and collective development, which tends to give way to the dominance of the patriarchal archetype. The great error and bias of humanism was to have identified patriarchal dominance with progress and with the finality of history. Archetypal evolution exists, but it can only occur normally and creatively if patriarchal dominance is conceived as being followed by the dominance of the archetype of alterity which relates the matriarchal and patriarchal archetypes dialectically on equal terms.

When we realize that the matriarchal archetype, although frequently dominated by the patriarchal archetype in later childhood (from ages 2 to 12), depending on the nature of each family and culture, continues to participate in symbolic elaboration throughout life, it becomes clear that it participates in many important features of psychological development and its dysfunctions. In this sense, the psychopathic and perverse manifestations accurately related by Freud to pathological expressions of the perverse polymorph are not due exclusively to fixations prior to repression (patriarchal dominance) but also to matriarchal pathology itself, which may become manifested at any time during the process, even during patriarchal dominance with organization and repression.

The problem is that the matriarchal archetype, being the coordinator of all sensuality and expressing itself through lust, aggression, and desire, may become dominant in pathology even or sometimes because it is hurt by the violence implicit in the repression of patriarchal dominance. Therefore, the perverse polymorph can exist also after patriarchal dominance and frequently as a reaction to patriarchal repression. Freud's view then is comparable to educators who always view transgression as a lack of discipline, when many times it is a reaction to arbitrary and exaggerated organization.

What must be explained now is the problem of the voluntary acting out of a defense, characteristic of the psychopathic disturbance. We can amplify greatly the range of the psychopathic defense to include all pathology acted out voluntarily and guided by desire and detecting when it is present in addictions and eating disorders. Together with defensive volition that obeys the shadow compulsively, we have also a fixation of the feeling function, which can be defensively repressed and/or deformed on the subjective and objective levels. In all such cases the psychopathic defense is never as morally or emotionally empty as it may seem for the lack of guilt or feeling reactions it presents. On the contrary, it frequently is full of lack of consideration for others due to intense hate and destructivity, frequently fixated on rejection and abandonment.

The Voice of the Shadow

Considering the concept of the shadow as an equivalent of defense and evil, as we are doing in this perspective, gives us a strategic way to really know the dark side of humankind. When we listen to the shadow of the psychopathic defense in active imagination, we can come to know that it is neither empty nor morally and affectionately indifferent but, on the contrary, always full of hatred and destructivity and absolutely open to the satisfaction of all selfish desire, of which it admits no restraint whatsoever (see, for example, the films *The Exorcist* [1973] and *In Cold Blood* [1967]).

The point is that consciousness under patriarchal dominance assumes such a polarized position vis-à-vis the shadow that it classifies its manifestations with many attributes but does not really experience it. This attitude of "scientifically" saying things about the shadow without really experiencing it from within, mainly in the case of the psychopathic shadow, brings us to such conclusions as that it is "an empty soul" without morality. These are outward intellectual impressions without inner experience.

In this sense, I invite the reader to animate any shadow content and use active imagination with it, mainly with the psychopathic shadow so as "to let evil speak psychologically." When we do so and if we really penetrate deeply into the core of the shadow, we see that hell is never an empty place, without feelings or ethics. On the contrary, it is full of all life events and emotions expressed through fixated structuring symbolic complexes, functions, and systems, guided by defenses to express terrifying evil distortions of the Self.

Chapter 8

THE HISTORICAL PROBLEM OF THE
MATRIARCHAL-PATRIARCHAL POLARITY

Based on the conception of the archetypal positions of consciousness, the choice of the matriarchal-patriarchal polarity as a basic reference for the symbolic elaboration of the process of individuation and humanization springs from its being sufficiently encompassing to participate in all instances of symbolic elaboration. This polarity has been the main mediator between consciousness and the central archetype in the symbolic axis even during patriarchal dominance. It can also be detected in neurophysiology in the polarities existing between the limbic system and neuro-vegetative processes on one side and cognitive processes on the other.

For the matriarchal-patriarchal archetypal polarity to be conceived with such amplitude, it must be perceived equally in the masculine and feminine psyche such that the matriarchal archetype can be liberated from its reduction to the mother and the feminine and the patriarchal archetype to the father and the masculine. In addition to correcting this reduction to gender, it is also indispensable to correct the distortions that have stigmatized the matriarchal and patriarchal archetypes due to their reduction to their roles in history and their final evolutionary relationship. All this is worthwhile in order to conceive an archetypal structure to guide the formation of individual and collective consciousness, first in structuring of ego and other identity, and afterward in its dialectical and systemic relationship. Indeed, we shall not find a theoretical conception for consciousness becoming aware of being-in-the-world if we do not begin by conceiving the structuring of consciousness in terms of the sensuality that feeds it (matriarchal) and in terms of an abstract capacity that organizes it (patriarchal).

The concepts of structuring symbol, complex, function, system, archetype, and symbolic elaboration are the main pillars in our understanding of the psychological formation of consciousness coordinated by archetypes. The perceived bipolarity of these concepts is essential for articulating the ego-other polarity as the center of consciousness and of the shadow with the archetypes. At the same time the man-woman polarity is one of the main psychological polarities representing two of the most important symbols and structuring functions.

Man and woman each carry one half the genes of their future children. Their relationship is the basis for the genetic and emotional formation of the child. The search for an affectionate relationship between them is the central emotional theme of adult life and the necessity of their companionship lasts until the last good-bye of the existential process. It is natural then that their characteristics and social functions are very important in forming their identities and the identities of their children in the process of existential self-fulfillment.

Over the millennia, the identities of man and woman have been superimposed on their family and social roles. Once humankind began to form settlements in the societies that gave rise to civilization, women were characterized by their domestic attributes and men by the commanding role in the family and by other social functions away from home. It is evident that under these conditions there prevailed between them an immense asymmetry of social power, which historically oriented their identities in the individual, family, and cultural Selves. In the same way, although in a manner not so rigid, the social classes functioned, based on socioeconomic stratification. Social categories of minorities such as homosexuals in many cultures, the untouchables in India, the gypsies in modern Europe, immigrants everywhere, Native Americans and African Americans in the New World, and also women generally have had difficulty separating their authentic identities from countless prejudices and attributes arising in these historical circumstances.

The Swiss lawyer and mythologist Johann Jakob Bachofen (1815-1887) became known for his thesis that feminine dominance had preceded the masculine dominance that prevailed in modern Europe in the nineteenth century. He developed this theme in his 1861 book *Mother Right*, based on myths and customs of ancient cultures (Bachofen 1967). Unfortunately, he applied his idea to anthropology and sociology and postulated that in ancient cultures there had existed societies ruled by women, which he referred to as matriarchy. This thesis had great impact on European culture at the end of the nineteenth century, an impact that was natural in a society with traditional patriarchal dominance but also, perhaps, for the fact that women were beginning to participate in civil right's movements.

With the idea of mother right, Bachofen discovered the theme that I refer to here as the matriarchal-patriarchal polarity. However, three serious reductions asphyxiated his grandiose intuition: the identification of the matriarchal with women, the conception of a social matriarchy ruled by women, and the evolutionary connotation he attributed to the matriarchal-patriarchal relationship. Because such a matriarchy was not found either in anthropology or in sociology, the idea brought him fame initially and, soon afterward, total discredit. Bachofen is now seen in anthropology as a nineteenth-century romantic who imagined societies dominated by women that never really existed.

The studies by Bachofen of myths that he designated matriarchy because they included important goddesses coincided with studies by Lewis H. Morgan about the Iroquois in the United States, in which he described typical patterns of family relationship such as the cross-cousin marriage (Morgan 1871). Attention was called to different roles of men and women in these societies, among which, for instance, the figure of authority in matrilineal marriage is carried out by the mother's brother and not by her husband (Radcliffe-Brown 1950). These studies initially reinforced Bachofen's ideas and influenced the work of Friedrich Engels, who wrote *The Origin of the Family, Private Property and the State* (1884), in which he described the beginning of patriarchal dominance. Although Engels's ideas seem to me now to be quite correct, he wrote as though the establishment of patriarchal dominance confirmed the preexistence of matriarchy, an association that contaminated his work. As I try to demonstrate in this book, patriarchal archetypal dominance succeeded matriarchal dominance in many cultures but is not related to the existence of matriarchy or to the discovery of the end goal of history.

The erudite works by the great names in classical anthropology at the end of the nineteenth century and the beginning of the twentieth century were entangled in the spiderweb of the matriarchal archetype and the puzzling epistemological dilemma it proposes. On the one hand matriarchal mentality and magic seemed ignorant and retarded, and so it was treated; on the other hand, as we are seeing more and more, mainly in ecology, it is full of natural wisdom.

Lucien Lévy-Brühl (1857-1939), Edward B. Tylor (1832-1917), and James G. Frazer (1854-1941) practiced an academic anthropology generally based on the reports of travelers about cultures that they themselves mostly never saw. Although very learned, their work, ideas, and conclusions about the tribal cultures they studied presented a great bias full of ethnocentrism and prejudices, which started by designating the members of these cultures "primitives." The center of this ethnocentric bias can be archetypally understood by these academics being caught in the elitist bias of patriarchal dominance labeling matriarchal characteristics pejoratively without really understanding their dynamics.

Tylor (1871) concluded that animism was a primitive form of religion in which magic manipulated the divine force to the subject's favor. Instead of "my will be done," which is the religion of magic and animism, he postulated "thy will be done" (patriarchal monotheism) as a more advanced form of religion. The magic practiced by tribal cultures was labeled by Frazer (1890) a "bastard science," because of a false interpretation of reality. Lévy-Brühl (1938) saw in tribal societies a sort of inferior thinking, a prelogic thinking of primitive mentality based on a mystical experience of reality which was practiced together with logical thinking. Jung adapted Lévy-Brühl's term experience mystique, calling it participation mystique as a synonym for unconscious identity.

These studies lacked the direct field observation that characterizes modern anthropology. First, they did not experience directly the cultural habits, rituals, and ideas they studied; second, they did not situate the symbols to which they referred systematically within the ethnic groups they studied. This traditional anthropological perspective was subsequently fiercely repudiated because its ethnocentrism was associated with the xenophobic theories of the twentieth century, some of them explicitly racist. All this coincided with the great cultural impact of Darwin's theory of evolution on European thought. It led many researchers to reduce anthropology to a radical ethnocentrism that placed Europeans at the top of a scale of evolution and non-Europeans, mainly tribal cultures, in varying degrees of inferiority in a clear analogy to the relationship of Homo sapiens to other hominids. Classical anthropologists were trapped in this evolutionary bias although they were at least partly conscious of it. Bachofen, for instance, writes in a letter to Morgan:

> German scholars propose to make antiquity intelligible, measuring it by popular conceptions of the present time. They only see themselves in the creations of the past. To penetrate in the structure of a mentality different from ours is a hard task. (Turner 1969, p. 15)

Three centuries of the exact sciences, in the 1500s, 1600s, and 1700s, were necessary to win over the power of the Inquisition in the university. In the nineteenth century the way finally opened for science to begin the study of the subjective dimension.

Although endorsing the criticism of the ethnocentrism of classical anthropology, I want to stress that the content of this ethnocentrism is very precious because it recognized the existence of the magic-mythic dimension of thought, which I consider to be a pattern of the ego-other position in consciousness which I call the insular matriarchal position. This was a great discovery, despite the ethnocentric bias, which was based on a pejorative comparison of the mentality of tribal cultures with the Cartesian logic of science (polarized patriarchal position).

Simultaneously to the study of tribal cultures in the nineteenth century, the subjective dimension was studied by science in the domain of mental health. Mental disease was recognized by Philippe Pinel as a separate condition from the criminal mind, and psychotics were removed from prisons and hospitalized. This observation of subjectivity led to the discovery of conscious and unconscious imagination.

It is important to note, as an illustration of the psychodynamics and psychopathology, that anthropology's discovery of magic in the cultural Self and psychology's discovery of imagination and hypnosis in the individual Self both did not duly recognize the value of their subject matter. Magic was considered a bastard science and hypnosis was reduced to hysteria, initially by Charcot and later by the Paris Academy of Sciences (Zilboorg and Henry

1941). The imagination was also disqualified. When we have a systemic bird's eye view of science's defensive reaction to subjectivity, we register an immense acting out of the subject-object dissociation of the Western cultural Self. Likewise, we must not forget that before the subject-object dissociation that generated scientific prejudice against the subjective dimension, our religious tradition was also greatly deformed in regard to the subjective-objective dimension with the Christ-devil dichotomy (see chapter 13). In this way, both science and religion limited the full perception of the matriarchal archetype and its individual and collective importance in psychological development.

The nineteenth century discovered two fundamental issues in subjectivity. The collective dimension of tribal cultures described an overall divinization of nature called pantheism and animism, an intense magic relation to things in daily activities based mostly on desire and a mentality that draws the ego and the other into such intimacy that it frequently fuses and confuses them, which was called mystical experience or magic-mythic relationship. In the individual dimension of unconscious processes, the repressed unconscious was discovered, expressed through symptoms, the transference relationship, the moral function, infantile sexuality, and the formation of ego identity through primary relationships. Thus, the study of subjectivity led to the discovery of a different way of thinking found in tribal societies' unconscious processes that form individual identity.

We may conclude then that the scientific study of subjectivity in the nineteenth century discovered that which today I formulate as the insular matriarchal position of the matriarchal archetype. Bachofen considered it to be a feminine-commanded society of the past (matriarchy). Classical anthropology restricted it to magical thinking and the divinization of nature, and psychoanalysis reduced it to sexuality, desire, primary process, the Oedipus complex, and the perverse polymorph. Jung reduced it to participation mystique and unconscious identity. Based on Jung's theory of archetypes, Erich Neumann (1949a) was the first to relate the matriarchal archetype to lunar consciousness, although still reduced to the feminine dimension.

We may therefore consider that the reductive and pathologizing deformations of the individual and collective subjective dimension present from the beginning of dynamic psychology and of traditional anthropology were very much influenced by a subjective-objective dissociation coordinated by the patriarchal archetype, which disqualified with ethnocentric prejudice the phenomenology of the discovery of the matriarchal archetype in the nineteenth century.

To avoid ethnocentrism, Franz Boas (1924) proposed to center modern anthropology on fieldwork and to study each culture as a meaningful whole avoiding at all costs evolutionary comparison with other cultures as was persistently practiced by classical anthropology. With such fieldwork, anthropologists found many different forms of family relationships, matrilineal and patrilineal, but nothing that could be called a matriarchy, that is, a society ruled by women.

Anthropology continued the study of different roles of men and women in tribal societies, for instance, the importance of the mother's brother in matrilineal and matrilocal contexts related in the studies of Lowie (1919), Radcliffe-Brown (1924, 1950), and later, Malinowski (1979). The question of the relationship of man and woman, far from receding in importance, became the complex study of kinship and language in human societies within the symbolic dimension (Lévi-Strauss 1958).

Erich Neumann (1905-1960) was an important follower of Jung and founder of the Israel Association of Analytical Psychologists, who unfortunately died at the climax of his brilliant career. Studying myths from different cultures, Neumann took up the studies of Bachofen with the thesis that myths of the great mother archetype would have anteceded patriarchal solar myths. He did not situate his thesis in the social reality of matriarchy as Bachofen had done, but rather positioned it within psychology in a supposed mythological history through the concept of archetype. Unfortunately, like Bachofen, Neumann equated the matriarchal world with the feminine and gave it a reductive historical evolutionary connotation related to the patriarchal world. In his book *The Origins and History of Consciousness* (1949a), he related great archetypal themes, which he considered representative of polytheism and of the great mother, to illustrate the historical period to which he attributed the birth of consciousness. Next, he collected solar myths, grouped under the theme of monotheism and of the father archetype, to illustrate the posterior period of the history of consciousness. It seems to me that his identification of the matriarchal with the feminine, of the patriarchal with the masculine, and their rigid evolutionary relationship are the main limitations to his theory.

The Post-Patriarchal Evolutionism of Alterity
The Concepts of Matriarchal and Patriarchal Dominance

When we consider the transformation of species within Darwin's theory of evolution today, we admit that mutations give rise to natural selection and the survival of the fittest, maintaining the characteristics which most favor ecological adaptation. The genetic transmission of the qualities acquired by mutations substitute for other characteristics, which cease to exist. Reptiles, for instance, acquire lungs and stop breathing through gills, and the gills disappear from the species. This is a structural modification.

The thinking model of evolution postulates the substitution of ancient structures with new ones that impose themselves through their adaptive capacity. The model thus adopted is that in evolution more archaic structures are transcended and can be abandoned and substituted by newer ones.

The evolutionary model served as a reference for Freud's development of the libido with the oral, anal, and phallic (genital) phases. However, within the archetypal dimension, this perspective is inadmissible because the matriarchal dominance at the beginning of life, which is generally followed by patriarchal dominance, does not diminish its importance, much less atrophy or disappear. On the contrary, even when hurt, repressed, and tortured in extreme cases of patriarchal domination, the matriarchal archetype will manifest itself in the individual and cultural Selves, albeit frequently through symptoms.

The evolutionary paradigm in psychology must be adopted with great care so as not to repress and sublimate the matriarchal archetype or treat it either as something only of the past or stigmatized as undeveloped. Be it in individual or collective development, the evolutionary model in psychology, although registering matriarchal dominance followed by patriarchal dominance, must be seen as a development toward the archetype of alterity, which will relate the matriarchal and patriarchal archetypes dialectically and activate the anima-animus syzygy (Jung 1950). Any theoretical formulation that disqualifies the matriarchal archetype in any existential dimension-be it ideas, emotions, the body, or nature-must be viewed with great suspicion of scientific bias, prejudice, and defensive intolerance.

As we know from the laws of genetics, acquired characteristics are generally not hereditary. However, the archetypal modifications of collective consciousness are transmitted through culture from generation to generation, incorporating and improving acquired knowledge. In such a way, genes and archetypes generally do not inherit acquired characteristics but culture and history do with great abundance. After the settlement of societies that accompanied the agro-pastoral revolution more than ten thousand years ago, the patriarchal archetype became dominant, and societies were organized through private property, social classes, institutions, and laws that slowly developed into cities and nations. Under the same archetype our species conquered the planet and went on the create an international binary system of communication which reunited humankind.

We can go back to Bachofen's and Neumann's thesis of the primordial dominance of the matriarchal archetype prior to the subsequent dominance of the patriarchal archetype, in many cultures, with three great differences from their approach: first, the matriarchal and patriarchal archetypes are bi-gendered in nature; second, from an evolutionary perspective, the matriarchal is not of lesser importance nor reduced to the past; third, the patriarchal archetype is not the last stage of the evolutionary process.

At the same time that the matriarchal is not reduced to women or the patriarchal to men and both are described as bi-gendered, I have conceived the matriarchal archetype as the archetype of sensuality and the patriarchal archetype as the archetype of organization, representing two different types of archetypal intelligence in the functioning of consciousness. The matriarchal expresses itself through the insular position of the ego-other polarity and the patriarchal through the polarized position. In this manner, we can see that Descartes's proposal to separate the *res cogitans* (thinking) from the *res extensa* (nature), which was necessary to initiate the scientific method in the seventeenth century, had already begun many thousands of years before when certain cultures started to substitute the magic-mythic relationship to nature with a relationship to nature that affirms itself in a causal, reflexive, and objective manner.

It seems to be a possible hypothesis that patriarchal dominance supplanted matriarchal dominance in history when, through the agricultural pastoral revolution, hunter-gatherer groups began to settle and organize the villages that became cities and nations. However, although it brought immense technological progress to humanity, we cannot equate this increasing patriarchal dominance with absolute progress and the final goal of history.

On the contrary! We are seeing more and more that this patriarchal dominance also brought a very unbalanced relation with nature, something which does not occur under matriarchal dominance and animism. The historical transition from matriarchal to patriarchal dominance has been progressing for approximately more than ten thousand years, and in many cultures it substituted magical causality by reflexive causality for dealing with reality. Cultures that developed patriarchal reflexive causality formed cities, nations, and empires while cultures that retained the matriarchal pattern of the magic-mythic mentality continued to live in tribes.

We know that water and rain are fundamental for agriculture. Mircea Eliade, in *From Primitives to Zen* (1967), describes the magic mentality of the Karamundi, who live in the banks of River Darling in Australia. They had a rain-making ritual that went as follows: one should open the vein of a man's arm and collect a few drops of blood on a gourd shell; one should then add some gypsum and mix it to form a paste; next, one should add to this mixture a few beard hairs and place it between two pieces of tree bark and stick it in the bottom of a river or lagoon. Until rain comes, the men must refrain from sexuality. When drought is very intense, the whole tribe practices this ritual.

As Lévi-Strauss, Malinowski, and many other anthropologists have reported, magic does not exclude scientific procedures, which can be simultaneously undertaken with great efficiency. There is no doubt, however, that a culture that practices magic on a daily basis in order to face actual difficulties on one hand calms emotions but on the other hand remains limited in ability to face difficulties objectively. A culture that faces such difficulties rationally through reflective causality will more likely work them out productively on the objective level, but quite possibly at some cost to their peace of mind. This is what happened to those cultures that developed irrigation to fight droughts and ended up building empires based on irrigation (Ribeiro 1968).

Bringing the perspective of Jungian symbolic psychology to bear on the study of the matriarchal-patriarchal polarity, I am quite conscious of entering into controversial territory. However, a return to this study from this perspective seems very important for many reasons, the main one being to relate this basic archetypal polarity with the five archetypal positions of consciousness. Another reason is to show that within the humanities there are two great basic archetypes in the psychological elaboration of all symbols and complexes: the matriarchal and patriarchal archetypes, which need to be differentiated in the countless situations in which they present themselves.

Precisely because the matriarchal and patriarchal archetypes are so extraordinarily involved in the structuring of consciousness, their normal and defensive manifestations accumulated throughout history emerge with great intensity whenever they are studied. In approaching them, Bachofen and Neumann possibly did not realize the extent of the cultural connotation they were entering and therefore inadvertently stepped on mines, formed by a shadow highly charged with defensive complexes full of wounds of injustice and tragedy. These include racism along with colonialism and slavery covered up by a defensive ethnocentric evolutionary theory, the oppression of women and minorities, ecological devastation, dictatorships, and wars. Both Bachofen and Neumann honored the feminine, but in doing so through ideas about cultural and mythological evolution which were not subsequently confirmed they discredited their studies and the importance of the very matriarchal archetype to which they dedicated a great part of their work in order to promote it.

Based on the false premise that the technological parameter is the reference point of progress (Ribeiro 1968), many intellectuals were led to endorse the superiority of industrialized societies over tribal societies and, in final analysis, of the patriarchal archetype over the matriarchal archetype.

A well-known racist and ethnocentric intellectual of the nineteenth century was Joseph Arthur de Gobineau (1816-1882), who wrote many books, of which the best known is *An Essay on the Inequality of the Human Races* (1853; Bachofen's *Mother Right* was published just a few years later, in 1861). Gobineau became a diplomat and came to represent France in Brazil, being a frequent guest of Emperor Pedro II, who disagreed with his ideas. Gobineau detested the rest of the diplomatic corps and Rio de Janeiro for "cockroaches, rats, bats, idleness, and . . . miscegenation." The sentence "I do not believe that we descend from apes but we certainly are walking in their direction" was attributed to him; he affirmed the supremacy of the white race and within it considered the Nordic blonds of Aryan descent superior to all others. He interprets the French Revolution as a victory of the inferior Celtic-Roman race over the French-Germans. An anti-Semitic fanatic, his seminars in Paris were attended by many renowned intellectuals, including Nietzsche and Wagner (Gobineau 1853).

The main disciple of Gobineau in Germany was the Englishman Houston Chamberlain, who wrote *The Foundations of the Nineteenth Century* in 1899. Expressively anti-Semitic and against miscegenation, he formulated many fantastic interpretations of history with these central themes. The fall of the Roman Empire, for instance, he attributed to the decadence begun by the miscegenation of the Romans with the defeated enemies. This anti-Semitic and racist ideology was the cradle of the theory of eugenics of the *Third Reich* (Hitler 1925-26).

We must also take note that in the nineteenth century, Europe was in the third century of its repressive and predatory colonialism, justified sadistically and psychopathically by false Christian moralism according to which the inferior nations of pagans needed salvation (Gambini 1988). All this was unwillingly corroborated by the ethnocentric perspective of classical anthropology. It was in this devil's cauldron of racist and anti-Semitic shadow that Bachofen and Neumann entered with great erudition and enthusiasm for the feminine.

We must add to this picture the praiseworthy fact that Bachofen and Neumann drew attention for having given to women and the feminine a privileged position in the remote past of a culture in which they were oppressed and disqualified. This praise of the feminine opened space to examine the privileges of man within patriarchal dominance, an analysis that would each time further reveal with this apparent superiority of man the oppression of woman, ideological racism, ecological destruction, class exploration, savage capitalism, slavery, war, and genocide. For all these reasons human sciences still today present innumerable fixations and defenses that resist the anthropological symbolic archetypal analysis of cultures through these two fundamental archetypes.

It is important to recognize that Freud's description of repressed sexuality in the Victorian period, the discovery of infantile sexuality, and his reduction of the id and dreams to wish fulfillment, as well as Jung's description of participation mystique or unconscious identity and dreams as unconscious expressions, were only the tip of the iceberg of the matriarchal archetype, which had been disqualified and repressed millennia before the advent of Christianity.

My concept of the cultural Self (Byington 1986) within a symbolic and systemic perspective of the process of humanization (Teilhard de Chardin 1947) allows us to return to comparative anthropology, trying to avoid any ethnocentric or racist frame, to amplify the symbols of one culture with the help of symbols from other cultures to better understand these symbols in both cultures. This is a return to comparative anthropology, condemned by modern anthropology but now redeemed by fieldwork and a systemic approach that tries as much as possible to study symbols within symbolic archetypal anthropology in their cultural contexts (Byington 1998). In this manner the concept of the cultural Self is a contribution relating Jung's concept of the individuation process with the work of Lévi-Strauss as well as the works of Mircea Eliade and Joseph Campbell.

When we conceive normal and defensive comparative anthropology within the notion of evolution and history based on the relationship of the matriarchal and patriarchal archetypes, we have an extraordinary bird's eye view of culture that radically invalidates traditional notions of progress. Historians from antiquity (Morgan 1877) to modern times have tended to identify the concept of progress with that of technology. Instead of trying to include the subjective dimension in that concept, we have limited it to objectivity. In this manner, it was impossible to escape ethnocentrism and to consider collecting hunting groups and tribal cultures as other than retarded, barbaric, savages and primitives with all the inferior connotations implied when compared to industrialized societies. One of the great difficulties was the absence of access to language in archaeology because written languages began only a few thousand years ago. This prevented archaeologists in many instances from realizing the complexity of ancient cultures. However, when other parameters are chosen to evaluate progress, for instance, the relationship to the environment, this notion can be modified and even radically inverted.

Considering that two dimensions in studying the fear of extinction of our species are ecology and social cooperation, tribal cultures are by far more developed than industrialized cultures. Animism or pantheism considers sacred every animal, tree, stone, or natural phenomenon and respects them accordingly. The absence of animism in modern humanism of industrialized societies has been one reason why we have destroyed so many animal species and forests. Indeed, we know that the most industrialized countries are the most destructive regarding nature (visit www.worldwatch.org).

In tribal cultures, due to daily sensory intimacy with the natural forces through animism, the symbiotic ego-other relationship (mystical experience) respects and preserves nature in a way unthinkable by patriarchally dominant industrialized societies. The culture of the Gagudju in northern Australia, for instance, lived and preserved flora and fauna for forty thousand years. In contrast, the colonization and "progress" brought by the patriarchal dominance of Europeans in only four hundred years caused great pollution and ecological devastation, including the destruction of the Gagudju culture (*Australia's Aborigines*, 1997).

Together with the immensely valuable discoveries and social development as a result of the coordination of consciousness by the patriarchal archetype, it is important to acknowledge that exactly because it can delimit, organize, and produce so many remarkable things, it can also form a shadow like no other. This fact calls our attention to how societies with patriarchal dominance are prone to plundering nature, to ecological destruction, to elitism of social classes, to oppression of minorities, to repressive political regimes, to homicidal and suicidal policies, and finally to terrorism, war, and genocide.

The study of the matriarchal and patriarchal archetypes and their relationship including the virtues and shadow aspects of both the individual and collective dimensions becomes very fertile and promising when we base our perspective in the dialectical position of the alterity archetype. This archetype coordinates the normal and defensive relationship of all polarities, including the matriarchal-patriarchal polarity, which allows us to study in great detail their productive functions and pathological dysfunctions.

The theory of polarities adopted by Jung, when employed systemically to analyze the whole psychic dimension, allows us to postulate that the matriarchal and patriarchal archetypes form the basic polarity of all dimensions of the Self. However, we have a long way to go and it will require much good will to rescue these archetypes and their polarity from the conceptual confusion and discredit in which they have been involved. To understand the non evolutionary and dialectical relationship between the two fundamental archetypes, it is necessary to know their corresponding archetypal ego-other positions in consciousness, their dialectical articulation through the archetype of alterity, and their systemic relationship in the contemplative position of the totality archetype, which we shall examine further in the following chapters.

Chapter 9

THE MATRIARCHAL ARCHETYPE

An old bathing trunk
A whole day to bum around
A sea which has no size
A rainbow in the sky (Toquinho and Vinicius de Moraes,
Afternoon in Itapoã)

The matriarchal archetype, as the archetype of sensuality and fertility, through the insular ego-other position in consciousness, coordinates all representations associated with the physiological functions: the senses, the vegetative nervous system, the limbic system, and the neuroendocrine system. It is the archetype of the senses, the emotions, and the vegetative life of the body as well as being the archetype of the imaginal, musical, and intuitive functioning of the right hemisphere of the brain. It is so basic and participates so much in all our senses that we live it conscious and unconsciously most of the time. At any moment, if we pay attention, for instance, to the functioning of one of the senses, we become aware of countless functions that participate in it and that we are not otherwise conscious of. This is what happens with the trees and the leaves of a forest: from a distance we see them all as one green form, but when we come near and look at them one by one we see an infinite variety of forms and colors.

In *yoga*, meditation is frequently used to expand consciousness through the differentiation of body sensations. Any single sensation can be observed through introspection: a little itch, pain, breathing, posture, or any other sensory moment. Many different body stimuli can be used to intensify different perceptions, such as pressing the tongue against the roof of the mouth, or pressing a finger inside the ear, or assuming one of the countless body positions of *hatha yoga*, like the lotus position or standing on one's head. As with the leaves of the forest, our senses, apparently so little differentiated and monotonous, when focused present countless unique characteristics. Thus we have a small idea of what the matriarchal archetype coordinates in symbolic elaboration. When we suffer pain or feel lack of love or desire, we pay attention to that specific leaf in the forest, but when we don't, we are completely unconscious of what is going on. Because it is the archetype of sensuality, it permeates psychic life consciously and unconsciously with subliminal perceptions like breathing, for instance. This archetype includes eroticism and aggression, two of the most important structuring functions, which, as I have mentioned, were emphasized by Freud defensively in the Oedipus complex. However, although they are most important, they are only two of the countless structuring functions that develop consciousness.

When Kant wrote the *Critique of Pure Reason* (1781), perhaps his major work, he came to the conclusion that reason is incapable of explaining the dimensions of space and time, and he therefore characterized them as things in themselves (*Ding an sich*). From there on, reason no longer operates and gives way to intuition. This limit, which Kant demonstrated, is one of the boundaries between the patriarchal archetype of reason and rational organization and the matriarchal archetype of the senses, dominantly of intuition, sensation, and feeling.

To circumambulate an archetype we have to imagine it from four perspectives. The first is the genetic component, which is always the same unless we suffer genetic mutations. The second is its circumstantial collective and historical expression, the daily transformations of which are passed on from generation to generation. The third is to feel it operating in individual and collective symbolic elaboration at the unique moment in question within the totality of the Self and its developmental process. The fourth perspective is to see whether the archetype is coordinating symbols normally, that is, freely in the process of individuation, or whether it is coordinating symbols fixated and expressed in defenses pathologically through repetition compulsion in the shadow. These four variables interact within the conscious-unconscious relationship in varying degrees.

To know the coordinating nature of the matriarchal archetype is very important for the symbolic developmental perspective for two reasons: first, because the ego-other identity is formed in primary relationships in the beginning of life dominantly through it, and second, because it continues to take part in all symbolic elaboration during the rest of life.

When psychoanalysis reduces the id to wish fulfillment, to pleasure, to sexuality, to aggression, or to the life and death drives, this becomes a perspective that conceives the matriarchal archetype in a very limited way.

I have already mentioned that the insular matriarchal position, due to its high degree of dispersion, does not have a codified conjugation of the poles of polarities and therefore can easily enter into symbiosis and mythical-magical thinking. This happens because the ego and the other are not polarized, coordinated, and separated in a rational (Cartesian) way as in the polarized patriarchal position and so can be easily confused with each other.

I had the opportunity to observe a woman of the Tapirapé tribe in central Brazil during a much delayed labor of childbirth. The shaman was summoned. He danced, singing and playing his drum; he blew smoke over the patient and invoked the spirits. Up to this point, this was a ritual of conjuring; now began a ritual of magic. He placed a gourd with a corn husk stopper near the patient, and at the end of more dancing and singing he pulled out the stopper. Some time after this, the child was born. The shaman received gifts, thanks, and went away.

Magical thinking believes that the ego can modify the other according to desire, emotion, and faith. Magical causality operates through the emotional causality of desire and not through the reflective causality based on the characteristics of the other, the object. According to James Frazer (1890), magic is carried out in one of two ways: the first is imitative magic based on a concrete metaphor, the second is contagious magic, when the object of magic has had contact with the person to whom the magic is directed, as in the case of hair, nails, photos, or clothes used in the rituals. In the above case, the gourd is an imitation of the womb and the stopper is an imitation of the labor difficulty, and therefore this is a case of imitative magic. The womb was stopped up and the magic ritual caused birth because it took off the stopper. There are shamans who do tricks-this shaman could have withdrawn the stopper without anyone seeing it and then presented the gourd without it, but that would be magic through illusion, like they do in the circus, and not genuine magic. The procedure is all the more powerful because the shaman pulled the stopper out in front of the whole family and they all saw it come out and afterward the baby was born. That is good and sound magic. No tricks about it. This makes us relate magical thinking with magical causality. Frazer did not relate magic with emotion, only with objective reality, and therefore called it a bastard science and could not see the efficiency of magic and how it productively expresses the subjective dimension.

Claude Lévi-Strauss in his book *La Pensée Sauvage* (*The Savage Mind*, 1962) has affirmed that magical thinking (magical causality) can operate side by side with scientific thinking (reflexive causality). I once had an experience among a Xavante Indian tribe in Central Brazil (Goiás) that confirms his assertion. The Xavante had gone out before dawn to hunt a jaguar whose tracks had been seen in the neighborhood. Before going, they drew the jaguar image on the sand, danced and sang around it, and flung spears and arrows at its image. This is imitative magic. Next, they went out, following the jaguar tracks, and after a while they abandoned the tracks and veered away in a circle. When one of them told me this afterward, I asked why they had left the tracks and gone around. He explained that it was a way to come near the jaguar against the wind so it could not smell them. This is scientific thinking based on reflexive causality.

As Victor Turner writes in his book *The Ritual Process*:

> In the dimension of religion, as well as art, there are not ethnic groups more complex. There exist only technologies simpler than ours. The imaginative and emotional life of mankind is always in any part of the world rich and complex. It is part of my work to show how rich and complex can be the symbolism of tribal myths. It is also not correct to speak of a structure of a mentality different from ours. It is not the question of different cognitive structures, but of one identical structure articulating very different cultural experiences. (1969, p. 15)

When the concept of the insular matriarchal position is used to understand magical thinking, we see that it does not exist only in tribal cultures but is also very common in anyone and in any culture, including ours. The psychodynamics of magical thinking are such that it deals with objects as if they had subjective characteristics that obey the ego. It does not differentiate ego and other strictly as Descartes proposed for the polarity thinking (subjective, *res cogitans*) and nature (objective, *res extensa*), to think correctly (*pour bien penser*). Therefore, when we employ scientific thinking and clearly separate the subjective from the objective, the ego from the other in a polarized way, we invalidate magical thinking. This is what happened when Frazer realized that magic includes the motivation of the subject within objective reality and called it a bastard science.

When we observe people around us who think frequently within the insular matriarchal position we realize that they frequently think magically although they can also easily express Cartesian thinking. In such instances they follow magical thinking believing that their desire will influence objective reality. They say that faith can move mountains, and literally think so. Acts of faith and miracles, for example, express the realization of magical thinking. The number of educated people who guide their thinking by magical causality and through absolute faith in the realization of their desire is most impressive. Instead of Descartes's famous "I think, therefore I am," their motto seems to be "I desire, therefore, such and such will happen accordingly." It is this experience that may make games so attractive, especially games of chance. When one hits the jackpot, one experiences the wonder of magic as objective reality, one experiences a miracle. This is why games of chance can be so fascinating and even addictive.

The utility of magic lies in the emotional reinforcement of the ego which helps to resist frustration and adversity and improves hope, patience, dedication, and performance. To cheer for a team, to undertake an exam, sign an important contract or get better from sickness are situations in which magical thinking can reinforce self-trust, optimism, and health. No doubt, the performance with such reinforcement can be better than without it, as we can easily see from the statistical results of soccer games between two teams played at home or away. This is also the reason why placebos function as medication. Suggestion has a placebo effect because positive emotional reinforcement improves physiological results. In this sense, the placebo is symbolic and magically affects the subjective and objective dimensions.

A ten-year-old goes to school to take an exam in geography. His mother puts a picture of his grandfather who had traveled around the world inside his textbook for luck. This is contagious magic. The boy gets a good grade, and they attribute the result to his studying (science) and to his grandfather (magic). For the next exam, the boy wants to take along his grandfather's picture because he has learned contagious magical thinking. Mother and son in this case are not doing anything different from someone in a tribal culture who employs contagious magic in daily life. Therefore, we can conclude that magic is an expressive technique that acts on emotions reinforcing self-assurance. Today it has become not only an important part of any book on self-help that wishes to be a best seller, it is also the essence of marketing that is responsible for an important part of sales in business.

As I have described in my book *Education from the Heart* (Byington 2004), emotional participation and reinforcement in education are part of the transference relation in education and can be a very important factor to improve learning.

Magic becomes negative when magical causality absorbs the relationship with objective reality to the point of preventing the practice of objective reflexive causality. In the case of the student and his mother, this would happen if they thought that it would suffice to take the grandfather's picture to the exam without having to study. The extensive self-help literature, which sells hundreds of millions of dollars yearly, is mostly based on magical causality, generally of the imitative kind. Due to the extraordinary growth of consumerism during globalization and to the corresponding activation of the insular matriarchal position, people use more magical thinking every day to reassure themselves. This is certainly one of the reasons why the Harry Potter books, about the apprentice magician, became such extraordinary best sellers.

Knowledge of psychosomatics and of the psychology of emotions brought a great contribution to the study of magic. When we say that the effect of a drug is due not to its chemical components but to its placebo effect, we are referring to the magical effect of the drug. Supporters responsible for the extraordinary growth of antidepressive medication were quite surprised by the results of research involving fifty-seven reports whose final numbers showed a therapeutic tie between placebo effect and objective medication (Kirsch and Sapirstein 1998). Increasingly, we recognize the importance of emotions in our daily life (Goleman 1995), and we become ever more aware that suggestion can influence people intensely for good and for evil.

In this sense, the magic of the Tapirapé shaman can also be considered scientific when we take into consideration that psychology is also the science of emotions. When we do so, we can expand our concept of science and of magic beyond materialistic objective science and conceive symbolic science, where we deal with magical causality to influence the subjective dimension together with reflexive causality to influence the objective dimension. This expansion of the philosophy of science to encompass symbolic science allows us to conceive symbolic humanism, which is the core of Jungian symbolic psychology.

Case Example

A businessman had a phobia about flying. He needed to travel frequently, and this symptom limited his professional life. He came for therapy, and we saw that he had an intense defensive aggression, which came from a primary defensive identification with his father, who had exhibited many outbursts of rage in front of him during childhood. This defense made him insecure with men and with his own emotions. He made the association that his symptom (the phobia) came from not trusting pilots. We elaborated the fixation, with the pilot being a metaphor for a father figure, but the phobia continued.

Elaborating the symptom through the imagination, we discovered that he fantasized that he had to control the flight magically because of the pilot's perceived incompetence, and therefore he always sat in the front row. We soon became aware also that the figure of the pilot fused with a figure of his father and himself who were not competent to control their emotions. I prescribed anxiolytic medication, which had some good result, and went on to elaborate the symptom further with expressive techniques.

I asked him to bring in a tape with the sound of an airplane in flight. Lying on the couch with his eyes closed and listening to the tape, I suggested that he imagine himself inside the plane. I read for him a summary of the career of a commanding pilot and then asked him to mime picking up a phone on his seat and telling the pilot that he now knew of the pilot's competence and could begin to trust him and let himself be taken care of. To demonstrate this, he would continue in his imagination by sitting in the middle of the plane and detaching himself from a controlling attitude. After two sessions, the phobia was brought relatively under control, and he could stop taking the medication. I recommended that he repeat the exercise during the week preceding a flight.

This is a common treatment of a phobia using a cognitive behavioral expressive technique applied within the symbolic psychodynamic context of the symptom. The initial rational, logical objective explanation-that planes are much safer than cars and, as he did not fear driving his car, he had no reason to fear traveling by plane-had not the least influence on the symptom. Only the emotional fantasy and suggestion were decidedly efficient; therefore, in this case, treatment by symbolic elaboration within the rational polarized patriarchal position through reflective causality did not work, but the fantasy within the insular matriarchal position through magical causality rapidly brought the phobia under control. It is very impressive from clinical experience that the majority of cases function this way.

As I pointed out in a paper on compulsive obsessive behavior (Byington 1996), when cognitive behavioral techniques are applied within the symbolic meaning of the symptom, the therapeutic effect is greater and lasts longer.

In my book on education (Byington 2004) I noted that the pedagogic transference is highly efficient due to its magical characteristics, just as cheering for a team or emotional coaching for an exam is. A known artist appears on television wearing a special T-shirt for merchandizing a product, and in the following weeks sales increase considerably. This is imitative magic based on the popularity of the artist. It is extraordinary how people love to compete for the bride's bouquet or sometimes pay fortunes to buy superstars' personal belongings in auctions. This is contagious magic.

The phenomenon of transference was discovered by Freud and employed to describe and treat the defensive projection of neurotic contents of the patient on the therapist. However, as Jung (1946) demonstrated, transference is the basis of every human relationship through empathy. In this sense, every human relationship may have in greater or lesser degree a component of suggestion. Children in particular, but also the general public, have an important part of their personalities that operate through suggestion, which can have very positive or negative results. In a general way, all magical procedures refer to emotions, wish, pleasure, sensuality, and the intimacy and interchange of the ego-other position in the insular matriarchal position.

Many parents lose emotional control when their children misbehave. In this way, they weaken the archetypal charge they carry due to the parental transference, which is one of the strongest in life. This is why I recommend that parents address their children, in these highly charged emotional situations when they misbehave, with a distant, emphatic, disapproving, and firm attitude but without sermons and without raising their voices and then pull out of the emotional setting, allowing the transference to produce its effect. In other words, they should never lose their temper and become aggressive because this morally lowers their attitude in front of the child and weakens the emotional power of the transference. In cases where parents become aggressive, children may submit through fear, but the loving bond that fosters deep education is then weakened and wasted.

Mental health statistics show that around 70 percent of medical consultations worldwide involve psychosomatic complaints, which means that they present emotional issues that belong to the matriarchal dynamic.

Case Example

A middle-aged, very distinguished lady began having palpitations (ventricular extrasystoles), which worried her cardiologist because they could not be controlled by medication. He indicated psychotherapy to examine "a certain emotional component" which he felt in her symptom.

Right in the first session, she told me that she had had a few episodes of extrasystoles in the past but that lately their frequency had increased greatly due to a strong tension she was undergoing in her marriage. The relationship with her husband had always been difficult, but she had continued in the marriage because she had two children. However, the children were now grown up. They had married and moved away, and her marriage difficulties increased considerably. Her husband started coming home late from work. One day she followed him and discovered that he was enjoying a happy hour drink with his secretary. She did not say anything, but she felt much hatred and began living inside a pressure cooker.

I explained to her that aggression produces adrenaline and that possibly this repressed rage was causing her extrasystoles. She seemed to understand my explanation rationally but nothing changed. We then began to employ the expressive technique of dramatic acting out the shadow within active imagination. Her heart should tell her husband how she felt. In that moment we magically and dramatically "animated" her heart, which acquired an autonomous personality such as a stone, a tree, rain, or fire could do in a tribal culture through the imagination in daily life.

She began acting the voice of her heart, speaking very softly. Normally I interact with patients during expressive techniques to involve the transference energy in the magical procedure. In her case I told her that her heart was speaking so softly that it was not convincing me of her disgust. Suddenly she began to yell, calling her husband names, using cuss words that I had not imagined she knew. After a few sessions with the voice of the heart the extrasystoles went away and never returned. Months afterward they divorced.

The medication used from the polarized patriarchal position had the intention of eliminating the extrasystoles and would have repressed the "heart's voice" and therefore fortunately had no effect. The emotional acting of the expressive technique based on the magical causality of the insular matriarchal position, on the contrary, opened the possibility of expressing her "heart's voice" and magically cured her. In this manner, magic and magical causality can be included in science when they are employed to express emotions within the dialectic position of the alterity archetype. This was possibly the magia naturalis described by the philosopher Marsilio Ficino (1433-1499) during the Renaissance.

We must emphasize that this magic elaboration with expressive techniques must be carried out within the symbolic elaboration process of the Self and not simply for an adaptation to a politically correct social convention and at the convenience of the persona. In the case above, had we acted along with the cardiologist and used cognitive behavioral suggestion or even hypnotism to get rid of the extrasystoles, we would have been trying to silence the "voice of the heart" with a great danger of aggravating the symbolic content of the symptom and producing serious alienation. (One cannot avoid speculating that this alienation might have led to a heart attack, possibly a fatal one.)

It seems to me that many psychosomatic symptoms are defensively magic. That is, they are the defensive emotional expression of fixations as shadow formation in the insular matriarchal position. We can only understand this defensive magic of psychopathology, however, if we understand the structuring function of normal magic, the magic of the shaman, of the Xavante jaguar hunter, of the teacher who motivates students with smiles, of the marketing specialist, or of the therapist who elaborates symptoms with expressive techniques. Only in this manner can we see that the magic of the extrasystoles of the woman in the case above were defensive, that is, a shadow acting out that was cured when the voice of the heart was allowed to speak freely. The neuropsychological path used defensively by the symptom was the same that normally causes palpitation when we see our beloved in the early stages of a romance.

It is necessary to cultivate detachment from countless prejudices accumulated in our culture in order to assimilate all the extensions of the matriarchal archetype as one of the five great forms of intelligence of the psyche. It is especially difficult to understand how the insular matriarchal position can create such variety of symptoms when fixated and also cure them by the magic elaboration of expressive techniques.

Side by side with the typological functions of sensation and feeling, the matriarchal archetype also employs intuition. The fact that islands of matriarchal conscience are surrounded by unconsciousness elects intuition as the messenger connecting these islands to each other and to the central archetype. Intuition is therefore the great matriarchal structuring function of centroversion. This is difficult to comprehend because the insular matriarchal position is characterized by intimacy, symbiosis, and attachment, and it seems paradoxical that it would be capable of transcendence and spiritual life. The key to understanding this paradox is that intuition exercises this connection through the metaphors of the imagination and not through rational explanation. Follow a child's play and you will understand many messages from the center of its being. Having access to an extraordinary fountain of sensuality-the intuitive conscious and unconscious transcendent function of the imagination-creates metaphors that are representations, magical, emotional, and enchanted. This is the world of Peter Pan, of Santa Claus, and of myth and religion for billions of people. In this manner, the matriarchal archetype is not only the archetype of emotion, feeling, intuition, and magic but above all it is the archetype that best expresses the structuring function of faith and religiosity.

Intuition united to feeling, sensation, and sensuality generates empathy based on matriarchal exuberance and spontaneity, creating a cornucopia of magical meanings to represent the world through infinite images. These are the leaves of the forest of every individual and of all cultures. The insular matriarchal position is remarkably capable of propitiating empathy because it breathes intimacy. It is the best function for becoming aware of what someone else is feeling, something logical thinking is incapable of doing. This happens due to the great intimacy of the ego and the other in the islands of consciousness. This (con)fusion is frequently taken for unconscious identity or sheer unconsciousness, but this is a huge mistake. To think so is to miss the point that the insular matriarchal position is a very creative, profound, and important intelligence of being in the world, consciously and unconsciously. On the one hand, it is a disadvantage that it operates mostly out of consciousness, but on the other hand, it is of great advantage for the Self because it collects information from the deepest unconscious sources to feed consciousness. It is like the lotus flower whose beauty appears in the sunshine with such glamour because its roots reach the prodigious fertility of the mud at the very bottom of the lake.

Fixation and Defensive Attachment in the Insular Matriarchal Position

Coordinated by sensuality and desire, the insular matriarchal position can present great spontaneity and pleasure. This attachment to sensuality, however, as we have seen, may produce automatism and conditioning, which can become stereotyped, fixated, and present strong resistance to change. For example, in the Western diet we have three poisons-too much salt, sugar, and fat. In spite of all education, our habitual consumption of these substances in excess, conditioned through generations, stubbornly resists change. The same thing happens with many habits that are not healthy, and this affects nature negatively. This is also the case with ignorant behavior, including superstitions, absurd religious practices, hate, and intolerance, which resist change tenaciously due to a high degree of attachment and conditioning coordinated by the fixation and defensive expression of the insular matriarchal position.

When this attachment becomes clearly fixated and defensive, it is very difficult to treat precisely because the insular matriarchal position expresses so strongly sensuality and instinctive behavior in such symbiotic intimacy. People are so attached that they become literally possessed by their symptoms, defenses, and compulsions. This is the case, for instance, with alcoholism and drug addictions, as well as with eating disorders, sexual perversion, kleptomania, and compulsive gambling. The compulsive conditioning of the defenses justifies group therapy in these situations, because the social harmony of the matriarchal archetype provides rituals that favor ego detachment and reinforcement.

Fixations of the insular matriarchal position cause dissociations-splits between the ego-other and other-other polarities-which are from then on expressed through defensive projection and introjection in dissociative, hysterical reactions. Defensive projection may give rise also to persecutory paranoid reactions; defensive introjection may result in hypochondriacal reactions, which are found in many cultures that treat the projected shadow as an obsessive spirit, called an incubus in the Middle Ages. These projections were treated as diabolical spirits capable of possessing people. When introjected, this shadow was referred to as a succubus.

During the European colonization of the African continent, the many different ethnic groups were not considered separately and were assembled and repressed artificially into modern nations; these nations are now exploding in genocidal wars to establish frontiers within the bloodshed of ancestral rivalry and hatred accumulated during colonialist repression. In such cases, the ancestral attachment to the land and the shadow split was defensively projected onto the neighbor as enemy to express the defensive insular matriarchal archetype, while the genocidal wars are symbolically organized under the defensive polarized coordination of the patriarchal archetype.

The Muriqui Symbol

To end this chapter I want to mention a very significant matriarchal symbol related to the Olympic Games to take place in Rio de Janeiro in 2014.

The Muriqui (pronounced mooreekey) of the South is the name of a monkey considered to be the chimpanzee of the Americas (Brachytteles arachnoide). Its name in Tupi Indian language means "people who swing the hips." They are also known as "the gentle people of the forest" because they love to hug each other. They are five feet tall, live in groups, and are very friendly. Threatened with extinction, they are now being protected. In the contest to choose a symbol for the Olympic Games, they won first place.

Gilberto Gil, a composer, singer, and former ministry of culture of Brazil, during political exile composed a song called *A Big Hug*, which became very popular. After the selection of Muriqui as a symbol of the Games, Gil offered his song, free of charge, to accompany the monkey during the games. *Hello Rio de Janeiro, a big hug / a big hug* . ... is how the song goes.

Chapter 10

THE PATRIARCHAL ARCHETYPE

Taking the crown from the hands of Pope Pius VII, Napoleon crowned himself. (Interrupting the institutionalization of the Republic through the dialectical position of the alterity archetype, Napoleon's self-crowning transformed France into a warring patriarchal empire.)

The *Enûma Eliš* of Assyrian-Babylonian mythology and the *Old Testament* are two great creation myths relating the beginning of the world and of humanity through images of the matriarchal and patriarchal archetypes that result in a clear patriarchal domination.

The *Enûma Eliš*, an epic poem, was found on seven clay tablets in the library of King Ashurbanipal in Nineveh. They date from the seventh century B.C., but probably repeat older versions of oral tradition. They tell that Apsû, the sweet waters, united with Tiamat, the salt waters, and bred the gods. Apsû is somewhat of an abyss which surrounded the earth, like Oceanus in Greek mythology, whom Homer calls the father of all things. Tiamat is the feminine earth. From them were born Mummu (the roaring of the waves) and a pair of serpents Lahmu and Lahamu who bred Anshar, as a masculine principle, and Kishar, the feminine principle. They had children named Anu and Enki, who became the father of Marduk, the great patriarchal hero-god who created and organized the Babylonian world.

One of the intentions of Jungian symbolic psychology, in bringing the mythological dimension to amplify the basic archetypes, is to describe the matriarchal-patriarchal polarity within the concept of dominance, present in

219

every culture. Although most settled cultures present a great patriarchal exuberance that determined their social organization and technological development, it is very misleading to consider this to be the final goal of historical evolution. Patriarchal development was always accompanied by the presence of manifestations of the matriarchal archetype. The important issue to register is that patriarchal development generally formed a significant shadow due to the oppression of the matriarchal archetype, which one day would have to be rescued through the coordination of the alterity archetype.

It is important to note that the *Enûma Eliš*, as it is told, includes the consecration of Marduk as the great patriarchal hero-god. Therefore, the symbolic meanings that register his crushing victory over Tiamat belong to the patriarchal perspective, which described not only its victory but also the shattering of the matriarchal to give birth to the world and mankind.

Apsû and Tiamat were disturbed by the noise of their descendants and thought of destroying them. Enki learned of their intention and allied himself with Apsû and Mummu. This made Tiamat furious. She created an army with dragons, serpents, and many other monsters armed with hurricanes under the leadership of Kingu. Enki united with his father Anshar and delegated to his son Marduk the command of the natural forces against Tiamat and her army. Mounting the tempest and armed with the hurricane, Marduk threw his net around Tiamat and imprisoned her, and she exploded with the winds; he then cut her up and trampled on her. He imprisoned Kingu and his army with his net and threw them to the bottom of hell.

With the upper half of Tiamat's body, Marduk built the heavens, and with the inferior part he built the earth. In the heavens he placed the gods and their images, which are the stars. He then fixed the duration of the year and the course of the stars and created humanity, forming the first human being with Kingu's body (*Larousse Encyclopedia of Mythology* [1959]).

The amplification of the patriarchal archetype through myth and history identifies it naturally with man. This happened because man is physically stronger than woman, is capable of erection, penetrates her sexually, and is the champion of physical aggression. At the same time, with pregnancy and breast feeding woman became the depository of matriarchal fertility and sensuality. These projections were subsequently maintained by habits and traditions, and even by the humanities (Gray 1992).

Each person and each culture has a unique Self with a characteristic matriarchal-patriarchal polarity that can be better known and studied in comparison to the Self of other persons and cultures. The evolutionary perspective of the patriarchal over the matriarchal has limited and deformed their relationship.

This pseudo-evolutionary paradigm has been the suicidal fallacy of the humanities in practically all cultures on the planet throughout history and may cost us the destruction of our species. Conversely, the true evolutionary paradigm is here referred to as the measure to which the matriarchal and patriarchal archetypes relate dialectically with equal rights to express their differences coordinated by the archetype of alterity (see chapter 11).

In the Assyrian-Babylonian mythology, we have an expression of patriarchal dominance with extraordinary violence in the organization of creation, in the centralization of power by physical force, and in the rigid polarization of victor and defeated. The conquest is led by the hero Marduk who ends up sending Kingu and his armies to hell, which has many matriarchal characteristics. However, it is of special interest that humankind, cobbled together from Kingu's body, ends the creation myth with an emphatic component of the alterity archetype. This is so much so that, as the myth points out, to deal with human reality within such patriarchal dominance is to recognize and rescue the repressed matriarchal archetype from the bottom of hell, representing the shadow.

To become aware of the extent to which this myth is real today, an illustrative example is the recognition and rescue of the symbolic body in the study of the subjective components of diseases. Indeed, we ignore, disregard, and impose stressing demands on our bodies until one day we find ourselves taking them for a walk in the park every morning on our cardiologists' recommendation...

We know that dreams and myths can express historical representations of cultures, but they are not history. Myths are the dreams of cultures. The archetypal foundations of the psyche proposed by Jung, allied to the prospective capacity of symbols (which he also pointed out), allow us to examine myth and history and to see in them a structuring function of individual and collective consciousness. How and when these influences occur depends on circumstances. Although myths may refer frequently to historical events through fantastic stories, their symbolic component, capable of interfering in the structuring of consciousness, is undeniable. For an example, it is sufficient to think of the Christian myth and its influence on modern humanism.

Comparative symbolic anthropology is very important for studying the matriarchal-patriarchal relation in myths and cultures. Generally, the greater the patriarchal dominance, the more a culture tends to have figures with centralized authority in its mythology, and to have a monotheistic tendency and a corresponding matriarchal hindering. When matriarchal exuberance prevails, the tendency is plurality and polytheism. Finally, the dominant presence of the alterity archetype propitiates a combination of matriarchal plurality and patriarchal unification. Greek mythology is an outstanding example of this third instance, in which side by side with great polytheistic richness we have the clear administration of the centralizing figure of Zeus. Indian and Egyptian mythologies share this characteristic.

The Yoruba culture of the Nago, who came as slaves to Latin America from West Africa, expresses a great matriarchal polytheism and a mythological matriarchal-patriarchal conflict almost the opposite of the one described in the Assyrian-Babylonian mythology. However, the intense and central dialectical manifestation of the archetype of alterity in its pantheon expressed by the Orixá (god) Exu, shows the polytheistic aspect together with the unifying monotheistic tendency of the supreme principle represented by the Orixá Olodum or Oxumaré (Byington 2007).

When Olodum decided to create the earth, he called Obatalá the masculine principle and gave him the gourd of existence (*apó-iwa*) and instructed him. Obatalá gathered all Orixás and also called Odudua, whose gender varies. Odudua told Obatalá that he (or she) would go only after accomplishing the proper rituals. During Obatalá's journey, Exu asked him if he had undertaken the proper rituals. Obatalá answered that he had not done anything, and Exu declared that his actions would be completely unsuccessful. Obatalá lost control and began to feel thirsty; he passed by a river and did not stop; he passed by a village and was offered milk and did not accept it. His thirst became unbearable. He came by a palm tree (*igi-ope*), thrust his ritual staff (*opa-soru*) into the trunk, and drank the sap until he passed out; he then slept deeply.

Meanwhile, oriented by the priests (*babalawos*), Odudua carried out his (or her) ritual obligations and then brought a ritual offering (*ebó*) to Olodum. He opened his seat cushion and realized that he had not put any soil in the *apó-*

iwa he had given to Obatalá. He gave the soil to Odudua to take to Obatalá. Finding Obatalá still asleep, Odudua picked up the *apó-iwa* which was on the ground and brought it back to Olodum, who filled it with soil. He charged Odudua to form the earth and Obatalá to form all beings.

Obatalá and Odudua each founded his own nation. They competed and almost came to war, threatening all creation. Orunmilá, patron of the Ifá oracle, made them face each other and offer sacrifices; this settled their agreement. From then on, their union was represented by the *gourd igbá-odu*, whose halves are respectively this world (*aye*) and the beyond (*orum*) (Elbein dos Santos 1975). These are very important to the meaning of the myth because they represent symbols, complexes, and structuring functions that were projected onto the historical figures of man and woman. In this manner, the change of sex of Odudua in different cultural traditions shows a great opening for the interaction of the founding gods as well as the relationship of man and woman.

In this manner, we see that the creation myth of the Yoruba culture presents a great primordial conflict between the two basic archetypal polarities, but the myth, from the beginnings, leads the conflict toward a ritual integration of their opposing positions. The conflict was so serious as to threaten creation. The activation of the alterity archetype expressed through the oracular god Orunmilá creates the ritual gourd *igba-odu*, symbol of the union of opposites and model for the dialectic relationship of the matriarchal and patriarchal archetypes in the development of culture.

Obatalá's flaw, which caused him to get drunk and lose the primacy of creation, was that he had not made the correct offerings coordinated by Exu. This god is the master of crossroads, a companion of the Greek Hermes and patron of the sacrificial offering (*ebó*), which richly expresses the alterity archetype in the Yoruba pantheon, caring especially for the relationship of opposites (Byington 2007). Disrespecting Exu unbalances the primordial polarity of Obatalá and Odudua, which needs Orunmilá's intervention to restore its balance. What is most extraordinary in the Yoruba's creation myth is the explicit representation of this loss of balance and the search to restore it in the very origin of creation.

These two creation myths, the Assyrian-Babylonian and the Yoruba express the basic matriarchal-patriarchal conflict through very different imagery and meanings in quite unique symbolic paths that illustrate the diversity of possibilities of individual and collective development. The many cultures I have studied and the many people I have accompanied in their development all have shown unique situations in the confrontation of these two great archetypes.

The polarized patriarchal position propitiates an extraordinary increase in the capacity of consciousness to control nature, society, ideas, emotions, and the body, as well as all other symbolic dimensions of the psyche. Its main typological function is thinking, allied to sensation and intuition and leaving feeling far behind. Due to its vocation for organization and control, the patriarchal archetype is intimately associated with the power drive, to which Adler (1914) gave central importance in psychological development.

The polarized ego-other and other-other positions that characterize the patriarchal archetype articulate in a hierarchic way all the poles of structuring functions. They establish clear rational associations to be memorized and applied in daily living. The relations of poles elaborated in this manner form logical systems of opposites, which from then on operate productively to administer mental life and behavior. The typological functions of intuition and sensation are subsidiary to thinking in symbolic elaboration; sensation operates to control in the here-and-now that which is already known, and intuition functions as a strategy to foresee and operate the new. At the same time the feeling function is left far behind, very much controlled, injured, repressed, and frequently forming the shadow, as we see in the dissociative syndromes formerly called hysteria.

The intense and intimate attachment of the insular matriarchal position expresses the primacy of sensuality, affection, and desire and the satisfaction of drives and instinctive reactions. It generally creates habits of behavior that operate mostly through intuition and sensation and in which predominate symbiosis and intimacy are subordinated to the feeling function. "I want you to warm me in this winter and that everything else go to hell" goes the popular song (by Roberto Carlos). With the adoption of the polarized patriarchal position, however, there follows detachment from sensuality and affection without which one cannot abstract polarities so intensely. Articulating hierarchically one pole with the other to deal with objective reality, the polarized patriarchal position registers its elaboration of space and time, which explains its aversion to spontaneity and its praise for tradition, often in a very rigid and even obsessive way (Byington 1996).

It is difficult to follow the general implantation of the polarized patriarchal position as the archetype of organization and of power. Still more difficult is to admit that a pattern of such importance remained practically latent in our brain during so many millennia of prehistory. It began to be activated prodigiously only around ten thousand years ago with the agro-pastoral and the cultural revolution. From then on its operation flourished and frequently occupied a dominant position in the historical developmental process.

Symbolic Anthropology: A Third Phase

Having recognized the ethnocentric bias that deformed classical anthropology, modern anthropology since the work of Franz Boas (1924) began adopting field research and avoided comparative anthropology, restricting studies to each culture as a whole. Exceptions to this rule were the works of Mircea Eliade, Claude Lévi-Strauss, and others, including Jung's method of amplification for better understanding archetypes.

Jungian symbolic psychology proposes a third phase in anthropology, which we might refer to as archetypal anthropology, in which anthropology is practiced trying to identify normal and fixated symbols and complexes (shadow) in one culture and compare them to symbols in other cultures that do not have such fixations. This approach, applied to the matriarchal-patriarchal polarity, is very productive for the study of normal and defensive development. Instead of fearing ethnological methodology deformed by ethnocentrism, a fear that motivated modern anthropology's tunnel vision, we can employ archetypal comparative anthropology to understand further the normal and pathological development of Western culture based on knowledge of other cultures.

Organization and the challenge of accomplishment form the context that activates the patriarchal archetype. One may lead a calm and simple life and become known as a humble person; however, if given a post of leadership, authority, and responsibility, in no time one can develop arrogance, rigidity, intolerance, and a exaggerated sense of authority. The same happens in the cultural Self. Nations can have periods of peace and tranquility, but if forced into urgent organization due to a threatening situation, the degree of intolerance and patriarchal authoritarianism can rise incredibly fast. We experienced this in Latin America with patriarchalization activated during the political movements of the 1960s and 1970s. The United States experienced this in a most intense way after the terrorist attacks of September 11, 2001.

The more power our species gained over nature, the more the patriarchal archetype was activated, to the point where, in many cultures, it inverted radically the dominance of the matriarchal archetype. The important issue is to reason in a systemic and dialectic way, and not in a linear way of thinking that would have it that the patriarchal came to substitute the matriarchal archetype and that this is a synonym of progress and the goal of evolution. The more the patriarchal archetype is activated unilaterally, and the more the power of the ego in individual or collective consciousness rises, the more the matriarchal archetype is threatened and wounded and suffers generally in the shadow.

The consequences of our historical transformation over thousands of years can be seen from two different perspectives. From the matriarchal perspective there was a corresponding wounding and plundering of mother Gaia that accompanied devastating wars of conquest and oppression (Lovelock 1979). From the patriarchal standpoint, there was an extraordinary development of technology, an immense increase of power to control nature, and the organization of society for production.

This reasoning becomes clearer when we realize that archetypes exist in virtual form and are activated by circumstance, place, and time. Although archetypes are activated today depending on existential circumstances as they have always been, they do so within historical circumstances and respond accordingly.

The polarized patriarchal position can be systemic, that is, it can elaborate symbols and complexes within totality, but it is different from the systemic perspective of the alterity archetype. The patriarchal systemic perspective refers to totality but does not expose unilaterality, elitism, and shadow and may even increase them, whereas the alterity archetypal perspective recognizes the type of interaction between polarities, endorsing their democratic relations and exposing their fixations and defenses, that is, confronting their shadow.

Take as an example a family in therapy to deal with a serious economic problem. They had handed over the money saved by the parents and by two sisters to the eldest son; he worked in the money market but his ethical behavior was untrustworthy. In one session in which we were elaborating the separation of each family member's money to be managed individually, I said, "Before the house falls down . . ." and one sister immediately replied, "If all of us continue warmly holding hands, let it fall." The feeling function maintained such attachment within the family unit that the suggestion to detach to elaborate the honesty-dishonesty polarity precipitated a defensive matriarchal reaction. This frequently occurs in family business where a shift from private to professional management is needed.

Initiation rites serve to praise resistance, especially of men, to pain, stress, and danger, stimulating them to undertake difficult deeds (see the film *A Man Called Horse* [1970]). The warrior model of Sparta in Greece became famous, and rigid teaching of the young still today is sometimes referred to as Spartan education. In such rituals, masculine identity is strengthened by the constellation of the patriarchal archetype through missions that activate the hero archetype and hinder the matriarchal archetype through coercion. The absence of analogous rituals for women illustrates the degree to which the polarized patriarchal position was historically implanted asymmetrically and related to the man-woman relationship based on the development of manhood. This hierarchy caused an erroneous identification of man with the patriarchal archetype and woman with the matriarchal archetype, examples of which can be found in Bachofen and Neumann, in the social sciences, and also in popular culture, as we see in the best-selling *Men Are from Mars, Women Are from Venus* (Gray 1992). This fundamental error has greatly contributed to limiting the understanding of the matriarchal and patriarchal archetypes in culture and in the identities of men and women.

In my experience following the individuation process of countless persons, within the symbolic perspective, I have not found one single structuring function that cannot be expressed by both men and women in psychological development. On the contrary, when one has a theoretical opening for understanding the symbolic richness and variety of the individuation process, it becomes clear that any structuring function can be symbolically lived in any elaboration. This includes pregnancy and nursing, which are functions absolutely exclusive to women on the objective level, and erection and penetration, which are exclusive to men. A very affectionate woman told me that if it were not for her husband, she certainly would not have been able to carry any of her three pregnancies to the end. Another woman, who had a psychotic episode after giving birth to her first child, told me that the same would have happened following the births of her next two children if she had not asked her husband for help and if he had not intimately participated in the pregnancies, births, and breast-feeding periods. There are many situations in which men must adopt a passive attitude and patiently wait for a situation to mature, and there are also occasions in which women must exhibit phallic behavior and penetrate problems with a sword of intelligence, competence, courage, and impulse.

The Typological Matriarchal-Patriarchal Dominance

Once we are convinced that the relation of the matriarchal and patriarchal archetypes exists in different combinations in the personalities of men and women as well as in cultures, we can perceive that they form a psychological archetypal typology side by side with the four functions and two attributes described by Jung (1923). It is easy to see that there are men very gifted at domestic activities, including cooking and child care, decoration, dress making, dancing, fashion, and many others in which the insular matriarchal archetype tends to be predominant (see the film *Billy Elliot* [2000]). We can observe, too, in growing frequency, the many women who have an intense professional call for administration, organization, finances, management, control, law, and even military activities and leadership, all of which are based on the dominance of the polarized patriarchal position (see the film *Joan of Arc* [1948]).

Two new psychological types emerge from this discovery. They are the types of matriarchal dominance and patriarchal dominance, in both the masculine and feminine personalities. This helps demonstrate how many characteristics that come from historical circumstances and are not structurally present are attributed to the identities of men and women. Given the opportunity to follow the natural call to a profession within their individuation process, men and women can develop professional abilities and ways of being centered on structural functions that were traditionally attributed to the other gender.

This fact is very important for the psychodynamic study not only of the individual personality but also of marriage, family psychology, and culture. In the individual process, this typology is useful for working out resistance to authentic development due to historical prejudices accumulated over thousands of years of patriarchal dominance. In marriage therapy, the same occurs and is of extraordinary importance especially when one or both members have a typology that is contrary to stereotyped tradition. In such cases, special understanding is necessary to incorporate such typological differences into the affectionate relationship of daily living, especially as they become pronounced over time. In family therapy, we can also employ very productively the knowledge of this typology in the relationship of the personalities of the different members of the family. In the well-known film *Billy Elliot* (2000), we see this problem dramatically represented by a youngster who has a dominant matriarchal typology expressed in a dance vocation within a British working class family exhibiting a pronounced patriarchal dominance.

One of the difficulties and prejudices to admitting and developing this archetypal typology in men and women is the projection of homosexuality, which can be quite defensive. This defensive projection is more frequent in matriarchally dominant men like the character Billy Elliot, because the stereotyped identity of patriarchal dominance in men is traditionally more strict and commonplace than in women.

Detachment in Patriarchal Dominance: Examples

Let us not think, however, that the intense detachment described in the polarized position is complete. On the contrary, because polarized patriarchal detachment is centralized on sensuality, feeling, and in the emotions, this happens in direct proportion to an intense attachment to the thinking function, to organization, power, control, authority, and to hierarchically organized pairs of opposites. The great detachment from sensuality, spontaneity, and pleasure cultivated, for instance, in religious and military institutions is strictly related to attachment to discipline, authority, and obedience.

For example, a chief of the department of human relations in a firm threatened with bankruptcy came out of a general board meeting with the mission to cut personnel expenses drastically. Twenty percent of the employees had to be fired, beginning with those who received higher salaries. Examining the list, he saw that many of the employees to be fired were his close friends and among them was his boss, who had hired him fifteen years before. He had a sleepless night and came to his therapy session the next morning feeling that he was not dismissing employees but destroying the firm. He concluded that he could not think about it, because if he did, he would quit himself before firing anyone. He elaborated on the effort he had dedicated to achieve to this position in his career. He remembered sadly the worn-out shoes he walked home in after classes to save money and the glass of water he drank before going to bed to fight hunger. Was it worthwhile, he asked himself, seeing the inhumane task he now had to perform?

In the ritual of circumambulation of the sacred mountains in Japan, the Buddhist monks took along a knife and a rope in case they failed to end their pilgrimage successfully (Corrêa Pinto 2007).

Because Prometheus stole fire and gave it to humankind, Zeus chained him to a rock in the Caucasus and sent an eagle to devour his liver daily.

One of the most meaningful examples of the integration of the polarized patriarchal position through the coordination of the structuring functions of obedience, faith, and submission is found in the *Old Testament*.

> And it came to pass after these things that God did tempt Abraham, and said unto him, Abraham: and he said, Behold, here I am.
> And he said, Take now thy son, thine only son Isaac, whom thou lovest, and get thee into the land of Moriah; and offer him there for a burnt offering upon one of the mountains which I will tell thee of.
> And Abraham rose up early in the morning, and saddled his ass, and took two of his young men with him, and Isaac his son, and clave the wood for the burnt offering, and rose up, and went unto the place of which God had told him.
> Then on the third day Abraham lifted up his eyes, and saw the place afar off.
> And Abraham said unto his young men, Abide ye here with the ass; and I and the lad will go yonder and worship, and come again to you.
> And Abraham took the wood of the burnt offering, and laid it upon Isaac his son; and he took the fire in his hand, and a knife; and they went both of them together.
> And Isaac spake unto Abraham his father, and said, My father: and he said, Here am I, my son. And he said, Behold the fire and the wood: but where is the lamb for a burnt offering?

> And Abraham said, My son, God will provide himself a
> lamb for a burnt offering: so they went both of them together.
> And they came to the place which God had told him of;
> and Abraham built an altar there, and laid the wood in order,
> and bound Isaac his son, and laid him on the altar upon the
> wood.
> And Abraham stretched forth his hand, and took the
> knife to slay his son.
> And the angel of the LORD called unto him out of
> heaven, and said, Abraham, Abraham: and he said, Here am I.
> And he said, Lay not thine hand upon the lad, neither
> do thou any thing unto him: for now I know that thou fearest
> God, seeing thou hast not withheld thy son, thine only son
> from me. (Gen. 22:1-12)

The competition for physical performance is another dimension in which the ambition of the patriarchal power is outstanding. It becomes a worldwide festivity every four years in the Olympic Games.

The patriarchal ambition in ancient Greece was frequently exaggerated and became hubris, defensive omnipotence and inflation, severely punished by the gods. The story of Icarus illustrates this: seeing the sun, he wanted to get near it, and he flew each time higher until his wings melted, and Icarus fell to his death from the heights.

"We are seeing a shift from car accidents to sports injuries," said orthopedist Flavio Murachovsky at the Albert Einstein Hospital in São Paulo. According to him, at least 40 percent of orthopedic consultations in São Paulo at the time came from sports injuries, twice as many as five years earlier. "There are patients to whom I show the x-ray with the injury, and even then they say that they will not stop" ("The more exercise, the better?" *Veja*, February 6, 2008; my translation).

Murachovsky also relates the story of a twenty-four-year-old man who had become a gymnast when he was eight years old. By age eleven, he was training five hours a day, six days a week. He was operated on twice-a knee and a foot. He broke his sternum and his wrist (two or three times, he lost count). He hurt his hands and fingers frequently in addition to collisions with gymnastic equipment and muscle tears.

In these diverse individual and collective examples we see an extraordinary attachment to ambition and power coordinating polarities that establish a rigid control of one pole over the other in both normal circumstances and in instances of pathology, with planned, rational, and rigid detachment from the affectionate bond involving oneself, one's body, emotions, nature, and other people.

This detachment by abstraction of the affectionate function, however, does not need to be cruel nor result in terrible and disastrous events. In most initiation rituals, the initiated transforms and strengthens his identity, referring afterward to his trials with great pride, especially if they leave marks or scars to be exhibited (see, for example, the film *A Man Called Horse*). However, wounds are not obligatory. Many conquests are glorifying and bring only generous prizes. If we consider the many discoveries over the years that have greatly increased the welfare of humankind, we see the normal and productive side of ambition, tenacity, and devotion propitiated by the normal attachment to power within the coordination of the patriarchal archetype.

The Polarized Patriarchal Position
and the Hero Archetype

Joseph was called upon to discover the meaning of the pharaoh's dream, in which seven thin cows devoured seven fat ones (Gen. 41:1-57). He interpreted the dream prospectively, saying that times of abundance would be followed by times of need. Designated second in command of Egypt by the pharaoh, Joseph built storehouses all over the empire and prepared for times of need, which were probably related to the irregular flow of the Nile.

Joseph's career as a ruler of Egypt and the interpretation of this dream expressed in the biblical tradition the relation of the functions of intuition and sensation with organization and planning subordinated to the thinking function in administration and economics. To coordinate and control the structural function of feeding, which is the essence of the insular matriarchal paradigm, the polarized patriarchal archetype became dominant in many cultures through social and economic measures organized through thinking and planning. In this sense, Joseph, in the dimension of economics, is an example of the productivity of the patriarchal hero of all times.

The change of paradigm brought about by patriarchal dominance, probably established after the shift in human culture from nomadic to settled, produced an extraordinary increase of human power over nature and of mental organization and social relationship. The symbol that best represents this increase of power and its consequence on behavior was the hero, duly recognized as a most meaningful archetype.

As Campbell illustrates in *The Hero with a Thousand Faces* (1949), the archetype of the hero coordinated by the patriarchal archetype is a cultural phenomenon subjacent to civilization. The mythology of the hero-with the hero's divine filiations, threatened birth and childhood, and miraculous life-represents this structuring function with immense capacity. Through the heroic patriarchal paradigm, anyone can feel like a prophet, a soldier of God, or a national leader and the heroic call will support the mission. The incorporation of the patriarchal pattern coordinating the hero archetype, when manifested in the religious dimension, activated the structuring functions of transcendent spirituality to such a degree that the ego empathizes with the Lord, feels to be his prophet, and speaks in his name. The hero frequently identifies and is possessed by the Lord to submit the other to the Lord's will or to obey the other and follow him blindly. From this state to fanaticism and suicidal or homicidal terrorism is merely a question of gradation in defensive expression.

Although most grandiose features of the patriarchal hero make an appearance in the history of civilization with many landmarks, the archetype of the hero or any other archetype is not exclusive to the coordinating action of the patriarchal archetype. The myth of Dionysus and the discovery of wine, for instance, is a beautiful example of the hero archetype participating in the symbolic elaboration of the creativity and fertility of the matriarchal archetype through play. In the dimension of the alterity archetype, we also find outstanding expressions of the hero archetype, as for instance in the myths of Christ, of Buddha, and of Exu. Last, we have also the representation of the hero archetype coordinated by the archetype of totality, illustrated by the myth of Lao-Tzu.

The Patriarchal Archetype and the Shadow

The creative force of the patriarchal archetype and its fantastic conquests during history are associated with the human suffering and matriarchal wounds that accompanied its implantation and formed the great shadow of civilization. The creativity-destructivity polarity of the patriarchal archetype presents an ethical drama so extraordinary that it requires intense conceptual effort to admit that it is subordinated to the central archetype.

To elaborate this ambiguity, Freud postulated the existence of a death instinct which attacks the life instinct, forming the Thanatos-Eros polarity. However, a dualist constitution that intellectually solves this huge polarization within the Self by separating two basic and antagonistic instincts is unacceptable from the biological and humanistic perspectives. How can we accept that a science dedicated to studying and describing the immense creativity of the psyche be used to postulate that its psychobiological essence is normally dissociated and intrinsically incompatible with unity, equating it psychodynamically with schizophrenia, the most serious of mental diseases? At the same time, how can we equate within a coherent whole an extreme polarity that includes in one polarized patriarchal position the heroic deeds of people who daily sacrifice themselves to save others and the invention and usage of the gas chambers?

Freud's dualist proposition divides the psyche and ignores the fact that the fixations and destructive defensive functions that form the shadow are not autonomous, expressing a primary death instinct, but are the result of the life force fixated and defensively subordinated to repression. In this manner, Freud overlooked the fact that his very recommendation of repression and sublimation of the perverse polymorph are at the root of fixation and shadow formation. When cattle men mow down thousands and thousands of square miles of gigantic trees in the Amazon forest to increase pastures, do we need a death instinct to explain such destruction of nature, or is it obvious that the life instinct has been fixated in the structuring function of greed and formed a very defensive and destructive shadow? Do we have to go any further than this obvious reality to see evil in defensive greed?

The theoretical way I choose to include creativity and destructivity that is both good and evil in human nature is the symbolic path of duality in unity which sees good as equivalent to full self-realization and evil as the result of fixations and defenses that form the shadow (see chapter 7).

The patriarchal archetype occupying the main structuring position in psychoanalysis is the archetype that forms more shadow during symbolic elaboration. This is so because the polarized position is normally hierarchical and establishes a great tension within polarities through perfectionism, puritanism, intolerance, and rigidity, which easily transform contention into defensive repression and shadow containing the disqualified pole.

The patriarchal defensive division between the poles ("the opposites") is equivalent to the dissociation of polarities and may lead to defensive projection, such as we find in the scapegoat complex, or to a defensive introjection giving rise to depressive symptoms.

The basic characteristics of organization and control of the patriarchal archetype are stimulated by the relation of totality with the central archetype and acquire a connotation of being at the service of wholeness. The relation to duty permeates the archetypal field and activates the impulsive tendency of the hero archetype for which the mission transcends pleasure, well-being, and life itself. The ego suffers in this position because it may feel superior or inferior but is always rigidly submitted to authority, power, and totality through perfectionism, intolerance, and an absolute lack of compassion. Because of this, submission and suffering inflicted to oneself and others are conceived as inherent to reality as expressed in lex talionis (the law of talion, an eye for an eye, or retributive justice). Freedom is seen as precious but this is illusory in the patriarchal paradigm because its missionary nature is permeated by an enslaving idealism of tasks. Without matriarchal spontaneity, there is no real freedom. However, the more the ego suffers, the more its mission is exalted, and it feels elected mainly if the price of victory is life itself. Therein lies the glory of Valhalla, of the heroes who die fighting, or of any suffering caused to others in the line of duty.

The sacrificial death of the patriarchal hero becomes the death of the ego and thus expresses its predisposition to repression, homicide, suicide, and war. This may explain in part why Freud finally adopted death as the ego instinct that culminates psychological development (Freud 1920).

The polarized patriarchal position, through the structuring functions of duty, honor, and victory establishes the notion that success in performance is the most important thing that can happen in life. Within the code of honor of the Japanese samurai, atonement for public shame and failure could only be accomplished through the suicidal ritual of seppuku. At the same time the heroic death through triumph in mission is proof of the grandiosity of God, of the central archetype, expressed in life. Inferiority is equivalent to failure and cannot have dignity and therefore should not exist. The imposition of the will at the service of power is the way to well-being of which authority and superiority are consequences. We thus understand why the persona and social status are the highest values for so many people and why chronic feelings of social inferiority created the terrorist ideology of the human bomb. In suicidal bombers, humiliation and the ransom of self-esteem walk hand in hand with the martyrdom coordinated by the hero archetype defensively expressed by the patriarchal archetype.

Within the patriarchal perspective, in a general way, there does not exist loose, happy, and pleasant work. All occupation is a call to fulfill an obligation:

> In the sweat of thy face shalt thou eat bread, till thou return unto the ground; for out of it wast thou taken: for dust thou art, and unto dust shalt thou return. (Gen. 3:19)

Failure during performance is always accompanied by guilt and punishment for which there is no forgiveness. Its atonement does not happen by understanding and compassion, but by its elimination through self-punishment and the search for perfection. The ideology of eugenics is one of its extreme defensive expressions (Avian 2007).

The gigantic shadow constructed in culture by the patriarchal archetype was formed, wounding in different ways the matriarchal archetype, which participates with it in the basic regency of the structuring archetypal quaternio of the Self. Everything is simplified if we, like Freud, postulate a death instinct to hurt and destroy. But when we instead adopt a dialectical and systemic reasoning, we then have to understand how the patriarchal archetype is deformed and how it functions pathologically, as we see in its many tragic dysfunctions throughout history. Each matriarchal wound spreads through suffering into all other dimensions. These wounds often are not even registered with any degree of suffering because they can occur amid great commemoration, arrogance, and pride of patriarchal success.

The compass and gunpowder were until recently equally praised by humanity. Coordinated by the polarized patriarchal position and the patriarchal hero, they came from China and were used to guide Europe's colonization of the planet, massacring its own and other cultures and raising war to devastating conditions. The internal combustion engine celebrated our victory over nature and increased the power of the ego in geometrical proportions in what came to be the industrial era. Our greatest scientific deed was nuclear fission, which gave the patriarchal archetype the power to destroy our species. What will happen if it is once more turned against humanity by the patriarchal hero fills us with terror. Never before have light and shadow, good and evil come so close to the possibility of an apocalyptical confrontation.

The legendary and tragic testimony of Chief Seattle in response to U.S. President Franklin Pierce in 1855 in over the proposition to acquire the territory of the Duwamish tribe provides an example of archetypal comparative anthropology. Although no original document or transcription exists, the version that was published is nonetheless full of wisdom and possibly expresses the ideology of a culture steeped in the insular matriarchal magic-mythic position criticizing Western culture with its "progressive" industrialized paradigm and exposing the shadow of its patriarchal dominance with great clarity. It is, in a way, an answer to the arrogance of normal and defensive patriarchal dominance, which considered tribal cultures primitive:

> The Great White Chief in Washington sends word that he wishes to buy our land. He also sends words of friendship and goodwill. This is kind of him since we know he has little need of our friendship in return. But we will consider your offer. The Great White Chief can count on what I say as truly as our white brothers can count on the turning of the seasons. My words are like stars: they do not set.
>
> How can you buy or sell the sky or the warmth of the land? The idea is strange to us. We do not own the freshness of the air or the sparkle of the water, so how can you buy them from us? We will decide in our time, but every part of the Earth is sacred to my people. Every shining pine needle, every sandy shore, every mist in the dark woods, every glade and humming insect is holy in the memory and experience of my people.
>
> We know that the white man doesn't understand our ways. One portion of the land is the same to him as the next, for he is a stranger who comes in the night and takes from the Earth whatever he wants. The Earth is not his brother but his enemy, and when he conquers it he moves on. He leaves his fathers' graves behind and doesn't care. He kidnaps the Earth from his children. His father's graves and children's birthrights are forgotten.
>
> His appetite will devour the Earth and leave behind a wasteland. The sight of your cities pains the eye of the red man. But perhaps this is because the red man is a "savage" and doesn't understand.
>
> There is no quiet place in the white man's cities. No place to hear the leaves of spring or the rustle of insects' wings. The clatter insults the ears. But perhaps I am only a "savage" and don't understand. And what is there to life if a man cannot hear the lovely cry of the whippoorwill or the argument of the frogs around a pond at night?

The Indian prefers the soft sound of the wind darting over the face of the pond, and the wind itself cleansed by the midday rain or scented with pinion. The air is precious to the red man for all things share the same breath: the beasts, the trees, and the man. The white man doesn't seem to notice the air he breathes. Like a man dying for days, he is numb to his own stench.

If I accept, I will make one condition: the white man must treat the beasts of this land as his brothers. I am just a "savage" and don't understand any other way. I have seen a thousand rotting buffaloes on the prairie, left by the white man who shot them from a passing train. I am a "savage" and do not understand how the smoking iron horse can be more important than the buffalo whom we kill only to live. What is man without the beasts? If all the beasts were gone then men would die from a terrible loneliness of the spirit. For whatever happens to the beasts also happens to the man. All things are connected. Whatever befalls the Earth befalls the sons of the Earth.

Our children have seen our fathers humbled in defeat. Our warriors have felt shame. After defeat they turn their days in idleness and contaminate their bodies with sweet food and strong drink. It matters little where we pass the rest of our days; they are not many. A few more hours, a few more winters, and none of the children of the great tribes that once lived on the Earth, or that roamed in small bands in the woods, will be left to mourn the graves of a people once as powerful and hopeful as yours. One thing we know that the white man may one day discover: our God and your God are the same. You may think now that you own Him as you wish to own our land, but you cannot. He is the God of man and his compassion is equal for the red man and the white.

The Earth is precious to him, and to harm the Earth is to pour contempt on its creator. The whites too shall pass, perhaps sooner than other tribes. Continue to contaminate your own bed and you will one night suffocate in your own waste.

When the buffalos are all slaughtered, the wild horses all tamed, the secret corners of the forest heavy with the scent of many men, and the view of the ripe hills blotted by telegraph wires. Where is the thicket? Gone. Where is the eagle? Gone. And what is it to say goodbye to the swift and the hunt, the end of living and the beginning of survival.

We might understand if we knew what it was that the white man dreams, what hopes he describes to his children on long winter nights, what visions he burns into their minds so that they will wish for tomorrow. But we are "savages." The white man's dreams are hidden from us. And because they are hidden we will go our own way.

If we agree, it will be to secure the reservation you've promised. There, perhaps we may live out our brief days as we wish. When the last red man has vanished from the Earth, and our memory is just the shadow of a cloud passing across the prairie, these shores and forests will still hold the spirits of my people, for they love the Earth the way a newborn loves its mother's heartbeat.

If we sell you our land, love it as we've loved it. Care for it as we've cared for it. Hold in your mind the memory of the land, as it is when you take it. And with all your strength and all your might and with all your heart preserve it for your children, and love it as God loves us all. One thing we know: our God is the same as yours. The Earth is precious to him. Even the white man cannot be exempt from our common destiny.

The Patriarchal Archetype, the Central Archetype and Spirituality

The relation of the central archetype, the four regent archetypes, and the ego-other polarity brings about the articulation between the coordinating capacity of these archetypes, the formation of identity, and the operation of consciousness.

We cannot evaluate only the organizing capacity of the patriarchal archetype through its strategy of control, planning, articulation, and administration that propitiated the extraordinary degree of civilization together with so much tragic suffering. It is also necessary to follow its roots into the central archetype to understand fully the profundity of its nature.

"I am who I am" was the first great revelation of the god Yahweh to Moses (Exod. 3:14). Patriarchal abstraction endows the ego with an overall experience so extensive that consciousness relates to totality as the very being. This is the maximum possible detachment from sensuality. It goes beyond all entities and material forces and reunites everything in an ontological experience -"I am who I am."

The first and foremost heroic mission of Moses is to amplify his consciousness to realize its encounter with the universal being.

Height and solitude symbolically represent detachment from symbiotic and intimate involvement with sensuality. Because of this, the search for ascension of the spirit is represented by the most varied rituals aimed at moving away from desire, such as abstinence from eating meat and many other types of food, from owning property, from sleeping, sexuality, or human presence. Think of the vows of chastity, poverty, and obedience made by Catholic priests and the mendicant monks of India, completely deprived, walking along with their rice gourd, surviving at the mercy of public charity.

In the humanization voyage of the cosmos, the patriarchal archetype coordinates the elaboration of symbols, complexes, functions, and systems in a way that fosters the interaction of consciousness with the central archetype to a most extraordinary degree of abstraction. Spiritual ascension takes us to the experience of the heavenly kingdom and from there to a vision of the universe. The mountain heights are sublime because they are near the clouds and have a sight of endless extension. Telescopes such as Hubble, when seen symbolically, express a grandiose meaning. From a point in cosmic space the intelligence of the spirit is directed to infinity and eternity.

However, as immensely great as the spiritual ecstasy of the polarized patriarchal consciousness can be, it cannot have a relationship of compassion with life and the universe. The Brahmans who meditated in the forests of India and became hermits transcended the patriarchal dynamics to live in the contemplative position of the totality archetype (see chapter 12). The abstraction of the polarized patriarchal position allows mystics to receive their revelation in solitude but exhorts them to return to the world and live in it. So did Moses, who returned from Mount Sinai with the tablets of the law and a heroic mission to lead his people to the Promised Land.

The greatness of the creativity, of detachment and of the productive results of the patriarchal archetype, as we have seen, are proportional to its terrible capacity to generate a great part of planetary shadow that threatens to destroy our life on earth. Our survival depends upon the activation of another archetype capable of relating this extraordinary productivity of the patriarchal archetype to the fertility of the matriarchal archetype accumulated during civilization. This is the archetype of alterity.

Chapter 11

THE ARCHETYPE OF ALTERITY

Follow the middle path loving thy neighbor as thyself.

That which is below is like that which is above. And that which is above is equal to that which is below to realize the miracles of only one thing. (Hermes Trismesgistus, Emerald Tablet, second century)

Within the five archetypal positions of consciousness, the dialectical position of the archetype of alterity is the main contribution of Jungian symbolic psychology (Byington 1992b). If the essence of Jung's thought is the archetypal search for totality within the meaningful interaction of all polarities, including good and evil, that is, consciousness and shadow, the archetype of alterity is a pattern that reveals the Ariadne's thread in his work.

The Historical Conception of the Alterity Archetype

Due to the importance of the concept of the archetype of alterity in Jungian symbolic psychology, I shall briefly describe how the concept arose. It was in writing my graduation thesis for the C. G. Jung Institute of Zurich that I first felt the pattern of relationship of polarities in alterity to be an archetype.

The first step in the phenomenology of "otherness" is to notice the other, and then to realize somehow its role or importance enough to give it the right to manifest itself; having recognized the necessity of the other, the next step is then to see that it is intimately related to the one. From this will finally

follow that the one and the other form a whole together, and
in fact, do not exist without each other. (Byington 1965, p. 11)

I titled my thesis *Genuineness as Duality in Unity* and included in it the
relationship of many polarities and their meaning in unity. The two main
polarities explicated in the thesis were the complementary relationship between
Freud and Jung and the interaction between the individual and the collective,
which later became the polarity of individuation (Jung) and humanization
(Teilhard de Chardin).

Freudian psychology tends to overvalue the determining role of the
ego, and it is well known how Freudian analysis can imprison a creative
personality by interpreting unconscious material reductively as belonging to
ego formation in childhood. Jungian analysis tends to overvalue the opposite
pole. Cases are known of neurosis being treated exclusively with excellent
interpretation of archetypal motifs, while defense mechanisms and defensive
parental identifications formed in childhood, which sabotage creativity and
personality development, are not elaborated.

The great influence in my conception of the alterity archetype was
Jung's theory of polarities, which I always felt followed Heraclitus's and Hegel's
logic, where thesis relates to antithesis to become synthesis.

For the first issue of *Junguiana*, the journal of the Brazilian Society for
Analytical Psychology, I wrote an article entitled "A Symbolic Theory of
History: The Christian Myth as the Main Structuring Symbol of the Alterity
Pattern in Western Culture" (1983). In this article, I described the historical
amplification of the concept of alterity in the mythological dimension with
the Christian myth, an idea I later expanded by describing alterity as an
archetypal pattern of consciousness in the individual and cultural Selves
(1992b). I initially referred to alterity also as a post-patriarchal pattern of
psychotherapy (1986).

The archetype of alterity can be amplified by the knowledge that it
coordinates the relationship of the ego and the other (and of all polarities)
through the dialectical position in which each opposite can express itself with
all its symbolic potential. This dialectical relationship varies in a spectrum
from radical opposition to equality and is therefore capable of representing
all the meanings symbols can have, even their most profound and complex.

Because Jung described the anima and animus as the leading archetypes
of symbolic elaboration relating conscious and unconscious polarities, the
alterity archetype encompasses them in its phenomenology. In this way, the
alterity archetype is capable of apprehending the mystery of the opposition as

well of the equality of opposites and of coordinating the dialectical interaction of the basic archetypal polarity of the psyche formed by the matriarchal and patriarchal archetypes, within the individual and collective Selves. The archetype of alterity coordinates symbolic elaboration dialectically and systemically always as a function of totality. In this manner, it relates consciousness and shadow within the psychopathology of the processes of individuation and humanization, searching to rescue fixated symbols and reintegrate them in individual and collective consciousness. This capacity to rescue symbols fixated in the shadow endows this archetype with the potential to reintegrate the divided Self, which in psychotherapy means finding the normal meaning of symbols fixated in the shadow and reintegrating them with their normal structuring functions. In the religious dimension it is identified with the confession of sin, repentance, and the messianic structuring function of salvation.

The Three Principles of Relationship

The archetype of alterity includes the syzygy described by Jung as an expression of the conjunction archetype (Jung 1951). The archetype of alterity, as well as the archetype of totality (see chapter 12), allows consciousness to understand the principle of synchronicity defined as acausal by Jung (1952). Interrelating dialectically the matriarchal and patriarchal archetypes, the archetype of alterity includes the insular matriarchal position within the principle of magic causality and the polarized patriarchal position within the principle of reflexive causality. In this manner we see that there are three basic principles through which we interact with the world: the causal magic, the causal reflexive, and the acausal, or synchronicity, which is coordinated by the archetype of alterity (diagram 12).

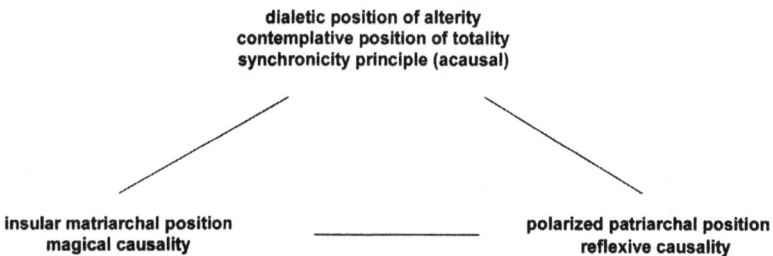

**dialetic position of alterity
contemplative position of totality
synchronicity principle (acausal)**

**insular matriarchal position
magical causality**   **polarized patriarchal position
reflexive causality**

Diagram 12

The magical causal relationship is subordinated dominantly to the omnipotent experience of control of reality through the imagination, greatly inspired by the subjective emotional dimension, mostly desire (insular matriarchal position). Causal reflexive and probability relationships occur between ego-other and other-other polarities after they have undergone detachment from the insular position and begun functioning with the strict separation of subject and nature, according to Descartes's recommendation within the polarized patriarchal position. In the third situation, the acausal encounter of the ego with the other, and of the other with others, produces meanings without any specific causality, which makes the synchronicity experience unique, that is, impossible to stereotype or repeat. Encompassing the insular matriarchal and the polarized patriarchal positions, the dialectical position of alterity and the principle of synchronicity include countless causal connections in such a way that not a single one can be selected as the cause, and this rends the whole system acausal.

Wu wei (from Taoism, doing without doing) is a way for consciousness to open up to understanding synchronicity; it admits the intention of the ego in the insular matriarchal and polarized patriarchal positions but detaches from them. Therefore it does ... without doing. Acting in the world without desire and without thinking that one knows and controls events, *wu wei* is a way for the mind to function within the mystery of synchronicity and thus to become conscious of life's reality in the way of Zen and Tao.

Alterity and Immunity

Medical thinking about the relation of health and disease, within the dialectical relationship of alterity, slowly developed the notion of immunity through the interaction of antigens and antibodies, which gave rise to vaccination. The transition from the polarized patriarchal position to the dialectical alterity position was very difficult because in the polarized position health is radically opposed to disease, and so it was logically impossible to think that a disease could produce health. For this to happen, we had first to admit that disease and health were in some way equal.

This is a good example of the mysterious secret of the equality of opposites, a concept transmitted in alchemy since antiquity, and the observation that only the dialectical position of alterity can formulate in a comprehensible, logical, and rational way. We see here clearly that the five ego-other positions of consciousness are forms of intelligence, although logically very different from one another. In this manner, the dialectic position of alterity can explain vaccination, which is an incomprehensible paradox in the polarized patriarchal position.

Smallpox was the most feared and deadly of all the diseases, worse than yellow fever, cholera, and even bubonic plague, which were referred to as "God's wrath" in the Middle Ages. The preventive treatment of inoculating individuals with the secretion of smallpox lesions had been practiced in India since the eighth century and in China since the tenth century. We see how vaccination as an example of alterity was already in the medicine of ancient cultures before it was activated in Europe in the eighteenth century.

In an instance of synchronicity, some English farmers, who like everyone else were terrified of smallpox, observed that some of their cows had lesions that resembled smallpox, and that the maids who milked these cows also had them on their hands. Strangely, these maids did not catch smallpox. We know today that the cowpox virus is less virulent than the smallpox virus, and it can immunize humans against smallpox. The fear of the disease was such that some of the farmers, through reflexive causality thinking, began to vaccinate themselves and their families by scratching their skin and rubbing it with the secretion from the cows' blisters. Benjamin Jesty was one of such farmers who, in 1774, vaccinated himself, his wife, and his two daughters in this manner. Twenty-two years later, the surgeon Edward Jenner used James Phipps, the eight-year-old son of his gardener, as a guinea pig. He first scratched the boy's arm and applied the secretion from the hands of Sarah Nelmes, who had been infected with cowpox milking the cow Blossom. Afterward, Jenner infected Phipps with smallpox and saw that the boy had been immunized. This is a historic example of the psychopathic shadow of the alterity archetype, because Jenner used a child to experiment with a deadly virus. Mr. Phipps, James father, supposedly had not known nor had he agreed beforehand to allow the experiment and the risk of his son's life. Had things gone wrong and Phipps become seriously ill or even died, we quite possibly would have never heard of him or of Edward Jenner for that matter. As the experiment was highly successful, all involved became famous: Edward Jenner, Sarah Nelmes, James Phipps, and even the cow Blossom. Once Jenner realized that Phipps had been immunized, he performed the experiment with twenty-three more subjects, described them in a paper to the Royal Society, and was recognized as the inventor of the vaccine against smallpox. Thanks to him, smallpox is under control worldwide.

This fantastic event, which marked the introduction of vaccination into Western medicine and has been saving millions of lives ever since. Besides being a psychopathic acting out of the shadow, it also calls our attention to one very specialized condition within which the opposites are equal in the dialectical position of alterity. The equality of opposites is such a treasure and a mystery cultivated since antiquity because it occurs only in the most extraordinary conditions, which must be searched for with the greatest creativity, intelligence, care, and attention. This is probably the reason why the Emerald Tablet was a hermetic teaching.

Today we know that if we were simply to adopt a general attitude of considering the opposites equal and vaccinate other diseases with live virus, millions of people would die as a result. Microbes cause diseases and are generally opposed to health. Therefore, in most cases, the polarized patriarchal position is valid. The dialectical position is correct in very special cases and even then in nearly unique conditions. Many vaccines are made with the virus alive, others are made with attenuated forms of the virus, and still others are made with dead virus. Just like love, democracy, and freedom, alterity in immunology only works under very special circumstances. Rigorous laboratory requirements demonstrate the importance of the polarized patriarchal position as a base from which to exercise alterity. In the same way, the very rich and exuberant behavior of live organisms shows that the insular matriarchal position is indispensable for the dialectical position of alterity.

Alterity is the most complex and difficult dialectical position for consciousness precisely because it has no limits to its production in symbolic elaboration. The limit for the meaning of a symbol is infinity because all symbols are archetypal and, in last analysis, they express the central archetype, the totality of being in the universe. In this sense, the dialectical position of alterity, within the structuring archetypal quaternio, suffers competition from the matriarchal and patriarchal archetypes, which are much simpler and require less energy to coordinate symbolic elaboration. This competition is due to a polarity of the central archetype: speed versus quality. On one hand the central archetype favors the production of meanings that are relatively simpler but have immediate usage (symbolic elaboration by the matriarchal and patriarchal archetypes), and on the other hand meanings that are more refined, complex, and profound need more time and more work to be produced (symbolic elaboration by the alterity archetype).

Frequently, results obtained with great dedication, time, courage, intelligence, patience, sacrifice, and sensibility within the dialectical position of alterity are reduced to the patriarchal or the matriarchal (either normally or defensively) to save time and energy. However, this process often is not carried out by the same individual or by the same generation. This is found in the case of very intelligent and creative persons who make discoveries or have new insights coordinated by the dialectical alterity position whose followers use these discoveries or insights in matriarchal or patriarchal patterns in ways that can be normal or defensive.

Modern technology presents many examples of this process. Modern devices, such as cars, refrigerators, televisions, or computers, are created as the result of discoveries within the scientific dialectical position of alterity. But they are multiplied within the patriarchal pattern on a production line for use by countless consumers, most of whom will use them simply for pleasure (according to the insular matriarchal position) or for duty (according to the polarized patriarchal position) without the least idea of how they work. This situation can be quite normal, but it way also turn defensive.

Let us imagine an antibiotic discovered within the dialectical position of alterity and produced in great quantities within the patriarchal position. It should be prescribed by physicians operating within the dialectical position after the pathological type of bacteria has been identified and its reactions to specific antibiotics have been tested in antibiograms. To take or to prescribe antibiotics for a common cold, for instance, has become a habit in many Western cultures, even though we know that common colds are caused by viruses which do not respond to antibiotics. As a result, bacteria present in the body may mutate and develop resistance to antibiotics.

This medical example of patriarchalization of alterity-the irresponsible usage of antibiotics - is quite defensive and is becoming a dangerous shadow. It has significantly increased bacterial resistance to antibiotics, rendering a few types of bacteria totally resistant and sometimes deadly. The situation has worsened in many countries to the point where several of the finest hospitals have these resistant bacteria. This is very impressive, and although the risk of infection is difficult to estimate, many doctors are now limiting their patients' hospital stays for fear of contamination by resistant bacteria, today called super bacteria.

Because we are dealing with archetypes, the matriarchalization and patriarchalization of alterity can manifest itself in many existential dimensions. In medicine, for instance, plastic surgery is a practice in which the matriarchalization of alterity may become quite defensive. People who are defensively vain and who resist any signs of old age may search their appearance, may deform them grotesquely, sometimes with tragic consequences.

Alterity and Paradox in Christianity

The logic of the polarized patriarchal position can give rise to paradox. Frequently the dialectical logic of alterity can solve these paradoxes and unravel important meanings for the development of individual and collective consciousness. This is so because the logic of alterity employs opposites not only in opposition but also in equality, which makes sense in the alterity position but not in patriarchal discourse.

Entering a Christian house of worship, for example, it is common to see the letters α (alpha) and ω (omega), which represent the beginning and the end, under the figure of Christ (Christ Pantocrator). Many may read this inscription patriarchally and interpret its meaning as Christ being everything. Others, however, may see in the inscription a reference to the paradox that Christ is the smallest and the greatest, an idea that requires the alterity position to understand it.

The logic of alterity is more encompassing than that of the patriarchal position because it frequently uses reason side by side with emotion and relates polarities in a spectrum that varies all the way from opposition to equality. This frequently turns the alterity position into an initiatory procedure because it needs experience to understand its deeper content. Recall the Gnostics who practiced initiatory knowledge to understand the passion of Christ (Hoeller 1982). Following this logic, we have to empathize with the life and the teachings of Jesus and experience with mind and heart that which he tried to transmit with his kindness, suffering, and sacrifice. In order to do it, we can be helped by the concept of non action from Buddhism and of *wu wei* from Taoism to become aware of Jesus' disposition toward offering his emotion and his will. We are very near to understanding alpha here and will be able to do it when we feel Jesus' humbleness, which from the perspective of power transforms him in the weakest and most vulnerable of all creatures.

But what of omega? Continuing our initiatory experience, we become aware of the degree of sacrifice and extraordinary courage that made him surrender to the Father's will and carry the cross amid humiliation and torture toward his own crucifixion, which makes him the greatest. The message of alterity in which paradoxically the smallest is equal to the greatest reveals itself to us joining alpha and omega as we understand the meaning of Jesus' passion transformed in the myth of Christ.

Continuing this gnosis, we experience the miraculous encounter of Mary Magdalene, which Christ, announcing the Resurrection, confirmed symbolically and prospectively by the historical influence of the myth through the millennia. We can now see the Messiah crucified and revered between alpha and omega. The logic of paradox is clearly revealed through the identity of opposites within the dialectic position of the alterity archetype.

Alterity and the Paradox of Good and Evil

The theory of polarities encompasses all symbols, complexes, functions, systems, and archetypes. This is relatively easy to admit with polarities in a general way, but when it comes to the polarity of good and evil, the question is much more difficult. How can we understand that at the same time we situate good and evil within the central archetype, we know that the structuring function of ethics normally structures conscience and good and that the Self is deformed by the formation of shadow and evil?

As we saw with the alpha and omega in association with the figure of Christ in many churches, the paradox of good and evil coordinated by the central archetype can also be understood by the dialectical position of the alterity archetype.

We know that the shadow formed by the fixation of symbolic elaboration is expressed in individuation and humanization. We know also from this perspective that the central archetype coordinates all the processes of symbolic elaboration, forming consciousness through normal structuring functions and forming the shadow through these same functions when they become fixed and defensive. Beyond this, we realize that the central archetype expresses the shadow and evil through repetitive compulsion of defenses because it cannot do without the symbols they contain. This dissociation (Laing 1960) brings suffering to the Self, which activates the central archetype to bring the ego and consciousness to help. This is the paradox of the central archetype. Following the dialectical pattern of alterity, the ego and conscience act on their own behalf, because somehow they know that in rescuing fixations from the shadow, that is, from evil, they are searching and integrating something that belongs to them.

In this way, we understand the paradox in which evil is also good. It admits fixations and evil but also the creativity needed to rescue their contents through symbolic elaboration. In this manner, the central archetype propitiates the rescue of symbols from evil and the realization of good. We then have to admit that the processes of individuation and humanization show a messianic aspect of the central archetype. When it cannot avoid fixation, it expresses evil but at the same time propitiates the effort to ransom fixated symbols because they are indispensable for the developmental process.

Alterity and Ecology

When we understand von Bertalanffy's conception (1969) of a feedback mechanism in biological systems (multiple biofeedback system) within the patterns of relationship of consciousness, we see that this interdependence of mechanisms and also of species, which can be friends as well as enemies, can be understood within the dialectical position of alterity. When the ego realizes how much it depends on the other, it can better respect it and try to improve their relationship. In this way we become aware of many defensive and destructive consequences in human relations within the ecosystem caused by the unilaterality and omnipotence of the matriarchal and patriarchal positions.

Visiting the Moholoholo Wildlife Rehabilitation Centre in South Africa, I saw some hyenas now considered a species threatened with extinction. I received the following explanation by a zoologist specializing in ecology. A few decades ago it was observed that a type of vulture, the biggest bird in South Africa, was diminishing so quickly that it was suspected to be threatened with extinction. These birds are very useful because they are the only ones that can pierce the thick hides of big animals such as hippos, elephants, and rhinos with their strong curved beaks. Without them to act as butchers of nature, dead animals rot and can cause diseases that infect other species.

Ecologists began mountain climbing expeditions to examine the vultures' nests in the mountain peaks and found young vultures suffering from rickets, surrounded by all sorts of pieces of plastic bottles. They imagined (using reflective causality) that they lacked calcium in their diet and that the parents were trying to make up for it in this clumsy way. Research was begun to examine the vultures' food cycle and the dysfunction was discovered.

Cattlemen had become worried about the number of cattle killed by hyenas and had begun to hunt them down. The hyenas' numbers diminished drastically, and they practically disappeared. When an animal dies in the wild, the vultures, after opening the hides, share the food with the hyenas, whose potent jaws are strong enough to grind the large bones as they participate in eating the viscera. Small pieces of bone are carried by the vultures to their nests to supply the calcium needed by their young. Once this flaw in the food cycle was discovered, the farmers compensated for the lack of hyenas by grinding bones of cattle and leaving them beside the corpses of big animals, thus partially solving the problem.

This small example shows how the interaction of species can be severely affected by lack of knowledge of the reality of the other within systemic thinking, that is, without considering the dialectical relationship of the part among them within the whole.

At this same wildlife rehabilitation center we can also see how our matriarchal intervention in nature with all good intentions can also negatively affect the biological system. Many people gather young abandoned animals to rear without knowing how negatively this can affect the animals (see the film *Born Free*, 1966). Living with humans and being fed by them, the animals lose not only fear of us but also the capacity to live and hunt in their own habitats, being thus condemned for life to either artificial protection or a zoo.

The patriarchal intervention in agriculture, as for instance with the use of pesticides, also has to be understood within the life chain of nature in order to avoid becoming destructive by interrupting the interdependency of species within the ecological dimension.

Alterity and Sustainable Economy

The artificial matriarchal and patriarchal interference with nature has produced dysfunctions that threaten our survival more and more. This is a convincing example of the structuring capacity of these archetypes. The pollution and destruction of the environment and the limits of natural reserves such as minerals, forests, biofuels, and even water have launched a massive activation of the dialectical position of alterity in the planetary Self in order to understand better and to confront and elaborate this shadow of civilization.

The progress of the conscience of alterity together with economic globalization and the geometric growth of communications have stimulated the perception of our shadow as never before. The destructivity of wars has never brought consciousness of the patriarchal shadow to the same degree as ecological devastation, because after wars are over, the dead are gone and the victors celebrate their glory with their spoils. In nature, however, the dead remain on the battlefield, exposing devastation and pollution, which forces us to face the destructive consequences of the shadow.

The ethical perception of our ecological shadow grows greater every day. The reactionary strategies of the economic and political forces interested in the maintenance of this shadow are being increasingly identified, mapped, and exposed. This confrontation with the shadow is being presented to the new generation as a question of survival, and the current tendency of education is to increase significantly the number of people who become conscious of what the issue really is and engage themselves in the confrontation of this shadow (*Worldwatch Institute* 2010). In this manner, the activation of the structuring function of supraconsciousness, which concentrates attention on the relationship of conscience and shadow, is increasing, transforming the problem of our survival into an ethical question.

It is within this epic confrontation between good and evil, conscience and shadow propitiated by the dialectical position of alterity that thesis and antithesis have produced a synthesis whose ideology is a mixture of the one side, backing up capitalism and market economy, with the other side, promoting government control, social welfare, and ecology.

It is within this epic confrontation between good and evil, propitiated by the modern rise of the survival theme based on the dialectical position of the alterity archetype, that the thesis of continuing to plunder and devastate nature for the sake of consumerism and the antithesis of controlling the economy has given rise to the concept of a sustainable economy (*Worldwatch Institute* 2010).

Within sustainable economy, one of the innovations brought by the conscience of alterity is the responsibility of every industry to handle the waste it produces. This pattern of relationship of the ego taking care of the shadow regards the whole ecological dimension and calls forth the individual, the family, and society to become responsible for the waste produced. In this manner, we establish a dialectical relationship between consumerism and waste, which begins within each home and culminates in the diminution of pollution at all levels of production as well as in the recycling of the maximum amount of waste. Indeed, one of the great aims of sustainable economy is the inclusion of waste and the prevention of pollution not only in the cost of production but also in the technology of production. The difficulty of implementing sustainable economy lies in the fact that the implantation of the alterity archetype is a true change of paradigm in the relationship between industrial production, nature, and society.

I can think of nothing more illustrative of the differences of the matriarchal, patriarchal, and alterity patterns of intelligence than the manner in which waste is disposed of. In the matriarchal pattern we simply consume what we want and throw away the remains anywhere. This pattern is so spontaneous and so subordinated to immediate convenience that we have ruined many of our environments with trash. In the patriarchal pattern we select places where we transport and dispose of trash. This mentality is so generalized that it has included burying atomic waste in the deserts or throwing it into the oceans. These two patterns of consciousness are characterized by unilateral omnipotent attitudes that privilege either the subject (narcissism) or the other (echoism). The polarity in question is consumerism-trash in which consumerism is privileged and trash is disqualified and ignored, frequently forming the shadow. In the patriarchal pattern trash becomes the scapegoat to be sent somewhere far away. "Sweeping the dirt under the carpet" illustrates this attitude. In such disqualified position, it is common that the inferior pole becomes fixed and defensive and forms part of the shadow. In this case, trash causes the pollution that poisons the cultural Self and sickens our way of living, just as Chief Seattle described (see chapter 10). One terrifying example of this dysfunction among many others is the poisoning of underground water reserves (aquifers) by lead residues leaching out of obsolete gasoline tanks that were thrown away and simply buried.

The Archetype of Alterity in Education

The search for the dialectical position of alterity among people at all social levels characteristic of democracy should not exclude the theory and methods of education. I have explained these in *Education from the Heart: A Jungian Symbolic Perspective*"(2004).

Here, the search for alterity tries to transform the traditional patriarchal paradigm of teaching, wherein the subject-object dissociation is maintained and reinforced in the body of students paralyzed in the classroom, the transference relationship between the teacher and the student is ignored, evaluation is almost exclusively carried out by tests, discipline is dealt with primarily by sermons and punishment, rational objective teaching is privileged, emotional expressive techniques are considered superfluous, and teachers are identified with knowledge and students with ignorance.

In order to attain full alterity, the diffusion of alterity in teaching, stressed by the Swiss pedagogue Jean Piaget in his theory and method of constructivism, must also include the emotional dimension and become symbolic constructivism. This method makes us aware of the enormous creativity of the teacher-pupil relationship and of the pedagogic transference, which are more or less wasted in the patriarchal repetitive method (see the film *Dead Poets Society* [1989]). Within alterity we can resume the ludic, spontaneous, sensual, and pleasant characteristics of the insular matriarchal position through expressive techniques and teach them together with the duties and teaching programs of the polarized patriarchal perspective. The dialectical relationship between teacher and student elaborated through the concepts of the normal and defensive transference can significantly identify the shadow in teaching and contribute to making it a lively process in which what is learned is difficult to forget.

Alterity in Marriage and Love

The dialectical position of the alterity archetype is quaternary, and this can be experienced in the case of love and marriage. The activation of the insular matriarchal archetype at home is necessary to care for so many things needed by the household and by children. The polarized patriarchal archetype in the active position is also intense due to all the responsibilities duties and tasks to be undertaken in a marriage (see chapter 5). Love in marriage frequently declines as a result of so much repetitive routine and so many obligations on the two sides of this situation.

Similar to interest in life, intelligence, and creativity, love is also a function that does not have limits to its development. When it diminishes, it is either because the potential for growth is not receiving the necessary investment in quantity and quality or because a fixation has occurred and it has turned defensive. Both possibilities make for frustration, disinterest, or grief, and this is the moment for the couple to sit down and elaborate the situation in a quaternary attitude that includes suffering, frustrations, and complaints. Each one must relate dialectically to the creative growth and shadow of the other. The results are never a simple matter and frequently mean a long journey of "accompanied solitude," which requires dedication, patience, faith, and hope of improvement.

Alterity in Sports and Games

Within the historical patriarchal dominance, rivalry and aggression among nations were experienced mainly in war. Sports, games, and tournaments within a culture were often very violent and risky, frequently ending in death. The ball game played by the Mayas is illustrative; the game ended with the sacrifice of the captain of the losing team.

The implantation of alterity in Western culture can be registered through many events among which we find sports and games. They include matriarchal pleasure within patriarchal rules which turn games into a dialectical interplay of archetypal polarities. The cultural transformation from the patriarchal to the alterity paradigm opened many opportunities for the symbolic expression of aggression, ethics, competition, ambition, courage, and notions of victory and defeat in which the ego-other polarity experiences these functions in a dialectical relation characteristic of alterity. In this way, sports came to perform a civilizing pedagogic function with association of ludic and sensuous performance in the matriarchal position with patriarchal codification of behavior without repression. This is an outstanding cultural acquisition for taming competition and aggression and transforming war in sporting contests.

In Latin America, Europe, Africa, and increasingly in Asiatic countries and North America, soccer (or association football) is a sport that has an extraordinary capacity to educate even illiterate persons in ethics. The fact that it is played with the head and the feet gives special emphasis to the body below the waist, a function occupied by dancing, generally by women, since time immemorial. The big difference is that soccer includes the functions of competition and aggression, which can be exercised mainly by men. Together with globalization, the growth of soccer and alterity implantation have been extraordinary (Byington 1982).

Soccer began in England, exactly why we do not know. One possibility is that it came from the harpastum in which Roman soldiers kicked around the decapitated head of their enemies. It is also interesting to make an association here with the fact that it was also in England that the first social-political European movement toward democracy began.

British soccer was, from the very beginning, revolutionary and contrary to the prevalent patriarchal dominance that trained armies for war. The matriarchal archetype in Scotland has traditionally been vibrant. In the Middle Ages, in the city of Midlothian, a very popular ball game took place between married and single women. With its distance from the cult of virility, class privilege, and authoritarianism, soccer had a great popular attraction and moved away from the war mentality. In 1227, for instance, a war between England and Scotland was avoided because the soldiers of Lancashire, traditional enemies of the Scots, disobeyed their commanders and chose to express their rivalry in a soccer game instead of on the battlefield. The legend goes that king Edward I was one of the players (Byington 1982).

This dialectical and antiwar attitude led to a reactionary patriarchal response by the monarchy and during the reigns of Edward III, Richard II, Henry IV, Henry VIII, and even Elizabeth I in the sixteenth century, many prohibitive edicts were decreed against soccer because it led young men to neglect the practice of archery and this weakened the army. The fact that soccer ransomed the repressed matriarchal archetype and related it dialectically with the patriarchal archetype made it irresistible. Unlike religious education, which was accomplished through puritanical sermons and threats of going to hell and which limited the revolutionary alterity of the Christian myth by defensive patriarchalization (see chapter 13), soccer, without catechism, implanted alterity in collective consciousness with great exuberance through competition, sensuality, play, and pleasure.

Looked at symbolically, the soccer field is a mandala that contains the dramatic dispute of eleven players on each side and the referee. All are focused on the ball, a sphere, which according to Plato is the most perfect of all forms, a symbol of totality and completeness. The highly energized mandala of the field is separated from another mandala around the stadium that contains the public, which participates in the game through rational and emotional massive identification, cheering and ethically evaluating and judging all the events of the game, agreeing or not with the decisions of the referee. The judgment of the referee by the general public is extraordinarily useful in the teaching of ethics. The elaboration of playing through reflexive causality imposes limits and rules that allow fans to cheer with the most varied repertoire of emotional reactions in favor of their team and against the adversary and sometimes also against the referee; all this emotion propitiates an intense magical causality that affects everyone present. Players respond with intensified vigor dialectically in biofeedback rhythm to this emotional energy of the public participating in the game. Finally there is a third mandala operated through television that connects the first mandala to a much larger public around the world. All of them drinking beer, eating popcorn, and . . . cheering. (Byington 1982).

The ethical structuring functions within the dialectical relation of alterity is coordinated by the referee through polarized patriarchal regulations and decisions, which include light fouls, serious fouls (yellow card), extreme fouls which are punished by expulsion (red card), off-sides, and the most feared punishment-the penalty. This is a true pedagogy of ethics because everyone inside and outside the field elaborates these regulations and agrees or disagrees with the referee. An important detail is that fans outside the field can yell anything they feel like at the referee, whereas the players can agree or disagree with his decisions but must do so in a respectful attitude and tone of voice and always obey the decision. In this manner players educate society to control and direct aggression creatively.

The dialectical tension of polarities is so intense in soccer because in every goal scored the symbiotic relationship between scoring player and fan, goalkeeper and fan, clashes in the dramatic experience of victory and defeat, life and death. After penetrating the enemy's lines, whose guardian, the goalkeeper, is the only privileged player to touch the ball with his hands, everyone experiences the ecstatic penetration and fecundation of the adversary through a goal that is the equivalent of his death. The game is interrupted. Victors cheer and many of the defeated cry. The ball returns to the center of the field. Life ends and prepares for rebirth. The teams rearrange. The referee whistles, and the game starts again, configuring a ritual of death and resurrection within alterity.

During the week, the press energizes the symbiosis of the insular matriarchal position by relating players and fans. As days go by, the ritual is heated by provocative commentaries from fans, players, and press specialists. During the game, radios and televisions describe the best kicks with metaphorical expressions to the audience's delight. Announcers become famous for the popular poetry they create. "Tim Donovan crosses the midfield like a hurricane and fires a cannon shot. Gooooal!!! Neymar dribbles the goalkeeper and shakes the bride's veil. Goooooal!!! Messi dribbles four defenders and shoots, crumbling down the enemy's citadel. Goooal!!!"

Showing exuberantly the dialectical and synchronistic complexity of the alterity archetype, soccer games present unpredictable incidents hard to imagine, which make it fascinating. Conscience sways between magic causality of fans and players enthusiastically dedicated to win, the reflexive causality of the coach's strategy which includes rehearsed plays, and the acausal synchronicity of the unfolding mystery, which reveals the truth of the final reality through sometimes unpredictable and miraculous goals in the last moments of the play.

Matriarchal and Patriarchal Dominance in Alterity

The dominance of one of the two basic archetypes in alterity does not mean a fixed hierarchical relationship, which would be incompatible with the dialectical position, but rather an archetypal leitmotif during symbolic elaboration. It is like a musical composition that can be played in the key of C, F, or G. This can be seen in the basic difference between art, religion, and science. All three of them can be dialectically very creative and profound, each following a different archetypal dominance.

Myth and art have an insular matriarchal substratum because they are basically sensual, imagery, fantastical, emotional, intuitive, and highly irrational. They can be experienced without having to demonstrate or prove anything. Myth and religion as structuring functions of consciousness seek a direct revelation of the central archetype as to the nature and purpose of life and the world basically through imagination and magical causality complemented by reflexive causality, which interrelates issues logically. This does not mean that myth and art, although with a matriarchal foundation, cannot present an intense patriarchal dominance in symbolic elaboration. In the myth of Marduk, in Assyrian-Babylonian mythology, and in Islamism and Judaism, for instance, we find a very intense polarized patriarchal influence which does not prevent them from having a magic-mythical substratum expressed by the insular matriarchal position.

When art is seen as a structuring function of consciousness, we understand it as the search to express the nature of life and the profundity of being through the aesthetic dimension. Because visual and hearing sensuality are the essence of this expression, the insular matriarchal archetype dominates its foundation. However, the codification of the arts frequently submits its symbolic elaboration to quite intense patriarchal coordination, which often becomes traditional.

Science presents in its very essence the matriarchal archetype during observation but also the patriarchal archetype for detachment, organization, abstraction, and general rationalization. Although the dominance of the coordination of symbolic elaboration is carried out basically by the alterity archetype during the creative period, afterward, during the post-creative period (that is, during the practical use of the discoveries made), frequently the matriarchal or patriarchal archetypes take over.

Alterity and the Trickster Myth

As Paul Radin asserts in his book *The Trickster* (1956), very few myths have such an ancient and extensive distribution. The trickster is found among the myths of ancient Greeks, Chinese, Japanese, in the Semitic world, and in Indian culture and survives today in the image of the court fool and the clown.

Commenting on this symbol, Karl Kerényi (in Radin 1956) calls attention to the dumb-cunning polarity and illustrates it with the complementarity between Prometheus (who reflects before acting) and Epimetheus (who acts and then reflects). Prometheus deceives Zeus and steals fire, giving it to humanity, and is punished with imprisonment in the Caucasus. Epimetheus marries Pandora, who brings calamities with her to the world. Amidst creativity, good and evil, shrewdness and dumbness are in such a way intermingled that Kerényi asserts that "in mythology we hear the world telling its history" (in Radin 1956, p. 175). He adds that the theme of the divine deceiver is inherent to mythology, illustrated vividly by Hermes in ancient Greece.

Also in Radin's book, Jung writes a symbolic commentary on the trickster figure and amplifies it with the carnival feast in the Middle Ages together with the figure of the devil as God's monkey (símia dei) and the feast of the fools. Going further, he associates the trickster with figures of fairy tales such as *Stupid Hans* and *Tom Thumb*, ending with the mercurial spirit of alchemy which he studied in detail (Jung 1948a). Jung, Radin, and Kerényi were aware of the messianic characteristics of the trickster.

From the perspective of the archetypal positions of consciousness, we can say that the trickster myth is coordinated primarily by the insular matriarchal position mainly through the functions of desire and deceit. Expressing creativity without limits, his only motivation is self-satisfaction. In this way obstacles along the way must be surpassed through cunning, without measuring consequences for himself and others, including death. His pleasure is feasted triumphantly with a laugh of lustful satisfaction, which may include debauchery.

In his book *The Trickster*, Radin tells a myth of the Native American Tlingit:

> Raven was the son of a man named Kit-kaositiyi-qa, who gave him strength to make the world. After he had made it he obtained the stars, moon and daylight from their keeper at the head of Nass by letting himself be swallowed by the keeper's daughter and be born of her. He obtained fresh water by tricking its owner, Petrel. As he was flying out through the smoke hole, however, Petrel made his smoke-hole spirits catch him and lighted a fire under him, turning him from white to black. Raven scattered the fresh water out of his mouth to make rivers and streams. Because some people who were fishing for eulachon would not take him across a river, he let the sun forth, and they fled into the woods or ocean, becoming such animals as the skins they wore had belonged to. Next Raven

stole fat from some boys who were throwing it back and forth. He found a piece of jade bearing some design, stuck it into the ground, and pretended to a spring salmon that the object was calling it names. The salmon came ashore and Raven killed it. Then he got the birds to procure him skunk cabbage so that they might eat the fish, but instead of feeding them, he sent them away a second time and ate it himself, burying the bones in the ashes. After that the birds dressed and painted themselves up.

Raven came to the bear, and the latter fed him on some of his own flesh, a proceeding which Raven tried to imitate in vain a little later. Then Raven went out fishing with Bear and Cormorant, killed the former by cutting off a piece of flesh, and pulled out Cormorant's tongue so that he could not tell anybody. Afterward he killed Bear's wife by inducing her to eat halibut bladders which he had filled with hot stones. He came to some fishermen and stole the bait from their hooks, but was finally hooked in the nose and had to recover his nose disguised as another person. Now he came to some deer with fat hanging out of their nostrils, pretended that it was mucus, and obtained it. He started along by canoe, and all of the animals wanted to accompany him, but he accepted only Deer. Coming to a deep valley, he laid some dried celery stalks across, covered them with moss, and induced Deer to try to walk across. Deer did so and was precipitated to the bottom, where he was devoured by Raven. Afterward Raven began mourning for him. (1956, pp. 104-105)

In this intense matriarchal dominance, the function of voracity is so prominent that the ego uses the other for total satisfaction, and desire is so greedy that it frequently devours even the ego. In this version of the myth, the hero raven creates the world but to obtain it from Nass's head he lets himself be eaten up by his daughter. The ego, the other, good, and evil exist but desire encompasses everything to satisfy itself. Raven cuts Cormorant's tongue so that it cannot tell anyone that he killed Bear. The notions of right, wrong, and guilt exist, but Trickster inverts their position whenever he feels like satisfying his desire.

When patriarchal exuberance increases in the myth, the trickster, in its heroic function becomes clearly a transgressor. In situations where his performance is permitted, as in the case of the court fool or the fool's pope in the Feast of the Circumcision of Christ during the Middle Ages and in modern humorists, he does it in a clearly compensatory role to the polarized position of the patriarchal archetype permitted by legal authority.

In the alterity pattern, however, the trickster exerts its heroic function as an unauthorized transgressor. It confronts the patriarchal canons through cunning, humor, and creativity, upsetting established traditions. Without exerting radical patriarchal antagonism, the trickster transcends conventional duties and unites polarities, including life and death, in the process of self-realization.

Hermes steals Apollo's cattle and disguises the theft by turning his footprints around. From a systemic viewpoint, the cattle, as symbol of Apollo's strength, needed to be stolen. This god patriarchalized increasingly his role in the Greek pantheon, replacing Helios. Hermes was destined to steal Apollo's cattle and go beyond the radical patriarchal separation of polarities. Indeed this is what he actually does, becoming the messenger of Zeus, symbol of the transcendent function that unites polarities. On accomplishing this task, he receives the function of psychopomp, guide of souls to the beyond. However, once his theft is discovered, Hermes does not defy Apollo but, on the contrary, gives him the lyre, which he had just invented. This is the creative way through which the trickster transcends the patriarchal pattern in the position of alterity when the thesis (the theft) is confronted by the antithesis (Apollo's wrath), forming a new synthesis (the lyre).

Analyzing alchemy Jung compares the trickster to the spirit mercurius, that miraculous substance capable of mixing with all others and propitiating the transformation of matter to realize the opus (Jung 1948a). Within alterity the trickster can shrewdly mingle with any function to serve the archetypal search for totality (Jung, in Radin 1956).

Through this archetypal labyrinth, we can approach the interpretation of the symbol of the trickster within the dialectical position of alterity to arrive at Christ as a dialectical transforming hero of history. Although his message is highly contesting and revolutionary, he transcends the polarized patriarchal position without antagonizing it to the point of affirming that he did not come to change one iota of the scriptures (Matt. 5:17-18). Confronting the stoning of the prostitute, he does not prohibit it; on the contrary, he permits it by those who have not sinned. Facing the thesis (stoning) and the antithesis (forgiveness), he introduces a synthesis (self-reflection of shadow) whereby before stoning, the aggressor has to confront his own soul and understand a new ethic that can substitute patriarchal aggression by compassion through self-reflection within alterity.

The heroic message of Jesus as trickster establishes the interaction of the opposites in a dialectical relationship of alterity that includes the polarities sin and salvation and life and death. Jesus realizes this extraordinary all-embracing feat by offering himself in sacrifice to be united with the Father. In so doing, he implants in history a new archetypal paradigm, in which the thesis as the father and the antithesis as the son transform in synthesis represented by the paradox of the Trinity in which three are one and father and son relate in the dialectical of the alterity archetype through the Holy Ghost.

Alterity, Medicine, and Psychotherapy

We saw how in immunology the dialectical position of consciousness was fundamental to discovering vaccination. In the same way that the food chain and countless other associations among plants, animals, and minerals exist in nature, so the cells of the human body and its constituents interact systemically.

Systemic thinking, which articulates the parts as a function of the whole, must be conjugated with the meaningful, that is, symbolic relationship of the parts among themselves, including the shadow. When we do so, we become aware of the importance of the association of the archetype of totality (see chapter 12), which relates all symbols with wholeness, with the archetype of alterity, which articulates the poles of polarities dialectically among themselves, including the shadow, all of them within totality.

The dialectic-systemic perspective is being implanted in medicine to an ever greater degree, stimulated by molecular biology. The growing anatomic, physiological, and neurochemical mapping of neurotransmitters and the production of drugs that affect them have lately undergone an extraordinary development. Unfortunately, however, this growth has been occurring unilaterally and patriarchally because it has not been accompanied by the symbolic view of the body and the dialectical relation of the mind-body polarity. The study of psychosomatic medicine has not been sufficient to overcome this epistemological bottleneck and, to this day, remains far below its human possibilities.

The psyche encompasses the representations of the mind, which are subjective (such as ideas and emotions), and representations of body (society and nature), which are objective. Through these representations, which make up the symbols, complexes, structuring functions, and systems, the psyche includes the subjective and objective dimensions, that is, the polarities mind-body, mind-nature, and mind-society.

Take as an example a forty-five-year-old man who had hepatitis C. He was infected when he was twenty-five through the use of cocaine. He was treated with interferon, and although he was not cured, he now has a viral count that is relatively low and stable. Frequently when he is alone he drinks beer or whiskey and occasionally snorts cocaine. His life story showed a pathological fixation on his primary quaternio with very negative experiences of the mother and father complexes and the bond between them. His parents divorced when he was five. He lived four years with his mother and then came to live with his father. He felt his mother to be emotionally unbalanced, affectionately distant, completely centered on her suffering, and incompetent to take care of him and his brother, who was four years older. His father came from Europe, had a German education, and was very hard, caring but never holding his two sons and never missing an opportunity to demean their mother.

He never adapted to school life because his behavior had been since early childhood very aggressive, expressing his negative identification with his father complex. His self-esteem was very low, and he was never able to take care of himself, living out his negative maternal complex intensely. His relationships with women were very limited, and he was attracted to women who were clumsy and incompetent, and to whom he was critical, reproducing his parents' marriage bond, failure, and defenses. During his therapy, his sick liver and his defensive attacks on it with alcohol and cocaine were often associated to his aggression against regulations, allied to his incapacity to behave correctly and to take care of himself efficiently.

We can send such a patient to a hepatologist or to a clinical psychiatrist. One way or another we must treat his liver symbolically, to be taken care of within the mind-body polarity. What we see is a liver attacked by virus, alcohol, and cocaine, which is a consequence of physical and emotional complexes. They need to be addressed psychologically together with laboratory exams. To consider him as just one more case of hepatitis is to limit his treatment considerably.

In another example, a forty-six-year-old married woman, without children, felt depressed, could not go to work, suffered from insomnia, was socially irritable, lost her appetite, and laid in bed for most of the past two weeks. She had had a similar episode in her youth, which lasted for a month, when her father was transferred to another town, and she had to separate from her boyfriend. There were no other cases of depression in her family. This time the depression began after an intense quarrel with her boss, with whom she'd had a warm and pleasant relationship for the past five years. There is no doubt that her case is one of pathological depression (DSM-IV) and that she needed medication. Her anamnesis showed that she had a significant fixation in her primary quaternio, in which she experienced an intense rejection of her mother, who showed overt preference for her older sister. At the same time she had a very affectionate and trusting affinity with her father. Her relationship with her husband had many aspects of the relationship with her mother, and the professional relationship with her boss clearly compensated for the lack of affection in her marriage. The quarrel with him as father figure may have precipitated a regression to a fixation of her negative mother complex accompanied by the depressive rejection. The symbolic elaboration of her depression included sessions of couple therapy, which dramatically improved her marriage and allowed her to return to work with a significant increase in self-knowledge. Of course her antidepressive drug therapy must have helped, but the symbolic approach was essential for the change of personality she experienced after she understood the full meaning of her depression.

These two clinical cases-one of hepatitis, the other of depression-are ordinary cases in medical consultations. Unfortunately, such patients frequently return home with drug treatment that does not include the disease symbolically and systemically in the individuation process. The exclusively objective treatment of psychological symptoms through medication and cognitive behavioral therapy passed from psychiatry to other specialists, and today many cardiologists, neurologists, and gynecologists are prescribing anxiolytics, hypnotics, and antidepressants with little or no symbolic elaboration of symptoms within the existential process.

To elaborate the opposites of any polarity in a dialectical position in which they interact meaningfully, for instance the mind-body polarity, the reasoning of the therapist must be subordinated to the archetype of alterity. This is very difficult for it includes the dialectical elaboration of the conscious-unconscious, subjective-objective, cognitive-emotional, and normal-pathological polarities. This implantation structures consciousness with symbolic humanism, no doubt one of the major conquests of the individuation and humanization processes.

When we see symbolically components of the mind-body polarity within the shadow formed by the fixation of structuring symbols, complexes, functions, and systems, we have a reference for relating polarities within dialectical practice of symbolic humanism in medicine and psychology.

Synchronicity is largely used in Jungian symbolic psychotherapy to amplify consciousness through symbolic elaboration coordinated by the dialectical position of the alterity archetype.

Jung described as case in which he was treating a young patient with good academic education, which she used to act out a defensive patriarchal Cartesian logic that prevented any deep symbolic comprehension of her existential reality. After a certain moment in therapy, he gave up trying to go through this defensive logical system which "knew and controlled everything" and waited for something that could allow her to experience life symbolically on a deeper level.

> My example concerns a young woman patient who, in spite of efforts made on both sides, proved to be psychologically inaccessible: The difficulty lay in the fact that she always knew better about everything. Her excellent education had provided her with a weapon ideally suited to this purpose, namely, a highly polished Cartesian rationalism with an impeccably "geometrical" idea of reality. After several fruitless attempts to sweeten her rationalism with a somewhat more human understanding, I had to confine myself to the hope that something unexpected and irrational would turn up, something that would burst the intellectual retort into which she had sealed herself. Well, I was sitting opposite her one day, with my back to the window, listening to her flow of rhetoric. She had had an impressive dream the night before, in which someone had given her a golden scarab-a costly piece of jewelry. While she was still telling me this dream, I heard something behind me gently tapping on the window. I turned round and saw that it was a fairly large flying insect that was knocking against the windowpane from outside in the obvious effort to get into the dark room. This seemed to me very strange. I opened the window immediately and caught the insect in the air as it flew in. It was a scarab beetle, or common rose chafer (*Cetonia*

aurata), whose gold-green color most nearly resembles that of a golden scarab. I handed the beetle to my patient with the words, "Here is your scarab." This experience punctured the desired hole in her rationalism and broke the ice of her intellectual resistance. The treatment could now be continued with satisfactory results. (Jung 1952, par. 982)

We can suppose that this unexpected event paralyzed circumstantially, within the transference relationship, the reflexive causality of the polarized patriarchal archetype which gave support to her defensive system. This technique is frequently used by masters of Zen Buddhism, who break the exaggerated polarized control of the patriarchal archetype through *koans* that reveal the profound reality of Zen.

A candidate to become a Zen master had to pass an examination. He went to bed the night before worried. He tried to empty his mind in order to be able to live Zen during his presentation and then went to sleep. The next morning, he entered the room, saluted the Zen masters present, and opened his mind to live Zen. An absurd intuition invaded his mind like lightning, and he immediately expressed it. He knelt down, picked up his sandals, put them upside down over his head, and stared at the masters attentively and very seriously. He then put his sandals back on and left the room. He was heartily approved and became a great master.

If we elaborate this little story from the perspective of reflexive causality, we can say that the *koan* the candidate used to live Zen was a double inversion of reality to free the mind of its normal conditioning: first, the inverted the position of the sandals, and second, putting them on his head. However, this is an explanation after the occurrence of the *koan*. From the perspective of magical causality, we could say that the candidate showed total spontaneity, which impressed the masters greatly. However, these two explanations, although plausible, do not encompass the richness, the profundity, the effect, and the uniqueness of the *koan*, which only the principle of synchronicity can grasp.

Zen is an experience of synchronicity within the dialectical position of alterity that transcends magic and reflexive causality. When Jung put the scarab on the patient's lap, he shocked her the way a Zen master would and this allowed her to transcend reflexive causality, which defensively dominated her mind, and open herself up to dialectical symbolic elaboration.

For example, a forty-five-year-old patient was elaborating the end of our analysis. We recapitulated everything we had worked through, how much effort we had invested, and the results we harvested. After this session, he dreamed about his graduation in economics, and we understood that this symbol probably was synchronistically related to the end of our analysis. Leaving the session and going to the garage of the building, he had a great surprise. He met a girlfriend whom he had loved a long time ago and had not seen for many years. They kissed affectionately. Going home, he suddenly recalled that she was the girl with whom he had danced the waltz at his graduation party twenty years before.

We see the opening of consciousness coordinated by the dialectical position of alterity. In this case during psychotherapy it propitiated an extension of consciousness which endowed the person with the ability to experience synchronicity and understand symbolically a profound revelation of being.

In order to better understand the meaning of the alterity archetype, it is important to imagine why it is the deepest form of human intelligence. Remembering that the psyche develops to form consciousness and the ego in order to become aware of being as the creative force of the universe, we can realize that the ego and the other relating dialectically within totality form the most complex and profound model to experience and know being.

Chapter 12

THE ARCHETYPE OF TOTALITY

The only sin of my old age was to have written the Tao Te Ching (legendary confession of Lao-Tzu)

The experience of death is the most profound of life.

To begin, we have to differentiate the archetype of totality from the central archetype. The archetype of totality is a regent archetype and, as such, is subordinated to the central archetype. The archetype of totality mainly coordinates the expressions of the relationship of consciousness with the totality of the symbolic dimension, whereas the central archetype coordinates every symbolical elaboration from the beginning to the end of development through the interaction of all archetypes to form ego and other identities.

This does not mean that the symbols that commonly represent the potential of the central archetype and the totality of the Self-such as the diamond, the sphere, mandalas, infinity, eternity, the pearl, the tree and so many others-cannot be common to both. Although any symbol can express any archetype, some symbols end up being associated more frequently with a particular archetype, while others are associated with more than one archetype, always depending on the context in which the symbol is being elaborated. However, it is important to emphasize that all symbols in the final analysis also express the central archetype.

It could not be otherwise because of the fact that the central archetype is the chief coordinator of the four regent archetypes and of all individual and collective symbolic elaboration. This evidently includes the dysfunctions of the developmental process, the fixations and defenses that form the shadow. Although the central archetype does not form defenses causally, it registers their occurrence and activates the mechanism of repetition compulsion to express them. While fixations and defenses operate, the central archetype coordinates the Self interacting with the normal and defensive structuring functions.

Ancient cultures of China, India, Japan, and Tibet developed the ritual of introspection through meditation directed at the most varied symbolic experiences. One such ritual consists in detaching one's attention from focusing on any object and concentrating in emptiness. In doing so, consciousness experiences the all encompassing extension of the central archetype and, consequently, of the totality of the Self. Repetitive prayers, phrases, or words employed as mantras have the same function, that is, to empty the symbolic axis circumstantially and to permit consciousness to experience directly the intensity of the central archetype.

As the tai chi mandala ☯ expresses particularly well, the dilution of the frontiers of the ego-other polarity creates the perception that one is the other. This, however, is not the ego-other symbiotic characteristic of the insular matriarchal position, where fusion between them is so frequent, but a very clear state of consciousness that captures the identity of the ego with the other in what they secretly were and now realize they really are: the universal being. Indeed, did they not emerge among countless other polarities from the differentiation of the cosmos to propitiate the processes of individuation and humanization reunited in the essence of being? And is it not this being, permanent and immutable, described by Parmenides and rescued in modern times by Heidegger that permeates everything and reveals itself to consciousness now when the boundaries of polarities fade?

In this manner, contrary to the anxious restlessness of multiplicity, meditation focused on the void is invigorating and highly relaxing, because it allows us to experience unity underneath endless diversity.

The contemplative position of the totality archetype, on one side, has the practical function of crowning symbolic elaboration of any situation and even of the existential process; on the other side, however, when seen in all its symbolic extension, it has the virtue to reveal to us all things, including ourselves, reunited in the one. Through the function of sensation we are led to experience a glorious perception of wholeness. Through intuition, the psyche grasps infinity and eternity. Thinking propitiates ecstatic admiration in the face of the unlimited intelligence of creation and feeling enchants us with the full satisfaction of being totality.

When one of my daughters was five years old, we went on a vacation, and she loved to stay for hours in the swimming pool, learning to swim with her sisters. One morning she told me: "Daddy, I spent the night dreaming with a pizza. It flew around me for a long while. Can we have pizza tonight?" As Fordham (1944) described, it is common for children to express images of the totality of the central archetype in drawings. He attributed this to archetypal ego formation from the beginning of life. At five years of age, my daughter's ego was probably in full acquisition of the symbolization capacity, and the swimming pool was the temenos where she learned to swim and dive with great pleasure. Her interpretation of the dream was compatible with the insular matriarchal position of sensuous desire because she loved pizza. On a more profound level, however, the dream expresses in a picturesque way, through the image of a circle flying around the child, a genuine representation of a symbol of totality, a mandala structuring her ego.

A young man, seventeen years old, suffered from terminal leukemia. All possible treatments had been undertaken. He was in a hospital waiting for death, and one day asked his father if he could to take him home where he could watch the sea. He explained that he wanted to see "one last sunset." His doctors and his mother were against it, because whenever he moved around, bruising and bleeding increased. His father, however, was moved and prepared his transportation. The bruises and bleedings increased, but the young man smiled when he saw the sunset. That night he died.

In this case, the sunset symbol expressed the totality archetype at the end of the existential process. The archetype of totality coordinates the last phase of symbolic elaboration in any life event and also at the end of life. It functions as an accountant-auditor who comes to examine and authorize the end of the operation and the integration into consciousness of the meanings produced. During the performance of this function, the totality archetype employs the evaluating function to accomplish its task. Whenever we do any business, we need reassurance. Many times when we are about to finish a deal, we suddenly notice that something is missing-a certain document, the signature of the partner's wife, another banking form, and we run to fetch it. This is the result of the evaluating function operating within the totality archetype, which at the last moment structures consciousness with the one missing item before concluding the operation.

The archetype of totality remains relatively frustrated in many cases where a very long symbolic elaboration is needed. Many of the elaborations of certain symbols remain incomplete because of their nature, as is the case, for instance, of the parental complexes. In such cases, premature interruptions of elaborations cause fixation and defensive attitudes that will operate in the shadow.

In David Lynch's film *The Straight Story* (1999), a retired man in old age decides to visit his brother with whom he has unsolved questions. As he has no car, he decides to travel on a lawnmower. He undertakes a heroic journey to elaborate and conclude important symbols and complexes that had remained fixated during his individuation process.

It is very difficult to end many elaborations even when they are precious and necessary as in the case above. There are so many elaborations in our symbolic axis that some are left behind due to fixation or lack of time and/or disposition. This is not wise, because when we do so, we are prone to increasing our shadow. This occurrence is more frequent in symbolic elaboration coordinated by the matriarchal and patriarchal archetypes, because they have a significant degree of unilaterality, which favors disregarding the ego-other bond and naturally limits the effort to pursue symbolic elaboration to the end.

In this manner, symbolic elaboration coordinated by the dialectical position of the alterity archetype is nearer to the contemplative position of the totality archetype, because its tendency for compassion and consideration tends to recognize that which is important for wholeness and prompts one to dedicate oneself to completing elaboration, making it holistic and systemic.

The Unitarian Contemplative Position of the Totality Archetype

The process of symbolic elaborations leads to increasing detachment of consciousness from circumstantial events to prepare it for the final attachment to totality. The non differentiated position of the central archetype begins detachment from the whole by focusing on the symbol to start its elaboration. This is followed by the insular matriarchal position, which differentiates islands in consciousness establishing focal attachment and symbiotic relationships.

The polarized patriarchal position presents a great detachment of the sensuality of the insular matriarchal position in exchange for a greater attachment to power. The dialectical position rescues the importance of attachment of the insular matriarchal position and establishes a relative detachment of the matriarchal and patriarchal positions to establish their dialectical relationship coordinated by the archetype of alterity. Finally, the contemplative position of the totality archetype has a greater detachment than the previous positions because its only attachment is to totality and completion and nothing else.

Detaching from the other four archetypal positions, the ego and the other approach the central archetype and the perception of their frontiers diminishes progressively. The focus of consciousness is on wholeness, which encompasses the ego and the other, and because of this, their boundaries increasingly fade. This fact has confused many authors, especially those dealing with Eastern cultures, who have described the phenomenology of consciousness in the search for wisdom. Many of them have referred to the highly detached consciousness of the archetype of totality, in describing the state of Nirvana, as consciousness without an ego. This confuses the phenomenology of consciousness and of the ego, because if consciousness does not have an ego, it cannot orient its owner to tie his or her shoestrings, much less find the way through a door. With all that we have seen of the archetypal positions of consciousness differentiating them throughout life but always and inevitably expressing the regent archetypes, to speak of consciousness without the ego is the equivalent of ignoring the developmental process. Even in schizophrenia, when the ego is frequently shattered, it is still there.

In Jungian symbolic psychology, the human psychological development process is always archetypal and inseparable from consciousness, whose central polarity is the ego-other relationship. The phenomenon described by the masters then cannot be explained by removing the ego from consciousness because this is archetypally, that is, structurally impossible. It can be explained however describing a state of consciousness in which the ego and the other are more detached than in any other position of consciousness and form a unity with the whole. This is the contemplative position, which is always present when we end any symbolic elaboration. Consciousness can also amplify this perception, experiencing itself one with that which was elaborated.

Imagine yourself in an apartment by the beach, contemplating the sea. In the first plane you see the swimmers, the waves, and perhaps a little boat and the clouds. The separation of the ego and the other is quite clear. Continue to contemplate the sky and the sea in all their immensity. Open your conscious to totality and feel the immense extension of being. The ego and the other begin to fuse. This was the only experience of transcendence admitted by Freud, who, following Romain Rolland, called it oceanic feeling (Freud 1929). Continue the experience and realize that you detach from any other perception and enter fully into the contemplative position of consciousness, feeling yourself one with the world; and yet, pay attention to the fact that you are plainly conscious. At the same time you do not have any notion whatsoever of a boundary between your ego and the other because you are one with totality. This is the contemplative position of conscious and your ego, although motionless, is fully there.

A young engineer is driving his car, going home after work. He is driving automatically, his mind in between the non differentiated position and the insular position. Suddenly, when passing a bus which had just stopped, a middle-aged woman crosses the street in front of the bus and is in front of his car. He is startled, brakes, but cannot avoid the collision. He gets out of the car. Many people gather, and they realize that the woman in the street is alive and conscious but hurt. Someone calls the police; someone else, an ambulance. All this occurs mainly in the insular position, but now there is a hurt person to be taken to a hospital, the police asking for his driving license, his car in the middle of the street, and the need for him to call his lawyer and the insurance office. To organize all this, the polarized patriarchal position is activated.

In court six months later, the woman, who recovered from a broken leg, sits among witnesses, including the bus driver. The young engineer is being judged. The woman's health insurance company is the plaintiff and accuses him of being responsible for the accident. His lawyer argues that the woman crossed the street in front of the stopped bus, completely oblivious to the traffic, and so, in reality, she was the one who caused the accident. The engineer pleads innocent. The lawyer for the health insurance company counters this argument, saying that, according to the bus driver, the engineer took too long to brake, and because of this he is guilty.

The dialectical position of alterity is now active in court; contrary elements are weighed by the judge. Other witnesses are called, yet the situation is not conclusive. The judge now calls the victim as last witness. She identifies herself and swears to tell the truth. The judge asks her if she recognizes the accused as the driver of the car of the accident. She answers yes and says that she is thankful to him for being the first person who helped her. Then, the judge asks the decisive question to elaborate the responsibility for the accident.

"Did you know that there were cars moving on the other side of the bus when you crossed the street?" "Yes I knew, but I looked in the wrong direction and so did not see his car." Verdict: innocent!

A year goes by and the engineer decides to visit the scene of the accident. By chance, there is a bus parked in exactly the same place. For a few moments, the scene of the accident flashes through his mind, from the crash to the verdict. And then he thinks, "What a scare. How nice that it is all over!" He looks at the cars passing the parked bus. Suddenly, he is the bus, the woman, himself, his car, the judge, the lawyers, and the verdict. He is all this because the elaboration of the accident has come to an end and his conscious is now in the contemplative position of totality.

The Shadow of the Contemplative Position

We have seen that the psychological energy of the shadow and its defenses are proportional to the energy of their corresponding normal structuring functions. Because of this, the shadow formed by fixation of the contemplative position of the archetype of totality is very intense and threatens the balance of the Self. It is intense because its symbols, complexes, structuring functions, and systems can encompass the whole process of development, and it is threatening because when the process nears the end of life, which involves death, its defensive expression can lead to self-destruction.

In this sense, senile depression generally includes two important components: on one hand the difficulty of going forward and facing death; on the other hand, the resistance to regressing, to going back and confronting unelaborated fixations full of guilt and suffering. The experience of regression here is part of the symbol and structuring function of the final judgment, whose elaboration includes a true existential account.

At the end of the process, the detachment coordinated by the contemplative position leads to a great sacrifice of attachment, which includes the physical body and one's own life. In this phase, the traditional way of dealing with death in one's culture is most important, together with the relation to its mythical roots. It is also very important for the spiritual life of the person and the experience accumulated to elaborate important existential situations regarding frustration, transgression, and ambiguity.

The Contemplative Position and the Unitary Vision of Being

Through the millennia, the contemplative position and the archetype of totality have propitiated cultures to formulate extraordinary concepts such as Tao in Taoism, Zen in Japanese Buddhism, Moksha in Hinduism, Nirvana in Buddhism and the state of grace in Christian mysticism. Searches for these in daily life have become paths of wisdom for guiding life. Each of these is of great complexity and has been described by wise men in many ways and in countless books to describe ontological identity and the finality of being. Their many expressions-such as wisdom, enlightenment, way, peace, balance, full realization, and many others-point to the essence of the psyche, which unites the smallest and the greatest, the multiple and the unique, and change and permanence within the unitary nature of creation.

The Tao Te Ching and Heidegger's Ontology

Heidegger's search for being (*Sein*), which transcends and encompasses all things (*Seiende*) within the contemplative position, is analogous to the concept of Tao. However, in the same way that Tao is not restricted to transcendence because it is also the way, the here-and-now, Heidegger reunites the incommensurable dimension with life's reality, postulating that the here-and-now (*Dasein*) is also being-in-the-world (*Sein ist in-der-Welt sein*). Heidegger expresses the contemplative position with the notion that being transcends and includes all things, and Lao-tzu enhances it with the notion that Tao transcends and expresses itself in all things.

Taoism is the millenary philosophy of China. Centralized in the concept of Tao, it describes the unitary essence of being which transcends polarities within the sense of development. In this way, Tao is the whole and at the same time the way (Bloise 2000).

The preoccupation of detaching from the ego as causal agent (matriarchal and patriarchal positions) is propitiated by the concept of *wu wei*, non action, which situates consciousness at the service of Tao. The description of Tao which is the way and has sense, leads consciousness to an extreme detachment that prevents the ego from directly intervening in symbolic elaboration through the insular position (desire) and the polarized position (control). This fact places consciousness through *wu wei* at the service of happening, not by causality, but by synchronicity (alterity and totality). Thus, the ego is prevented from desiring and from any pretension to control or explain Tao, and polarities are used to neutralize unilaterality and to open the way to reveal totality (alterity and totality).

In the Tao Te Ching, six centuries before our era, Lao-Tzu conceived eighty-one chapters in which he formulated the essence of Taoism and the unitary way of seeing life, the world, and truth. This commentary is only a small synthesis to amplify with Taoism the contemplative archetypal position of the totality archetype.

1

The TAO that can be expressed
is not the eternal TAO.
The name that can be named
is not the eternal name.
'Nonexistence' I call the beginning of Heaven and Earth.
'Existence' I call the mother of individual beings.
Therefore does the direction toward nonexistence
lead to the sight of the miraculous essence,
the direction toward existence
to the sight of spatial limitations.
Both are one in origin
and different only in name.
In its unity it is called the secret.
The secret's still deeper secret
is the gateway through which all miracles emerge.

With this first chapter, Lao-Tzu invalidates the rational notion of transcendence and transposes the dimension of being from rational consciousness to the unconceivable, which must not be seen as the unconscious but rather as the conscious-unconscious incapacity to conceive. He ends this verse affirming that the nominated is in the dimension of things that is the mother of all things and situates the origin of the universe in the nameless.

2

If all on earth acknowledge the beautiful as beautiful,
then thereby the ugly is already posited.
If all on earth acknowledge the good as good,
then thereby is the non-good already posited.
For existence and nonexistence generate each other.
Heavy and light complete each other.
Long and short shape each other.
High and deep convert each other.
Before and after follow each other.

Thus also is the Man of Calling.
He dwells in effectiveness without action.
He practices teaching without talking.
All beings emerge
and he does not refuse himself to them.
He generates and yet possesses nothing.
He is effective and keeps nothing.
When the work is done
he does not dwell with it.

Unlike Heidegger, who abandoned all polarities to avoid unilaterality, reduction, and deformity of being, Lao-Tzu enters into polarities in the polarized patriarchal position to deny and transcend them through the concept of *wu wei* (doing through not doing), which detaches conscience from the matriarchal-patriarchal polarity. It is at the end of life that we can best admire the wisdom of Lao-Tzu and of Heidegger, because then we realize that the most difficult thing of life is our preparation to leave it.

4

TAO is forever flowing.
And yet it never overflows in its effectiveness.
It is an abyss like the ancestor of all things.
It mellows their acuity.
It dissolves their confusion.
It mitigates their brightness.
It unites itself with their dust.
It is deep and yet it is real.

I do not know whose son it is:
It seems to be earlier than God.

The transcendence of Tao and its identity with all things can be associated with the concept of ontological identity, the identity of being (see chapter 4). It is complementary to ontic identity, the identity of things, accessible to attachment in the matriarchal and patriarchal positions. The problem of the truth of being is also inherent in the contemplative position. Heidegger formulates it through the concept of genuineness (*Eigenartichkeit*) and Lao-Tzu refers to it in many ways, including nonviolence.

8

The highest benevolence is like water.
The benevolence of water is
to benefit all beings without strife.
It dwells in places which man despises.
Therefore it stands close to TAO.
In dwelling benevolence shows itself in place.
In thinking benevolence shows itself in depth.
In giving benevolence shows itself in love.
In speech benevolence shows itself in truth.
In ruling benevolence shows itself in order.
In working benevolence shows itself in competence.
In movement benevolence shows itself in timing.
He who does not assert himself
Thereby remains free of blame.

The Contemplative Position
and the End of the Physical Body

As the end of life draws near, the contemplative position is increasingly activated in symbolic elaboration together with detachment from the anterior positions, now including the personal body, and the existential process. The experience of death is no doubt the most profound of life.

The transcendent structuring function of the imagination is intensely activated and conceives the end of life and life after death in the most varied ways, which depend largely on one's myth and culture one lives in. The sacrificial function has a special role here because detachment includes the separation of the physical body, which will be left behind. In this sense, old age is a powerful structuring function destined to prepare final detachment through the diminution of physical vitality together with the countless diseases that accompany the body until its end. All these experiences are highly symbolical, and if elaborated, understood, and integrated, they structure consciousness with meanings to undertake this fundamental transformation.

The contemplation of the process as a whole brings memories, suffering, and longing from past events, which slowly come to an end and open space for the imagination to elaborate symbolically that which is yet to come. Western culture has largely estranged itself from the Christian myth (a theme that will be expanded on in the archetypal theory of history in the next chapter) and therefore has little to contribute to elaborate this passage. The life of Christ offers the experience of death and resurrection, but few Christians have been educated to access and consult Christ about existential problems such as sin, faith, and death and to be guided by him to understand this transformation spiritually, that is, symbolically.

Jung's individuation process has the great virtue of symbolizing life and death during the stages of life, and this contributes significantly to the acquisition of the symbolic capacity to elaborate one's own death at the end of the process (Jung 1928, Byington 1996).

The contemplative position once turned defensive is prevented from closing symbolic elaboration because of fixations that condemn it to repetition compulsion. These fixations can encompass extensive existential parts of the personality including all symbols and complexes that form the shadow and all psychopathology. The personality is then divided by the shadow (Laing 1960), which limits its search for plenitude.

We have seen that each archetypal position structures consciousness normally and in the path of good or, when it eventually becomes fixated and defensive, in the path of pathology, sin, and evil. In case consciousness functions defensively in the contemplative position, it contaminates daily activities with pessimism. "Nothing will come out right." "Everything I do turns out a flop." "Life has no sense and no justice." "The corrupt are glorified and the evil ones always have the upper hand. Good always ends up in the gutter."

Pessimism, depression, and cynicism endorsing evil are sometimes symptoms of a defensive depression. However, I could not disagree more with Aaron Beck (Beck, Rush, Shaw, and Emery1979) when he attributes depression to depressive thinking, which would then be the cause and not the result of depression. For all we have seen of fixations and defenses in shadow formation, to attribute depressive symptoms to autonomous pathological thinking and to try to modify them by changing thinking through cognitive behavioral techniques, without elaborating the emotional conscious and unconscious symbolic contents fixated, seems to me to be artificial and highly alienating. With such therapy, we are prone to create conditioned robots dissociated from what they feel. It seems to me that in so doing, the therapist imprisons patients in a theoretical straightjacket in which, to free themselves from depressive symptoms, they have to acquire obsessive symptoms. They are prohibited from having depressive thoughts and are conditioned to have only "healthy thoughts." This is very different from seeing depression as a structuring function and following it, in the shadow if it is fixated or normally if it is not fixated, to understand and elaborate the symbols and complexes it contains, and only then to use cognitive behavioral exercises to encourage detachment of defensive functioning (Byington 2007).

The Contemplative Position and Preparation for Death

Cultures exist in which religion is exercised through living symbols and rituals can favor normal symbolic elaboration of death and life after death. Our unfortunate Western culture, tragically uprooted from its mythical imagination due to the defensive patriarchalization of the Christian myth, suffers severely from the subject-object dissociation described earlier and is not prepared to deal with this profound undertaking. For centuries, countless Christians who truly believe in Christ have been conditioned not to have direct emotional contact with him and, therefore, cannot let themselves be guided by him beyond life. With rare exceptions, even Catholic priests who give the extreme unction do not know how to exercise the archetypal positions of alterity and contemplation to elaborate the life process within light and shadow (sin) to prepare people to be led by Christ into eternal life. Frequently, their persona is so artificial and defensive that it shows them incapable of experiencing the resurrection.

The preparation for death in Western culture for the majority of people who do not live the Christian magic-mythical dimension of the insular matriarchal position or of any other religion is a question of initiatory education. The first lesson is that death is part of life and that they walk hand in hand during every minute we live. Psychologically this means that the archetype of life and death is part of the central archetype (Byington 1996).

Sexuality begins and is taught during childhood, but it is in my view a gross error to think that children, after being theoretically taught, know what sexuality is. As Freud (1905) described, sexual libido is transformed during oral, anal, and phallic phases until it reaches genital maturity in puberty. Only then do young people begin to know what sexuality is. Therefore, although children "learn" earlier and earlier how babies are born, beginning with "a little tiny cell that Papa puts into Mama," they will only be initiated into sexuality existentially after adolescence when they start to experience sex. In this manner, we must protect our children not from the cognitive knowledge of sex, which is all over the media, but from having precocious sexual experiences, such as witnessing the intimate life of their parents or of adults who can molest them. A precocious sexual experience for a child, especially if it is of sexual abuse and, worse of all, if the abuse is incestuous, is a devastating experience for the personality, and bound to produce intense fixation and shadow.

The gravity of the fixation from sexual abuse is not initially felt because these experiences occur mostly in the insular matriarchal position and can be accompanied by pleasure. The gravity is felt when the older child begins to elaborate it in the polarized position, which makes it antisocial, abominable, and highly charged with guilt, for, as Levy-Strauss (1958) explains, the incest taboo is the cornerstone of the social root of civilization. The union of matriarchal pleasure and patriarchal guilt is the reason why most sexually abused children feel responsible and hide this fixation.

In analytical psychology, the pseudo-separation of a personal and an archetypal unconscious prevented the recognition of ego archetypal structuring until the 1950s, when it was discovered that the ego is formed by archetypes. One of the consequences of this ego-archetype dissociation was the concentration among Jungians on the symbolic archetypal mythological form of incest to the detriment of emphasizing the devastating power of defensive incest during ego formation in childhood.

Analogous to sexuality, the precocious experience of death by the child can be very traumatic and the cause of serious fixation and defense formation. Like the structuring function of sexuality, the structuring function of life and death is initially known only cognitively. The child knows that death exists but does not know what it is. Like sexuality, sometime during childhood, the child is likely to experience death emotionally. A grandfather dies, someone hit by a car and the body is seen on the street, or a little animal or the family pet dies and the first experience of death is consummated. Jung discovered it when he was four years old with the corpse of a man who had drowned in the Rhine. This is very frightening, and the child must be protected and oriented; it is the beginning of the elaboration of the life and death polarity.

In my view it is contraindicated in our culture for the contrasexual parent to appear naked in front of their children after about the second year of age because the image of the nude parent can become part of the imaginary life of the adolescent and inhibit sexual development, especially during masturbation.

In the same way, the child must be protected, whenever possible, from the precocious experience of death. In small Brazilian towns, in the mourning of the deceased, the family leaves the door open and the whole town, including children, comes to see the dead person. This is a very creative collective event that dilutes this first experience of death and is completely different from situations when parents who take children to the cemetery "to learn what death is like," which I find artificial and inadequate. Death is very traumatic for children because the relation with their parents is so symbiotic that they imagine the next person to die will be their parents. I do not relate this to an oedipal feeling, which may also be present, but to the fear of loss of either of the parents. This unbearable threat can cause severe fixations and defenses.

Adolescence brings existential sexuality, and this is the time when the learning of death also begins. It can be taught within the theme of death as a part of life and illustrated by many biological examples, starting with the death of the gametes when they form the zygote. This example was given by Sabina Spielrein in her paper "Destruction as the Cause of Transformation" (1912), which contributed to Jung's (1912) and Freud's psychological conception of death. Another example that illustrates this theme are the millions of skin cells that die daily and are replaced, along with countless examples of self-renewal in nature, such as the transformation of butterflies and the change that occurs in the leaves of trees every autumn and spring.

Meditation is of great importance for spiritual development and can be employed to imagine any life experience whatsoever, including the death and replacement of body cells. Active imagination, developed by Jung, is the best expressive technique for ransoming the magic-mythical imagination that we left behind with Santa Claus and the Easter bunny in childhood. It allows us to relate the insular matriarchal position and the polarized patriarchal position within the dialectical position of the archetype of alterity, which is indispensable for the symbolic transformation of life in death and death in life.

When we use active imagination with the dead, we can experience life after death. This is an experience which I recommend only during and after the sixth stage of life (from 40 to 60 years old) in order to prepare for one's own life after death. This is very different from the experience of relating with the dead such as in education, when we use active imagination to establish an emotional relationship with important historical figures of the past. This can be done using photographs and biographical details that show their lives to be like everyone else's. Instead of only reading about Newton, Darwin, Columbus, and Gandhi, it is very useful for students to look at their pictures, do active imagination with them and with their ideas, to have the experience that although dead, they continue to be so much alive. In this way, we prepare people from adolescence on to live with death within the existential process. This method transforms the great masters of the past into spiritual guides, gurus, as happens in India. This is most important for beginning to understand symbolically the Indian concept of reincarnation, whose literal interpretation with ants and flies may seem unconvincing.

To start with, it is important to know that active imagination with the dead is an expressive technique that can only be employed with someone after forty who has proven to have a strong ego capable of undertaking regression. A step further in this process is active imagination with intimate persons who have died, starting with grandparents and later with uncles, parents, siblings, and important friends. In this case, it is not advisable to practice active imagination with dear ones who have died recently, because the magic-mythical relation through the imagination can become a hallucination and start a psychotic episode. Where the deceased was an intimate acquaintance, the mourning rituals must be undertaken first, and at least two years should pass before practicing active imagination with them.

Only in extreme cases can active imagination with a recently dead person be carried out to elaborate the death of a very dear relative or friend. These are tragic cases in which the loss precipitates the imminent threat of suicide. Great care is necessary in such cases because the constellation of the archetype of death can be so intense that it may threaten to possess and kill the person in mourning. Such active imagination is very dangerous and should only be practiced if accompanied by an experienced analyst and when the person in mourning has had a period of analysis that showed a strong ego capable of regressing, confronting, and elaborating the shadow.

The elaboration of past, fixated, and defensive pathological mourning can also be carried out therapeutically through active imagination, also with the same careful procedures mentioned above (Byington 2005b).

The Myth of Death in Egyptian Mythology Psychostasia

Inspired by the death and resurrection of Osiris, the symbolism of the existence of death after life was so important in ancient Egypt that people prepared for it carefully and concretely during their lifetime. After death, the ritual of mummification was most carefully carried out. The weighing of the soul, the ceremony of psychostasia, positions consciousness in the insular matriarchal position and in the polarized patriarchal position in the final judgment. This custom in ancient Egypt is useful for comparing the elaboration of the symbol of death and the transition to the beyond, matriarchally and patriarchally coordinated, to its elaboration by the coordination of the dialectical position of the archetype of alterity as proposed in the Christian myth and in Jungian symbolic psychology.

Together with the mummy, the soul must present talismans and magic words written in the *Book of the Dead* in order to cross the frightening distance that separates the realm of the living and of the dead. In the final judgment, the dead person is taken by Anubis or Horus to Osiris, who receives the person seated in a great room. In the center there is a large scale, and Ma'at, goddess of truth and justice, prepares to weigh the heart of the deceased. By her side is Ammit, the devourer, a hybrid monster, part lion, part crocodile, and part hippo, ready to devour the guilty. Around the large room, on the right and left sides of Osiris, sit forty-two figures dressed in gowns, each with a sharp sword. Some have human heads, others have animal heads. They correspond to the provinces of Egypt, each one in charge of examining one special aspect of the personality of the dead person.

The deceased begins the ritual with a negative confession addressing every judge by name to show that he has nothing to fear and confessing himself without sins. There follows the psychostasia, the weighing of the heart. In one of the dishes of the scale, Annubis or Horus places Ma'at or her ideogram, the feather, symbol of truth and justice, and on the other, the heart of the dead person. Thoth checks the weight and writes it on a tablet, communicating the result to Osiris. In case the dishes remain even, Osiris declares the dead to be virtuous and grants the person eternal bliss in his kingdom with the special duty of caring for dams and channels (Larousse 1959, p. 41).

The myth expresses the insular position of the matriarchal archetype and the polarized position of the patriarchal archetype in the elaboration of the life of the dead person. This may be applied to any symbolic elaboration during the process of individuation or to the end of life.

The ceremony is an ethical evaluation of the good and evil polarity to verify patriarchally the state of the soul. Osiris, as an expression of the patriarchal archetype, coordinates the final elaboration and the forty-two judges stand for the cultural Self. They are symbols of the structuring functions with whom the deceased must interact. The fact that they have human and animal heads refers to the amplitude of their symbolic nature.

The heart of the dead person is a symbol of his or her psychic life, and in the case where it weighs more than justice and truth it will be devoured by Ammit, a monster equivalent to the patriarchalized devil in Christianity. The weighing is idealized because any sin, fixation, or defense forming a shadow will make it heavier than Ma'at's feather, symbol of truth and justice, and will exclude it from Osiris's domain. The patriarchal nature of the elaboration is quite clear when we see that good and evil are radically separated and evil, sin, and shadow are thoroughly excluded from the elect and afterlife.

The patriarchal coordination of the Egyptian ritual is idealized and does not admit sin or evil. In this way it is incompatible with the dialectical position of the alterity archetype and does not allow sufficient detachment from organization and power to operate in the contemplative position of totality.

This is very different from the extreme unction of Christianity, which, instead of a pure heart, is a ritual for a sinful heart that through confession elaborates the fixations of the shadow in alterity to be able to detach sufficiently and attain the contemplative position of the archetype of totality. Unfortunately, a great many Catholic priests do not elaborate anything and automatically give their blessing for those who are about to die even when their condition is such that they are still physically able to elaborate their shadow in confession. This shows the degree to which patriarchalized institutional Christianity has allowed the ritual of confession to deteriorate, which prevents the dialectical encounter of Christ and devil, good and evil, during and at the end of life.

The Myth of Those Who Cannot Die
The Legend of Dracula

Symbolically, the legend of Dracula refers to fixations that prevent the end of symbolic elaboration. Not to be able to die, in this context, is not to be able to end the life process nor to have peace and harmony. In cases of significant gravity, one is tormented by fixations and defenses of pathological complexes that many religions project onto the images of dammed spirits, tormented souls, incubi, and succubi which persecute the living. These "entities" correspond to the repetition compulsion of defensive projections.

Every fixation includes the defensive prevention of death of an attachment that cannot be completely elaborated. To be fixated in the archetype of life and death means not to be able to go forward in creative life and not to be able to deliver to death that which has already been used and must be left aside. One of the components of psychopathology is anxiety due to fixation of the life and death archetype, which cannot execute its normal functions and becomes persecutory. Defensive fear of death in such cases becomes a great form of anxiety and sometimes causes people to worry about countless things, some of which are not at all important, running around compulsively and disoriented. It is a great acquisition in the process of individuation and humanization to discover that we must not fear death because it is part of life. This led me to conceive the structuring function of the archetype of life and death within the central archetype in Jungian symbolic psychology (Byington 1996).

In cases where the elaboration of death becomes fixated and cannot be realized, the disturbance is so compulsive that it prevents the ending of the elaboration of being.

In the romance *Dracula* by Bram Stoker, published in 1897, the author imagines a story in which Count Dracula is the legendary prince Vlad Tepes, who was born in 1431 in Transylvania and ruled the territory of Wallachia, today Rumania. He fought many battles with Ottoman Turks and became famous for torturing his enemies with much cruelty, preferring impalement. Stories of vampires based on the image of Dracula are numerous and most of them are about survival after death by protection of the devil. The conditions for survival are to be alert only by night, that is, hidden from normal daily life, and to feed on the blood of the victims, luring them to serve the devil.

This theme refers to a fixation of the archetypes of alterity and totality from which people cannot escape. The dialectical interaction of the polarity life and death becomes fixed so that the opposites cannot be lived separately. In the case of the Dracula complex, the fixation is associated with lack of affection and aggression caused by frustration due to separation and abandonment. The acting out of this shadow can lead to the repetition compulsion of sadomasochistic behavior expressed by criminal night life. These cases can present extreme psychopathic gravity, as for instance the legendary Jack the Ripper in London.

The legend of *The Flying Dutchman* probably originates from seventeenth-century nautical folklore and has many variations. It refers to a ghostly ship with a ghostly captain and crew. One famous version is Wagner's opera *Der fliegende Hollände (The Flying Dutchman)* in which a ship sails across the seas with its damned crew. They are condemned to sail forever and only love can bring them death and peace.

In this case we have the fixated wound of hurt love that paralyzes the individuation of so many people because, as we see in the legend, not only the captain but all his crew are cursed for life. *The Flying Dutchman* can be associated with the fixations of the wounds of love that can dehumanize creatures and make them "fly over the high seas of life," disseminating false seduction and adventure, contaminated by poisoned love amidst pain and desperation.

The Myth of Those Who Do Not Accept Death

Son of Aeolus, Sisyphus was the founder of Corinth, grandfather of the hero Bellerophon. He told the river god Asopos that the river god's daughter Aegina had been kidnapped by Zeus. The god avenged himself and condemned

Sisyphus to death, ordering Tantalus to take him to Hades. Sisyphus however, was very cunning. He imprisoned Tantalus in such a way that only Ares could free him. Finally, he was taken to Hades, but before he went, he forbade his wife to undertake funerary rites for him. Upon arriving, he complained of this to Hades so intensely that the god let him return to life to prepare the rites. The situation became so queer that only Hermes could be summoned to solve it. Sisyphus was condemned to push a stone to the top of a mountain in Hades. It rolled down before reaching the top, and he had to push it up again. This repetition compulsion is an excellent example of the incapacity to elaborate creatively the life and death polarity.

Meditation: Part 2

There are many different meditations to prepare for death; in chapter 4, I described the first part of one, which I call "Contemplation of the Miracle of Life" (page 113). In it, the mind first detaches itself from the executive nervous system and concentrates on the sympathetic functions of breathing, circulation, and photosynthesis. In this second part, we practice mentally going out of the body on the voyage to the profundity of the universe. This journey prepares for the experience of life after death and should be practiced by people after age 40 who have undertaken analysis and proved to have an ego capable of regression and shadow elaboration.

Experiencing the Eternal Home

> Lay not up for yourselves treasures upon earth, where moth and rust doth corrupt, and where thieves break through and steal: But lay up for yourselves treasures in heaven, where neither moth nor rust doth corrupt, and where thieves do not break through nor steal: For where your treasure is, there will your heart be also. (Matt. 6:19-21)

Return for a moment to the first part of the meditation, below your life tree, and imagine the sun's rays participating in the oxygen production through the photosynthesis in plants. Leave your body and follow the sun's rays. Travel through the atmosphere and enter the outer space. See the blue earth very far away, your body in the pose of meditation, and the little monkey lying on the first branch over it.

Pass by the sun and watch the Milky Way all around you with its four hundred billion stars (Sagan 1980). Continue on and leave the Milky Way. Now you are in outer space among the hundred billion galaxies of the universe. You see Orion, Andromeda, and countless others. You experience the infinity of the cosmos. Contemplate the immensity of the universe. Let this feeling of admiration, intimacy, and delight turn into love for creation. When you feel it, you will recognize that you are in your eternal home. Although not knowing it before today, you have always been there. It is infinite and eternal and will continue to shelter you after you die. Now you know the way. In the days to come, you can visit it frequently as part of your ritual for learning how to live and die. You will be always welcomed.

Go back now to your body on earth. Tell the little monkey to begin brushing his apples. Say good-bye to the gnome and thank him for the experience.

These meditations can be enhanced with visits to a planetarium.

The Cosmic Coniunctio of Contemplative Consciousness

The cosmic experience of the separation from the body in this meditation prepares the entrance to the great home of being as the final coniunctio of the life process. The preparation for this encounter, which is the essence of life after death, occurs through the exercise of contemplative consciousness that commands without commanding (*wu wei*) the detachment from everything else and the final deliverance to become ready for the final attachment.

The climax of this ritual for the final coniunctio is the active imagination with creation within the eternal home, during which parts still obscure in the process of individuation and humanization will emerge and become more elaborated in each return to earth and to your body after meditation.

This ritual teaches that the imagination of life after death accompanies the processes of individuation and of humanization in the search for the final union with creation in infinity and eternity.

Chapter 13

THE ARCHETYPAL THEORY OF HISTORY

The Christian Myth and the Alterity Archetype

The Christian myth is a hero myth that expresses in the highest degree the transition from patriarchal dominance to the humanization of the dialectical position of the alterity archetype. This fact is meaningful in that it illustrates the prospective relationship of myth, evolution, and history (Byington 1983).

When I first read Hegel's lectures on history almost fifty years ago, I was fascinated by his prospective view of history as the search to attain freedom and unite reason with the world spirit (Hegel 1899). My fascination increased when Hegel conceived the logic of development through the dialectic of opposites whereby thesis and antithesis forms synthesis. Later, this fascination for Hegel subsided when I read Marx, who declared Hegel's theory idealistic and proposed instead that the end goal of history be communism, attained through the dialectic of class warfare. Seeing, however, that in *The Communist Manifesto* of Marx and Engels (1848) the democracy of the socialist movement inspired by dialectical materialism had been patriarchalized and deviated into dictatorship, I returned to Hegel to better understand history prospectively.

Jung's theoretical inclusion of the relationship of polarities in the individuation process reinforced the importance of the interaction of thesis and antithesis in psychological development. My formulation of the cultural Self, together with Teilhard de Chardin's concept of evolution through humanization, led me to see mythology in history beyond Neumann's patriarchal myths. Where could I situate the myths of Christ and of Buddha?

> The nineteenth and twentieth centuries (from their beginning) were mainly dedicated to discovering the past of humanity. The result of these investigations established that the birth of reason (la pensée) on earth corresponded biologically to a humanization (hominization) of life. Today, these researches are directed to the future, based on the development of the human phenomenon, and reveal the appearance in this direction of a perspective still more impressive: the progressive humanization of humankind. (Teilhard de Chardin 1959; my translation)

My conception of the archetypal positions of the ego-other relationship in individual and collective consciousness, coordinated by the matriarchal and patriarchal archetypes, led me to recognize the dialectical position of the alterity archetype in the coordination of these two archetypes as the foundation of freedom as originally conceived in socialism and in democracy (Byington 1992b).

Thus, I came back to Hegel's philosophy of history and its prospective goal of freedom as the expression of the incarnation of the alterity archetype in history. Evidently, with my Western background, it would not take long to see the Christian myth as the mythological expression of the archetype of alterity in the West and the Buddha myth as the same in the East. In this manner, the archetypal theory of history was born.

The historical transition toward the implantation of the alterity archetype in culture will here be described passing through the dominance of the patriarchal archetype mainly within the Christian myth. There is, however, another path toward alterity though the dominance of the matriarchal archetype, which we find expressed in India, for instance, in the myth of Krishna.

In Indian mythology, the transformation of the godhead is represented through ten avatars which are incarnations of Vishnu. In Sanskrit, the word avatar is formed by *ava*, which means "down," and *tarati*, which means "passing beyond." Avatar thus refers to the succeeding incarnations of the divine.

Krishna expresses the transition toward the alterity archetype through the dominance of the matriarchal archetype in the eighth avatar which precedes the ninth avatar of Buddha.

It was my wife, Maria Helena Mandacaru Guerra, who called my attention to the profound experience of alterity in the love relationship of Krishna and Radha. This mythological amplification occurred during her study of Jung's *Red Book*, which led her to write *The Red Book - The Love Drama of C. G. Jung* (2011).

We can also conceive this transition through a mixed path of matriarchal and patriarchal symbolism such as we find in the Latin novel *The Golden Ass* from Apuleius (Neumann 1952a) . Its matriarchal components are the structuring function of beauty and vanity present in the competition between Psyche and Aphrodite, and its patriarchal symbolism lies in the works prescribed by Aphrodite to Psyche. Finally, the alterity, anima, and animus characteristics are present in Eros and Psyche's search for equality in the masculine and feminine relationship and the blessing of their coniunctio granted by Zeus, which transforms them into a divine couple within wholeness.

The occupation and oppression of the land of Israel by Rome in the beginning of the Christian era represented the aggressive confrontation of two outstanding cultural traditions, both with intense patriarchal domination. Rome, with its military power, dominated a great part of the Western world and the Middle East. Israel, with the religion of the chosen people oriented by a sacred book, had an extraordinary pride and dignity; in spite of its small population, it had one of the richest spiritual traditions of antiquity.

This conflict existing within the polarized patriarchal position could only lead to the genocide of the Jewish people. This had been the model of confrontation between conflicting ethnic groups for more than ten thousand years of patriarchal dominance. When Corinth in Greece rebelled against Roman occupation in the year 146 B.C., all its men were slaughtered, its women and children were sold as slaves, and the city was looted and destroyed. Finally, its ruins were covered with salt so that nothing would flourish there again.

The archetypal polarized patriarchal model of handling ethical conflicts by aiming for the destruction of the enemy clearly demonstrated that the day humanity acquired sophisticated weaponry, as could be foreseen by developing technology, a war of catastrophic dimensions would end the process of civilization. Unfortunately, this obvious truth has been only partially assimilated and is one of the great threats to our survival.

The Jewish mystical tradition had long cultivated the messianic coming of a hero who would give back to Israel the past glory lived under the leadership of David and Salomon. But how could Israel face the immensely greater military power of the Roman Empire? Wouldn't an armed rebellion lead to the massacre of Israel and to the destruction of the second temple, as it in fact happened in 70 A.D.?

This tragic and threatening atmosphere activated in the Jewish cultural Self an archetype that mediates opposites more profoundly and creatively than the exclusively polarized position of the patriarchal archetype. As with all archetypes, it had always existed virtually, but now, on the eve of genocide, it was activated in the history of collective consciousness through a myth of incarnation: not the incarnation of a patriarchal hero bringing war and victory or defeat but rather the incarnation of a messianic hero who would offer salvation to humankind through self-sacrifice. Had anyone or anything caused such a myth? No, and the proof of this is that both sides of the conflict, thesis and antithesis, repudiated such a synthesis. It was kairos, the archetypal historical tension of the Jewish cultural Self that constellated the incarnation of the messianic hero of the dialectical position of the archetype of alterity through the principle of synchronicity.

Within the numerous mystical sects that existed in Palestine, many of which cultivated heroic dreams of fighting Roman oppression, one more prophet announced a revolutionary message and was crucified during the festivities of Passover. He bothered Jews who were either negotiating Roman occupation or preparing the revolt to fight Rome as well as Romans, who thought only of maintaining social order so that they would continue receiving their taxes.

By synchronicity, too, a Roman citizen of Jewish descent was converted to the message of the carpenter's son and continued to preach it within the Roman Empire as catholic, that is, universal. When Paul abandoned the ritual of circumcision, he renounced the dominance of the patriarchal archetype and the myth of the chosen people. He preached the "good news" of the dialectical position of the alterity archetype to elaborate sin, which is the shadow, in the search for salvation of humankind.

The Conversion of the Roman Empire and the Institutionalization of Christianity

The employment of the principle of synchronicity within the dialectical position of the archetype of alterity allows us to relate acausally many unforeseeable meanings of events, also prospectively.

The synchronicity in the implantation of Christianity would be most influential in its institutionalization. The Roman Empire had always forcefully repressed all those who defied its ruthless domination. Christians were considered subversive and pitilessly persecuted. They met in secret in catacombs that grew rapidly around Rome. Many were imprisoned and delivered to lions in the Colosseum. However, they distinguished themselves from other prisoners, for they entered the arena singing and holding hands in the face of their martyrdom. It is not difficult to imagine the impact this had on the people and how much the martyrs contributed to spreading the new religion. Fascination for the "good news," which eventually converted a great part of the planet, can be better understood today when we realize that its central message was to implant in history an archetypal position in collective unconsciousness that can save our species.

Jesus' message of love is permeated with compassion for the less favored parts of society. He preaches love for the other as for oneself and that we are to turn the other face to our enemy, that is, to elaborate the understanding of aggression within acceptance. We have here three characteristics of the dialectical position of alterity. One is the democratic integration of all members of society, which psychologically means the articulation of all parts dialectically and with equal rights within the whole. The second is the integration proposed through the dialectical interaction with the social shadow represented by the poor and the sick in society, so well illustrated by the Sermon on the Mount. The third, and perhaps the most important, is the message of salvation through the elaboration of sin, that is, the shadow, which dissociates one from God that is from the totality coordinated by the central archetype, to rescue human integrity.

One of the most remarkable events in Western history was the conversion of the Roman Empire. In 312 A.D., Constantine's armies were preparing to fight the armies of Maxentius in what became known as the battle of the Milvian Bridge near Rome on October 28th. According to Christian apologist Lactantius, Constantine had a dream the night before the battle in which he was told to mark the shields of his troops with a sign of Christ, most likely the Chi-Rho. The historian Eusebius related a different version in which Constantine saw in the sky the Christian sign with the legend, *Cum hoc signo vincent* (In this sign, conquer). In 313 A.D., with the Edict of

Milan, Christians were no longer persecuted, their confiscated properties were returned, and the conversion of the Roman Empire began.

The Mythologizing of Jesus' Message

The mythologizing of Jesus' life allows us to amplify his preaching in a much more extensive dimension than its factual transmission would have done. In this way, we can see the relationship of fact, myth, and history, which is essential to the understanding of the archetypal theory of history. This theory is also essential for explaining the formation of myth and for understanding the modifications of the meanings of myths throughout history, which can be creative or defensive as we see with the myth of Christ. The mythologization involves the symbolic amplification of fact through the transcendent structuring function of the imagination, which includes the miracles, the greatest of which was the Resurrection. It is indeed the Resurrection that best expresses the relation of the Christian myth with history symbolically, because through it we become conscious of the millennial transformation of Western culture toward the bourgeoisie, the conquest of modern civil rights, modern art, and science.

The symbolism of the Christian myth occurs within the hero myth. The threatened birth, the double paternity, the virgin mother, and the miracles are classical components of the heroic saga. The visit of the three kings following a star confirms it. The heroic feats begin with the miraculous Dionysian transformation of water into wine at the marriage in Canaan and include the curing of cases of possession and blindness, the multiplication of bread and fish, and the resurrection of Lazarus. The hero's death is a paradox because he is tortured and crucified by those to whom he offered love. Finally, the Resurrection is seen and recognized only by a woman, and his reencounter with humanity is announced for the future.

The dialectical position of the alterity archetype in the myth establishes the encounter (*Auseinandersetzung*) of consciousness and sin, that is, the shadow in the search of salvation. The transformation is so great that it occurs through the life-death and rebirth polarity within the individuation and humanization processes. The central sacrifice of the myth is that of the whole personally, through which the death of the son, as thesis, transforms the role of the father, as antithesis, into the Trinity with the Holy Ghost (synthesis). This initiating experience through symbolic death forms the mystery of the Trinity, which expresses the transformation of the matriarchal and patriarchal paradigms into the paradigm of alterity in the world.

In my view it is a gross psychological misunderstanding to consider Christianity to be monotheistic because its whole mystery of transformation through death and resurrection goes beyond patriarchal dominance, which is the archetypal essence of monotheism. The Christian myth expresses the archetype of alterity because it ransoms the insular matriarchal position characteristic of polytheism through the incarnation and relates it dialectically to the patriarchal polarized position characteristic of monotheism. The polarized dynamic expression of the life-death polarity in the transformation of the personality well illustrates the patriarchal dominance in the perspective of psychoanalysis and its difference from analytical psychology. Whereas psychoanalysis established a rigid polarized dualistic separation of the life and death drives, analytical psychology situated life and death within a symbolic dialectical relationship of duality in unity in psychological development (Jung 1912; Byington 1965, 1996).

The archetypal theory of history allows us to imagine that the implantation of the archetype of alterity in Western culture had a most important structuring civilizing function, from which originate most of the important issues of modern humanism including democracy and the modern sciences.

The structuring function of the Christian myth in the historical implantation of the dialectical position of alterity, however, has not been duly recognized and valued. Its consequences were found in all dimensions of modern life, but its archetypal pattern, and above all its historical root in the myth, has not been identified due to the historical deformation of the myth during institutionalization.

The archetypal theory of history uses the concepts of the cultural Self, of structuring symbols, complexes, functions, and systems, and of fixation and defenses forming the shadow to understand the normal and pathological development of collective consciousness.

The connections between the Christian myth, the alterity archetype, and modern humanism in Western culture have not been duly assessed due to the defensive patriarchalization of the myth, which gave birth to the Inquisition. The myth, so deformed, has been identified with the Inquisition and most unjustly blamed for a reactionary approach to the revolutionary ideas of science and modern humanism, which it had itself created. It is hard to see and understand that, from the perspective of the cultural Self, Christianity is a divided institution just like the neurotic individual personality. One part is the myth, the other is the institutionalized myth and its shadow with great deformities as a result of defensive patriarchalization (Byington 1991a).

The dialectic of alterity is extraordinarily creative and difficult for the ego to understand, to practice, and above all to maintain. It calls for great openness to the new and, to evil and also to the detachment from the old, which has died and needs to be delivered to death. The dialectic conscious position of alterity calls for the permanent and intense usage of the structuring transcendent function of the imagination, of the sacrificial and the ethical functions to live the paradigm of symbolic humanism (Byington 1997). Due to these difficulties, the acquisition of the dialectics of alterity preached by the myth are frequently reduced to the matriarchal and patriarchal archetypes (the matriarchalization and patriarchalization of alterity), which sometimes become fixated and defensive and thus form shadow.

From the Christian Myth to the Inquisition

Christianity and Buddhism have hundreds of millions of adherents worldwide, side by side with Hinduism and Islamism. However, the myths of Christ and of the Buddha are still far from being implanted in civilization. Their central teaching is compassion, which is very difficult to assimilate because it requires transformation of the world vision of the patriarchal paradigm to live the dialectical relationship of the alterity paradigm.

Anyone who has understood the prospective aspect of the concepts of structuring symbols, complexes, functions, and systems within the dimension of myth, dream, and fantasy will find the notion of the intervening time between the constellation of a myth and its integration in collective consciousness perfectly normal. The myth of Christ has had approximately two thousand years and the myth of the Buddha approximately two thousand six hundred years, which is a relative short historical time for the implantation of their extraordinary proposition, whose messianic transformation involves such a radical change in the religious, socioeconomic, political, and ecological dimensions in the individual, family, cultural, planetary, and cosmic dimensions of the Self.

However, another important factor that delays the implantation of the myth in history, besides this natural implantation time, is the phenomenon of fixation, which delays elaboration of the symbolic content and forms defenses within the shadow exactly as it does in the individual psyche as described by Freud. These defenses act out the fixated symbols in a deformed way that can be very destructive, even to the point of expressing the opposite meaning they normally have. This happened during the institutionalization of the Christian myth in which the fixated symbols came to express defensively the devil, appropriately also called the Antichrist. This fixation of the myth created the Inquisition, which expressed the shadow of Christianity in history (Byington 1991a).

The great difficulty of institutionalizing Christianity occurred synchronistically and paradoxically with the patriarchal historical conditions of the implantation of its myth. Constantine's miraculous facility for converting the Empire from top to bottom was made possible by the rigid social stratification coordinated by the dominance of the polarized position of the patriarchal archetype. It was only natural then that after the conversion, the organization formed to implant the myth, that is, the Church, assumed the same patriarchal model. How was the Church going to implant the paradigm of alterity to transform the dominant patriarchal model, when the Church itself was organized according to that paradigm? This was the great dilemma of the historical implantation of Christianity, and it was for this reason that the Church did not always have the capacity to differentiate Christ and Antichrist.

Understanding the difference between the Christian myth and institutionalized Christianity is of the utmost importance for relating myth, archetype, and history in the way proposed by Jungian symbolic psychology. A frequent misunderstanding that arises during the interpretation of symbols of Christianity, including Jung's writings, is the nondifferentiation of the myth from the Church (Jung 1940, 1948b).

We must realize then that the great difficulty of implanting the structuring symbols of the Christian myth socially, from the beginning, arose from the historical conditions of its institutionalization. We already mentioned that Constantine converted to Christianity before the battle with Maxentius. When he had the Christian sign painted on the shields of his soldiers before battle, he clearly placed the cross at the service of the sword, in total opposition to the teachings of Jesus. This was, no doubt, the first great occurrence of the patriarchalization of the myth, synchronistically linked to the conversion of the empire.

The political system that best expresses the social implantation of the archetype of alterity is democracy. Christianity did not have the least chance to be institutionalized democratically, because the political system that accepted it had a pyramidal structure characteristic of the polarized patriarchal position which had been practiced traditionally through the social political reference of imperial Rome. Christianity adopted this hierarchical model of Roman administration and organized an army of priests, bishops, and cardinals under the command of a unique leader, the pope. Although on the one hand, it was permeated by certain democratic characteristics, such as the election of the pope by vote, on the other hand, the lifelong mandate, the administration through papal bulls, and the vows of poverty, chastity, and total obedience clearly belonged to the patriarchal model. In this way, the ecclesiastic organization that was formed was more cohesive than any army. The power of the pope was exalted to the point of divinizing his special decrees ex cathedra. In this sense, the pope was magically-mythically considered the representative of God on Earth, like many kings, emperors, and pharaohs of patriarchal regimes. According to this patriarchal hierarchy, women occupied a much lower position than men in the institution.

The patriarchalization of ritual restricting religiosity to sermons and obedience to priests cut off at the root the dialectical communication of Christians with God, that is, of the ego with the central archetype through the archetype of alterity. There followed the repressive legislation of sin undertaken mainly through papal bulls expressing canon law with the requirement of absolute obedience and threatened in many ways.

Confession is the great Christian ritual for elaborating the dialectical relation of virtue and sin, good and evil before God, that is, psychological totality. Patriarchalization weakened confession and reduced it grotesquely to the enumeration of transgressions and to penalties codified through prayers in order to receive absolution and grace. This reduction deformed the ritual of confession and prevented it from being lived as the encounter of the devil-tormented soul with Christ. The weakening of the structuring function of confession through defensive patriarchalization was so great that it corrupted absolution and culminated in the selling of indulgences.

It is impressive how frequently Christian education uses condemnation to hell as a threat to obtain good behavior from children. This patriarchal attitude separates children from the intimate dialectical relation with Christ, causing repression and shadow formation through fear instead of dialectical integration.

Mentions made here to the defensive patriarchalization of Christianity during institutionalization refer mainly to the Roman Catholic Church, but this does not mean that much that is here considered cannot also be applied to Orthodox Christianity and Protestantism in varying degrees.

A few years ago I went to visit a dear friend on her deathbed. She had suffered very much during her life and was a very delicate and kindhearted person. She was loved in her Catholic community because she visited families, taking the image of the Virgin Mary to pray with them. Suddenly, in the middle of our conversation, she took my hand tightly and told me that she was afraid to die. I told her that she needed to talk to Jesus about this and let him show her the way. She then became very serious and remarked: "But I do not know how to do this!" I was very surprised and replied: "But it is so easy. You lived your whole life with Him. You only have to talk about all that you lived and include your fear of death." She became even more serious and scared and repeated: "But I do not know how to do that." I felt as though she were telling me that she did not have permission to do it because it was sinful.

The Church stimulated the faithful to worship the victimized crucified Christ. This is praiseworthy within the history of the Christian faith, but its exaggeration and the way it was used repressively to manipulate power frequently prevented the community from experiencing the glory of the Resurrection and of living with Christ. If this had been done, Christianity would have become a religion of love, joy, and creativity emotionally attuned to the myth and not a religion that emphasizes sadness, repression, sin, guilt, submission, and fear of hell.

The experience of the Passion of Christ includes good and evil to elaborate sin, that is, the shadow, in the search of totality. In this way the relationship of Christ with the devil within the dialectics of alterity belongs to the essence of the myth, which is at the center of the ritual of confession.

When Jesus is prevented during confession from a confrontation with the devil in the dialectical relation of sin and virtue within the religious experience, the polarized patriarchal position takes over in the figure of the priest and establishes an antithetical relation between good and evil which paralyzes the redeeming action of Christ in the symbolic elaboration of sin through repentance.

Imagine a patient elaborating a mother or father complex amid rage and tears, and the analyst interrupting to say: "Now you will promise in the name of your health and well-being that you will never again experience these emotions." The patient would answer: "I promise." And the analyst would add: "You may go now."

The Inquisition

Cruelly persecuted in the Roman Empire for almost three centuries, Christianity was finally tolerated beginning in 313 A.D. with the Edict of Milan. After the official beginning of institutionalization, the Church changed from being persecuted to being the persecutor, and the religious dimension came to be experienced within the social status and the articulations of political power. This could not be otherwise because the myth, which represented the incarnation of the dialectical position of alterity, had to be compressed into the patriarchal polarized position in order to be institutionalized. Up until then, Christians were victims of persecution by the patriarchal authorities. However, once in power, Christians assumed the traditional patriarchal pattern to control and codify the myth. The initial codification of faith with the passing of time became canon law (*Corpus juris canonici*) to control the exercise of all religious activity. Anyone who came up with an idea or religious practice that was considered to be in disagreement with canonic law was subject to the accusation of heresy and subject to punishment, including the death penalty (Byington 1991a).

It is obvious that symbols as powerful as those contained in the Christian myth needed different ways of elaboration during its institutionalization in order to experience, understand, integrate, and transform collective consciousness. Thesis could not become synthesis without entering into a dialectical encounter with antithesis. This undertaking, however, collided with the necessity of maintaining a political and ideological stability within the Church, so that the community could receive a uniform orientation. The easiest way to accomplish this was through a non constructive directive and repetitive way of teaching in which people were trained and oriented without actively participating in the experience of the learning process. This, of course, was teaching based on the polarized patriarchal position, which could not in any way be pedagogically constructive (Byington 2004).

In this manner, the concept of heresy - from the Greek hairesis, which generally means a school of thought and which originally was the very expression of the dialectical creativity in the elaboration of the myth - was considered sinful and used to persecute anyone who thought or felt differently from the orientation established by the Church. In that manner the Church maintained the exclusiveness of the elaboration of the myth with absolute control and prevented the participation of the community in any elaboration whatsoever of its extraordinary symbolic vitality. Heresies as different ways of elaborating the myth grew, and this resulted in increased persecution, intolerance, and repression, and in the great schisms of Christianity within the cultural Self (Byington 1991a). I include within these schisms the separation of science and religion in the university at the end of the eighteenth century.

A psychodynamic study of the structuring symbols, complexes, functions and systems contained in these countless heresies, would certainly reveal a great many meanings of psychological importance for the understanding of the myth. We know for instance, that the Gnostics, a sect that was persecuted and destroyed as heretical, were very creative mystics (Hoeller 1982). Possibly, one of the characteristics for which they were considered heretics and persecuted was their direct contact with Jesus through the imagination. Countless Christian mystics who had visions of Christ and interacted with Him in meditation must have also practiced active imagination. As we know, Jung practiced this method extensively and adopted it as the main expressive technique for symbolic elaboration (Jung 2009; Guerra 2011). The well-known meditations found in the spiritual exercises of St. Ignatius of Loyola show the patriarchal control of psychological creativity of symbolic elaboration to remain within the bounds of canonic law.

The fact that the paradox of the Holy Trinity is the theoretical center of the Christian myth made it the subject of many heresies. Among them we distinguish the heresy of Arius, who considered the nature of the Father different from that of the Son (homoiousian). This idea was considered heretical already by the Nicean Council of 323 A.D. when the concept that the nature of the Father and the Son are one (homoousian) was established as canon. This polarity between equality and difference of the Father and the Son in the Holy Trinity is very creative from the perspective of the dialectical position of alterity. If the Father and the Son are one, both become God and the polar opposites father and son are conceived as one. However if the Father and the Son are different, we have much more scope for amplifying the extraordinary symbolism of the incarnation of the Holy Ghost, who, through the Passion of Christ, united the Father and the Son as duality in unity (Byington 1965). Indeed, the symbolism of the Holy Trinity most profound and meaningful to me is reached when the opposites are equal and also different, that is, when the Father and the Son are equal and, at the same time, different and related through the Holy Ghost. Had that been accepted as canon law, the Arius heresy might well have been adopted by Christian theology, side by side with the approved version, enriching it greatly.

When the mystery of the Trinity is seen symbolically in this manner, we cannot say that the Christian religion is a monotheism, a category which suits the unified abstraction of the patriarchal position. The Christian myth is a reunion of monotheism and polytheism like so many other mythologies, including Greek, Indian, and Egyptian, all of which express many characteristics of the alterity archetype.

Although the Inquisition proper was not established until the twelfth and thirteenth centuries (the creation of the Holy Office for the Questions of Faith occurred in 1229 during the papacy of Gregory IX), already at the beginning of institutionalization in the fourth century deliberations and laws against heretics arose and flourished with astonishing frequency and regularity. In the reigns of Emperor Valentinian I (364-375) and Theodosius I (379-395), heretics were subject to exile and confiscation of property and were disqualified to inherit and finally subject to the death penalty. The Spanish bishop Priscillian was judged guilty of heresy by his congregation and condemned to death by order of Emperor Magnus Maximus of the Western Roman Empire in 385 A.D. (Byington 1991a).

The Inquisition then was not only a time of especially repressive Christianity, but indeed the carefully and legally codified expression of the defensive patriarchalization of the myth, which terrified Western culture. It lasted, incredibly, for fourteen centuries if we count from Priscillian's death to the decapitation of the last woman accused of witchcraft on 18 June 1789 in Glarus, Switzerland (Zilboorg and Henry 1941).

The death penalty was decreed by the Church and implemented by the government. Although the death penalty has been abolished, the Holy Office continues to be active because it is not necessary to kill the flesh when one can kill the spirit. An example of the continuing defensive patriarchalization of the Church in Brazil, which is the largest Catholic country in the world, occurred after the publication of the book *Church: Charism and Power* by Brazilian theologian Leonardo Boff in 1984. He first received from the Holy Office the order to remain for a year in "obsequious silence," which meant that he could not lecture or publish anything. This repression ended by him leaving the Church. According to the Brazilian press at the time, Boff affirmed that during his audience with Cardinal Ratzinger, today Pope Benedict XVI, in the hall of the Congregation for the Doctrine of the Faith in Rome, he became aware that he was sitting in the same chair occupied by Galileo almost four hundred years earlier.

One must bear in mind, however, that throughout the centuries of patriarchalized defensive repression of Christian theology, the Church preserved the core of the myth in the holy mass and communion. It is true that frequently the Host is given to the believer and the wine is taken exclusively by the priest, but the miracle of the Eucharist and the mystery of the Passion and Resurrection have remained intact in the ritual of the Catholic mass for two millennia. This has been perhaps one of the greatest contributions of the Catholic Church to favor the genuine implantation of the myth during its institutionalization. In this sense, many Protestant sects resulting from the Reformation, which was formed to abolish celibacy, the selling of indulgences, and papal power, among other things, patriarchalized the myth still further with the elimination of the cult of saints and holy images of the cult of Virgin Mary, of the Eucharist, and even of communion during the mass. With this increase in the patriarchalization of the myth and repression of its matriarchal aspects, Protestantism favored the defensive tendency to consider Christianity to be monotheistic.

The Christian Myth, the Renaissance, and the Birth of Modern Science

From the perspective of an archetypal theory of history, I see the great creative contribution of the Christian myth, in addition to the progressive implantation of the search for social democracy, to be the birth of modern science.

During the first millennium of the elaboration of the myth, we find the predominance of introversion in monastic life. Within the intense patriarchal control of the social elaboration of the myth, as described above, its creativity was preserved mostly in the mass and in monastic life. Because the Church limited the elaboration primarily to the victimization of Christ, concentrating on his suffering and his death on the cross, and in the martyrdom of the saints, the elaboration of sin through the introversion of monastic life and depression became a permissible way to experience the message of the myth dialectically.

This could be done in compassion and detachment from power through the humility and solidarity of mysticism in the monastic community life.

Neoplatonic philosophy, especially the ideas of Plotinus (204/5-270), contributed to this tendency, along with the work of Augustine (354-430). Introversion, feeling, intuition, and spiritual creativity met in the translation of erudition from antiquity and led to monastic medieval philosophy through Aristotle toward extraversion. Taking on the study of Aristotle, Thomas Aquinas (1225-1274) conceived the Aristotelian-Thomist synthesis in the thirteenth century, which united Aristotle and Christian theology in the *Summa Theologica*.

Long centuries of discussions in the monasteries of the Middle Ages developed the thinking function and the art of arguing (dialectics) in the elaboration of the myth (Eco, 1980). One of the great if not the greatest conquest of this introverted journey, which united old and experienced monks and young novices, was the precise examination of emotions and feelings. This examination of consciousness evaluated their intimacy and correctness of their understanding of and faith in Christ, so well described in St. John of the Cross's dark night of the soul.

It was this examination of consciousness practiced in the monasteries within the dialectics of faith and sin that incorporated the alterity archetype's dialectical way of thinking into the Christian myth. It was this extraordinary acquisition that, centuries later, influenced by Aristotle, extraverted to examine nature and became the scientific method.

The second millennium of elaboration of the myth presented an increasing extraversion which used the elaboration obtained in introversion through feeling and intuition in the first millennium to explore nature through thinking and sensation and the social dimension through feeling and intuition. The monasteries became modern universities and the excessive control over subjectivity by the Holy Office favored the extraversion of libido to study the outer world instead. The acquisition of the dialectics of alterity to study the different states of consciousness regarding sin and virtue through confession in the monasteries became extraverted and fostered a dialectical examination of the nature of truth and error through the scientific method. The rescue of the insular matriarchal position, greatly repressed concerning wealth, social status, and sexuality, became extraverted in the observations of nature and the experiments of alchemy. This elaboration of the natural forces through the sensuality of the insular matriarchal archetype allied with the monastic discipline, organization, and coherence of the patriarchal archetype, originated the scientific method and modern science, exercised in the dialectical position of the alterity archetype. Thousands of years after the epoch-making pastoral agricultural revolution, another extraordinary cultural transformation was launched.

The Second Great Revolution

His erudition acquired in the universities of Krakow, Bologna, and Padua encompassed all the knowledge of the Renaissance. He worked during the day in the parish of his uncle, the prince-bishop of Warmia, and at night he examined the stars. He observed, imagined, measured, and calculated, but he did not dare to conclude. Something was missing. However, he felt deeply that the dialectics between truth and error was fundamental for the knowledge he searched. And so he continued to observe, measure, imagine, calculate, and correct. Possibly in a dream or a vision, which was more like lightning between one patient and another in the bishop's parish, he suddenly saw the earth circulating around the sun. As the *Emerald Tablet* had revealed, polarities relate in opposition, but also in equality. The apparent movement of the sun around the earth, which we see daily in the sky, is certainly true because we see it so, but the movement of the earth around the sun, which is the opposite of what we see, is also true. One is the apparent truth, the other is the truth of reality. He waited for the night, looked again at the stars, and again he measured, calculated, and corrected. This time everything fell into place. With this new perspective, error disappeared. He looked at the starry heaven now and felt that God, the universe, confirmed the truth revealed to him through the scientific method.

The importance of the discovery of the central position of the sun, with the planets, including the earth, around it, by Nicolaus Copernicus (1473-1543) symbolically inaugurated the revolution of modern science. Contrary to the perception of the senses expressed by the insular matriarchal position and the magical-mythical imagination and established by tradition, science discovered reality beyond appearance and established a new paradigm to express the transcendent relation with God and the universe through the dialectical position of error and truth of the alterity archetype.

The extraordinary paradigm of the agricultural-pastoral revolution with its miraculous power to transform civilization through the settlement of nomadic life millennia later gave way to the scientific paradigm. The first revolution produced the conditions necessary for the establishment of the polarized position of the patriarchal archetype in the organization of social life. The second revolution permitted symbolic elaboration to go beyond the sensual appearances of the matriarchal archetype and the organizing patterns of the patriarchal archetype in order to implant the dialectical position of the alterity archetype in science and to methodologically study the essence of reality. The patriarchal paradigm led humanity to control nature and human life. The alterity paradigm led us to know them.

The structuring effect of the Christian myth revealed in introversion the reality of emotions behind appearance. Through confession, meditation, and the dialectical method of examining the mind it revealed the presence of sin, that is, of the shadow in the relationship with God. Its extraversion employed the same method to identify and go beyond error, the shadow of knowledge, and establish a relationship of truth with the universe, that is, with God. In this manner, the elaboration of error followed that of sin and evil (the shadow) in the search for truth and totality. This revolution culminated four hundred years later in the intuition of another great genius to express the dialectical position of alterity in the equation $E = mc^2$ that could establish the energy-matter and mind-matter polarities as the fundamental parameter of the knowable universe.

The hypothesis that modern science originated from the Christian myth follows the overall idea that myths are the symbolic root of the transformation of collective consciousness.

One bit of strong evidence that the creation of modern science was rooted in the Christian myth is that for the pioneers of science there was not the least antagonism between science and religion. On the contrary, they felt that the dialectic of alterity between virtue and sin present in the myth was totally consonant with the dialectic of truth and error inherent in the scientific method. Discoveries were related systemically with wholeness through the structuring functions of truth, ethics, and love. Each new discovery was a symbol of a new behavior of a structuring function which increased the complexity of the whole and the miracle of creation, being one more proof of the glory of the Lord and of the generosity of Jesus' sacrifice. Science and religion united to save humankind and redeem it from sin, error, and sickness. All the great geniuses, such as Copernicus, Galileo, Descartes, Kepler, Newton, and Leibnitz, were deeply religious and Christian.

It was not mathematics that separated science from religion, because mathematical equations were proof of the divine grandiosity of the harmony and beauty of the universe. The search for truth by the scientist fighting error and the battle of the mystic against sin in search of salvation were consonant because both expressed with great clarity the dialectics preached by Jesus. In this manner, error had to be identified and corrected to know the truth within science in the same way that sin and evil needed to be scrutinized in confession to be rescued from fixations in the shadow and integrated into goodness, freedom, and salvation. The necessity of experiencing sin and correctly separating it from virtue requires that one enter profoundly into the nature of the fixed structuring function in order to discriminate its normal function from its distortion. This can be done only through the elaboration of sin in confession, which is what we do today in treating symptoms with expressive techniques in analysis in order to rescue the personality from neurosis.

Case Example

A fifty-year-old man sought medical help because he was becoming more and more irritated and aggressive every day. He was treated with an anxiolytic, but that did not help. He started drinking. He had been very kindhearted and affectionate, but was now becoming cold and cynical.

He came to therapy, and in his first dream he was holding and carrying his brother who was five years older. In early youth, the brother had been diagnosed with juvenile diabetes, became blind, and died at the age of twenty-five. For years, the two brothers, along with a sister and their parents, cried daily over the suffering and eminent death of the sick brother. After his death, they swore never to cry again.

I tried to show to my patient that his feeling function had suffered a serious fixation, which kept him from suffering for many years. He had repressed his feeling function, but now he was missing it. He was aggressive and constantly irritated because that was the way he expressed frustration through his distorted feeling function. He took the anxiolytic medication and then started drinking to literally drown the feeling function once and for all.

I explained to him that his first dream of analysis showed that he needed to draw near to his brother again, even though he suffered, because that was the price of rescuing his feeling function. He resisted this suggestion, remembering that he and his family had sworn never to go back to that suffering and observing that this attitude had worked well for years.

I asked him to bring a picture of his brother to our next session. After he looked at the picture, we started active imagination. I asked him to look into his brother's eyes, showing him the state of aggressive irritation he was in, and ask for help. The brother answered that this was the result of their emotional separation. The patient understood that death had separated the brothers, but that the moment had come for them to feel that suffering again. It contained the love that was now lacking in his life and making him suffer. The impact was so strong that we cried. The patient was convinced. He opened himself to suffering, his feeling function returned to its normal expression, and his symptoms subsided.

The lesson this case teaches is that the aggression and irritation that were destroying his life were a fixation and a defensive way of living the feeling function he had repressed. The cure lay within the wound. Had we eliminated the aggression and irritation with drugs or cognitive behavioral therapy, he would have blocked his feeling function still further, with crippling consequences for the rest of his developmental process.

This is why the elaboration of sin through confession is so important, because within it is the hurt function that must be rescued to secure salvation. In this sense, the ritual of confession and elaboration of sin are analogous to the elaboration of symptoms and their underlying fixations and defenses in symbolic psychotherapy.

Louis Pasteur (1822-1895) was named director of sciences at the École Normale Supérieure in 1856. At the time, there was no scientific explanation for fermentation and the theory of spontaneous generation of putrefaction had many adherents. Pasteur had an intuition about the dialectical relation of the putrefaction of meat and microbes and went on to prove that putrefaction could be avoided by heat. He thus discovered the process of pasteurization and proved definitively that spontaneous generation does not exist.

It is as though Pasteur had an extraordinary vocation for the archetype of alterity expressed by his capacity to see the duality raw meat and putrefied meat operating within unity. In this manner, microbes could transform raw meat into putrefaction, which meant that the duality of fresh meat and putrefied meat did not present two absolute different and separate dimensions. Through the action of microbes the same meat can appear in two different states (duality in unity). This discovery made Pasteur the founder of the science of microbiology and inventor of many vaccines, which culminated in the vaccine against rabies in 1885.

It is important to assert that science and the Christian myth have the same root in the dialectical position of the alterity archetype. This perception allows us to understand that the modern opposition, estrangement, and incompatibility between science and the Christian myth are not archetypally true. It originated historically with the Inquisition and was followed by the subject-object dissociation begun at the end of the eighteenth century when science identified the myth with the Inquisition and eliminated it from the university together with the whole of subjectivity. This dissociation of the cultural Self developed into the rational materialism and positivism of the nineteenth century.

Materialism and the Subjective-Objective Dissociation
Science as the Greatest of All Heresies

The increasing antagonism that developed between science and religion, or better put, between religion and science, was not originally structural due to their nature. On the contrary, the archetypal foundation of science and of the Christian myth is one and the same. The conflict was institutionally established when the defensively patriarchalized Inquisition possessed the Church and began persecuting scientists as heretics (Byington 1991a).

Although Copernicus made his first observation in 1497, the publication of his complete works didn't occur until 1540, and according to legend, he looked at the last version in 1543, on his deathbed. He parted having left the celestial worldview upside down, something that could not be more heretical. The Holy Office fell upon his scientific heirs, the noblest of whom was Galileo. In this manner, science became the great heresy, so great indeed that 250 years later it defeated the institutionalized Christianity and locked the doors of the temples of knowledge to all subjectivity.

The pioneers of science were not materialists, not a single one of them. On the contrary, their spirituality was so great that they transcended the truth of appearances to search for truth (God) in the dimension of essence. They all were emotionally one with the Christian myth because their search for truth and love of totality were the same. It was the Church that had always considered the scientists to be suspected of an atheist heresy. The Christ of the scientists was the Christ of truth, glory, and resurrection, while the Christ of the Inquisition was of the tortured victim, nailed, and immobilized on the cross and used to manipulate and paralyze creativity. This Christ was revered dead, speechless, and never resurrected. His image on the cross was used to sustain the dogmatic authoritarianism of the Church and to persecute anyone who disobeyed. The Christ of the myth whom scientists loved and revered was the Christ of the glory of the Resurrection to be lived fully in the dialectical position of the Son and the Father through the transcendent function of the imagination represented by the Holy Ghost. The Christ of the Inquisition was used to manipulate people's guilt for being alive, for enjoying sex and pleasure, and to submit them as obedient sheep to the puritanical authority of the Church, coordinated by the defensive polarized position of the patriarchal archetype which submits completely the community to the Church. The great symbol elected for this holy and archetypal war was the heliocentric system, which expressed the might of science as the greatest of all heresies.

During this war between science and the Inquisition, the symbol of the heliocentric system was most important for three reasons. First, it invalidated the Ptolemaic astronomical system from the second century A.D., which was a traditional way of seeing heaven and God as old as the Church. Second, the Copernican revolution shook the basis of knowledge of the heavens, of God's domain, structured on the defensive power position which used the magical-mythical mentality of the insular matriarchal position to impose the religious perspective as the only way to seek truth. Third, the elaboration of error and sin through the dialectic of alterity would sooner or later be applied to the cultural Self and would certainly expose the immense shadow of the Inquisition and of the Church.

The condemnation of Giordano Bruno, burned at the stake in the center of Rome in 1600 after being transported in a wagon through the crowds, gagged with his tongue pierced, illustrated vividly to the scientific community the risk of practicing the dialectical position of the alterity archetype in the search of knowledge.

Confirming the heliocentric theory after observing the heavens with an eyeglass, Galileo became the center of knowledge and depository of the scientific heresy. The use of the eyeglass illustrates the increasing employment of the insular matriarchal position in the scientific method. It was no longer a question of imagining mythically and then repeating patriarchally how the heavens should be, but rather using sensuality through amplified vision to see

and describe (insular matriarchal position) side by side with all other observations systemically organized (patriarchal position). In this manner, the observations made by Tycho Brahe and Copernicus were precious to Galileo. The humiliation of this prince of scientists, compelled to kneel before five cardinals of the Holy Office and deny his discoveries and conclusions, was a historic example for the whole scientific community of the arrogance, authoritarianism, ignorance, cowardice, and repressive capacity of the Inquisition. The condemnation of Galileo to house arrest until his death sealed the rupture between the Church and modern science.

When Descartes published his *Discourse on the Method*, which became the new paradigm of the scientific worldview, one century after Copernicus's discovery, he established the polarized patriarchal position as a basic condition for the practice of the dialectics of alterity in the scientific method. In this manner, he broke the hegemony of the magical-mythical matriarchal position in the formulation of truth. Within the Cartesian method, imagination is free but not so much as to affirm subjectivity as reality. First it needs to be patriarchalized to strictly separate the ego (the subjective) from the other (the objective). *The Method* separates thinking (*res cogitans*) from nature (*res extensa*) "to think well," which is fundamental for separating the magical-mythical position characterized by the insular matriarchal position from the polarized patriarchal position.

To say that the pioneering scientists believed in the Christian myth does not mean that they reasoned exclusively within the magical-mythical dimension of reality. The Church admitted this reality but patriarchalized it defensively, whereas the leading scientists operated it parallel to the separation of the subjective-objective reality as Descartes proposed.

The Implantation of the Archetype of Alterity and the Renaissance

Within this process of mythical extraversion, which began in the thirteenth century and continued into the Renaissance, we register a significant flood of energy into social life and the study of nature. After a millennium of introversion and centuries in the monasteries to elaborate through depression the suffering and the sacrificial death of the Messiah, there erupted the spectacular volcanic creativity of the Renaissance as the mythological expression of Christ's Resurrection and glory. Creative depression had done its work, and now creative progression took over (Byington 2007). The synchronistic label of *Renaissance*, which means a retake of the art of antiquity, is an analogy of the mythical Resurrection. It is a pity that we have so much difficulty seeing the Renaissance symbolically as the Resurrection within the continuing implantation of the Christian myth.

The dialectical relation of opposites within the cultural Self expressed by thesis and antithesis, nobility and serfdom, produced a synthesis, a third element, the bourgeoisie, a new social class, which promoted common citizens to owners of production and capital. The dialectical position of alterity brought a great differentiation of individuality and crowned the bourgeois, the new citizen of the world. This volcanic transformation launched the Reformation, which shook the structure of the Church, provoked the Protestant schism, and was followed by the Counter-Reformation, which tightened again cultural control and censorship, a reintensification of the defensive patriarchalization of the Christian myth.

Another creative social manifestation of the myth that intensely expressed the feeling function, transformed many social customs, and influenced Western art, giving birth to literature and romantic love, were the troubadours and the legends of knighthood, mainly the grail legend. This creativity exemplifies the expression of the anima-animus archetype within the archetype of alterity.

The answer of the Church to science and art in the Renaissance was significantly different. The insular matriarchal search of the myths and arts of antiquity to represent dialectically the archetype of alterity, although pagan, found relative acceptance and support within the Church because works of painting, sculpture, and architecture not only embellished churches and palaces, they also consecrated the figures of bishops, cardinals, and popes before history. This reaction was very different from the one toward the discoveries of science, which not only did not court religious authorities but on the contrary stood up to discredit them and diminish their authority over truth.

The chronic antagonism between religious institutions and science after the Renaissance gave rise to an atmosphere of repression, persecution, and humiliation in the university with regard to control over knowledge with power. Publications should contain the stamps *nihil obstat* (nothing opposed) and *imprimatur* (print it) or else the authors were subject to prison or worse.

It so happened that science, the most threatened and threatening of heresies, won its long battle with the Church at the end of the eighteenth century. However, and this is one of the main insights of the archetypal theory of history, in defeating the Church in the laboratory, the altar of knowledge, science expelled the subjective together with the Inquisition and dissociated *labor* from *oratorium* in the cultural Self. This was a Pyrrhic victory. As we know, Pyrrhus (318/319-272 B.C.) was the king of Epirus who became famous for winning a battle against the Roman army, but because he lost so many soldiers, animals, and artillery, his victory was equivalent to a defeat. When we throw away something precious together with waste, we say we throw the baby away with the bathwater. In this case, together with the Inquisition, we threw away emotions, intuition, feeling, ethics, faith, that is, our emotional relationship with subjectivity and totality.

Expelling the Holy Office from the university, science extirpated subjectivity from the scientific method and lacerated the Western cultural Self. From then on, the scientific method practiced the dialectic of truth and error exclusively in the objective dimension, dissociated from the subjective dimension, and formed the huge shadow of materialism. Science entrenched itself in the truth of exclusively objective knowledge, which formed a monstrous shadow that exploded two and a half centuries later over Hiroshima and Nagasaki.

From the end of the nineteenth century on, science became rationalist and materialist, privileging the typological functions of extraversion, thinking, and sensation and dissociating from the functions of introversion, feeling, and intuition. This is one explanation for the dominant extraversion of Western culture compared to the exuberant introversion of ancient Eastern cultures. Separating itself from the intuitive relationship with totality, science lost the full imagination and faith inherent in the magical-mythical dimension. Estranging itself from feeling, science withdrew from love, the ethical pillar of the Christian myth. In spite of these mutilations, science maintained the dialectical position of alterity received from the myth but reduced it exclusively to objectivity.

Scientific ethics came to be practiced exclusively in the domain of objective truth. New discoveries were praised for the acquisition of knowledge and power frequently to the detriment of their ethical consideration for the welfare of humanity.

Withdrawing from subjectivity and from the symbol of Christ, science turned away also from the symbolism of the Antichrist, the devil, as the way of evil and therefore could not see error as symbolically analogous to sin in the shadow.

Nineteenth-century science was the mutilated heiress of the victory over the Inquisition. It appeared covered with glory and alienation, quite unconscious of its shadow. Its arrogance proudly announced the ideology of positivism and materialism, which soon defensively patriarchalized the socialist movement inspired by the Christian myth (Zoja 2000). It was not by chance that the socialist movement, rooted in the myth, which inspired the English, American, and French Revolutions to search for social democracy, was so defensively patriarchalized in communism. Basing itself on Christian socialism in its search for a humanization of society, patriarchalized socialism formulated the theory of the class struggle to construct history and ended up forming the political dictatorships responsible for the greatest slaughter of people known to history (Solzhenitsyn 1973).

The Nineteenth Century and the Rescue of the Subjective
The Return of the *Labor-Oratorium*

We can now return to our original topic with a better understanding of why reductions to the unconscious and to the cognitive behavioral dimensions were so limiting to modern psychology. What we needed, and still need, to rescue in the cultural Self is more than the unconscious dimension and conditioned behavior, no doubt very important discoveries. The full-blown rescue of the subjective dimension of the Western cultural Self can only occur within the paradigm of the symbolic dimension relating the subjective and the objective dimensions and the matriarchal-patriarchal relationship through the dialectical position of alterity.

What happened during the nineteenth century was the beginning of the healing of the subjective-objective dissociation through the rescue of the subjective dimension in practically all dimensions of the cultural Self. This rebirth of the subjective occurred in the insular matriarchal position, forming isolated sectors of society that were still greatly separated from the objective due to the defensive polarized position. The result is that a great part of scientific knowledge still maintains the subjective-objective dissociation and actively resists reborn subjectivity fighting its way back to the university in the search for full symbolic elaboration.

In this manner, a historic analysis of what happened to Western culture in the nineteenth century in the light of the archetypal theory of history shows us many reductions that prevent the symbolic dimension from being completely dialectical and systemic. We can say that an important part of the theoretical intention of Jungian symbolic psychology, with its symbolic and alterity paradigm, is the identification of the methodological difficulties going on in each cultural dimension within the search to become dialectical and systemic.

Woodstock, Alterity, and Defensive Matriarchalization

The first (1914-1918) and the second (1939-1945) world wars in the twentieth century brought so much destruction that it shook the confidence of the humanism inherent to the patriarchal dominance still prevailing in the traditions of Western culture. The symbol in which this cultural commotion culminated was the atomic bomb. The use of the crowning achievement of science to destroy two cities and thousands of lives demonstrated to all that the materialist development of science, whether through capitalism or communism, would lead humankind to extermination.

In spite of the justification of using the atomic bomb to end World War II and the post-war euphoria, this symbol marked forever many hearts and minds and decreed disillusion with the scientific materialist era.

Thus began, in the middle of the twentieth century, a countercultural movement. The cold war that followed World War II inherited the threat of nuclear weaponry and launched an arms race. The practice of democracy in the United States was greatly curtailed by fear of communism, and many important figures in the counterculture and the civil rights movement were persecuted by the reactionary policies of conservative sectors of society.

However, the defeat of the American military campaign in Vietnam (1960-1973), which followed French colonialism, was a great opportunity for the ideology of alterity to reunite various manifestations of rebellion and creativity, such as the hippie movement, within counterculture. It was a propitious time for important synchronistic events.

The rock and roll festival in Woodstock, a farm near Bethel in New York August 15-17, 1969, celebrated the coniunctio yearning of peace and love in an extraordinary musical event. Planned for fifty thousand people, four hundred thousand gathered in an explosion of musical creativity, enthusiastic, love, sexuality, and altered states of consciousness. Within a proposition of the dialectics of alterity to search for full human realization and favoring love and not war, the polarized patriarchal dominance gave way to the liberation of the insular matriarchal archetype, which turned Woodstock into a true Dionysian orgy.

Twenty-three years after Hiroshima and Nagasaki, American culture responded with a festival, within the musical dimension, that became a symbol in the search for a more human society concentrated on love in a healing attitude toward the brutal tragedies that marked the first half of the twentieth century.

The volcanic Dionysian explosion of the repressed matriarchal archetype produced an enantiodromia within the Western cultural Self in the relationship of the two basic archetypes which unbalanced the cultural Self. The just measure was upturned and hubris installed, sometimes bordering on chaos. There appeared many manifestations of a true defensive possession by the matriarchal archetype which revealed a pathologization of the alterity position by defensive matriarchalization. Drug addition, alcoholism, precocious sexuality, with many cases of precocious pregnancy and abortion in alarming numbers, social corruption on many levels, dissemination of sexually transmitted diseases (STDs), such as AIDS, HPV, syphilis, hepatitis B and C, and eating disorders, including obesity, anorexia, and bulimia.

The abrupt liberation of the repressed matriarchal archetype gave way to a compulsive wish to avoid frustration, expressed in disrupted family life and youth behavior, frequent divorce, and an onslaught of blended families. This was accompanied by the exaggerated usage of LSD and other recreational drugs and an increase in drug traffic, organized crime, social corruption, violence, and crime in big cities worldwide. And, above all, society experienced unbridled consumerism.

The implantation of the archetype of alterity together with the liberation of the repressed matriarchal archetype favored the civil rights movement and brought the end of colonialism and an increase in the rights of women, oppressed racial and ethnic groups, homosexuals, and other minority groups. This led to the search for identity by many repressed ethnic groups who began to search for their own national territory. This happened in the Balkans as a movement of post-communist liberation and in African countries as a consequence of post-colonialist repression. The clash between different ethnic groups rising up to search for national identity and territory expressed through frequent genocidal wars their traditional rivalries and aggression which were repressed during colonialism.

Alterity, Globalization, Consumerism and Sustainability

Technology forms culture and responds to cultural development. The discovery and implantation of the worldwide computerized system of communication forming the Internet at the end of the twentieth century gave new and limitless stimulus for the implantation of the alterity archetype within globalization (Brown 2000).

The implantation of the dialectical position of alterity favors the constellation of the totality archetype and systemic phenomenology. This world movement went beyond frontiers and social regimes. Although still politically controlled in many countries, it continues to develop and seek interchange on a planetary dimension, forming the logos sphere around the world as predicted by Teilhard de Chardin (1947).

There is an old trickster and Adlerian saying in the confrontation of opposites that also works in the relationship of the two basic archetypes: "If you can't beat them, join them."

We saw how in the French Revolution the liberation of the repressed matriarchal archetype together with the search for the implantation of the alterity archetype in the quest for liberty, equality, and freedom of the First Republic (1792-1804) ended in bloodshed, terror, chaos, and repression. The patriarchal repression of the revolution was brought about by a military movement under the leadership of Napoleon, and only after more than half a century of dictatorship did France see the return to the Second Republic (1848-1852) of democracy and alterity.

In the case of the matriarchal revolution that shook Western culture in the second part of the twentieth century, a similar enantiodromia with countering patriarchal repression would be expected. Why did it not happen and what happened in its place instead? There are three important issues to consider.

The first is that, in the French Revolution, there occurred a social class war armed with the guillotine in the center of Paris. Alterity was too revolutionary to be absorbed and politically implanted. Social enantiodromia launched bloodshed, and the clash between the new and the old was too tragic to be contained. Chaos ensued, followed by a countering patriarchal enantiodriomia and repression.

Second, in the last part of the twentieth century, Europe and the United Stares were exhausted by war, and their capacity for patriarchal repression was discredited by the war and the civil rights movement.

Third, the integration of many symbols expressed by the liberated matriarchal archetype were at this point historically well underway within the implantation of the alterity archetype, such as moral customs, artistic creativity, and civil rights claims. Therefore, although many aspects of matriarchal exuberance became exaggerated and defensive, as pointed out above, many others had already been acquired and could no longer be repressed as they had been after the French Revolution. Let us only think of the European Union, uniting the warring countries of Europe, and the civil rights movement in the United States, victorious in so many aspects.

However, such activation of the alterity archetype, accompanied by the liberation of many structuring symbols, complexes, and functions of the matriarchal archetype would, by the very definition of the structuring archetypal quaternio around the central archetype, also activate the patriarchal archetype. And it did, but not in a repressive way through radical enantiodromia.

This new encounter of the intensely activated matriarchal and patriarchal archetypes in the second half of the twentieth century occurred under the coordination of the alterity and the totality archetypes. This conjunction resulted in a new synthesis within the context of globalization, heavily supported by the development of worldwide communication.

Instead of the traditional pattern of repression that characterized the millenary patriarchal dominance, this new relationship of the matriarchal and patriarchal archetypes, coordinated by the alterity and totality archetypes, developed world globalization through consumerism as synthesis. Production rose together with sales, equally satisfying industry and market.

In spite of the dialectical relationship of the matriarchal and patriarchal archetypes having associated production and satisfaction among nations during globalization like never before, its shadow became threatening. Symbolic elaboration complemented by the archetype of totality waved a worldwide red flag regarding the limits of natural reserves. For the first time in history, human expansion was faced with the limitations of the planet to continue sheltering us in the future, given the damage we have done to it over the years (Lovelock 1979). Finally, we have now to admit the fallacy of the identification of patriarchal domination with progress and of patriarchal domination as the final goal of culture.

In order to satisfy productively the four structuring archetypes of the archetypal quaternio, the principle of sustainability was conceived to deal with the shadow of consumerism. This paradigm, highly expressive of the Christian and Buddhist myths of dialectical relationship through compassion, applied to the cultural and the planetary Selves calls forth two significant sets of phenomena: on one side, a new form of human production, and on the other, moral consciousness and an attitude based on recognizing and elaborating the shadow accumulated through thousands of years of patriarchal paradigm erroneously identified with progress and the end goal of history.

In order to implant the pattern of sustainability, the first set of phenomena-new forms of human production-must consider the limits of natural resources on the planet and, therefore, has to restrict the aim of material production to that which is strictly needed for human well-being.

The simple allegiance of the matriarchal archetype to satisfy human sensuality with the patriarchal archetype to produce quantity, even though within the dialectical relationship of alterity, is not sufficient for the future of mankind, because our planet cannot satisfy unbridled consumerism and must now learn the paradigm of economic sustainability. The mentality of the upper economic classes of the world, which identifies satisfaction with consumption, must change, because this ideal of consumerism requires resources of three planets to satisfy it (*Worldwatch Institute* 2010).

This means that the implantation of the dialectical position of the archetype of alterity must be associated with that of the contemplative position of the archetype of totality in order to relate human needs to the capacity of our planet. In this manner, the relationship of the matriarchal and patriarchal archetypes, which served as parameters for human development, must from now on be submitted to the coordination of the archetypes of alterity and totality in order to attain economic sustainability within the paradigm of symbolic humanism required for the survival of our species.

The second set of phenomena, also necessary to implant the pattern of sustainability, refers to the confrontation of the shadow formed during the thousands of years of patriarchal dominance. This shadow slowly built up a hedonistic narcissistic mentality of consumerism that became more highly developed during the four centuries that followed the industrial revolution and culminated in the population explosion and the extraordinary rise of consumption that has almost tripled in the last fifty years.

The change from consumerism to sustainability is the next great task in the implantation of the alterity archetype, now turned inseparable from the totality archetype, so as to situate the dialectical relation of the matriarchal and patriarchal archetypes within the capacity of the planetary Self.

Simultaneous with this search for the transcendence of consumerism and the implantation of sustainability within the planetary Self, other great focal points of tension make up important issues addressed by this archetypal theory of history. Every important issue in the lives of countries worldwide must be seen symbolically and archetypally related to the search toward alterity and totality.

No doubt the dispute over atomic weaponry and the political transformation of Islamic societies and their biblical confrontation with Israel are of utmost historical and mythological importance and must be analyzed and understood together with patriarchal confrontation and all we have described in the preceding chapters of its danger of war and genocide. The aggravating factor now is that the threat of patriarchal confrontation with atomic weaponry is so close to a catastrophe of worldwide proportions which reminds us of the beginning of our era when the archetype of alterity was revealed mythologically during the threat of genocide. We can only hope that two thousand years of the implantation of the dialectical relationships of polarities within compassion and love may bring tolerance and dialogue for the countries involved in this imminently patriarchal confrontation.

We worked hard on the elaboration of this resistance. We were about to give up when one day during meditation I broke the rules and, in desperation perhaps, I asked him bluntly why he could not love creation. "Because I am a lonesome being who has suffered and continues to suffer very much. Creation is so grandiose that I feel that I cannot possibly relate to it." Then, out of nowhere, or perhaps out of intuition and empathy, I asked him, "Have you ever considered the loneliness and the immense suffering undergone by the creative spirit since it all began?" His reaction was as though he experienced at the individual level the big bang moment of the cosmos.

Chapter 14

THE ARCHETYPAL DEVELOPMENT
OF THE PERSONALITY
THE SEVEN ARCHETYPAL
STAGES OF LIFE

Beware humans! Thy lot is to bear the encounter of good and evil in the developmental process of thyselves!

With the main concepts of Jungian symbolic psychology, described in the preceding chapters, we can now summarize the archetypal development of the personality within the systemic symbolic archetypal paradigm. This summary does not intend to include the whole development of the personality but only to highlight some of its main themes. The ages attributed to the stages should be regarded loosely as to the starting times of their contents.

The meaning of the word passive as it is used in the following discussion has to be understood with due care; for something to be passive it has to exist. However, the passive position of the ego here refers both to a state in which the ego exists but is not active and also to all historic situations that prepare ego formation.

The first idea to be taken into account is that the identity of the ego and of the other are formed by the archetypal coordination of the process of symbolic elaboration, first in the passive position and only afterward in the active position. This approach may be difficult to follow because it is quite different from the traditional one adopted in most schools of psychology in which psychological development is described from the standpoint of the ego and from the several dimensions of the Self which prepare to receive it. When many people are preparing a great party for an important visitor who has not yet arrived, is not this visitor already somehow present in the party?

This difference from the traditional approach is important because it allows for the insertion of identity formation, beginning with conception, in all dimensions of the Self and in the roots of all life experiences from the beginning of time.

In the traditional developmental approach, the ego is considered only after it appears, and consequently the theory of identity formation is mostly restricted to part of the child's individual Self, to the parental Self, and only relatively to the family Self. Body formation and other dimensions of the Self are considered only in a very limited way.

However, when we take into consideration ego formation in the passive position before the real appearance of the ego, the symbolic scope of identity formation is immensely increased and unconscious body, social and cultural symbolism acquire a much greater importance.

For example, consider the identity formation of gender symbolically. We know that gender is determined by genetic constitution, which we situate primarily in the sensual realm of the matriarchal archetype and that the ego does not have any active role in its beginning. However, within the symbolic elaboration of our individuation process, it is undeniable that the ego participates in the identity formation of gender initially in the passive position. How else would ego identity acquire most of the countless symbolic characteristics that will develop around gender identity during the whole of life? Of course, after the child becomes conscious of its gender identity around age two, it will participate actively in its symbolic elaboration, but it is undeniable that this elaboration begins in the passive position, before the ego existed in the sexual dimension of the personality.

At the point where a boy or a girl acquires gender consciousness and continues to develop gender identity through his or her activities, gender identity has already been largely formed passively and its passive development will continue together with what the ego actively does.

The passive-active polarity is of fundamental importance for the understanding of personality development. Consider in the above example that when we become conscious of our gender identity around age two, it had already been forming with many symbolic fundamental characteristics since conception and in the conception of our species since sexuality appeared in the evolution of life on earth two billion yeas ago (Sagan 1980). However, this passive symbolic elaboration, as important as it is, will be complemented by the active elaboration to a significant degree, so much so that it may even include the surgical change of sexual identity later in life.

The second idea of fundamental importance to consider in this conception of ego-other archetypal identity formation is that fixation of symbolic elaboration will form defenses and shadow that will deform identity during one's lifelong process and form one's evil part (Byington 1997). Therefore, within this theoretical perspective, the confrontation of evil with its fixations and defenses in our shadow comprises the ethical dimension of individuation (Jung) and of humanization (Teilhard de Chardin), which transforms human life into an ethical dramatic process (Byington 1997).

One significant example of this precocious fixation in the passive position is any genetic or congenital malformation of the fetus, which will produce defensive fixations and shadow in the very beginning of life. Any future fixation and shadow formation at any point of the individuation process, whether in the passive or active position, will also constitute a dysfunction to be elaborated through the ethical structuring function (Byington 2008c).

One of the greatest virtues of our nature, so contaminated by evil, is our capacity to develop supraconsciousness-awareness of normal and shadow formations and their interaction during development. However, the activation of the function of supraconsciousness depends greatly on the integration of the alterity archetype, which is possible only in the later stages of life, after the relative sensual integration of the matriarchal archetype and the organizing integration of the patriarchal archetype.

The First Archetypal Stage of Life
Intrauterine and Social Preparation for
Identity Formation from Conception until Birth

During pregnancy, the process of symbolic elaboration will form a most important part of our ego-other identity mostly in the passive position. This occurs in great measure through the formation of the body and through the dynamics of the symbolic cultural reality that will receive us after birth. Most psychological schools are still imprisoned in the individual-collective and mind-body dissociations that identify the psyche with the individual mind, leaving part of the body and culture out of it. Not so in Jungian symbolic psychology because, as we have emphasized repeatedly, its concept of psyche includes the polarities mind-body, mind-emotion, mind-nature, mind-society, and individual-culture, all represented in our brain by representations within the symbolic dimension.

Many recent studies have suggested that there are signs of mental development during pregnancy, although these phenomena could also be considered as mere physical reflexes without any emotional component. William F. Supple Jr., in *Becoming a Baby* (2002), describes these signs in the order of development. In day 38 of pregnancy, for example, a touch to the mouth area causes the head to turn away. This is thought to demonstrate an avoidance or protective reflex. In day 40 of pregnancy, the first detectable brain waves are recordable. This means that the brain is functioning in a complex coordinated manner with neurons activated in organized and functional patterns. Whether the embryo can think or have consciousness, we don't know for sure. In day 41, nerve fibers from the cerebral cortex form into a band (the internal capsule) and descend to the spinal cord. These neural cables will enable voluntary movement.

In day 79, fetuses suck their thumbs and have a preference for the right or left thumb, showing that lateralization of brain functions begins very early. The preference shown by 90 percent of fetuses for the right thumb coincides with right-handedness in adult life. In day 94, a bitter-tasting substance introduced into the amniotic fluid will cause the fetus to behave as though the substance were tasted and a reaction indicating dislike is evoked, complete with a facial response.

In day 134, the major organ of hearing-the cochleae-are mature and functional. The fetus hears the grumblings of the mother's digestive system, her heartbeat, and her voice. Experiments have shown that some of the intonations in the mother's voice will be incorporated into the baby's crying after birth. In day 154, blink and startle responses to outside noises are quite clear. A startle response involves a general contraction of major muscle groups-legs, arms, and trunks-and increased heart rate. Repetition of sounds decreases such responses due to habituation. While we spend 25 percent of our time asleep in REM, fetuses spend 80 percent. Are they dreaming all this time? If so, what do they dream about? In day 172, various studies have shown that fetuses will respond to male and female voices with a decrease in heart rate.

These intrauterine events, described among many others, revealed by modern research, show that mental activity exists and increases during pregnancy. How much of it is retained by sensual memory and will influence identity formation is difficult to ascertain.

Other significant and undeniable contributions toward identity formation, also passively prepared in the cultural surroundings of the pregnant womb, come from transindividual forms of the Self which are inseparable from pregnancy and will complement psychological development after birth. As the fetus acquires the capacity to develop its human potential, the cosmic Self, the planetary Self, the cultural Self, the family Self, and the conjugal Self prepare for the formation of the new being as one more heir to all the riches and miseries accumulated since life began four billion years ago and continued by civilization during the one hundred and fifty thousand years of the humanization process of the cosmos (Watson and Berry 2003). This conjunction of intrauterine and extrauterine life will concentrate within the cultural Self to form individual identity in the specific culture in which the child is born. Reducing the formation of identity to the presence of the ego after birth greatly limits our understanding of the development of consciousness because the roots of identity formation are infinitely older.

Specific characteristics of the cosmic Self, such as the day-night polarity, which coordinate the relationship of animal and plant life, and the awake-sleeping polarity (conscious-unconscious polarity) of the planetary Self together with nationality and climate will be hallmarks in the symbolic structuring of individual identity. The cultural Self will be of fundamental importance, contributing with important ethnic characteristics such as race, language, historical traditions and customs, social classes, and institutions. No less important will be the family Self, with its ethnical, social, and educational position, its history, its members and their relationships. Nearest to the child will be the conjugal Self formed by the physical, psychological, and cultural traditions of the parents' personalities and the bond between them forming the structuring primary quaternio (see chapter 5).

During pregnancy parents will begin to elaborate symbolically the relationship between themselves and their future baby, including its name, and many important emotions will be constellated which will afterward contribute to its normal or defensive (shadow) identity.

Case Example

Diane is now forty-five years old. When she was born, her father was working abroad and came home two months later to find that his wife had named the child Lucia. Very frustrated, he legally changed the girl's name to Diane. Years later the parents divorced, and the daughter lived with her mother, rarely seeing her father. She always felt her name to be Lucia, and she tried to change it legally but the judge did not find sufficient reasons to accept her request. How many meanings there are in this simple choosing of a child's name!

The regent archetypes as always are very active coordinating all dimensions of the Self, but they are especially meaningful in the cultural Self and in the family Self because the traditional patriarchal domination in many cultures reduces pregnancy, birth, and childcare to the matriarchal dimension. The greater the patriarchal domination, the greater reduction creates the syndrome of the emotionally dominant mother and distant father (EDMDF), which can fixate and defensively affect the identity formation of men and women and affect their relationship. This EDMDF syndrome has been implanted in the cultural Self of many cultures, including Western culture, which is our reference in this book.

Each new physical and emotional acquisition during identity formation makes the ego more capable of exercising the active position. This transformation can be seen during breast-feeding when sucking becomes more active and the child begins to press the breast with its hands and recognize its mother's features. This becomes even more conspicuous when bottle-feeding is started and the child holds the bottle with both hands. This transformation by the ego from the passive to the positive position will be enhanced with the physical acquisitions in the next archetypal stage, brought about by the maturation of the nervous system.

Due to the historical implantation of the alterity archetype in Western culture and the consequent development of civil rights and the democratization of the relationship between women and men, the EDMDF syndrome is being questioned, elaborated, and abandoned by many couples of the new generation. The social acquisition of the alterity pattern has led many women to university graduation and work outside the home and many men to intimate participation during pregnancy, birth, and child care. This change is also affecting the relationships of grandparents with their future grandchildren and will diminish the importance of the obstetrician, whose role as a father substitute was especially important in the EDMDF syndrome.

The Second Archetypal Stage of Identity Formation From Birth to 2 Years of Age

The syndrome of the emotionally dominant mother and distant father (EDMDF) is characteristic of patriarchal dominance in culture and therefore has been very influential in Western culture and in psychology. As has frequently happened, this historical circumstance in archetypal dynamics was wrongly equated with human psychological reality in the same way that masculine and feminine identities were equated with their roles within traditional patriarchal family and society (Gray 1992). This perspective affected greatly developmental dynamic psychology, incorrectly reducing the primary relationship to the mother-child dyad and wrongly establishing the relationship with the father as a later event. This theoretical error has negatively influenced the identity of men and of women and the relationship of parents in child development, exaggerating the importance of the mother and, at the same time, hurting and deforming the identity and the role of the father.

Within the perspective of the implantation of the alterity archetype, primary relationships structure ego and other identities through the primary quaternio formed by the maternal and the paternal complexes, the characteristics of the bond between them, and the reactions of the child (see chapter 5). This approach has led me to consider Freud's concepts of the Oedipus complex and of the perverse polymorph as fixations and defenses of the primary quaternio, that is, pathological and incompatible with normal development.

This stage occurs in a psychological field dominantly coordinated by the matriarchal archetype through the functions of sensuality and desire, with the ego mainly in the passive position but also in the active position, for instance, when the baby begins to suck the breast. This stage may also be affected by the patriarchal pattern of education and by pediatric hygiene measures dealing with the child's feeding and clothing.

In this stage, the ego-other polarity continues to be formed primarily in the passive position. Due to the nearness of the ego and of the other in the matriarchal insular position, identity formation occurs mostly through symbiosis and imitation, as was partly described by Margaret Mahler (Mahler, Pine, and Bergman 1975). The projection-introjection mechanism of identity formation starts operating mainly in the next stage.

The nature of the *insular* matriarchal position (*insular* means island) is dyadic and can include intimacy with the mother on one conscious island and with the father at the same time on another island from the beginning of life. The relationship with the mother and father complexes, when the father is intimately present, occurs in different islands of consciousness but with equal importance, so much so that frequently the first word the modern child pronounces is "daddy," to the surprise of tradition-conditioned psychologists and members of the family.

The structuring functions of union and separation and of loss and frustration permeate the whole process of transformation during development. According to its etymology, sacrifice (*sacer* "sacred" plus *ficare* "to make") means to make something holy, which symbolically implies the transcendent connection of things during the development of the incarnation of the totality of being. In nearly all ancient cultures, sacrifice was practiced, offering goods to the gods in exchange for their blessing (Viveiros de Sá, 2000). During psychological development the structuring function of sacrifice offers to the central archetype that which must die in exchange for the new acquisition of the personality or culture. The archetypal matrix of change is coordinated by the life and death archetype through which what dies and what is acquired are dynamically interconnected (Byington 1996). When the function of sacrifice becomes fixated and defensive this exchange is carried out inadequately and the function of sacrifice is deformed, frequently turning into mutilation doomed to repetition compulsion in the shadow. In such cases, for instance, as in pathological mourning, regression is necessary to reach the fixation and elaborate it correctly, so that the old dies and is buried and the new can freely flourish (Byington 2005b).

One of the first experiences of sacrifice for the child in the second stage of life is when it is weaned. Through the sacrifice of feeding from a nipple (whether breast or bottle) the child acquires the capacity to drink from a cup and eat from a spoon and, with the acquisition of teeth, to chew its own food.

The Third Archetypal Stage of Life
From 2 to 12 Years Old

Already in the last stage and continuing in this one we see the development of four very significant acquisitions in physical growth that will greatly contribute to the formation of identity with the ego in the active position. The first is bowel and urinary control due to sphincter maturation, the second is the perception of gender difference, the third is locomotion, and the fourth is the acquisition of speech.

Bowel and urinary control structure identity with the capacity to separate socially the intimate and the public dimensions, which will begin to form symbolically the persona and the superego dimensions through the parameter of that which is socially approved or not.

The physical sexual characteristics mark identity with the physical differences between boys and girls. These differences are of extraordinary importance also in the cultural Self because they will carry the gender differences historically established in every culture. Just imagine the difference of identity passively formed in women born in an orthodox Islamic culture and in a Western culture. These physical differences between boys and girls will greatly influence identity formation during matriarchal and patriarchal domination later in life and then will slowly diminish under the coordination of the alterity archetype when the importance of the physical differences between men and women diminish in importance and give place to their psychological differences, which vary considerably in every individuation process and consequently also in every conjugal relationship, whether homosexual or heterosexual.

In 1905, Freud described his epoch-making theory of infantile sexuality within the dominance of the patriarchal pattern which characterizes psychoanalysis. Incorporating traditional patriarchal male superiority in his theory, he defensively projected it onto women's anatomical differences and made them the source of an inferiority complex, a castration complex which was called penis envy. This misogynous approach reinforced by scientific authority delayed the implantation of the alterity archetype in modern psychology and deformed the study of feminine identity with the male prejudice of patriarchal tradition.

Later studies made during the twentieth century by Kinsey (Kinsey, Pomeroy, and Martin 1948; Kinsey, Pomeroy, Martin, and Gebhard 1965),

Masters and Johnson (1966), and Hite (1976) compensated to certain extent for Freud's cultural bias and called attention to the importance of the clitoris in feminine sexuality with its central role in feminine masturbation and orgasm.

However, we need to elaborate the symbol of prostitution within the cultural Self, which for millennia associated feminine financial independence and sexual pleasure with public exclusion and social discrimination, with women's sexual liberation and self-realization and men and women's equal rights. This perspective marked feminine sexual education, masturbation, and orgasm with defensive transgression and guilt. At the same time we need to elaborate the symbol of homosexuality, also in the cultural Self, which has been in various ways linked normally and defensively to the feeling function mainly of men (Byington 2001).

The rescue of feminine anatomical identity from the pejorative stigmatization of the castration complex and penis envy must begin with the education of the little girl at about two years of age, when she becomes conscious that she is different from boys for not having a penis and for having a clitoris. At that moment a true ritual of feminine initiation of the girl must take place, in which her mother will begin to teach her that she and her mother are different from her father and little brother (whom she saw with a penis), as are all women and men in the world. From then on, the girl and her brother will be separated when bathing and dressing just as grown-ups do. This initiation will reinforce the girl's identity, because the mother will tell her that, on account of what she learned, she has now become a little woman. The same will happen with the boy. After his father has explained how they are different from girls and from mother and begun to bathe separately, he will also tell the boy that he has become a little man. With the new types of parental couples formed by masculine and feminine homosexuality, new studies of identity formation will have to be undertaken to guide the development of personality of their children.

Because bowel and urine control are well underway and the intimate dimension will be actively differentiated from the public dimension, whenever the girl touches her genitals in school or in public, the mother or the schoolteacher will not scold her at all and will simply continue the initiation and tell her that just as she does not urinate in the classroom, she also should not touch her genitals in public and only touch herself intimately when she "washes" in the bathroom. This initiation ritual must be done very carefully, as with all initiations, to convey the intimate and symbolic revelation of the transcendent nature of excretory and genital activities without at any time giving them the connotation of something forbidden or sinful. On the contrary, for this ritual is of paramount importance in differentiating containment from repression and guilt in feminine education. The instruction continues and considers quite natural the little girl's pleasure in touching her genitals on her way toward masturbation. This education will be also important for dealing with cases of compulsive or defensive masturbation, because in such cases the elaboration of the masturbation can be done with the meaning of normal and defensive masturbation and not as if masturbation per se were the problem.

The description of a stereotypical attractive (incestuous) and aversive (parricidal) personal reaction of boys to the mother and father led to Freud's formulation of the Oedipus complex, which I consider a gross reduction of the normal richness and complexity of the primary relationship within the primary quaternio to an impoverished, personal, and defensive (that is, pathological) relationship.

Identity formation is rooted in the primary relationship and in many symbols that cannot be foreseen and programmed. Therefore, identity is a structuring function and an absolutely unique process that happens and at the same time is elaborated and integrated as it reveals itself symbolically and synchronistically during development.

This third archetypal stage of life occurs from approximately two to twelve years old and is characterized by the beginning of development of the social life of the child. During the preceding stage, symbolic elaboration and ego-other identity formation were coordinated primarily by the insular position of the matriarchal archetype in the passive position mainly through the functions of sensuality and desire. From then on symbolic elaboration will be carried out also by abstract mental organization and rules, coordinated by the polarized position of the patriarchal archetype. The intensity of this tension will depend greatly on the matriarchal-patriarchal relation within the family and cultural Selves and on the physical acquisitions of the developing organism.

The Symbolism of Incest

In this third stage of life, the child acquires many characteristics that will favor its autosomatic development (Neumann 1960). In comparison to the intense symbiotic relationship of the preceding stage, the child will now enter into the beginning of sexuality which will prepare him or her for adult copulation and the propagation of the species. At the same time, the child acquires speech, which will open the door to social life with humankind.

This gigantic leap from the womb to society occurs within the family structure of primary relationships generally experienced within the primary quaternio. The entrance into society will mark the existence of a new generation. The old will be aging, and the young are coming to replace them.

Jung (1912) and John Layard (1945) formulated the elaboration of the regulation of marriage, such as the cross-cousin union within many tribal societies, as a compromise between the endogamous and the exogamic libido (psychic energy) partly to continue in the family and partly to separate from it and live in the outside world. Jung called great attention to the structuring function of incest as an important representation of the union of the ego with the anima and animus archetypes and with the central archetype, which he called Self. The abundant incestuous relationships among the gods in mythology confirm the creative importance of this motif.

The fixation and defensive deformation of the structuring function of incest during the child's development in the third and fourth stages of life, however, is an event with extraordinary symbolic destructive power of the shadow which was not sufficiently described either by psychoanalysis or by analytical psychology.

As we know, Freud made the repression and sublimation of the Oedipus complex, encompassing incest and parricide, the center of his theory of psychological development. I do not mean to say in any way whatsoever that Freud considered the Oedipus complex normal in adult life. On the contrary, he considered its presence, that is, its non-repression and sublimation in adult life, as the basis of all psychopathology. However, because he described it as present in all children up to five years of age which makes them perverse polymorphs. He weakened in a very peculiar way the clinical recognition of the frequency and the devastating consequences of child sexual abuse .

Although Freud described pathology as the result of the lack of repression and sublimation of the Oedipus complex, the fact that he described it present in all children greatly diminished the perception of child sexual abuse by adults. This difficulty in recognizing and dealing with real incest by psychoanalysis was increased when many incestuous cases with children were interpreted as their fantasies. Masson's *An Assault on Truth* (1984) deals exactly with this question when he accuses psychoanalysis of covering up real cases of child sexual abuse with such interpretations.

Because Jungian symbolic psychology considers the Oedipus complex defensive, that is, pathological, it also considers abnormal any child's repetitive incestuous fantasy and recommends that such a child receive psychotherapeutic assistance. In this manner, it is much more difficult to overlook cases of sexual abuse.

Having treated many cases of sexual abuse and incest, my experience is that during the third stage of archetypal development, especially during intense matriarchal exuberance (age 2-7 years) when sexual abuse and incest occur through seduction and without violence, the incest wounds and their consequences may not be immediately felt. The devastating guilt and severe fixation of self-esteem occur later proportionally to patriarchal dominance after 8-10 years of age, when the child becomes increasingly conscious of what happened through knowledge of the incompatibility of incest with social life (Jacoby 1991).

According to Lévi-Strauss (1958), the incest taboo is the main organizer of family relationship and the pillar of civilized social life. The incest taboo organizes family and social life expressing the matriarchal archetype by the erotic structuring function inseparably from legal organization and the control of the structuring function of aggression expressed by the patriarchal archetype.

Freud united these two basic functions of eros (sensuality) and power (aggression) in the concept of the Oedipus complex which I consider defensive and pathological.

Instead of the Oedipus complex I attribute the social control of the erotic and the aggressive functions to the imitation and conditioning of the organization of family and social life naturally formed through millennia of customs which in time became tradition and taboo. With the further development of the rational systems of patriarchal organization, taboos were transformed into legislation. Jung's explanation of the incest taboo by the regulation of endogamous and exogamic libido (psychic energy) must also be taken into consideration (Jung 1912).

As already explained, the ego is not considered here exclusively the center of consciousness because it is inseparable from the other. The identity of the ego is formed together with the identity of the other as a result of the meaningful characteristics produced by every symbolic elaboration.

Consequently the center of consciousness is occupied by the ego-other polarity (see chapter 1, p. 250), which makes the concept of narcissism inseparable from the narcissism-egoism polarity. We can never say, for instance, that a child is feeling this or that without expressing what some else is doing to the child in that determined situation. The same occurs in any human relationship, for instance, regarding the feelings and emotions of the husband or the wife in marriage therapy. The attribution to Oedipus of incest and parricide without examining at the same time what Iocasta and Laius did to him was the fatal mistake that led Freud defensively to conceive the Oedipus complex as normally present in every child within a supposed theory of primary narcissism.

Social rules and conventions formed over millennia were the result of abstractions of the instinctive drives conditioned in customs and represented in language and the rational process we have come to call *mind*. These abstractions were assimilated in behavior sensually through imitation coordinated by the matriarchal archetype and organized rationally in polarities, which carry out symbolic elaboration mostly through the archetypal pattern of organization that I have conceived as the patriarchal archetype present in the personalities of both men and women.

This change from the dominance of matriarchal literal sensuality and kinesthetic perception to patriarchal abstraction expressed in language is the first great transformation of archetypal psychological individual development and must receive our full attention to understand what we mean by psychic reality within the symbolic archetypal perspective.

Psychoanalysis described this transition through repression and sublimation of the perverse polymorph and of the Oedipus complex to form the superego at around five years of age. This is radically different from the theoretical perspective of Jungian symbolic psychology, which considers Freud's concept of the perverse polymorph to be a defensive expression of the matriarchal archetype. In my view, the matriarchal dimension cannot and should not be repressed and sublimated because it is an archetype and as such should be creatively dealt with during the whole of life. Furthermore, the Oedipus complex is considered in the primary relationship a myth of psychopathy and psychosis that is a defensive pathological expression of Oedipus's primary relations and of his family Self.

When we consider that the ego-other polarity is formed initially passively within the primary relationships, it follows that we cannot fix the reactions of the ego in a stereotyped active position toward the maternal and paternal complexes in the beginning of life as psychoanalysis did with the Oedipus complex, postulating that at the beginning of life boys regularly feel incestuous and parricidal tendencies. Besides the variety of maternal and paternal complexes and the bond between them, the identity of the ego-other polarity is also formed by the countless reactions of the child, which cannot be foreseen and which contributes to form the ego within primary relationship mainly when it begins to operate in the active position. It is very important to remember that the maternal and paternal complexes are representations within the individual Self of the child and of real persons within the family Self.

When we take into account that the main drive of the child is to realize the potentiality of the central archetype, expressed by the conscious and unconscious urge to become an adult, we can imagine that this can be accomplished dominantly through imitation, which will teach the child what is right and what is wrong and does not need either repression or sublimation.

In this manner, development is here conceived as a natural and wishful process guided by the family, by culture, and by the child's urges and not as something culturally imposed on criminal instinctive drives. Of course, we must admit that social adaptation through the structuring organization of the patriarchal archetype collides with the playful, magical, and wishful spontaneity of the matriarchal archetype. However, through the richness of the symbolic dimension the central archetype and the alterity archetype can creatively coordinate transformation through imitation without necessarily employing repression and sublimation. Winnicott's description of the structuring function of play in the life of the child is one of the creative ways patriarchal organization and matriarchal spontaneity interact to propitiate conscious development and deal intelligently with adaptation (Winnicott 1971).

The normal healthy urge to grow and become an adult is best seen in a child learning to walk. The child falls, feels pain, and sometimes becomes bruised and cries. But in the next moment, it starts again the learning process with great motivation and enthusiasm. This urge to fulfill the capacity to be an adult and become human is a profound realization of pleasure, desire, and ambition helped by the power drive and creative envy and does not need either repression or sublimation to be accomplished (Byington 1996).

Consider also the game of hide and seek so popular in childhood. It alternates the capacity of visibility and control with the capacity to hide, that is, become invisible. Through this interplay of patriarchal organization and matriarchal wishful expression one can creatively elaborate countless symbols that propitiate development without repression. This is, for instance, exactly the way sexual development can occur in the ritual of initiation prescribed above, when the little girl can hide from social control in the "intimacy of washing" and enjoy sensual pleasure that is not acceptable when done in public. After graduation, I practiced clinical medicine and research among the Carajá Indians along the Araguaia River in Central Brazil. Living with them daily, I was intrigued by the way they educated their children, which did not include repression and sublimation. Probably because their matriarchal exuberance is so accentuated, their emotional intimacy, pleasure, and enjoyment were quite remarkable. Children were not separated in daily activities from adults. For more than a month, I did not see a single case of punishment or sermons such as we so frequently see in Western family life. Older children took care of younger children and, in all ages, the tendency to imitate adults was conspicuous and predominant. Children early on participated gladly in working together with adults, and what most impressed me was that their learning was not acquired as a duty and judged according to the success-failure polarity but was mostly regulated and evaluated through the pleasure of how well they could imitate adults, which included playing. I was much impressed by a game boys played that imitated their father's work. They would take small pieces of bamboo and turn them into bows and arrows. The play was ritualized and acted by groups of about six boys from around four to eight or nine years of age. The older children acted as leaders. They played near where their fathers built their bows and arrows. As they made bows and arrows, they would start shooting them at banana tree trunks amidst joy and laughter. Adults neither supervised nor evaluated their work, something very rare among us (Byington 2004). Their matriarchal ethical standards were much more compatible with the ethics of individuation than superego ethics abstractly and collectively imposed (Neumann 1949b).

Having had this pedagogical experience among the Carajás and later supervising teachers in grade school, high school, and college and treating children, grown-ups, and families in clinical psychiatry and psychotherapy, I came to the conclusion that the most important structuring function in normal and pathological identity formation of the ego-other polarity within primary relationships is imitation and not repression. At the same time, I also concluded that the main causes of ego dysfunction, besides the lack of holding and caring, are overprotection, power, and erotic abuse.

It seems to me that the theory of "normal and necessary" repression and sublimation to express transformation and development created by psychoanalysis is a great bias based on superego patriarchal organization acting unilaterally, defensively, and therefore repressively over matriarchal pleasure, spontaneity, and sensuality. This perspective ignores the existence of the central archetype coordinating teleologically the drive of the matriarchal archetype toward adult life through the imitation of grown-ups, which functions within play and pain but without repression.

Among many of Erich Neumann's creative ideas with which I agree and admire, there are a few I disagree with. One of them is in his book *The Child* (1960), published after his death. There, he states that "the wolf children, the human children raised by she wolves, do not develop in the manner specific to the human race" (p. 82). He goes on to explain that this happened because of the nonactivation of the matriarchal archetype. I disagree because I think that the quadruped posture and the howling to the moon adopted by these children were exactly an extreme demonstration of the function of imitation of the wolves coordinated by the children's matriarchal archetype. On the other hand, I quite agree with him that there are pathological cases in which archetypes are not activated as though they were due to a genetic failure. One example seems to me to be neurological autism, where children are incapable of empathy. This limitation can indicate a relative genetic absence of the matriarchal archetype.

Error is a fundamental teacher in learning. Likewise, frustration is the main vitamin for ego strengthening. When children do not have a normal contact with disease, their immunological system does not develop properly. When something is not learned through error, it is not really integrated. When the ego is not strengthened through frustration, it remains immature, weak, and incapable of dealing with difficult life situations. I do not mean by this that frustrations should be imposed on the child through education. I mean rather that when pain and frustrations naturally occur during development such as in learning to walk, they must be considered a part of life, without parents making a great fuss over the situation. In this sense the erotic drive of pleasure emphasized by psychoanalysis and the power drive chosen by Alfred

Adler as the main drive of individual psychology are both of central importance when seen spontaneously lived in the individuation process described by Jung. Frustration normally occurs within the life process. To learn to withstand frustration is one of the major acquisitions of the ego function and is completely different from repression, carried out based on the superego which is not natural to the child's emotions. Contrary to psychoanalytical recommendation, learning to contain emotions through the superego blocks creativity and produces robot-like alienation with artificial control.

In this sense the most difficult challenge for educators in the transition from the second to the third archetypal stage of life is maintaining the pleasure and spontaneity of the matriarchal archetype during the progressive integration of the patriarchal archetype with organization and learning of delimitation without repression.

Winnicott's (1971) emphasis on the importance of play in childhood can be understood as a recommendation to cultivate the matriarchal archetype parallel to the progressive activation of the patriarchal archetype during the third stage of life and afterward.

This same perspective is adopted by Erich Neumann when he writes: "The living functioning of the ego both without and within, which is its matriarchal as well as its patriarchal aspect, is the indispensable foundation of a productive integration of consciousness and an open personality capable of progressive transformation and growth." (1960, p. 79)

This is the essence of the method of teaching I have proposed in my book *Education from the Heart: A Jungian Symbolic Perspective* (Byington, 2004) in which I recommend the symbolic dimension of a patriarchally organized program and a matriarchal atmosphere of emotion, pleasure, and play to interact within the transference relationship of teacher and student.

The Difference between Boys' and Girls' Development

Besides the anatomical aspect, a great difference between boys and girls, which takes place in the third stage of archetypal development with great complexity and variation, within the heterosexual family of patriarchal tradition, lies in the fact that boys must separate from their mothers to affirm their identity, whereas girls must not. On the contrary, girls can reinforce identity with their mothers by playing at mothering with dolls very early in life.

The separation from mother is painful for boys and is accompanied by rough playing and aggressive competition that favors individuality and active behavior and will be synchronistic with penis penetration and rape symbolism later in life. This separation complex of boys limits the feeling function and stimulates the aggressive function. The greater the patriarchal dominance in the family, the more the hurt feeling function and the separation complex of boys can lead to severe fixation, repressive and aggressive defenses, mostly projected with paranoid behavior onto women. Due to this painful separation from their mothers, boys naturally prefer to relate through power whereas girls naturally favor eros (Gray 1992).

This defensive repression of feeling and exacerbation of defensive aggression is greatly responsible for defensive competition among males, especially in patriarchally dominant cultures, including initiation rituals. It restricts masculine affection in relationships with women and with other men. In the masculine dimension of the cultural Self, it favors professional competition, which in turn has promoted a misogynous and even a warlike disposition in the planetary Self.

Sexuality and Affection as Symbol and Structuring Function in the Masculine Personality

As with all structuring functions, sexuality can vary within a spectrum between polarities. One of such variations occurs within a spectrum which varies from dominant homosexuality to dominant heterosexuality with bisexuality in the middle. This spectrum includes all forms of sexuality, which can either function normally during the process of individuation or be fixated and therefore defensive (Byington 2001).

For purposes of studying affection (here conceived as a synonym for feeling) and sexual development, it is useful to recognize also a spectrum from homogeneous affection to heterogeneous affection, which can be associated in different ways with the sexual spectrum. In this manner, we can have normal and defensive variations of affection associated with normal and defensive variations of sexuality.

Homosexuality has existed in all cultures throughout history with varying degrees of acceptance. In Western culture masculine homosexuality has been considered sinful and sick, though presently it is recognized medically as a normal sexual manifestation (DSM-4R) although its genetic determinants, if any, are as yet unknown. As with all structuring functions, homosexuality is here considered to have the possibility of being normal or defensive.

The eroticism of homosexuality and the feeling in homogeneous affectivity tend to associate themselves in boys to compensate for the separation wound of the heterogeneous affection of the maternal relationship.

If the father complex is experienced affectionately, the compensation of the separation wound only through homogeneous affectivity can be very productive, but if the father complex is experienced as distant and cold, as within the EDMDF syndrome, the tendency of the boy to experience homogeneous affection together with homosexuality can be significantly stronger. This is so because the relationship with an affectionate and intimate father will diminish the impact of the EDMDF syndrome and compensate significantly the effect of the separation wound from the mother.

On the other hand, the homophobia frequently inherent in patriarchal tradition can neutralize the compensatory homogeneous affectionate search of the separation complex and increase the repression of feeling in the masculine personality. In such cases the compensatory tendency of the separation wound through defensive homosexuality in the shadow can be very intense, even more so because, lacking homogeneous affection, it will tend to be compulsive and pathologically promiscuous.

The "Latency Stage," "Penis Envy," and the "Castration Complex" in Feminine Sexuality

Freud (1905) described a "latency stage" during the third stage of development. I think this supposed latency is not natural and is the result of the patriarchal repression he himself prescribed for superego formation.

The theoretical hypothesis that the perverse polymorph and the Oedipus complex exist in all children and must be repressed and sublimated to form the superego and achieve maturity seems to me to be the basic defensive idea and bias to "explain" the creation of the concept of a "latency period" before puberty.

When this repression is carried out, however, it can have disastrous consequences, in particular on the sexual initiation of girls in which this defensive "latency period" is implanted with the interruption of sexual activity and pleasure and the introjection of guilt. This repression defensively implants the castration complex in girls and is the psychological equivalent of the clitoridectomy practiced in many tribal societies to repress sexual pleasure and orgasm in women. It also defensively constellates the prostitution complex, which lurks in the feminine historical background and becomes active whenever a woman rejoices in or is prohibited to have sexual pleasure.

Boys are not as affected by the idea of a latency period because the patriarchally dominant culture is very phallocentric and glorifies their sexuality, making them quite indifferent to the idea of such a latency period.

During this third stage of archetypal development, the process of individuation continues to further the formation of ego and other identities differentiating autonomy and individuality. Still very much contained in the family Self and traveling the masculine and feminine paths pointed out above, the child continues to exercise the passage from the passive to the active position of matriarchal and patriarchal structuring functions in the elaboration of existential symbols to produce meanings with which to further construct identity.

Still under the intense structuring influence of primary relationships, mostly through the imitation function, the child becomes increasingly active in dealing with society in the preparation for the revolution of puberty. It must be understood that the imitation function is not to be understood literally and can also produce many aversive variations, by which children may turn out very different from their parents.

The Identity Formation of Girls

Unlike boys, who suffer the separation wound from their mothers, girls do not have to separate from their mothers so early and can imitate them from the very beginning by mothering dolls. This enhances their identity formation through symbiotic identity with their mothers and maintains the integrity of their feeling function.

In the case of the emotional dependence of mother and of the distant father (the EDMDF syndrome), girls preserve their feeling functions much more than boys (separation wound) but tend to project greatly onto men their logos, animus, or abstract creative function on account of the distant father.

Due to the progressive implantation of the alterity archetype and the professional and sexual development of women, helped by the intimate relation with men in the primary quaternio of their children, women are integrating much more their animus and alterity archetypes with the increasing capacity to live their intellectual endowment in the most varied professions together with their emotional and sexual capacities.

The Fourth Archetypal Stage of Life
The Revolution of Adolescence
(from 12 to 20 Years)

Biologically an animal is considered adult (mature) when physical growth is advanced, and it can procreate. In humans adolescence begins with the onset of puberty with maturation of the sexual glands around twelve years of age.

Adolescence spans the period from puberty to adult. I situate the age of adulthood arbitrarily at twenty, although it can vary significantly. In many tribal cultures, for instance, adulthood is set at sixteen, when adolescents undergo the ritual of initiation into adult life and can marry and become part of the tribal council (van Gennep 1909). In Western culture adolescence for some has been prolonged due to the increasing number of years one needs for the education to become a specialist and work in many professions. On the other hand, for many and especially among the poor, adolescence is shortened or nonexistent when children begin very early to take care of the household and of younger siblings or drop out of school and take to the streets.

Symbolically and archetypally, adolescence is the stage of development during which a second birth occurs, whereby children undergo a process of separation from the parental complexes and enter actively into social life. The tension present in this separation is guided by a process of polarization that reacts against the original family and at the same time is attracted by social life, love, and adventure influenced by the hero archetype.

Jung had a dream when he was 12 years old that well expresses the polarization with the parental world in the beginning of adolescence.

> I saw before me the cathedral, the blue sky. God sits on His golden throne, high above the world-and from under the throne an enormous turd falls upon the sparkling new roof, shatters it, and breaks the walls of the cathedral asunder. (1961, p. 39)

Of course the dream is all the more meaningful when we associate the Basel cathedral destroyed in the dream with the head church of his father and realize that this was the first great manifestation that would from then on separate Jung from his father's religious views. Due to the fact that they did not elaborate this negative father complex, this dream probably shows a fixation and the formation of Jung's Oedipus complex (Byington 2011).

The archetypes that coordinate the polarization of adolescence are the anima, animus, and alterity archetypes. Because Jung discovered these archetypes only as an adult and did not systematically articulate ego formation with archetypal coordination, analytical psychology frequently confuses the anima and animus archetypes with the matriarchal and patriarchal archetypes as here conceived.

Jung associated his concept of the anima with a dream he had in 1912, which, according to him, was decisive in the development of his love relationship with Toni Wolff (Shamdasani, 2009).

> Then, around Christmas of 1912, I had a dream. In the dream I found myself in a magnificent Italian loggia with pillars, a marble floor, and a marble balustrade. I was sitting on a gold Renaissance chair; in front of me was a table of rare beauty. It was made of green stone, like emerald. There I sat, looking out into the distance, for the loggia was set high up on the tower of a castle. My children were sitting at the table too.
> Suddenly a white bird descended, a small sea gull or a dove. Gracefully, it came to rest on the table, and I signed to the children to be still so that they would not frighten away the pretty white bird. Immediately, the dove was transformed into a little girl, about eight years of age, with golden blond hair. She ran off with the children and played with them among the colonnades of the castle.
> I remained lost in thought, musing about what I had just

experienced. The little girl returned and tenderly placed her arms around my neck. Then she suddenly vanished; the dove was back and spoke slowly in a human voice. "Only in the first hours of the night can I transform myself into a human being, while the male dove is busy with the twelve dead." Then she flew off into the blue air, and I awoke. (Jung 1961, pp. 171-172)

The dream shows that the anima archetype can be expressed by many symbols, including animals, and that it can also be bisexual.

The differentiation of the anima, animus, and alterity archetypes from the parental archetypes is of fundamental importance in understanding archetypal development and the archetypal stages of life. Jung has emphasized that the anima and animus archetypes are psychopomps that guide the individuation process to totality in the second half of life. I want to point out here that this great differentiation of the anima and animus begins in puberty through the polarization process with the matriarchal and patriarchal archetypes.

The anima and animus archetypes associated to the hero archetype antagonize the remaining passive position of the ego in exercising the insular matriarchal position and the polarized patriarchal position, reinforcing the passage of these archetypes to the active position. Adolescents agree with general sensuality (matriarchal) and social organization (patriarchal), but resist passively repeating their parents and want rather to exercise them actively in their own way.

The anima and animus archetypes are here considered bipolar. They are the archetypes that lead the ego to encounter the other and all polarities, on equal terms, including conscious-unconscious and *yang-yin* polarities. For this reason I have considered them an expression of the alterity archetype which relates polarities dialectically with equal rights to manifest themselves (see chapter 11).

In the beginning of adolescence the anima and animus archetypes form separate group Selves of boys and girls which enrich individual identity through intimacy and imitation and the polarization with adults. Homogeneous affectivity is dominant during this stage, and homosexual involvements are common. Cases of dominant homosexuality generally reveal themselves plainly here. Soon heterogeneous affection and heterosexual relationships can arise and develop toward marriage and the formation of the new family. The progressive integration of the anima and animus archetypes includes affectionate and sexual association together with overall social involvement and the activation of a professional vocation.

All this happens with the anima, animus, and alterity archetypes mostly in the passive position. Although they enhance matriarchal and patriarchal ego expression in the active position, they themselves still express the ego in the passive position. Love relationships and professional vocations in adolescence generally happen to the young and are not specifically sought. Boys and girls feel attraction and kiss during a party. This relationship can end that night or develop into a love affair that may last a long time and even one day lead them into marriage. The professional call is similar. Adolescents feel inclined toward one profession or another and may change their minds many times before finding a satisfactory occupation. Only in the sixth stage of life (40-60 years of age), which I call the stage of maturity or second adolescence, will the anima, animus, hero, and alterity archetypes be actively lived.

This is so because the archetypal transformations of the individual and family Selves in adolescence are in great turmoil due to the intense polarization between the present and the past generations. As described above, the polarization between them obeys two purposes which frequently conflict. On one hand the tension between the generations favors a greater or lesser passage of the matriarchal and patriarchal archetypes from the passive to the active position. If they remain passive, the new generation merely repeats the old, and the process of individuation stagnates. On the other hand the anima, animus, hero, and alterity archetypes in spite of being in the passive position begin to favor profound individuality which may be helped or antagonized by the matriarchal and patriarchal archetypes, as in tragic romances such as Romeo and Juliet.

Along the development process, as Freud discovered, fixations and defenses, which contain poorly elaborated symbols, can be reactivated for countless reasons and unleash the dragon of regression. Amid the rich conquests of development so far, the shadow erupts in such a devilish way that it can usurp the leadership of the archetypal orchestra (see the film *The Exorcist* [1973]).

Case Example

An eighteen-year-old girl came for therapy because of depression and frequent suicidal fantasies. She was very intelligent and extraordinarily beautiful. Her schoolwork was excellent. All this could not compensate for an intense feeling that she was evil and did not deserve to live. She belonged to a middle-class well-structured family and had an older brother and a younger sister. The older brother had always been very jealous of her and taunted her with sadistic fantasies in which she was the daughter of a poor family who gave her as a baby to a trash truck that deposited her at their door. When she was five, she began to have tantrums. Whenever frustrated she became possessed, threw herself on the floor and bit whoever touched her. She began to have these tantrums also when accompanying her mother in shopping centers. Unable to cope with such behavior, her mother began to leave her stretched out on the floor and continued her shopping. In time the crisis subsided, but became fixated internally and created a severe defense mechanism, the basis of her powerful and threatening shadow.

As elaboration in analysis progressed, it became quite clear that her depression and self-recrimination with suicidal fantasies corresponded to her inadequate aggression expressing frustration and her mother's disapproval. The internalized imitation of her mother's behavior "left behind" her aggression, stigmatized as evil which deserved punishment with a death sentence, a symbolical equivalent to public abandonment in shopping centers by her mother.

At the age of eighteen she was praised for her beauty and intelligence and for her angelic voice and sweet behavior. Her aggression, however, which was a very important part of her soul, was imprisoned in hell (in the shadow) and acted out through her defensive depression. From time to time, like an imprisoned member of the family kept in jail, her shadow was visited through her defensive depression and reminded the prisoner of her ongoing trial which could end in a death sentence to punish her "criminal nature" (Lorenz 1963).

I worked through her defensive depression over the course of a whole year, using the expressive techniques of the marionettes of the Self, of dramatization and of active imagination. Sitting upright in front of an empty chair with a cushion, she was asked to invoke and talk to the little girl who was possessed by aggression during the tantrums (Byington 1993a). The little girl confirmed that she was evil because of her aggression, and in time it became clear that those fits were a reaction to her brother's sadism, to the rejection of her mother, and to the nonacceptance of her aggression in general. The dramatic technique was guided by me so that she would experience her aggressive drive as normal and be able to express it adequately whenever it was constellated. The aggressive dramatization was very intense and full of repressed hatred for her brother and her mother. During these exercises I never employ the technique of inverting role playing used in psychodrama because I think that this inversion can confuse the ego of consciousness with the ego of shadow.

After many analytic sessions with this elaboration, she came to the conclusion that her parents' love and intense admiration for her intelligence, beauty, and angelic persona prevented her from thinking of her aggression and depression as normal and reinforced intensely her feeling of being evil and condemned to die.

After a year of weekly analytical sessions, her depression subsided, and whenever she felt depressive she knew she had to regress and go down to hell to talk to her condemned child and bring her back to light.

This case illustrates the overall concept of Jungian symbolic psychology that the shadow and evil are formed by fixation and defensive formation of normal structuring functions. In this sense, evil or shadow must not be eliminated, as in a surgical amputation, but like any symptom, error, or sin must instead be rescued and restored to its normal functioning.

During therapy, our patient had to sacrifice her angelic defensive persona, to which she was very much attached, and build another persona that integrated her aggressive function adequately and allowed her to express herself fully, including radical disagreements with her parents. At first they were very surprised and even shocked by the transformation of their "sweet angel," but, after coming to a joint session with her, they finally had to admit that she was now beginning to express herself intelligently as an adult woman with a very strong personality.

The Fifth Archetypal Stage of Life
The Conjugal and Professional Choices
from 20 to 40 Years

From about twenty to forty years old, this archetypal stage of individual archetypal development in Western culture is centered on marriage, the making of a new family, and the development of a career or vocation.

Depending on how normal and differentiated the preceding stages of development were and on the gravity of fixations, defenses, and shadow formation, the personalities of the new couple will have moved from the passive to the active position of their matriarchal and patriarchal archetypes and begun integration of the anima, animus, alterity, and hero archetypes in the passive position.

As we observe the potential of the regent archetypes and their relation in the individuation process, one thing appears increasingly obvious. Psychological development leads toward alterity and totality through symbolic life, and important symbols that were left behind tend to reappear and force integration. That which was fixated and formed defenses and shadow will be acted out defensively by the central archetype through repetition compulsion and can exhibit regression and pathology, which can also be seen as a desperate call for salvation.

Individuation is our life and our inescapable destiny for better or for worse. We have an archetypal potential that will manifest itself as good or as evil. The central archetype is a ruthless commander of the development of the psyche. The normal ego as well as the imprisoned ego in the shadow are the soldiers of its existential army. Whether they are in good or fair disposition, hurt, sick, or imprisoned in hell, that is, in the shadow, at any moment they may be summoned by the central archetype simply because the symbols and functions they contain are needed in the journey toward totality. So, beware humans! Thy lot is to live the battle of good and evil in the developmental process of thyselves!

Although professional creativity and spiritual life are of fundamental importance in the fifth and sixth archetypal stages of life, in the case of heterosexuality, relationships between men and women continue to have a paramount function during the individuation and humanization process of the incarnation of being.

Men and women will relate in this stage of life, be it in marriage or in some other way, depending on their psychological development, primarily on the individual, family, and the cultural Selves. In spite of the great differences in these dimensions, I want to call attention now particularly to the different characteristics of their identity formation of their individual selves and the consequences of this in their affectionate relationships. The difficulty in men's capacity for love in the patriarchal tradition is so intense that our creation myth in Genesis relates Adam's eating of the tree of knowledge, seduced by the serpent and Eve, without even mentioning his falling in love with Eve. The temptation to acquire knowledge of good and evil is reduced to a moral transgression that does not include love.

There is an eloquent example of this in Jung's *Red Book*, published in 2009. The book was initially discussed and studied by many scholars, mostly men, as regards Jung's sanity, his separation from Freud, his mediumistic vision of the World War I, the discoveries of alchemy, the anima archetype, the transcendent function, and many other angles. All this happened until a woman (Guerra, 2011) laid bare the Ariadne's thread in the *Red Book* of Jung's love drama with Toni Wolff, his discovery of the importance of love, the difficulty he had in living with it, and his guilt about adultery. After reading her book, the emotional side of Jung's personality and his central search for love becomes so clear that one wonders why he hid the book and why so many scholars delving into it did not see Jung's love and guilt as the compass of his affectionate anima shadow (Salome) and the search to rescue the function of normal love from his shadow in his individuation process.

The existential elaboration of the separation wound from the mother in the personalities of men and of the permanence of the symbiotic fusion with the mother in the personalities of women during patriarchal domination are, in my view, the two main consequences of fixations which most frequently occur in their primary quaternio, which will influence decisively their affectionate relationship when they meet again in adult life.

Wounds cause pain and suffering which when fixated mark the relationship of the wounded with factors related to the cause of the wound. The separation wound from the mother will affect men's personalities in various and profound ways when they meet again with women. Men will bring Nemesis, the goddess of vengeance and of repairing injustice, to influence their behavior in their second meeting with women, now in adult life.

However, we cannot reduce the pain inflicted by men on women only to the separation complex of men in their primary relationship because it is the greater physical strength of men that also explains their domination of women and the abuse of power and sadomasochism that perverted their relationship throughout history and are being confronted by the rise of technology. It is undeniable that this factor also suffered the influence of the separation complex because it includes not only the separation wound but also weaknesses and sufferings lived in childhood, which are frequently associated with the maternal complex.

In this sense, the second encounter with women in their love relationship will include, if not direct feelings of vengeance, certainly a strong compensatory assertion to infantile dependence. After becoming adults men will compensate in varying degrees of power for their feelings of inferiority and dependence with control, betrayal, humiliation, and even rape and torture of women amid lust and love.

Men relate to women within this historical collective and individual dependence, and this will affect his individual Self in the development of affection and self-assurance. Women, on the other hand, have in their personalities the dominant influence of the mother complex in their identity formation. Within patriarchal tradition, the maternal symbiosis preserves their feeling function which they will live with their husband and children. However, if the feeling for the other can be fully lived, the same will not happen with her self-trust to be admired and favored in authority and intelligence and the capacity to realize themselves professionally in the relationship with their father, husband, and men in general.

The primary symbiosis can favor the affection, imitation, and identification of women with the mother role, but the high price paid for this intimacy with mother is the estrangement from father within the EDMDF syndrome. Within the family Self, women have to cope with the longstanding position of inferiority, abuse, and sadism to which they have been submitted during ten thousand years of patriarchal dominance. The important factor that will hinder their self-realization in a love relationship is the longstanding projection of authority, strength, self-support, creativity, power, and leadership onto men, which resists the integration of these functions. Another difficulty is the prostitute complex mentioned above which lurks in their shadow and threatens their social status of respect and honesty during their integration of sexuality.

Amidst countless individual and cultural variations in the personalities of men and women, these factors here mentioned are some examples of severe obstacles for them to respect and love each other and, at the same time, develop self-esteem and careers or vocations during the individuation process toward freedom, alterity, democracy, and self-realization.

Marriage, the Anima and Animus Archetypes, Adultery, and Polygamy

One immense problem in the Western system of marriage is defensive monogamy. When Jung discovered the anima, animus, and alterity archetypes, he had the courage to break up his monogamous Christian marriage and embark on first his love relationship with Sabina Spielrein secretly and afterward with Toni Wolff quite openly despite the traditional rigid morality of Swiss society.

Marriage as a structuring function can be seen in a spectrum that varies from monogamy to polygamy, passing through many other forms. The legal monogamous institution of marriage in Western culture has created a fixated and defensive model that does not encompass the whole individuation process of both men and women, and can lead to falsity, lies, treason, and all the other ingredients of the conjugal farce so frequently acted out in the shadow of Western marriages. According to Brazilian law, adultery is no longer considered a crime, as of 2005. Had Jung lived in Brazil he could have been punished with six months in jail.

The traditional love affairs of men conducted outside the official family, practiced for centuries in patriarchally dominant Western marriages, were maintained together with the defensive repression of women. However, the development of civil rights and the recognition of the anima, animus, hero, and alterity archetypes, developing equally in the personalities of men and women as part of the individuation process, has exposed this traditional patriarchal mystification and reopened the fidelity question in marriage for elaboration. New types of marriage and new family structures in modern societies have made relevant the fidelity question in its normal and defensive aspects.

During marriage, the couple reinforces the implantation of the matriarchal and patriarchal archetypes as much as possible in the active position. This means that they can live sensuously in the home and in social life as they like and according to the philosophy they think right. The more they are able to do so, the more they will develop their individuality, which is essential for continuing to implant the anima, animus, hero, and alterity archetypes in this stage and in the preparation for the next stage of life.

To implant the matriarchal archetype in the active position in marriage is to live at home with your own sensuality, that is, to enjoy eating, decoration, clothing, affection, sexuality, and leisure created actively by the couple. Regarding children, this means accompanying them intimately and warmly in their development, caring and holding them, for both normal and difficult situations alike.

To implant the patriarchal archetype actively in marriage is to partake of common ideologies and values, to plan the family's activities and finances together, to idealize investments for the future, and to share ambition and responsibility for realizing them. It means partaking of and organizing the moral orientation of their children and being responsible for their education in the present and in the future.

The problem with this performance is that even though it can be very productive, it is frequently not sufficient to maintain love and sexual interest and to avoid sameness and boredom if is not accompanied by the progressive implantation of the anima, animus, alterity, and hero archetypes with their creative experiences and innovations permanently enriching the relationship.

The greatest challenge to marriage in the individuation process is exactly the experience of anima, animus, hero, and alterity archetypes as lived by Jung, which may include the breakup of the marriage fidelity contract. The high number of divorces and new types of marriage and families being created has transformed the elaboration of fidelity in marriage contracts into a most relevant and inevitable question.

The Feminine, the Masculine, and the Identity of Men and of Women

The adjectives feminine and masculine have been traditionally used to designate characteristics of women and of men respectively. With the progressive implantation of the alterity archetype in culture, reduction to unilaterality diminished and polarities began to be increasingly employed regarding all symbols and structuring functions. Men and women were not excluded from this tendency.

Jung described the anima archetype as being expressed by the images of woman, but also of the snake, and as a pattern of conscious-unconscious relationship. However, the tendency to identify the anima with the feminine and the animus with the masculine became very intense in Jung's writings and in a significant part of the Jungian community.

However, when we consider the anima and animus archetypes as masculine and feminine respectively, this brings enormous confusion to the concept of the identity of man and of woman.

Before developmental psychology, human beings traditionally thought that they knew how they were. However, the more we know about the formation of ego and other identities in consciousness and shadow through the process of symbolic elaboration coordinated by archetypes during the processes of individuation (individual Self) and humanization (cultural Self), the more we see that identity is not an entity but a process revealed during life. No one that I know of can say that he or she knows who he or she is. Reality and its unpredictable events surprise us all the time, and we react symbolically in ways that we would not recognize as ours a day before. The same can be said about our life partners and intimate friends.

This being so, how can we ever imagine that we can define the extraordinary variety of the identity of man and of women as individuals by an abstract concept?

To make this issue still more complicated, we are realizing that, with the increasing integration of the alterity archetype replacing the dominance of the patriarchal archetype in the cultural Self, men's and women's traditional identities are rapidly changing and each gender is integrating more characteristics that traditionally belonged to the opposite gender (Byington 1986).

Although already very indiscriminate, the concepts of masculine and feminine identity became even more confused with the consideration of homosexuality as a normal expression of sexuality and the increasing formation of homosexual marriages.

Considering these variations and the growing notion that the identities of men and of women and their relationships are unique, cannot be defined by an abstract concept, and are revealed by symbolic elaboration during the individuation and the humanization processes, I propose the anima and animus archetypes to be applied separately to men and women, with their exclusive connotation of the masculine referring to man and the feminine to women. I propose also to conceive the anima and animus archetypes as bipolar and their main polarity to be *yang* and *yin*.

The Sixth Archetypal Stage of Life
Maturity or Second Adolescence
from 40 to 60 Years

This stage, from about 40 to 60 years of age, is characterized by the relative decrease in matriarchal and patriarchal dominance and a significant increase in the dominance of the anima, animus, hero, and alterity archetypes, which are now in the active position, the reason I call it a second adolescence.

This is a stage of development still not accessible to most people even in Western culture.

The decrease of matriarchal and patriarchal dominance accompanies the decrease of physical vitality and of the collective dependence on the persona and superego. One becomes increasingly independent of the opinion of others and feels that the moment has come at last to live one's own life. Those who come this far remember the pilgrimage through many tortuous ways of obeying conventions, which now entitles them to choose their own path. Development now includes preparing to detach from social dependence and political correctness. At the same time, the increase in the anima, animus, hero, and alterity archetypes in the active position means a significant differentiation of individuality and a growing creative perception of symbolic life the development of the function of supraconsciousness and the coordinating capacity of the central archetype.

Very few people and societies develop consciousness this far. There are many who do not integrate the anima and animus archetypes together with detachment and thus behave like teenagers, immaturely attached. They act out this second adolescence defensively as though it were the first. Black leather jackets, powerful motorcycles, and incestuous young girlfriends are typical of this defensive adolescence for men. In the film *Something's Gotta Give* Jack Nicholson and Diane Keaton live this stage with suffering, grace, and laughter (2003). Worst of all is when such people decide to invest their life savings in some "infallible and spectacular" new business and go bankrupt or fall into an incestuous and passionate love affair with unforeseeable consequences, as in Nabokov's *Lolita*.

The Seventh and Last Archetypal Stage of Life after 60 Years

This stage occurs approximately from age 60 to the end of life and is marked by increasing detachment which accompanies decreasing physical vitality, preoccupation with the diseases of old age, expectation of physical death, and the possibility of spiritual life after death.

As I have already mentioned, attachment and detachment are poles of the structuring functions of relationship and operate in every symbolic elaboration from the beginning to the end of life (van Gennep 1909). They interrelate with the life and death archetypes and are especially important in the transition from one archetypal stage to another (Byington 1996).

It is most important to remember that fixations and shadow formation tend to paralyze development, establish defensive attachment with compulsive repetition, and prevent detachment with great resistance. Due to the fact that the last stage of life functions mostly through final detachments, fixations are its major dysfunction, for they not only paralyze the last chances for development, but also favor severe regressions that may bring enormous guilt and suffering. One tragic event impressed me profoundly in the last year of medical school. The director of my college of medicine, a most respectable surgeon, married with three children and five grandchildren, was highly praised by the medical community. At the age of 75, he began to have senile depression and a compulsion to act out his repressed sexuality. People began to witness his compulsive flattering of young female students, which exposed him increasingly to ridicule. One day the shocking news came that he had committed suicide.

As has been pointed out, the individuation process starts with ego formation in the passive position and develops toward increasing ego formation in the active position. During this process, the function of supraconsciousness further develops the notion, for those who are psychologically developed, that human life forms consciousness and shadow.

Sanctity is a structuring function that recognizes and elaborates the shadow of oneself and others during individuation. In so doing sanctity diminishes evil in the world. Mythologically this corresponds to the call of Jesus for people to repent and seek salvation. Those who do not do this remain attached to fixations, defenses, or sin and continue to project and introject defensively their shadow and disseminate evil in the world.

The myth of the final judgment in Christian theology refers to the final symbolic elaboration of the shadow in individual and collective development. This elaboration is a projection of the last stage of the archetypal development of the individual. It is as though the central archetype had a final chance to elaborate many important symbols of individuation that were left behind, some of which remained fixated in the shadow. The extreme unction in Christianity is symbolically the last episode of this elaboration.

The shadow unelaborated during development sooner or later falls back on the ego with symptoms such as depression or is projected onto others, as for instance in paranoid reactions. Both defenses are forms of tormenting the ego of oneself or others and disseminating evil in life. Fixations prevent detachment and delay or stagnate psychological development. These considerations show the degree to which the individuation process is relative and give us an idea of the immense portion of the psyche's capacity that is individually and socially squandered. When we see the bloody trail of evil and destruction that marks the history of humankind and accept that it corresponds to the shadow formed by the fixation of symbols during the elaboration of normal life, we become aware of the great amount of creativity, beauty, and potential growth of the psyche that is daily wasted by our species.

The effort of the central archetype to activate and elaborate important symbols left behind in life frequently intensifies their fixations and defenses, in which they are entrenched, and aggravate clinical conditions. These are the psychological dynamics of countless cases of senile defensive depression that compel elderly people to self-destruction, as was the case with the dean of my medical faculty. Frequently these patients and even the doctors who medicate them do not have the least idea that their depression is the result of guilt and self-condemnation for potentiality and wounds unelaborated in the past, which have remained under the control of the shadow (the devil), and now come to collect their due on the last bend in the road.

Other patients project these unelaborated transgressions and wounds onto other people and become chronic aggressors of their family, of humanity as a whole, and of fate. I analyzed such a case in the figure of the musician Antonio Salieri in *Creative Envy* (Byington 2002a).

Among the billions who die precociously or remain to a greater or lesser extent fixated along the way, some come to the threshold of death asking for more life. Many do so conditioned by religious education, which has promised them an afterlife. A few, however, have had the experience of symbolic death and resurrection in the transformations undergone during the sufferings and joys of the long life process. For those who count on life after death due to religious education and conditioning, I do not have much to say. For those, however, who search for eternal life through psychological development, I can offer my own experience.

Meditation

Symbolic elaboration is the beating heart of Jungian symbolic psychology. Active imagination, as Jung described, is a method of directing the symbolic heart to propel blood to humanize unknown regions. Finally, meditation is the age-old discovery of the East, enabling one to detach and transcend Samsara or daily joys and sorrows and live the mysteries of worlds beyond.

In chapter 4 (p. 87) and chapter 12 (p. 269), I described a meditation for going out of the body and experiencing the eternal and infinite dimension of the cosmos as the home of the psyche. It has been our home during this incarnation, and in the final stage we will prepare to continue to inhabit it consciously after death, when our body has "returned to dust" and has become atomically pulverized in the universe.

To start the meditation, read it again in chapters 4 (p. 87) and 12 (p. 269). Tell the little monkey to relax on the first branch of your life tree as you leave your body, accompanying the rays of the sun in photosynthesis. Leave our galaxy, the Milky Way, and penetrate intergalactic space (Sagan 1980). This has always been the home of being, but it is not enough to know it. We must now experience it fully and encounter the spirit of creation that is the essence of infinity and eternity. This encounter will bring us union with the world spirit and the revelation of creation during initiation in the process of dying.

Concentrate your mind and imagine the hundred billion galaxies around you and the more than twelve billion years needed to create and develop this one universe until now (Sagan 1980). Let your mind be amazed by the grandiosity of creation. Your initiation will lead you to feel love, but this will only happen when your heart opens to the amazing miracle of being. The time has come for this ecstatic experience.

Creation is so extraordinarily great, and we are so infinitely small. How can one encounter the other? The psyche has the structuring function of the imagination to unite all opposites no matter how distant they are. Meditation is the great path toward union. Your mind is endowed with the capacity to imagine the distance from your minuteness to the extraordinary greatness of creation but only love can allow you to really experience this encounter. In order to achieve it, yoga and meditation must be exercised daily until your heart opens to creation and you become more and more familiar to each other. Only then will you feel at home with creation and acquire consciousness of life after physical death. This must be undertaken only in the seventh stage of life, lest death becomes more important than life. Now live the experience of the encounter.

Be ready. Imagine again infinity through the extension of this universe present in its one hundred billion galaxies. Imagine eternity thinking about the more than twelve-billion-year duration from the Big Bang until today as the life of only this one universe. Now touch the pulse of one of your carotid arteries and feel your heart beating and supplying blood to your brain. This is the way your psyche has to unite your heart to your brain, which in *Kundalini yoga* is the symbolic encounter of *Anahata*, the *chakra* of the heart and of love, with *Ajna*, the *chakra* of the brain and of the mind. Feel and imagine the blood being propelled by your heart to your brain. Imagine your encounter with the essence of creation when it will continue to contain you after the dissolution of your physical body. Enjoy this miraculous encounter through love joining your heart and your brain, your feeling and your imagination. Repeat this meditation frequently and prepare for life after dissolution of your physical body, discovering through love what it is to rejoice in the infinity of eternal life.

And yet, each person reacts to this exercise quite individually and many search for one's own way of living it.

I had a seventy-five-year-old patient who earnestly tried but could in no way experience the love relationship with creation. He could empty his conscience through detachment quite well, he experienced deeply the infinite and eternal vastness of empty space, but when it came to the emotional relation to the creative spirit, he backed up and literally froze, so abruptly that it reminded me of an autistic defense.

We worked hard on the elaboration of this resistance. We were about to give up when one day during meditation I broke the rules and, in desperation perhaps, I asked him bluntly why he could not love creation. "Because I am a lonesome being who has suffered and continues to suffer very much. Creation is so grandiose that I feel that I cannot possibly relate to it." Then, out of nowhere, or perhaps out of intuition and empathy, I asked him, "Have you ever considered the loneliness and the immense suffering undergone by the creative spirit since it all began?" His reaction was as though he experienced at the individual level the big bang moment of the cosmos.

The Mystery of Trinity and the Archetype of Alterity

A finance advisor and a university teacher in their late thirties had a nine-year-old daughter, a lovely girl. The parents were Protestants and leaders of a social organization that helped a large number of poor families. One day the girl went to spend the night with her maternal grandparents as she often did. At three o'clock in the morning, her father woke up to a phone call. It was his father-in-law, who said he was at the hospital with his granddaughter. Both parents rushed to the hospital. As entered, a pale-faced doctor received them. "I am terribly sorry to tell you that your daughter has died." The girl had suffered an acute and fatal meningoencephalitis. Both parents lost their faith and abandoned social work.

Fifteen years later the father came for therapy after hearing my lecture on active imagination with the dead in the treatment of pathological mourning (Byington 2005b). At the death of their daughter, the couple had gone through a two-year period of intense suffering, after which the mother became pregnant and gave birth to a boy, now entering adolescence, whom they loved very much.

The father's therapy with me lasted approximately three years. We elaborated their marriage complex, which had a serious fixation and defenses concerning the overprotective relationship of the wife with her father, but the central elaboration of the analysis was concentrated on his religious problem. He dreamed frequently about his daughter, Jesus, and the Devil.

During therapy I taught him to practice active imagination with many symbols, which finally included his daughter. With great emotion he told me that she was now an adolescent who seemed very mature and profound. We related this to his religious faith which, although lost after her death, continued to mature unconsciously. The girl told him that she loved and watched over him and her mother. Once a profound relationship between them had been reestablished within the imagination, she explained to him that he had been unjust to God and Christ because they could not be blamed for her death. They suffered with her parents' suffering but were not capable of avoiding it.

After many months of this spiritual and psychological symbolic work, he regained his faith after realizing how much God had suffered for not having been able to avoid the suffering of his own Son and how this sacrifice had been indispensable for their own transformation into the divine Trinity.

As we have seen in the individual and cultural archetypal psychological transformation throughout the book, elaboration of all structuring symbols and functions are subject to the coordination of the five archetypal intelligences, which include the structuring function of faith.

In the undifferentiated position of consciousness, which corresponds to the beginning of every elaboration coordinated by the central archetype, faith is the vitality expressed in the breath of life present in every new experience. In the insular matriarchal position the symbiotic intimacy of the ego-other relationship endows the ego with the capacity of animism, myth, and magic whereby faith is sensually and imaginally lived. The magic of prayer and wishful lighting of candles are expressions of the sensuous intimacy with faith.

In the polarized patriarchal position faith is lived through submission and obedience, to receive the protection, guidance, and approval of the Lord (Gen. 22:1-18).

In the dialectical position of alterity, faith is experienced during the revelation of the synchronistic experience of transcendence. The ego-other relationship is here lived in a spectrum that varies from opposition to equality. Faith becomes the emotional partnership of sinful imperfection with the magnificence of totality as the essential ethics of being.

The Mystery of Trinity

The Son had to die in sacrifice to transform the patriarchal rigidity of the Father into the compassionate and dialectical relationship with the Son within the soul of being.

"Father, why hast thou forsaken me?" was the experience of the death of the protecting and controlling authority of the Godhead to be transformed through the archetype of alterity into the dialectical and compassionate participation of humankind in creation through the energy of the Holy Ghost.

In the contemplating intelligence of the archetype of totality faith is lived in the ecstatic admiration for the miraculous existence of being in infinity and eternity.

Chapter 15

THE MYTH OF OEDIPUS
AND THE ARCHETYPE OF SANCTITY
INDIVIDUATION AND HUMANIZATION

To end this book, I present an interpretation of the myth of Oedipus, reuniting three main concepts: from psychoanalysis the Oedipus complex, from analytical psychology the process of individuation, and from Jungian symbolic psychology the archetype of sanctity. In this manner, we can clearly demonstrate how these concepts were dissociated by the emotional separation of the two great geniuses of modern psychology - Sigmund Freud and C. G. Jung (Byington 2005a).

From the perspective of psychoanalysis, we have the fixations and defenses formed in Oedipus's childhood, here situated as a pathological variant of the normal development of the primary quaternio (see chapter 7). The fateful occurrences in Oedipus's first years of life and their consequences in his adult life are further elaborated within the concept of the marriage quaternio (also described in chapter 7). These two parts of Oedipus's life serve as the basis for the tragedy *Oedipus Rex*, written by Sophocles in 429 B.C. at the age of 66.

From the point of view of analytical psychology we see the process of individuation in Oedipus through the elaboration of his shadow during his "dark night of the soul," which he crossed in exile as a blind pilgrim guided by his daughter Antigone. Confronting his shadow with the guidance of his daughter/anima, he is received and blessed in the sanctuary of the mothers, the fearful Erinyes, who were transformed to become the Eumenides, the benevolent. From then on, protected by King Theseus, Oedipus resists the temptation of repeating the actions of his father Laius and participating in filicide by allying himself to one of his sons against the other. Finally, having integrated his shadow and fulfilled his destiny, he walks into death in peace and sanctity.

Following the paradigm of Jungian symbolic psychology, the reunion of psychoanalysis and analytical psychology is here transcended to a more ample context than that of Oedipus's individuation process, because it includes his family Self, the cultural Self of Greece, and the planetary Self within the process of humanization conceived by Teilhard de Chardin. As Theseus, king of Athens, accompanies Oedipus to death, all these dimensions enhance the importance of the Oedipus myth in expressing the elaboration of the creativity and the shadow through the dialectical position of alterity to reach enlightenment within the contemplative position of totality. The expiatory pilgrimage is described in the play Antigone, written by Sophocles at the age of fifty-two, and further worked out in the play Oedipus at Colonus, written in 406 B.C. in his ninetieth year. In reality, the events of Oedipus at Colonus antecede those of Antigone, which takes place after the death of the hero.

In ancient Greece, the meaning of moral transgression, depending on the crime, established a true karma in the cultural Self that transcended the individual and included the genus, that is, the family and all descendents. Oedipus's pilgrimage will expiate his responsibility but not that of Antigone, Polynices, and Eteocles, who will die following the curse upon the Labdacids.

Everything begins when Laius visits the palace of Pelops and, on meeting Chrysippus, falls passionately in love with him, and the two fly away together. Feeling a terrible guilt over remembrance of his father, Chrysippus commits suicide. Laius's transgression violated the custom of hospitality, which was most cherished in ancient Greece. The importance of this crime was greatly increased by the death of Chrysippus. Because of this, Pelops's curse is fulgurant and tragically wounds the genus of the Labdacids in a devastating way.

In ancient Greece, homosexuality was acceptable when expressed parallel to the heterosexual family life, but Laius and Chrysippus lived it beyond the acceptable measure and thus committed great hubris, which provoked the wrath of Hera, the protectress of traditional heterosexual marriage.

Laius returned to Thebes and married Iocasta, making her queen, but Hera did not pardon him and sent the Sphinx against Thebes.

During patriarchal dominance, the heterosexual-homosexual polarity, coordinated by the polarized position, favored heterosexuality to the detriment of homosexuality in greater or lesser degree in most cultures. In Western culture through the progress of the elaboration of civil rights within the dialectical position of the alterity archetype, homosexuality began to be accepted in the nineteenth century, but it wasn't until the second half of the twentieth century that it was no longer considered pathological.

We still do not know whether homosexuality has a genetic basis but today, in Western culture, homosexuality is recognized as a normal variation of sexual identity, together with bisexuality and heterosexuality. As all structuring functions, these three forms of sexuality can be normal or defensive (Byington 2001).

When homosexuality is defensive, it is expressed inadequately, compulsively, and the couple is incapable of having a mature conjugal relationship. The discrimination between the normal and defensive forms, as in all structuring functions, is at times very difficult to detect due to preconceived and defensive reactions of the family or of the culture in question. These reactions frequently propitiate defensive homosexuality and prevent the living out of authentic normal homosexuality. In the case of masculine defensive homosexuality, we generally find fixations resulting from disturbances in the primary relationships, either a defensive identification with the mother or absence, abandonment, rejection, or radical aversion to the father figure.

In the course of thousands of years of patriarchal dominance, we frequently find limitations of affection, tenderness, charm, humor, and sensibility (Byington 2001). These limitations are used to disqualify as homosexual the undertaking by men of any profession traditionally feminine (see the film *Billy Elliot*). Within this psychological limitation, we generally find excess of power, mostly repressing eros and guiding the masculine personality toward defensive competition, arrogance, authoritarianism, and armed reaction to perceived threat. Parallel to this situation, normal affection between men, which I call homoaffectivity, may become defensive homosexuality when it is prevented from being freely expressed. This explains many cases of defensive homosexuality in which men express their tenderness, which they are forbidden to do in heterosexuality (Byington 2001).

It is within both the normal and defensive structuring functions of homosexuality, which includes homoaffectivity, that I situate the passion of Laius and Chrysippus and the reaction of Pelops and Hera. The limitation of homosexuality within patriarchal dominance resulted in its inadequate expression through the shadow and a great conflict with the cultural superego.

The shadow of the repressed feeling function coordinated by the polarized patriarchal archetype is also frequently expressed by rage in fratricide, parricide, and filicide defenses rooted in the masculine personality as a result of the unilaterality of the functions of power and aggression. It is frequently the case that the limited and undeveloped feeling function of men causes them to have a maternal dependence, an incestuous relationship with women that weakens their ego and makes it vulnerable to possession by the power drive and aggression. It is this complex of defensive reactions that Laius lives out with Iocasta and Oedipus after his relationship with Chrysippus was interrupted by traditional morality followed by tragedy.

I consider then that Oedipus's tragedy is the emergence of disturbances within the patriarchal dominance of the ancient Greek cultural Self expressed defensively through the personality of Oedipus, who will elaborate it heroically within his individuation process. The swollen feet, which will acquire world fame thanks to Freud, are of great symbolic meaning because they centralize his identity simultaneously in his physical deformity and in the central wound of the fixation of his primary quaternio. His feet were tied up and transfixed together with his death sentence. Today this crime is situated within the battered child syndrome. Presently in Brazil, Laius's and Iocasta's murder would be triply qualified because besides being a homicidal attempt, it presents characteristics of refined cruelty with a defenseless victim (Delmanto 2008).

The Delphic oracle, through the medium of its priestesses at the service of Apollo, intermediated the elaboration of individual and collective symbols, transmitting their messages in magical-mythical metaphors. In this manner, it expressed the structuring transcendent function of the imagination of the ancient Greek cultural Self for many centuries. Within synchronicity, the oracle prophesied which symbols in the individual and collective dimension constellated in their developmental processes without necessarily differentiating whether this elaboration was normal or defensive.

The Sphinx sent by Hera against Thebes is related to the relationship of Laius and Chrysippus, but she herself is also very meaningful. Daughter of the monsters Echidna and Typhon, according to Brandão (1991), or Echidna and her son Orthos, according to Kerényi (1951), she is the sister of the incestuous monsters Cerberus, the Chimaera, the Hydra of Lerna, and the Nemean lion. Her name means the strangler, and she represents the phenomenon of incestuous fixation, due to her incestuous monstrosity. As a symbol of that which is archaically non differentiated, incestuous, and therefore monstrous by virtue of being fixated in the insular matriarchal position, she comes to terrify Thebes with a riddle: an enigma about one being and its phases of life, which Oedipus deciphers as the human being. Indeed all that occurred in the drama of Laius, of Thebes, and now of Oedipus-including homosexuality, homoaffectivity, parricide, filicide, and incest-are structuring symbols, complexes, and functions to be elaborated along the individuation process, the stages of which are childhood, maturity, and old age, exactly the three phases of life described by the Sphinx to define the human being. Greek intelligence is brilliantly expressed in the heroic deed of Oedipus when he deciphers the riddle. Once it has been deciphered, the Sphinx goes back to the depths where she lives. Oedipus and the Thebans identified with logos celebrate her destruction and begin festivities for Oedipus's marriage with their queen Iocasta. One thing, however, is the rational mind; another, much greater and all encompassing, is being.

For Freud's fiftieth birthday in 1906, his followers commemorated the event with a supper during which they presented him with a medallion that moved him intensely. On one side was Freud's image and, on the other side, Oedipus in front of the Sphinx, with the inscription "He who deciphered the famous enigma and was a great man" (Jones 1953, vol. 2, p. 13). The identification of Freud with Oedipus is symbolic, and I want to point out two meanings, one in the light, the other in the shadow. The first is the power and the glory that comes from having established the unconscious dimension and the developmental process in psychology, a parallel to Oedipus deciphering the Sphinx's oracle and being crowned king in Thebes. One could say that on Freud's fiftieth anniversary his disciples crowned him king of psychoanalysis. The shadow side of this crowning occurred when Freud, like Oedipus, did not elaborate his incestuous complex by rationalizing the perverse polymorph as normal.

Crowned king in Thebes, Oedipus marries his mother and has four children: Antigone, Ismene, Polynices, and Eteocles. Believing wrongly that he had not merely defeated the Sphinx but destroyed it, Oedipus falls into its clutches and drowns in incest, adding to the parricide already committed. The Sphinx could not be destroyed because she is an archetypal image. Once her riddle was solved, she went down to her abode and waited for Oedipus to become conscious of the existential meaning of what he deciphered, or else to live it through his shadow instead. "Decipher me not only with the mind but also with your whole being or I will devour you," and so she did.

Deciphering the enigma of unconscious repression, Freud compared himself to Copernicus and Darwin and affirmed psychoanalysis to be on a par with the discoveries of those two great geniuses. His own genius is undeniable, but his identification with Oedipus also includes fixation, defense, and shadow to elaborate incest. Generalizing incest and parricide to all boys through the concept of the perverse polymorph and believing he could undo all the fixations of the id through rational interpretation and insight, Freud fell back into the rational omnipotence of the Enlightenment and was just as deluded as Oedipus. The filicidal elimination of Jung, Adler, and Wilhelm Stekel from his life and the defensive projection onto them as the parricidal sons of the primal hoard (Freud 1913) showed the extent to which he did not undergo any analysis to elaborate his father-son and mother-son relationships and their fixations and defenses.

On one side, Jung and Freud parted over Freud's reduction of libido to sexuality, which Jung conceived of as psychic energy. However, what predominated in the shadow of their separation was, in my view, the mutual defensive projection of their unelaborated father complexes. What else could explain the defensive separation of these two geniuses, whose joint creativity had so much to add to modern psychology but who never again spoke a word to each other during t 26 years (Byington 2011).

Oedipus lived happily with Iocasta and reigned in glory for many years, until Apollo sent the plague to punish Thebes. The play *Oedipus Rex* was the first detective story, describing the search for a criminal through a process of self-analysis. It is the very quest for justice and truth undertaken by Tiresias at the request of Oedipus himself, coordinated by the dialectical position of the archetype of alterity that guides him and the audience to the discovery of his parricidal and incestuous shadow. In a psychotic reaction, he plunges his mother's hairpins into his eyes and tears them out. In a psychoanalytic interpretation we can say that this self-mutilation was the acting out of his self-castration to expiate his guilt. Another interpretation is that Oedipus expresses psychotically that he cannot yet bear to see what everybody else is seeing: the horror of parricide and incest.

Oedipus followed his destiny. Instead of death, the way chosen by Iocasta who hanged herself, he chose pilgrimage in rags, helped by his daughter Antigone, and exposed his tragic shadow from city to city. The glory of the king famous for rationally deciphering the riddle of humankind and guilty of the two great crimes of patriarchal society is now exposed in the form of this humiliated beggar. That which he hid from the light in the psychotic reaction, he now exposes to the rich and the poor in many Greek cities. How can we not remember another pilgrim in India, who left the palace where he was a prince, detached himself fully from power, family, and riches, and became a mendicant monk in the search of enlightenment?

What did Oedipus mean by this pilgrimage, and what does it mean for us that instead of the expiatory suicide practiced by his mother, he chose to expose his shadow, abandon the persona of the powerful, and descend through shame to the deepest form of depression and detachment? In similar fashion, Dostoyevsky's Raskolnikov, in *Crime and Punishment*, purified his soul after living for years in the dungeons of Siberia until he could open his heart to receive Sonia's love. And Clamence, the lawyer in Camus's *The Fall*, who did not dive into the River Seine to save a drowning woman, ended his life in misery as a way to salvation (*heureusement*).

Did Oedipus know during his pilgrimage through social hell that he was practicing penitence in search of absolution and salvation, or was this only revealed to him at the end?

For Oedipus there was one last temptation. It did not come in the dimension of eros but rather concerned power. In the same way that Satan saw in the temptation for power his last chance to deviate Jesus from the light, Polynices comes to tempt Oedipus to join him against his brother Eteocles to regain the throne of Thebes. Oedipus resists the temptation by Polynices and King Creon's attempt to take him back to Thebes to strengthen his power as king. By chance, Oedipus is in the territory of Attica where Theseus reigns, and the king protects him from Creon's soldiers.

Oedipus is now at Colonus, the little town where Sophocles was born and wrote his last play, his farewell to life at ninety years of age. In the imagination of the poet there exists a sanctuary of the great goddesses. When they feel wrath they are the revengeful and feared Erinyes, but now they receive Oedipus as the Eumenides, the benevolent, meaning that they have accepted his extenuating confrontation with his shadow, admit his purification, and grant him pardon and grace. It is the experience of redemption and sanctity (Avian 2007).

Oedipus sees the end drawing near. His life is that of one of the great geniuses and saints of humankind who honor the place where they die. King Theseus is by his side and accompanies him toward the beyond. Finally, Oedipus separates from him and, now enlightened and sanctified, walks into glory and eternity (Greene 1940).

References

ADLER, Alfred (1914). *Individual Psychology.* Totowa, N.J.: Rowman and Allanheld, 1973.

ARIETI, Silvano (1959). *American Handbook of Psychiatry.* New York: Basic Books.

AVIAN, Silvia (2007). *Perdão. Uma Vivência de Liberdade [Pardon: A Question of Freedom].* Diploma thesis, Brazilian Society for Analytical Psychology.

BACHOFEN, J. J. (1967). *Myth, Religion and Mother Right: Selected Writings of J. J. Bachofen.* Translated by Ralph Manheim. Princeton, N.J.: Princeton University Press, 1992.

BAIR, Deirdre (2003). *Jung: A Biography.* Boston: Little, Brown and Co.

BATESON, Gregory (1972). *Steps to an Ecology of the Mind.* New York: Ballantine.

BECK, A. T., A. J. Rush, B. F. Shaw, and G. Emery (1979). *Cognitive Therapy of Depression.* New York: Guilford Press.

BLOISE, Paulo Vicente (2000). *O Tao e a Psicologia [Tao and Psychology].* São Paulo: Angra.

BOAS, Franz (1924). *Evolution or Diffusion? American Anthropologist.* 26:340-344.

BOFF, Leonardo (1984). *Church: Charism and Power: Liberation theology and the institutionalchurch.* London: SCM Press, 2011.

BOWLBY, John (1969). *Attachment and Loss*. New York: Basic Books.

_____ (1973). *Separation*. New York: Basic Books.

___.___ (1980). *Loss*. London: Hogarth Press.

BRANDÃO, Junito de Souza (1991). *Dicionário Mítico-Etmológico daMitologia Grega [Etymological-Mythical Dictionary of Greek Mythology]*. Petrópolis: Vozes, 1997.

BROWN, Lester R., et al (2000). *State of the World 2000*. World Watch Institute. New York: W. W. Norton.

BULFINCH, Thomas (2002). *Bulfinch's Mythology: The Age of Fable*. New York: Penguin.

BYINGTON, Carlos Amadeu Botelho (1965). *Genuineness as Duality in Unity*. Diploma thesis, C. G. Jung Institute, Zurich.

_____ (1975). "Freud e Jung - Dois Opostos que Formam um Todo" ["Freud and Jung: Two Opposites which Make a Whole"]. *Journal Planeta*. São Paulo: Ed. Três Rios.

_____ (1982). "A Riqueza Simbólica do Futebol" ["The Symbolic Richness of Soccer"]. *Journal Psicologia Atual* 5:20-32.

_____ (1983). "Uma Teoria Mitológica da História. O Mito Cristão como o Principal Símbolo Estruturante do Padrão de Alteridadew na Cultura Ocidental ["A Symbolic Theory of History: The Christian Myth as the Main Structuring Symbol of the Alterity Pattern in Western Culture"]. *Junguiana: Journal of the Brazilian Society of Analytical Psychology* 1:120-177.

_____ (1985). "O Conceito de Self Terapêutico e a Interação da Transferência Normal e Defensiva no Quatérnio Transferencial ["The Concept of the Therapeutic Self and the Interaction of the Normal and the Defensive Transference within the Transference Quaternio"]. *Junguiana: Journal of the Brazilian Society of Analytical Psychology* 3:5-18.

_____ (1986). "A Identidade Pós Patriarcal do Homem e da Mulher e a Estruturação Quaternária do Padrão de Alteridade da Consciência pelos Arquétipos da Anima e do Animus ["The Post-Patriarchal Identity of Man and of Woman and the Structuring Quaternary Alterity Pattern of Consciousness by the Anima and Animus Archetypes"]. *Junguiana: Journal of the Brazilian Society of Analytical Psychology* 4:5-70.

_____ (1991a). Preface. In: KRAMER. H. and SPRENGER, J. *Malleus Maleficarum: The Witches' Hammer* (1484). Rio de Janeiro: Ed. Rosa dos Tempos-Record.

BYINGTON, Carlos Amadeu Botelho (1991b). "A Realidade Psíquica da Dimensão Onírica" ["The Psychic Reality of the Dream Dimension"]. *Junguiana: Journal of the Brazilian Society of Analytical Psychology* 9:74-87.

_____ (1992a). "Marionetes do Self" [The Marionettes of the Self]. Paper presented at the Twelfth International Congress of Analytical Psychology, Chicago.

_____ (1992b). " A Democracia e o Arquétipo da Alteridade" ["Democracy and the Archetype of Alterity"]. *Junguiana: Journal of the Brazilian Society of Analytical Psychology* 10:90-107.

_____ (1993). "Uma Avaliação de Técnicas Expressivas pela Psicologia Simbólica Junguiana" ["An Evaluation of Expressive Techniques by Jungian Symbolic Psychology"]. *Junguiana: Journal of the Brazilian Society of Analytical Psychology* 11:134-149.

_____ (1996). "A Perspectiva Simbólica do Espectro Obsessivo-Compulsivo" ["The Symbolic Perspective of the Obsessive Compulsive Disorder"]. In Miguel, E.C. ed., *Obsessive Compulsive Disorder*. Rio de Janeiro: Guanabara-Koogar.

_____ (1997). " Ética e Psicologia" ["Ethics and Psychology"]. *Junguiana: Journal of the Brazilian Society of Analytical Psychology* 15:102-121.

_____ (1998). "A Identidade Multicultural da América Latina. Uma Introdução à Antropologia Simbólica" ["The Multicultural Identity of Latin America. A Introduction to Symbolic Anthropology"]. Anais do I Congresso Latino-Americano de Psicologia Junguiana. Punta Del Este, Uruguai.

_____ (2001). "Ternura, Sexo, Dignidade e Amor" ["Tenderness, Sex, Dignity and Love: A Study of Structuring Functions by Jungian Symbolic Psychology"]. *Junguiana: Journal of the Brazilian Society of Analytical Psychology* 19:79-91.

_____ (2002a). *Creative Envy: The Rescue of One of Civilization's Major Forces.* Wilmette, Ill.: Chiron Publications, 2003.

_____. (1996). "O Arquétipo da Vida e da Morte" ["The Archetype of Life and Death"]. *Junguiana: Journal of the Brazilian Society of Analytical Psychology* 14:92-115; revised 2002.

_____ (2003a). "D. Quixote e o Arquétipo da Esperança" ["Don Quijote and the Archetype of Hope"]. Third Latin American Congress of Jungian Psychology, Salvador.

_____ (2003b). "Psiquiatria e Política. A Psicopatia Individual e Coletiva no Nacional Socialismo" ["Psychiatry and Politics: Individual and Collective

Psychopathology in National Socialism"]. *Junguiana: Journal of the Brazilian Society of Analytical Psychology* 21:47-62.

BYINGTON, Carlos Amadeu Botelho (2003c). "No Funcionamento do Sistema Nervoso, o Símbolo inclui Matéria e Significado - Uma Contribuição da Psicologia Simbólica Junguiana" ["In the Nervous System, the Symbol Includes Matter and Meaning: A Contribution of Jungian Symbolic Psychology"]. Between Psyche and Matter, a Meeting of the Nucleus of Jungian Studies, Catholic University of São Paulo.

_____ (2004). *Education from the Heart: A Jungian Symbolic Perspective.*Wilmette, Ill.: Chiron Publications, 2010.

_____ (2005a). "Freud e Jung o que a Emoção não Deixou Reunir" ["Freud and Jung: That which Emotion Prevented from Reuniting"]. *Junguiana: Journal of the Brazilian Society of Analytical Psychology* 23:29-38.

_____ (2005b). "Imaginação Ativa com o Morto no Luto Patológico. Reflexões sobre a Morte no Brasil" ["Active Imagination with the Dead During Elaboration of Pathological Mourning: Reflections of Death in Brazil"]. In: CALLIA, M. and DE OLIVEIRA, M. F., eds., *Reflexões sobre a Morte no Brasil [Reflections on Death in Brazil]*. São Paulo: Ed. Paulus, pp. 185-195.

_____ (2006a). *Psicopatologia Simbólica Junguiana [Jungian Symbolic Psychopathology]*. São Paulo: Linear B, 2006.

_____ (2006b). "Eros e Poder na Relação Adulto-Criança" ["Eros and Power in the Child-Adult Relationship"]. *Junguiana: Journal of the Brazilian Society of Analytical Psychology* 24:67-76.

_____ (2006c). "Ciúme Construtivo" ["Constructive Jealousy"]. *Journal Psique Ciência e Vida* 1(3):46-51.

_____ (2007). "A Depressão Normal e o Futuro da Civilização" ["Normal Depression and the Future of Mankind"]. *Junguiana: Journal of the Brazilian Society of Analytical Psychology* 25:7-18.

_____ (2008a). *Introdução ao Estudo das Técnicas Expressivas.[Introduction to the Study of Expressive Techniques in Jungian Symbolic Psychology]*. Lecture in postgraduate studies of analytical psychology, Adolfo Ibañez University, Santiago, May 2008.

_____ (2008b). "O Quatérnio Primário e o Complexo de Édipo" ["The Primary Quaternio and the Oedipus Complex"]. *Junguiana: Journal of the Brazilian Society of Analytical Psychology* 26:7-16.

BYINGTON, Carlos Amadeu Botelho (2011). "O Parricídio Simbólico. A Ruptura Emocional entre Freud e Jung e seus Complexos de Édipo" ["Symbolic Parricide: The Emotional Separation between Jung and Freud and their Oedipus Complexes"]. *Junguiana: Journal of the Brazilian Society of Analytical Psychology* 29/2: 16-23.

CAMPBELL, Joseph (1949). *The Hero with a Thousand Faces.* 2nd edition. Princeton, N.J.: Princeton University Press, 1972.

CAROTENUTO, Aldo (1978). *A Secret Symmetry: Sabina Spielrein between Jung and Freud.* New York: Pantheon Books, 1982.

CASSIRER, Ernst (1944). *An Essay on Man.* New Haven, Conn.: Yale University Press.

CORRÊA PINTO, Gustavo Alberto (2007). *O Ritual da Montanha Sagrada [The Ritual of the Sacred Mountain].* São Paulo.

DE MASI, Domenico (2000). *O Ócio Criativo [Creative Idleness].* Rio de Janeiro: Ed. Sextante, 2001.

DESCARTES, René (1637). *Discourse on Method.* In Descartes: Oeuvres et Lettres. Paris: Bibliothéque de la Pléiade, Gallimard, 1953.

DINNERSTEIN, Dorothy (1945). *The Mermaid and the Minotaur.* New York: Harper and Row, 1977.

DOBZHANSKY, Theodosius (1955). *Evolution, Genetics, and Man.* New York: John Wiley and Sons, 1961.

DOSTOYEVSKY, Fyodor (1866). *Crime and Punishment.* Dover Publications, New York, 2001.

ECO, Umberto (1980). *The Name of the Rose.* New York: Knopf, 2006.

EDINGER, Edward (1972). *Ego and Archetype.* Baltimore: Pelican Books.

ELBEIN DOS SANTOS, Juanita (1975). *Os Nagô e a Morte [The Nagô and Death].* Petrópolis: Vozes.

ELIADE, Mircea (1967). *From Primitives to Zen.* New York: Harper and Row, 1977.

ELLENBERGER, Henri F. (1970). *The Discovery of the Unconscious: The History and Evolution of Dynamic Psychiatry.* New York: Basic Books, 1981.

ENGELS, Friedrich (1884). *The Origins of the Family, Private Property and the State.* New York: Penguin Classics, 2010.

FAIRBAIRN, W. Ronald D. (1952). *Psychoanalytical Studies of the Personality.* London: Tavistock.

FORDHAM, Michael (1944). *Children as Individuals*. London: Hodder and Stoughton.

_____ (1995). *Freud, Jung, Klein: The Fenceless Field*. London: Routledge.

FRAZER, James (1890). *The Golden Bough: A Study in Magic and Religion*. London: Macmillan, 1911.

FREUD, Anna (1927). *The Ego and the Mechanisms of Defense*. New York: International Universities Press, 1973.

FREUD, Sigmund (1895). *Project for a Scientific Psychology*. SE, vol. 1. Rio de Janeiro: Imago, 1971.

_____ (1900). *The Interpretation of Dreams*. SE, vols. 4 and 5. Rio de Janeiro: Imago, 1972.

_____ (1905). *Three Essays on Sexuality*. SE, vol. 7. Rio de Janeiro: Imago, 1972.

_____ (1909). *Five Lectures on Psychoanalysis*. SE, vol. 11. Rio de Janeiro: Imago, 1969.

_____ (1913). *Totem and Taboo*. SE, vol. 13. Rio de Janeiro: Imago, 1974.

_____ (1914a). *On Narcissism: An Introduction*. SE, vol. 14. Rio de Janeiro: Imago, 1974.

_____ (1914b). *On the History of the Psycho-Analytic Movement*. SE, vol. 14. Rio de Janeiro: Imago.

_____ (1917). *Introductory Lectures in Psychoanalysis*. SE, vol. 16. Rio de Janeiro: Imago, 1976.

_____ (1920). *Beyond the Pleasure Principle*. SE, vol. 18. Rio de Janeiro: Imago, 1976.

_____ (1929). *Civilization and Its Discontents*. SE, vol. 21. Rio de Janeiro: Imago, 1974.

_____ (1939). *Moses and Monotheism*. SE, vol. 23. Rio de Janeiro: Imago, 1969.

FREUD, Sigmund, and BREUER, Joseph (1893). *The Case of Anna O*. SE, vol. 2. Rio de Janeiro: Imago, 1974.

GALLBACH, Marion Rauscher (2003). *Learning from Dreams*. Einsiedeln: Daimon Verlag, 2006.

GAMBINI, Roberto (1988). *The Indian Mirror*. São Paulo: Axis Mundi.

GAY, Peter (2006). *Freud: A Life for Our Time*. New York: W. W. Norton.

GOBINEAU, Joseph Arthur de (1853). *Essai sur l'Inégalité des Races Humaines.* Paris: Edición Eletronique de l'Edition Pierre Belfond, 1967.

GOLEMAN, Daniel (1995). *Emotional Intelligence.* New York: Bantam Dell.

GORE, Al (2006). *An Inconvenient Truth: The Planetary Emergency of Global Warming and What We Can do about It.* New York: Rodale.

GRAY, John (1992). *Men Are from Mars, Women Are from Venus: A Practical Guide for Improving Communication and Getting What You Want in Your Relationships.* New York: HarperCollins Publishers.

GREENE, Graham (1940). *The Power and the Glory.* New York: Random House, 2005.

GUERRA, Maria Helena (2011). *O Livro Vermelho: O Drama de Amor de C.G.Jung [The Red Book - The Love Drama of C. G. Jung].* São Paulo: Ed. Linear B.

GUGGENBÜHL-CRAIG, Adolf (1980). *Eros on Crutches: Reflections on Psychopathy and Amorality.* Dallas: Spring Publications.

GUGGENBÜHL-CRAIG, Adolf, and HILLMAN, James (1995). *The Emptied Soul.* Dallas: Spring Audio.

HANNAH, Barbara (1981). *Encounters with the Soul: Active Imagination.* Wilmette, Ill.: Chiron Publications, 2001.

HEGEL, Georg Wilhelm Friedrich (1899). *The Philosophy of History.* New York: Dover, 1956.

HEIDEGGER, Martin (1927). *Being and Time.* New York: Harper, 1962.

_____ (1953). *Introduction to Metaphysics.* Rio de Janeiro: Tempo Brasileiro, 1966.

HERRIGEL, Eugen (1948). *Zen in the Art of Archery.* New York: Vintage Books, 1999.

HILLMAN, James (1966). *Senex and Puer.* Texas: Spring Publications, 1978.

_____ (1975). *Revisioning Psychology.* New York: Harper and Row, 1977.

HITE, Shere (1976). *The Hite Report: A Nationwide Study of Female Sexuality.* New York: Seven Stories Press, 1981.

HITLER, Adolph (1925-26). *Mein Kampf [My Struggle].* São Paulo: Ed. Moraes Ltda, 1983.

HOELLER, Stephan A. (1982). *The Gnostic Jung and the Seven Sermons to the Dead.* Wheaton, Ill.: Theosophical Publishing House.

HUGO, Victor (1862). *Les Miserables*. Signet Classic, Penguin Books, New York, 1987.

JACOBI, Jolande (1965). *The Way of Individuation*. New York: Harcourt, Brace and World, 1967.

JACOBSON, E. (1964). *The Self and the Object World*. New York: International Universities Press.

JACOBY, Mario (1991). *Shame and the Origins of Self-esteem*. London: Routledge and Kegan Paul, 1994.

_____ (1999). *Jungian Psychotherapy and Contemporary Infant Research*. London: Routledge and Kegan Paul.

JONES, Ernest (1953). *The Life and Work of Sigmund Freud*, 3 vols. New York: Basic Books.

JUNG, Carl Gustav (1912). *Symbols of Transformations*. CW, vol. 5. Princeton, N.J.: Princeton University Press, 1956.

_____ (1916). *The Transcendent Function*. In CW, vol. 8. Princeton, N.J.: Princeton University Press, 1960.

_____ (1921). *Psychological Types*. CW, vol. 6. Rio de Janeiro: Ed. Zahar, 1967.

_____ (1928). *The Relations Between the Ego and the Unconscious*. In CW, vol. 7. Princeton, N.J.: Princeton University Press, 1953.

_____ (1934a). *Meaning of Psychology for Modern Man*. In CW, vol. 10. Princeton, N.J.: Princeton University Press, 1964.

_____ (1934b). *Basel Seminar*. Psychology Club, Zurich, mimeograph.

_____ (1936). *Wotan*. In CW, vol. 10. Princeton, N.J.: Princeton University Press, 1964.

_____ (1940). *Psychology and Religion*. In CW, vol. 11. Princeton, N.J.: Princeton University Press, 1958.

_____ (1943). *On the Psychology of the Unconscious*. In CW, vol. 7. Princeton, N.J.: Princeton University Press, 1953.

_____ (1944). *Psychology and Alchemy*. CW, vol. 12. Princeton, N.J.: Princeton University Press, 1953.

_____ (1946). *The Psychology of Transference*. In CW, vol. 16. Princeton, N.J.: Princeton University Press, 1954.

JUNG, Carl Gustav (1948a). *The Spirit Mercurius*. In CW, vol. 13. Princeton, N.J.: Princeton University Press 1967.

_____ (1948b). *A Psychological Approach to the Dogma of the Trinity*. In CW, vol. 11. Princeton, N.J.: Princeton University Press, 1958.

_____ (1951). *Aion*. CW, vol. 9ii. Princeton, N.J.: Princeton University Press, 1959.

_____ (1952). *Synchronicity: An Acausal Connecting Principle*. In CW, vol. 8. Princeton, N.J.: Princeton University Press, 1960.

_____ (1954). *On the Nature of the Psyche*. In CW, vol. 8. Princeton, N.J.: Princeton University Press, 1960.

_____ (1955-56). *Mysterium Coniunctionis*. CW, vol. 14. Princeton, N.J.: Princeton University Press, 1963.

_____ (1961). *Memories, Dreams, Reflections*. New York: Random House.

_____ (2009). *The Red Book*. New York: Random House.

KANDEL, E. R., J. H. Schwartz, and T. M. Jessell (2000). *Principles of Neural Science*. 4th edition. New York: McGraw Hill-Medical.

KERÉNYI, Karl (1951). *The Gods of the Greeks*. London: Thames and Hudson.

KINSEY, Alfred C., POMEROY, Wardell B., and MARTIN, Clide E. (1948). *Sexual Behavior in the Human Male*. Bloomington: Indiana University Press.

KINSEY, Alfred C., POMEROY, Wardell B., MARTIN, Clide E., and GEBHARD, Paul H. (1953). *Sexual Behavior in the Human Female*. New York: W. B. Saunders, 1965.

KIRSCH, I., and SAPIRSTEIN, G. (1998). *Listening to Prozac but Hearing Placebo*. Prevention and Treatment 1(2), n.p.

KLEIN, Melanie (1932). *The Psychoanalysis of Children*. London: Hogarth Press, 1959.

LAING, R. D. (1960). *The Divided Self: An Existential Study in Sanity and Madness*. New York: Penguin Books, 1965.

LAO-TZU n.d. *Tao Te Ching*. English translation by H. G. Ostwald. Köln: Eugen Diederichs Verlag, 1978.

LAROUSSE ENCYCLOPEDIA OF MYTHOLOGY. London: Batchworth Press, 1959.

LAYARD, John Willoughby (1945). *The Incest Taboo and the Virgin Archetype*. Eranos Jahrbuch 12:254-307.

LEAKEY, Richard E. (1977). *Origins*. New York: Dutton.

LÉVY-BRÜHL, Lucien (1922). *La Mentalité Primitive [Primitive Mentality]*. Paris: Librairie Félix Alcans.

_____ (1938). *L'Experience Mystique et les Symboles chez les Primitifs [The Mystic Experience and Primitive Symbolism]*. Paris: Librairie Félix Alcans.

LÉVI-STRAUSS, Claude (1958). *Anthropologie Structurale*. Paris: Libraire Plon. English edition: *Structural Anthropology*. Chicago: University of Chicago Press, 1983.

_____ 1962. *La Pensée Sauvage*. Paris: Ed. Plon. English edition: *The Savage Mind*. Chicago: University of Chicago Press, 1968.

LORENZ, Conrad (1963). *Das Sogennante Böse [The So-called Evil]* Vienna: Dr. G. Barotha-Schoeler, 1973.

LOVELOCK, James E. (1979). *Gaia: A New Look at Life on Earth*. Oxford, UK: Oxford University Press, 2000.

LOWIE, R. H. (1919). *The Matrilineal Complex. American Archaeology and Ethnology* 16(2).

MAHARSHI, Ramana (1969). *Words of Grace*. Tiruvannamalai: Sri Ramanasramam, 2005.

_____ (2008). *Who Am I? The Teachings of Bhagavan Sri Ramana Maharshi*. 24th edition. Tiruvannamalai: Sri Ramanasramam.

MAHLER, Margaret S., PINE, Fred, and BERGMAN, Anni (1975). *The Psychological Birth of the Human Infant: Symbiosis and Individuation*. New York: Basic Books.

MALINOWSKI, Bronislaw (1979). *The Sexual Lives of Savages*. Rio de Janeiro: Francisco Alves, 1982.

MASSON, Jeffrey Moussaief (1984). *An Assault on Truth*. Rio de Janeiro: José Olympio.

MASTERS, William, and JOHNSON, Virginia E. (1966). *Human Sexual Response*. New York: Bantam Books.

MAY, Rollo (1958). *Existence*. New York: Basic Books, 1961.

MCGUIRE, William, ed. 1974. *The Freud-Jung Letters*. Princeton, N.J.: Princeton University Press.

MOCCIO, Fidel (1980). *Taller de Tecnicas Expresivas [Workshop of Expressive Techniques]*. Buenos Aires: Ed. Paidos.

MONTELLANO, Raquel Maria Porto (1996). "Narcisismo Considerações Atuais" ["Narcissism: Considerations today"]. *Junguiana: Journal of the Brazilian Society of Analytical Psychology* 14:64-69.

MORGAN, Lewis H. (1871). *Systems of Consanguinity and Affinity of the Human Family.* Lincoln: University of Nebraska Press, 1997.

_____ (1877). *Ancient Society.* Gloucester: World Publishing, 1974.

MORITZ, Rafael (2007). *A Relação Freud e Jung [The Relation of Freud and Jung].* Graduation thesis. Pontifícia Universidade Católica de São Paulo.

NEUMANN, Erich (1949a). *The Origins and History of Consciousness.* Princeton, N.J.: Princeton University Press, 1954.

_____ (1949b). *Depth Psychology and a New Ethic.* São Paulo: Paulus, 1991.

_____ (1950). The Moon and Matriarchal Consciousness. In Vitale, et al., *Fathers and Mothers: Six Studies of the Archetypal Basis of Family Psychology.* São Paulo: Símbolo, 1979.

_____ (1952a). *Eros and Psyche: The Psychic Development of the Feminine.* 3rd edition. New York: Bollingen, 1973.

_____ (1952b). "The Fear of the Feminine". *Quadrant, the Journal of the C. G. Jung Foundation for Analytical Psychology.* New York: John and Lucas, 1986, pp. 7-10.

_____ (1955). *The Great Mother.* New York: Pantheon Books.

_____ (1960). *The Child.* New York: Putnam's and Sons, 1970.

NIETZSCHE, Friedrich (1872). *The Birth of Tragedy.* São Paulo: Companhia das Letras, 2003.

OTTO, Rudolf (1917). *The Idea of the Holy.* Middlesex, UK: Penguin Books, 1979.

PARRISH, Rob (1996). *Battered Child Syndrome.* Salt Lake City, Utah: Children's Justice Division.

PERRY, John Weir (1974). *The Far Side of Madness.* Upper Saddle River, N.J.: Prentice Hall.

PIAGET, Jean (1954). *The Construction of Reality in the Child.* London: Routledge and Kegan Paul.

RADCLIFFE-BROWN, A. R. (1924). "The Mother's Brother in South Africa". *South Africa Journal of Science* 21.

_____ (1950). *African Systems of Kinship and Marriage.* New York: Oxford University Press, 1956.

RADIN, Paul (1956). *The Trickster*. Princeton, N.J.: Princeton University Press.

RIBEIRO, Darcy (1968). *O Processo Civilizatório [The Civilization Process]*. 3rd edition. Rio de Janeiro: Ed. Civilização Brasileira, 1975.

SAGAN, Carl (1980). *Cosmos*. Rio de Janeiro: Ed. Francisco Alves, 1992.

SÁNDOR, Pethö et al (1974). *Técnicas de Relaxamento [Relaxation Techniques]*. São Paulo: Ed. Vetor.

SARTRE, Jean-Paul (1943). *L'Être et Le Néant [Being and Nothingness]*. Paris: Ed. Gallimard.

SCHNEIDER, Kurt (1950). *Die Psychopatischen Persönlichkeiten [Psychopathic Personalities]*. Wien: Franz Deuticke.

SILVEIRA, Nise da (1981). *Imagens do Inconsciente [Images of the Unconscious]*. Rio de Janeiro: Alhambra.

SKINNER, Burrhus Frederic (1953). *Science and Human Behavior*. São Paulo: Martins Fontes, 2003.

SOLZHENITSYN, Aleksandr (1973). *The Gulag Archipelago*. Lisboa: Livraria Bertrand, 1975.

SPIELREIN, Sabina (1912). "Destruction as the cause of transformation". *Jahrbuch der Psychoanalytische und Psychopathologische Forschungen* 4:465-503.

SPITZ, René A. (1957). *Yes and No on the Genesis of Human Communication*. New York: International Universities Press.

SPITZ, René A., and CODLINER, Godfrey W. (1966). *First Year of Life: A Psychoanalytic Study of Normal and Deviant Development of Object Relations*. New York: International Universities Press.

SUPPLE, William F., Jr. (2002). *Becoming a Baby: How Your Baby Grows from Day-to-Day*. Latrobe, Penn.: Picket Fence Publishing.

TATTERSALL, Ian (1995). *The Fossil Trail*. New York: Oxford University Press.

TEILHARD DE CHARDIN, Pierre (1947). *Le Phénomène Humain [The Human Phenomena]*. Paris: Edition du Seuil, 1955.

_____ (1959). *L'Avenir de l'Homme [The Future of Humankind]*. Paris: Edition du Seuil.

TEIXEIRA, Roberto W (2008) (April 21). "Violência Mata Quatro Mil Crianças por Ano" ["Violence kills four thousand children every year"]. *O Estado de São Paulo* (newspaper).

TURNER, Victor (1969). *The Ritual Process: Structure and Anti-Structure.* Chicago: Aldine.

TYLOR, Edward B. (1871). *Primitive Culture.* London: Bradbury, Evans and Co. Printers, Whitefriars.

VAN GENNEP, Arnold (1909). *The Rites of Passage.* Princeton, N.J.: Princeton University Press, 1960.

VERGER, Pierre Fatumbi (1981). *Orixás.* Salvador: Ed. Corrupio.

VIVEIROS DE SÁ, Vera Lucia (2000). *Sacrifício, Sagrado Ofício de Elaboração Simbólica [Sacrifice, the Sacred Office of Symbolic Elaboration].* Diploma thesis, SBPA.

VON BERTALANFFY, Ludwig 1969. *General Systems Theory.* New York: Braziller.

VON FRANZ, Marie-Louise 1(957). *The Shadow and Evil in Fairy Tales.* São Paulo: Paulus, 1985.

WATSON, James D., and BERRY, Andrew (2003). *DNA: The Secret of Life.* São Paulo: Companhia das Letras, 2005.

WATZLAWICK, Paul, BAVELAS, Janet Beavin, and JACKSON, Don D. (1967). *Pragmatics of Human Communication.* New York: W. W. Norton.

WHITEHEAD, Alfred North (1929). *Process and Reality: An Essay in Cosmology.* New York: The Free Press, 1978.

WHITMONT, E. (1969). *The Symbolic Quest.* Princeton, N.J.: Princeton University Press, 1978.

WICKES, Frances G. (1927). *The Inner World of Childhood: A Study in Analytical Psychology.* New York: P. Appleton.

WINNICOTT, Donald W. (1964). *The Child, the Family, and the Outside World.* London: Penguin Books.

_____ (1971). *Playing and Reality.* London: Routledge, 1991.

WORLDWATCH INSTITUTE (2010). *The State of the World: Transforming Cultures: From Consumerism to Sustainability.* New York: W. W. Norton.

ZILBOORG, Gregory, and, HENRY, George W. (1941). *A History of Medical Psychology.* New York: W. W. Norton.

ZOJA, Luigi (2000). *The History of Arrogance: Psychology and the Limits of Human Development.* São Paulo: Ed. Axis Mundi.

Films

Australia's Aborigines, directed by Alexander Grasshoff. National Geographic, 1997.

Billy Elliot, directed by Stephen Daldry. Universal Studios, 2000.

Born Free, directed by James Hill. Columbia Pictures Co., 1966.

In Cold Blood, directed by Richard Brooks. Columbia Pictures Co., 1967.

Cries and Whispers, directed by Ingmar Bergman. Svensk Filmindustri, 1972.

Dead Poets Society, directed by Peter Weir. Touchstone Pictures, 1989.

The Exorcist, directed by William Friedkin. Warner Bros/Hoya Productions, 1973.

Joan of Arc, directed by Victor Fleming. RKO Radio Pictures, 1948.

A Man Called Horse, directed by Elliot Silverstein. Paramount, 1970.

Psycho, directed by Alfred Hitchcock. Paramount Pictures, 1960.

Samsara, directed by Pan Nalin. Miramax Films, 2001.

Something's Gotta Give, directed by Nancy Meyers. Columbia Pictures/Warner Brothers, 2003.

The Straight Story, directed by David Lynch. Walt Disney Pictures, 1999.

Vertigo, directed by Alfred Hitchcock. Paramount Pictures, 1958.

Winter Light, directed by Ingmar Bergman. Svensk Filmindustri, 1963.

Zelig, directed by Woody Allen. Orion Pictures, Warner Brosz, 1983.

Zorba, the Greek, directed by Michael Cacoyannis. Twentieth-Century Fox, 1964.

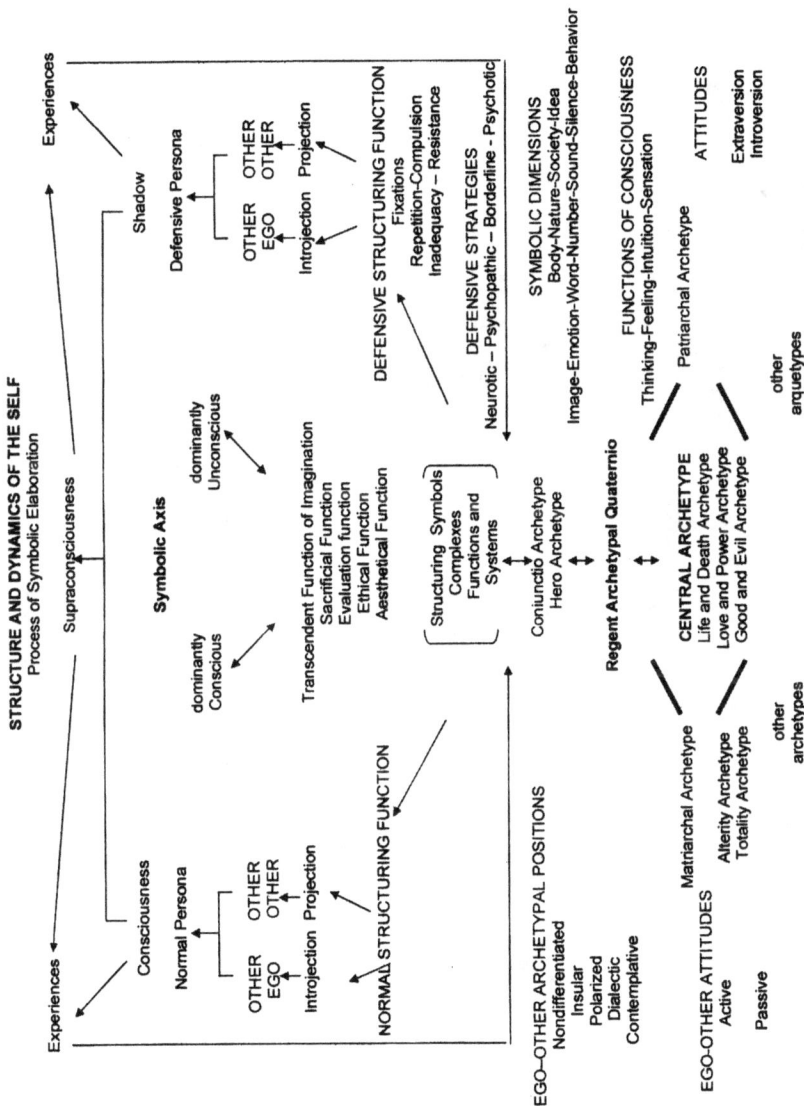

Diagram 13

STRUCTURE AND DYNAMICS OF THE SELF
Process of Symbolic Elaboration

Experiences

Supraconsciousness

Consciousness

Symbolic Axis

Normal Persona

OTHER EGO
OTHER OTHER

Introjection Projection

NORMAL STRUCTURING FUNCTION

dominantly Conscious

dominantly Unconscious

Transcendent Function of Imagination
Sacrificial Function
Evaluation function
Ethical Function
Aesthetical Function

Shadow

Defensive Persona

OTHER EGO
OTHER OTHER

Introjection Projection

DEFENSIVE STRUCTURING FUNCTION
Fixations
Repetition–Compulsion
Inadequacy – Resistance

DEFENSIVE STRATEGIES
Neurotic – Psychopathic – Borderline - Psychotic

Experiences

Experiences

Structuring Symbols
Complexes
Functions and
Systems

Coniunctio Archetype
Hero Archetype

Regent Archetypal Quaternio

SYMBOLIC DIMENSIONS
Body–Nature–Society–Idea
Image–Emotion–Word–Number–Sound–Silence–Behavior

FUNCTIONS OF CONSCIOUSNESS
Thinking–Feeling–Intuition–Sensation

Patriarchal Archetype

CENTRAL ARCHETYPE
Life and Death Archetype
Love and Power Archetype
Good and Evil Archetype

ATTITUDES

Extraversion
Introversion

other arquetypes

Matriarchal Archetype

Alterity Archetype
Totality Archetype

other
archetypes

EGO–OTHER ARCHETYPAL POSITIONS
Nondifferentiated
Insular
Polarized
Dialectic
Contemplative

EGO–OTHER ATTITUDES
Active

Passive